THE FIFTIES

LARGE
PRINT
EDITION

RANDOM
HOUSE

VOLUME TWO

THE

FIFTIES

David Halberstam

Published by Random House Large Print
in association with Villard Books,
a division of Random House, Inc.
New York 1993

Library of Congress Cataloging-in-Publication Data

Halberstam, David.
The fifties / David Halberstam. — 1st large print ed.
p. cm.
Includes bibliographical references and index.
ISBN 0-679-74725-7
1. United States—Social life and customs—1945–1970.
2. United States—Politics and government—1945–1989.
3. United States— Economic conditions—1945–
4. United States—Popular culture—History—20th century.
5. Large type books. I. Title.
[E169.02.H34 1993b]
973.92—dc20   93-19372
CIP

MANUFACTURED IN THE UNITED STATES OF AMERICA
FIRST LARGE PRINT EDITION

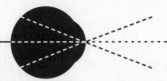

This Large Print Book carries the
Seal of Approval of N.A.V.H.

THE FIFTIES

TWENTY-NINE

BROWN V. *BOARD OF EDUCATION* had been the first great step in giving equality to blacks, but nonetheless only one of the three branches of government had acted. And yet the law, it soon became clear, was not merely an abstract concept—it possessed a moral and social weight of its own. So it was that the country, without even knowing it, had passed on to the next phase of the civil-rights struggle: education. The educational process began as a journalistic one. It took place first in the nation's newspapers and then, even more dramatically, on the nation's television screens. Those two forces—a powerful surge among American blacks toward greater freedom, mostly inspired by the *Brown* decision, and a quantum leap in the power of the media—fed each other; each made the other more vital, and the combination created what became known as the Movement. Together, the Movement and the media educated America about civil rights.

In Mississippi, the most reactionary of the Southern states, the resistance to integration was immediate and overwhelming on the part of whites. The moment the Supreme Court ruled in *Brown,* the existing white power structure moved to defy the law. White Citizens' Councils, often made up of the most respectable people in town, were formed to stop any attempts to integrate the schools. When blacks filed petitions in several Delta towns asking the local school boards to implement the law of the land, the citizens' councils struck back harshly. Their main weapon was economic power. For example, a local weekly, the *Yazoo City Herald,* printed the names, addresses, and phone numbers of blacks who signed such a petition, in an advertisement taken out by the local citizens' council. The result was the complete crushing of even this most tentative gesture. The blacks who had held jobs lost them. Their credit was cut off. One grocer who had a little money in the local bank was told to take it elsewhere. Of the fifty-three people who put their names on the list, fifty-one took their names off. Even then many of them did not get their jobs back. They had strayed. There was no forgiveness. It was the same in other Delta towns.

Elsewhere, the white response was open violence. Belzoni was known in the parlance of the day as "a real son of a bitch town." White people in other Delta towns marveled that in Belzoni "the local peckerwoods would shoot down every nigger in town before they let one, mind you just one, enter a damn white school." The Rev. George Lee and Gus Courts, officials of the NAACP, had gotten themselves on the local voter registration list, no small achievement in itself.

But when they had tried to vote in 1955, they were turned away by Ike Shelton, the sheriff, who refused to accept their poll-tax payments. Lee was a minister, and both he and Courts owned grocery stores. Lee was a man of particular courage. He seemed immune to the threats of the racists, though by local custom, people openly boasted what they would do to him if he continued his uppity ways. In Belzoni, as in many other Mississippi towns, the most violent racists frequently led dual lives: They were men who broke the law even though they were often officers of the law. No one knew this better than Lee. Nonetheless, he proceeded to threaten suit against Shelton unless the sheriff accepted his poll-tax payments in the future. With that he had crossed a critical line. There was a good deal of talk around town that something had to be done to stop him. Late on the night of May 7, 1955, Lee was driving alone in his car when he was killed. There was no autopsy. At first Sheriff Shelton said that Lee had died because he lost control of the car. The fact that there were powder burns on Lee's face and shotgun pellets in his car disproved that. Later, other people pieced together what had happened: Lee had been followed by another car, one of whose passengers shot out his right rear tire. As he slowed down, a second car pulled alongside and someone fired twice with a shotgun at point-blank range, blowing half his face away.

With the accident theory disproved, Sheriff

Shelton told reporters that it was surely a sexual thing, that he had heard that the Rev. Lee was playing around. The murderer, he said, was surely "some jealous nigger." No one was arrested. Though the murder seemed directly linked to the civil rights movement, the nation's press paid no attention. A few weeks later in Brookhaven, a black man named Lamar Smith was shot down in cold blood in the middle of the day in front of the county courthouse. Smith was a registered voter who had just voted in the state's primary election, and he had encouraged others to vote as well. A white farmer was arrested but not indicted. Again the national press did not cover the story. The traditional covenants of Mississippi seemed more powerful than the new law of the land. This was what Mississippi white men had always done, and therefore it was not news. Blacks in Mississippi seemed not only outside the legal protection of the police, but also outside the moral protection of the press.

Then just a few weeks after Lamar Smith was murdered, Emmett Till was killed in Tallahatchie County. It was this event that at last galvanized the national press corps, and eventually the nation. Emmett Till was a fourteen-year-old black boy from Chicago who had gone south for the summer; it was his second trip back to his family's home. His mother, Mamie Bradley, worked for the Air Force as a civilian procurement officer for $3,900 a year and had already been divorced from his father when he had died during World War Two. His father, it would turn out later, much to the embarrassment of some liberal journals who had proclaimed him a war hero, had actually been hanged by his superiors for raping two Italian women and killing a third. Mamie Bradley was a native Mississippian who joined the black migration from the Deep South to the great cities of the North. As Till and his cousin Curtis Jones had prepared to return to the Delta for a visit, she warned her son that the customs were very different in rural Mississippi than in urban Chicago, where Till had grown up. He had better behave himself at all times, she warned, even if he did not feel like it. Till and Jones were staying with Curtis's great-uncle, an aged sharecropper named Moses Wright, near Money, a hamlet on the edge of the Delta in Tallahatchie County.

Mississippi was a poor state, perennially either forty-seventh or forty-eighth in the union in education and per capita income ("Thank God for Mississippi," officials in Alabama and Arkansas allegedly claimed after the results of every census were published), and Tallahatchie, a county that was half Delta and half hill country, was one of the poorest areas in the state. Four fifths of its inhabitants earned under two thousand dollars a year. The educational levels were the third worst in the state. The average white adult had completed only 5.7 years of school, and the average black only 3.9. The largest town was

Charleston, one of its two capitals, which had 2,629 people.

Emmett Till was rather short but already possessed the body of a man and weighed 160 pounds. It was said by some who knew him that he was a sharp dresser and perhaps a little cocky. Neither of these qualities seemed criminal back in Chicago, but in Money, Mississippi, they were the kind of things that could easily get a young black in trouble. On Wednesday evening, August 24, 1955, Till and Jones drove in Moses Wright's 1946 Ford to a little grocery store called Bryant's Grocery and Meat Market. Indistinguishable from a thousand other tiny stores in the Delta whose customers were almost exclusively poor blacks, it sold fatback, snuff, and canned goods. Most of the sales were on credit. Business picked up on Saturday, when the blacks left the plantations and came in to do their meager shopping. The store, which had recently come on hard times because of increased federal food aid to blacks, was run by Roy and Carolyn Bryant, white people so poor that they did not even have their own car.

Even by Mississippi standards, the Bryants' life was hard. Roy Bryant worked as a trucker with his half brother, J. W. Milam, carting shrimp from the Gulf Coast to Texas, while Carolyn ran the store. The feelings about blacks and white women being what they were, there was a strict rule that Carolyn Bryant was not to be in the store alone at night by herself. Moreover, when her husband was away, she and her children were to stay with in-laws. She was twenty-one years old that summer, a pretty high-school dropout from nearby Indianola. "A crossroads Marilyn Monroe," the French newspaper *Aurore* called her.

The initial incident is still the subject of some debate. Apparently, on Thursday Till and his cousin were playing with some boys outside the store. According to Jones, at one point Till pulled a photo of a young white girl from his wallet and boasted that she was his girlfriend. It was regarded by the others merely as the boast of a city slicker to his country cousins. At that point one of the other youths said that there was a white woman inside the store—if Till was so good with white women, why didn't he go in and talk to her? Emmett Till did. According to some accounts, he whistled at Carolyn Bryant; according to others, he bought two cents' worth of bubble gum and as he left, he grabbed her, suggesting that they get together and that he had had white women back up north. According to the testimony of Mrs. Bryant herself during the trial (heard with the jury out of the room because it was so inflammatory in nature, it was disallowed by the judge), he grabbed her wrist and then made a lewd suggestion. "Don't be afraid of me, baby. I been with white girls before," she quoted him as saying. Then he left. An older black man who was playing checkers outside knew at once that something was desperately wrong, and he told Jones and Till that the woman would come out after them with a pistol and blow Emmett's brains out. The two quickly jumped in the car and drove away. As they did, Carolyn Bryant came out of the store looking for Emmett Till.

Mrs. Bryant told her sister-in-law, Juanita Milam, J. W.'s wife, what had happened. The women, fearing the consequences might turn violent, at first decided not to tell their husbands. Roy Bryant did not get home from his shrimp run until about 5 A.M. Friday. By then it was clear within the small universe of rural Tallahatchie that this was a major incident. The blacks were talking about it among themselves. Some relatives were already telling Till to get out of town as quickly as he could, that he was not safe. When Roy Bryant got to the store on Friday afternoon, a black outlined what had happened. In almost any other region of the country the incident would have passed quickly; but in the deep South a deadly serious code had been violated. Bryant would have been regarded as a lesser man had he not stood up for his woman and his own kind; the shame would be his.

Bryant and Milam were not men to cross anyway. Milam, who was six feet two inches and weighed 235 pounds, was nicknamed Big. A highly decorated veteran of World War Two, he was considered even meaner and more dangerous than Bryant. Everyone locally tried hard not to cross the two. Because he had no car, Roy Bryant told Milam that he would need his help. Could Milam come by with the pickup truck later? At first Milam balked. Saturday, he said, was the only day he could sleep late. Then Bryant told him what had happened. Milam was enraged. He said he would be by early on Sunday morning. He drove home, pondered what had happened, and decided not to go to bed. He packed his .45 Colt automatic pistol, drove by Bryant's house, and woke him. Bryant got his pistol, and off they went to Preacher Wright's house. There they demanded that Wright give up "the boy from Chicago." One of the two men, Wright later testified, asked him how old he was. Wright said he was sixty-four. "If you cause any trouble," the white man responded, "you'll never live to be sixty-five."

There is a relatively clear picture of what happened next, thanks not only to several black witnesses who, despite the threats against them, came forward to testify, but also because remarkably enough, Bryant and Milam later sold their version of the story to a somewhat roguish journalist named William Bradford Huie. Huie, who was considered more talented than respectable by many of his peers (whom he regularly scooped), represented *Look* magazine. And for the sum of about four thousand dollars, the two men, who had never taken the stand at their own trial, told the inside story of what had happened that fateful night.

Huie, who specialized in such eccentric journalism, was from Alabama. Shrewd, iconoclastic, he was proud of the fact that he was not, as he liked to point out, a liberal. He was looking for a story, not a cause. He had gone to Sumner after the trial, hoping to speak to a few of the defense attorneys and thereby piece together what had actually happened. He and the white Mississippi defense team had played cat and mouse for a while and shared more than a few drinks. One of the defense attorneys, John Whitten, said that he didn't know if the two men committed the crime. His partner, J. J. Breland, was more outspoken. Both men, he told Huie, were nothing but rednecks and peckerwoods. Bryant, he said, was a "scrappin' pine-knot with nuthin'." As for Milam, Breland said, "We've sued Milam a couple of times for debt. He's bootlegged all his life. He comes from a big, mean, overbearing family. Got a chip on his shoulder. That's how he got that battlefield promotion in Europe; he likes to kill folks. [But] hell, we've got to have our Milams to fight our wars and keep the niggahs in line." The lawyers had cooperated, Breland told Huie, because they wanted the rest of the country to know that integration was not going to work: "The whites own all the property in Tallahatchie County. We don't need the niggers no more. And there ain't gonna be no integration. There ain't gonna be no nigger votin'. *And the sooner everybody in this country realizes it, the better.*"

With that, the lawyers gave Huie access to the two men and told Milam and Bryant to tell Huie what had happened. Huie explained to them that because they had been acquitted, they could never be tried again. They were free men and his project would in no way change that. Then he suggested that he write an article based on their version of the events. Because the article would surely libel them—it would portray them as murderers—Huie said he would agree to make them a libel settlement in advance of four thousand dollars. This was not a payoff for their story, he emphasized. But just in case a film was made and the film libeled them as well, he made sure that they signed away the rights for would-be film libel, too. This was one of the most intriguing examples of checkbook journalism on record, and many people were appalled. "Others," Huie noted, "find this sort of thing distasteful and I have not found it particularly pleasing." Nevertheless, Huie hung around and talked with the two men over four nights, boasting to his editors, "I am capable of drinking out of the same jug with Milam and letting him drink first." Almost a decade later he would use the same method to get the cooperation of the two men who killed three young civil rights workers in Philadelphia, Mississippi.

There were no surprises in the story they told Huie: Moses Wright had produced Till. Milam had shined his flashlight in Till's eyes. "You the nigger who did the talking?" he asked. "Yeah," Till answered. "Don't say 'Yeah' to me: I'll blow your head off. Get your clothes on," Milam had said. Then they drove away with Till. They told Huie they did not intend to kill Till, they wanted merely to scare him and teach him a lesson. But when he proved to be unrepentant, only then, much to their sorrow, did they realize that they had to kill him. "What else could we do?" Milam explained to Huie. "He was hopeless. I'm no bully; I never hurt a nigger in my life. I like niggers in their place. I know how to work 'em. But I just decided it was time to put a few people on notice. As long as I live and can do anything about it, niggers are going to stay in their place. Niggers ain't gonna vote where I live. If they did, they'd control the government. They ain't gonna go to school with my kids. And when a nigger even gets close to mention sex with a white woman, he's tired of livin'. Me and my folks fought for this country and we've got some rights. I stood there in that shed and listened to that nigger throw that poison at me and I just made up my mind. 'Chicago boy,' I said. 'I'm tired of 'em sending your kind down here to stir up trouble. Goddamn you, I'm going to make an example of you—just so everybody can know how me and my folks stand.' "

They decided to kill the boy and throw the body in the Tallahatchie River. What Milam needed most was a weight. There was a cotton gin nearby where they had just brought in some new equipment, and he remembered some workers carrying out the old gin fan, about three feet long: the perfect anchor. They drove over to the cotton gin and found the fan. By then it was daylight and Milam boasted to Huie, for the first time, that he was a little nervous. "Somebody might see us and accuse us of stealing the fan," he said. Then he and Bryant took Till to a deserted bank of the Tallahatchie. Milam made the boy strip naked. "You still as good as I am?" "Yeah," Till answered. At that point, Milam shot him in the head with the .45. Then they wired him to the gin fan, which weighed seventy-four pounds, and they tossed the body in the Tallahatchie River.

Moses Wright did not call the police, as ordered by the two white men, but Curtis Jones did. The next day Jones went to the home of the plantation owner and called the sheriff to say that Emmett Till was missing. He also called Till's mother in Chicago. The local authorities began to dredge the river. It took them three days to find the body, heavily weighted as it was and snarled in tree roots. It was the body of a boy who had been badly abused: There was a bullet hole in his head, which had been bashed in. The body was so badly mangled that Moses Wright identified it primarily from Emmett's ring. The body was shipped north to Chicago, where Mamie Bradley opened the coffin and decided to hold an open-casket funeral. "Have you ever sent a loved son on vacation and had him returned to you in a pine box so horribly battered and waterlogged that this sickening sight is your son—lynched?" she told reporters. She delayed the burial for four days, so that the world could see "what they did to my boy." Thousands lined the black funeral home to see the body.

The murder electrified the large black communities in the nation's Northern industrial cities. White newspapers, aware of this new constituency and of the magnitude of the black emotional response, began to pay attention. White readers, as well, were stunned by the sheer brutality of the act and the idea of vigilante justice at work. In Mississippi, Milam and Bryant were arrested and charged with the murder of Emmett Till. For whatever reason—the brutality of the murder of a child, the public funeral in Chicago, or the vague sense among many in the North that something like this was bound to happen—the case became a cause célèbre. Here was what the Northern press had been waiting for: a rare glimpse beneath the deep South's genteel surface, at how the white power structure kept the blacks in line—using the rawest violence, if necessary.

The Till case marked a critical junction for the national media. Obviously, the Supreme Court decision had made a critical difference morally and socially; for the first time there was a national agenda on civil rights. The national media was going to cover not just the killers but the entire South. The editors of the nation's most important newspapers were men in their fifties, who by and large held traditional views of race but who, because of the *Brown* decision, were going to pay more attention to the race issue. Their reporters were different. They were younger men in their thirties, often Southern by birth, more often than not men who had fought in World War Two and who thought segregation odious. Moreover, they thought World War Two was, among other things, about changing America and the South, where things like this could happen. They had long been ready to cover the South. Now they had their chance. The educational process had begun: The murder of Emmett Till and the trial of the two men accused of murdering him became the first great media event of the civil rights movement. The nation was ready; indeed, it wanted to read what had happened.

Into the tiny Tallahatchie County seat of Sumner poured the elite of the Northern press, more than a little nervous to be in such alien and hostile territory. The reporters were easily recognized. They wore the journalists' uniform of the day: lightweight seersucker suits, button-down shirts, and striped ties, which advertised their former attendance at the nation's better schools. As the day wore on, the jackets might be shed and the ties loosened, but in the beginning those young men seemed to take their signals from one slim, graceful man.

Until then John Popham, of *The New York Times,* was the only full-time national newspaper correspondent working the South. Popham, then forty-five, had been covering the beat for eight years, at the request of the *Times'* managing editor, Turner Catledge, who was from Mississippi and who knew that profound changes were about to take place. Popham was a true American original: a Virginia aristocrat with a secret radical heart. Educated by the Jesuits, he was the son of a professional Marine officer and had served as an officer in the Marines himself. He was an utterly beguiling man, which was fortunate because his was clearly the most delicate of missions. He was endowed with such natural dignity that he seemed to bestow it on others. It was said that in the courtrooms of the South, all of them without air-conditioning in those days, the judge would give permission to the lawyers and members of the jury to take their jackets off. The judge would even take his jacket off. The only person left in the courtroom still wearing a jacket would be Mr. Popham, obvious to all as the gentleman from *The New York Times.* He had become, however involuntarily, the pioneer covering the region. When other reporters came down at the last minute, their contact, inevitably, was John Popham. Popham, by contrast, was connected throughout the region, and when a major event was breaking, he would arrive a week in advance to visit with local officials he knew, men from his vast network

of connections; everyone in the South knew someone or had been to law school with someone who
knew Popham. As such he was never a stranger.
So a week before the Till trial began, he called a
prominent businessman in Oxford, Mississippi,
who had been a fraternity brother of the Till trial
judge, Curtis Swango. Popham had visited Oxford, had dined with the businessman, and ended
up, of course, staying the night. So when he set off
to Sumner, he was already well connected. On his
first day, he went to lunch with Judge Swango.

Actually, Swango was almost desperate to
see him. "I've got all these reporters coming in—
seems like there must be one hundred of them,"
the judge complained, "and I've never dealt with
anything like this before. I can pledge to you that
as far as I can, I'll run a fair and honest trial, but
I'd like your help in dealing with the press." So
Popham agreed to be the liaison to the press, with
the judge setting the ground rules. In accordance
with the segregation of the times, he created one
press area for whites and one for blacks, finding
nonetheless that he was in constant conflict with
H. C. Strider, the local sheriff. He also became the
unofficial head of security for all reporters.
Sumner was not merely a community without motels, it was, after sundown, an extremely dangerous venue for journalists. Filled as it was with
smoldering resentments toward all these outsiders, it could explode at any time and a reporter
might easily disappear, not to be seen again. Rule

number one was: No reporter was to hang around the town at night. Instead, Popham decided, the white reporters should all stay in Clarksdale, some fifty miles away. He also instructed his colleagues on dress codes (once, Murray Kempton, of the *New York Post,* possibly the most talented man covering the trial, came down to dinner in British walking shorts. Popham went over and gently suggested that this was not the time or the place for shorts). He also made sure that the black reporters had a place to stay in Mound Bayou, an all-black community. When one of the blacks was arrested and put in jail for a minor parking violation by Sheriff Strider, it was Popham who got the judge to let him out.

The man who invariably embodied white political power in such small Southern towns was the county sheriff. His job was to protect the economic order for the ruling class and to maintain the racial and political balance, such as it was (but not to come down so hard on black field hands that they might miss a day of work). That was true all over Mississippi, but it was particularly true in the Delta. Sheriffs were rewarded for their stewardship: It was one of the highest paid jobs in the state, the salary coming from a percentage of the ad valorem tax and, also, payoffs from bootleggers (Mississippi was ostensibly a dry state). A Delta sheriff could officially make as much as forty to fifty thousand dollars in those days, and he could make almost as much again by permit-

ting a certain amount of bootlegging and gambling. In a state where five thousand dollars a year
was considered a good salary, that was an unusually handsome income.

Sheriff Clarence Strider seemed perfectly cast
for the role of this showpiece trial. Even more
than Milam and Bryant, he reflected the white-
power establishment in the deep South. He tried,
despite the decision of Judge Swango, to keep the
black reporters from covering the trial and
wanted to put the white press as far back in the
courtroom as possible. Almost every other word
out of Strider's mouth, in conversation with reporters and others, seemed to be *nigger*. "There
ain't going to be any nigger reporters in my courtroom," he told Popham in their first struggle over
media privileges. "Talk to Judge Swango," Popham answered. Strider did and only reluctantly
allowed the blacks to be seated.

Strider was a giant man, weighing at least 270
pounds. He was not pleased when Judge Swango
ruled against him on the black reporters, and he
was not pleased when others in the local white
establishment told him his behavior was not helping the county's reputation and he should be more
polite, especially to the black reporters. After
being told this several times, he finally walked
over to the black press table one day. "Morning'
niggers," he said. In fact, Strider was regarded as
something of an embarrassment among the local
planters; he had managed to accumulate land,

money, and power, but he was crude; and he did not know how to behave in someone's home or, even more important, how to accomplish the unpleasant parts of his job with a little finesse. Clarence, as former governor Bill Winter said years later, was the kind of man who felt threatened by the idea of a black man in a shirt and tie. Other sections of the country, after all, had their rednecks, but here was one who was the chief law enforcement officer. He listed himself in the yellow pages under the letter *P,* for plantation, and he housed his own sharecroppers in a series of shacks, painting S-T-R-I-D-E-R on their roofs. He had 1,500 acres of cotton, and thirty-five black families lived on his land. His sharecroppers bought their necessities from his own company store. He had three planes for crop dusting. As far as he was concerned, Strider told reporters, the entire case was rigged. Probably, it was all set up by the NAACP. Emmett Till was not dead, he said; rather, he had been whisked out of the county by the NAACP. Not only was he sheriff, he was a key witness for the defense. On the stand he testified that he could not identify the body because it had deteriorated so badly. Of course, he had done none of the elementary police work that would confirm whether or not it was Till's body.

When Charles Diggs, a black congressman from Detroit, showed up to witness the trial, Strider was furious. His deputies refused to believe that Diggs was actually a congressman. Jim

Hicks, a black reporter, took Diggs's congressional ID card to show one of his deputies in order to get Diggs a seat. "This nigger said there's a nigger outside who says he's a congressman," one deputy said to another. "A nigger congressman?" the other deputy asked. "That's what this nigger said," the first deputy added.

In the face of such behavior, the national press corps was prepared to judge Mississippi by the actions of Milam, Bryant, and Strider. That quickly caused a backlash. Soon there were bumper stickers that said: "Mississippi: The Most Lied About State in the Union." A defense fund easily raised money for the defendants. Racist jokes circulated: Wasn't it just like that little nigger to try and steal a gin fan when it was more than he could carry. Everyone knew the two men would go free. That was a given. As the trial wore on, the defendants and their families sometimes sat on the courthouse steps eating ice cream and playing with their kids, as if this were all a picnic. Portents of violence seemed to hang in the air. The real drama of the trial never involved acquittal or conviction but whether Moses Wright would have the courage to name in court, at the possible risk of his own life, the two white men who had come and taken his nephew from his shack. He was scared, and there was a good deal of talk early in the case that he might skip town. Only considerable effort on the part of Medgar Evers, the local NAACP agent (who would himself be murdered a few years later), kept him from fleeing. Wright received a number of threats saying that he would be killed if he took the witness stand. But without his testimony there was no prosecution case. Showing exceptional courage, he took the stand and named both Milam and Bryant. The trial lasted five days. Mamie Bradley took the stand and identified the body as that of her son. At one point she took off her glasses and dabbed at her eyes with a handkerchief. The all-white, all-male jury (nine farmers, two carpenters, and one insurance salesman) was not moved. "If she tried a little harder she might have gotten out a tear," the foreman, J. A. Shaw, said later. When a Clarksdale radio station referred to her as Mrs. Bradley (in the local lingo for blacks she should have been called "the Bradley woman"), people called for the rest of the day to complain.

The prosecutor, Gerald Chatham, told the court in summation there had been no need to kill Till. "The most he needed was a whipping if he had done anything wrong." In his summation John Whitten, one of the defense lawyers, told the jury: "Your ancestors will turn over in their graves [if Milam and Bryant] are found guilty and I'm sure every last Anglo-Saxon one of you has the courage to free these men in the face of that [outside] pressure." The jury deliberated sixty-seven minutes and then set them free. "Well," said Clarence Strider to reporters. "I hope the Chicago niggers and the NAACP are happy." It would have been a quicker decision, said the foreman, if we hadn't stopped to drink a bottle of pop. Later it was said that the jury deliberately prolonged its decision at the request of sheriff-elect Harry Dogan, in order to make it look better to outsiders.

The trial was over. Milam and Bryant stood acquitted in Mississippi and convicted by most of the nation. Their white neighbors, who had stood by them during the trial, now turned on them almost immediately afterward, when the two men took money from Huie and bought themselves new cars. They were told in effect to get out of town. Milam was refused a loan by the Bank of Tallahatchie the next year, which limited his ability to rent land. The Money store was one of three owned by the Milam-Bryant family, and soon after the trial it was boycotted by blacks in the area. Within fifteen months all three stores were closed.

If Milam's and Bryant's trial was over, a different and larger trial had just begun. John Popham left Sumner as stunned as the local residents at the size and power of the national press there. Other events in the past had drawn a large press corps, but this was something different, Popham thought, in the talent and professionalism of the journalists. With as many racial incidents taking place throughout the South as there were, and with more surely about to happen as blacks pressed for greater freedom and whites resisted,

Popham had a sense that the pace of life and the pace of change in the region was beginning to accelerate. In much of the past eight years he had worked alone, but he thought that would now be the case less and less. Something new was being created, the civil rights beat it was called, for this new and aggressive young press corps.

THIRTY

MOSES WRIGHT had not slept at home since the kidnapping of Emmett Till. In fact, he never even went back to his sharecropper's shack in Money. Right after the trial, he gave away his dog, drove his car to the train station, left it there, and boarded a train to Chicago. He no longer wanted to be a terrified, celebrity witness; instead, he became one more anonymous figure among millions of other blacks who were part of one of the greatest but least reported migrations in American history. If the dramatic and historic process of ending legal segregation was by journalistic definitions a major story, the migration of poor rural blacks from the rural South to the urban North, which was taking place at the same time, was not. Journalists, as the noted *New York Times* columnist James Reston once noted, do a better job covering revolution than they do evolution. Most of the reporters from the North who came south to cover this story arrived by airplane in whatever Southern city was momentarily under siege, rented a car, and sped off to the center of conflict. They did not, by and large, travel by bus or train; but if they had, they might have noticed another story: At the Memphis bus and train stations every day, large families of poor blacks clustered, often two or three generations huddling together. They were dressed in their best, but their poverty was plainly visible. They carried everything they owned, lugging their belongings in cardboard suitcases or wrapped in bundles of old newspapers and tied together by string; they carried food in shoe boxes. They behaved tentatively, as if they did not belong and were vulnerable to whatever authority was in charge. They went north largely without possessions and yet they left behind almost nothing.

This mass journey, which had begun at the time of World War One, marked the beginning of the end of a kind of domestic American colonialism. The other great industrial powers, like Britain and France and Holland, had established their exploitive economic system in distance places inhabited by people of color. America prided itself that it was not a colonial power, but, in fact, our colonialism was unofficial, practiced upon powerless black people who lived within our borders. When Britain and France ended their colonial rules in the middle of this century, they merely cut all ties to the regions they had exploited. In America, the exploited were American citizens living on American soil, mostly in the South. Thus a great migration began from the rural South—the colonial region—to the great metropolitan centers of the North, which they saw as a new homeland. But they came north with terrible disadvantages;

most particularly, they had been denied the education that would allow them to make an easy transition to a more prosperous life.

They were going to Chicago, Detroit, Toledo, and Cleveland, where the work force had previously always been made up of immigrants— Slavs and Germans and Italians. In the late nineteenth and early twentieth centuries, European immigrants had poured into America at an annual rate greater than the entire black population of the North. But when the supply of Europeans finally dried up, America's great employers turned quickly to the blacks in the South. The migration had been going on for some four decades, accelerating greatly during World War One, when the war virtually stopped immigration. World War Two saw the next big surge as white workers left in the hundreds of thousands to fight overseas. During the thirties and forties, the political and economic establishment of the South fought back desperately to hold on to its cheap black labor and there was an all-out effort to stop the flow North, which meant arresting, if need be, those representatives of the Northern factories who were there trying to enlist workers.

For much of the century the *Chicago Defender* was their voice. A black weekly, founded by Robert S. Abbott in 1905, it had been the driving force behind the early part of the black migration. Until then Southern blacks had had no form of public communication save word of mouth, but the *Defender* changed that. Below the Mason-Dixon line it had been regarded by whites as a subversive publication, for it printed the news, banned from Southern papers, about lynchings and murders, and it also printed help-wanted ads. If blacks joined the migration and came north, pledged Abbott, "they could get the wrinkle out of their bellies and live like men."

Abbott and others like him believed that in the South a black man was not treated as a human but as a mere economic possession. In Chicago during World War One, he liked to report, black men just off the train went to employment shops, where the jobs paid $2 and $2.50 a day. Why, the minimum wage in the packing houses in 1918 was 27 cents an hour, soon to go to 40 cents. That was a high wage for men who were accustomed to long hours of back-breaking work for subsistence wages. A black man working on a cotton plantation might make that in a month, and even then there was a chance that his boss would somehow manage *not* to pay him and to show, through the magic of white Southern bookkeeping, that the black employee in fact owed the boss money.

Abbott caught the feeling of rage that many blacks felt about their lives, and the stories he printed, from a large number of correspondents throughout the South, told of the almost daily violent racial incidents. The word *Negro* was not used in the paper, because it was too close to the pejorative *nigger;* instead, in his pages a black man was a *race man.* Critical to his success was his skill in distributing the paper through a vast network of black Pullman car porters. There were periodic attempts on the part of local Southern officials to suppress it, and much of its circulation in rural areas was accomplished clandestinely. When Abbott visited his home in Georgia, he always went in disguise, lest he be arrested. In many parts of the South it was dangerous even to be found with a copy of the paper in one's possession: "A colored man caught with a copy in his possession," wrote Carl Sandburg in the *Chicago Daily News,* "was suspected of having 'Northern fever' and other so-called disloyalties." Its circulation grew parallel to the migration: in early 1916, the circulation was 33,000; by 1919, it was 130,000. Abbott's biographer Roi Ottley thought the numbers were even higher, that by 1919 it was 230,000. It was estimated that two thirds of the readers lived outside Chicago, most of them in the rural South.

The more that white Southerners tried to suppress the *Defender,* the greater its legitimacy grew with blacks: They reasoned, and not wrongly, that what the white man feared so much and wanted to stop must contain the truth. The most important thing that Abbott did was to articulate the case for the migration from the South to the North. To Abbott, it was like the great biblical flight out of Egypt, and Ottley called it nothing less than "a religious pilgrimage." The

Great Northern Drive, Abbott called it. "Come North where there is more humanity, some justice, and fairness," he wrote. The voyage was terrifying. Southern blacks were hardly prepared for the urban condition. They left the South, the *Defender* wrote in 1918, "with trembling and fear. They were going—they didn't know where— among strange people, with strange customs. The people [the white Southerners] who claimed to know best how to treat them painted frightful pictures of what would befall the migrators if they left the land of cotton and sugar cane."

As the migration gathered force, local Southern towns tried to stop it by arresting work-force recruiters. But the migration was too powerful a force for local police to stop: a work-force agent need only walk down the street of a small Southern town, never turn his head, and yet say in a low tone, "Anybody who wants to go to Chicago, see me." That was it. They had lived close to the land, but Southern blacks were hardly rooted in any material sense; they had no homes and possessions to sell, few cars to get rid of in those days. All they had to do was pack a few belongings, some clothes, a photograph or two, and slip onto a late-night Illinois Central train to Chicago when no one was looking. So they went: first a few adventurous individuals, then whole families, church groups, sometimes it seemed, whole towns. Thanks to Abbott's negotiations with the railroads, there were better rates on the trains for large groups. One member of a family usually had gone ahead, and when others arrived later, they at least had a room waiting. The pioneer member of each family usually knew of work.

Chicago the great railhead, became, more than any other city in the country, the beacon for black Americans during the first half of the century: It had not only steel mills and other heavy metal shops, but it had the great meat-packing houses. Often there were grisly work conditions; factories were poorly lit, too cold in the winter and too hot in the summer. During World War Two, there had been a desperate need for labor and labor agents continued to scour the South, handing out free railroad and bus tickets to prospective black employees. But it was after World War Two that the migration began to accelerate even faster. There were a number of forces contributing to the change. Some of it was the reluctance of black workers to go back to a colonial agrarian economy after serving in the Army, or perhaps black people sensed that the repeated election of Franklin Roosevelt meant they had a right to greater freedoms. But the greatest impetus was a technological innovation that ended Southern resistance overnight. In fact, the very Southerners who had fought the migration hardest suddenly wanted only to speed it up. The reason was the invention of the mechanical cotton picker.

The list of technological and scientific

changes that transformed America in those years is an extraordinary one—the coming of network television to almost every single home in the country changed America's politics, its leisure habits, and its racial attitudes; the arrival of air-conditioning opened up Southern and Southwestern regions; the early computers were transforming business and the military; the coming of jet planes revolutionized transportation. But perhaps no invention had so profound an effect on the future of American life and was written about so little as the mechanical cotton picker.

As with many inventions, many people worked on it over a long period of time and there was no single inventor. But the inventor of record is John Daniel Rust. As *Fortune* magazine noted, if Rust was not the first man to invent a cotton picker, his early prototypes were so much better than anything that had gone before that "he was the first one to show the world that the idea would work." For more than a century, a machine to separate cotton from the boll without destroying the cotton had eluded inventors. In the end, that breakthrough was Rust's. He was a wonderfully eccentric genius, with more than a touch of the older Henry Ford to him; he was one of those uniquely American dreamers, and for much of his career he seemed more a dreamer than an inventor.

John Rust was born in Texas in 1892, the son of a poor farmer who had fought in the Civil War.

One of his jobs as a boy was to help pick the cotton on his farm; it was, he confided to his brother, Mack, the worst job in the world. He was always a tinkerer, though almost never a successful one. As *Fortune* magazine once noted of him, "at an early age he built an unworkable steam engine, later an unworkable airplane with a clockwork motor, patiently went on to invent a cotton chopper (to thin out cotton plants) and a suction device that would not only catch boll weevils but harvest cotton bolls. None of these things quite worked out either." But none of his early failures stopped him.

Rust spent his youth drifting: He worked as a migrant hand, and he took classes from correspondence schools on mechanical drawing and engineering. Gradually, the engine-driven cotton picker became his obsession; he knew from his own experience that there was a desperate need for one. He knew some eight hundred patents had been taken out on cotton pickers since the Civil War, none of them successful. If anything, that simply made his pursuit even more dogged. Like others, he conceived of a long spindle with teeth that would, while spinning, hit the boll and tear the cotton out. The problem was how to get the cotton off the spindle. It got caught in the machine's teeth and remained stuck there.

His own early designs featured a serrated or barbed spindle that would pull the cotton off. That, he finally decided after a long series of failures, was not the way to go. For the cotton seemed to obey its own laws and not the laws of man-made machines. It was not so much a machine that picked cotton as a machine that made a mess of cotton. Then one night in 1927, Rust lay in bed pondering his dilemma. There had to be, he was sure, some simple answer. Then he remembered his own experiences back in Texas picking cotton. In the morning when he had picked the bolls, his hands were still wet from the dew and the cotton had tended *to stick to his fingers.* He got out of bed, went downstairs, found a nail, wet it, and stuck it into a clump of cotton. The cotton stuck to the nail. He was stunned that it was all so simple. "I knew I had hold of something good," he said years later. "I was so sure of it, I thought I'd be able to build a salable machine inside of five years." Not everyone else was so confident. One hardware-store clerk who sold him parts asked him what he needed them for. When he explained, the clerk answered, "Good heavens, Rust. You can't do that! Some of the biggest companies in the world have been working on that for years and they haven't got anywhere yet. If they can't build a cotton picker, what makes you think you can?" The big companies, Rust answered, were all going in the wrong direction. With that the clerk sold him the material. "But I still think you're wasting your time," he noted.

Rust had budgeted five years for the task, but it turned out to take much longer than that. As he worked on the machine, he survived on the kind-ness of friends and relatives (but always kept a careful record of his debts). By the time his ma-chine came to market, he had spent perhaps $200,000—but the mighty Harvester Co., his chief rival, had spent an estimated $5 million. He was always underfinanced; he was essentially a tink-erer, working out of his own garage. His one part-ner during this long, difficult search was his brother, Mack. Like many inventors, he was fiercely independent and wary of big corpora-tions, which he was sure were corrupt. Though he could easily have sold his idea to a large company and seen his machine go to market more readily, he would not even consider the idea. A group of local businessmen once offered him $50,000 for a half interest in his invention, but he preferred to go it alone with his brother.

It was a long, hard journey from drawing board to production. The picker was, in fact, an engineer's nightmare: a complicated and delicate machine that had to work on rugged terrain. The possibilities of things going wrong were endless. When the Rust machine first went to market in 1927, it contained some 25,000 parts—3,000 in the spindles alone. It worked well in theory, but it was not dependable in the field. Small parts con-stantly broke down, and if there had been too much rain, the early machines were so incredibly heavy that they sank in the mud. The sixth Rust prototype, completed in 1933, was the first significant success; it was shown at an agricultural station in Stoneville, Mississippi, and it picked more cotton in one hour than an ordinary worker could pick in a week. W. E. Ayres, the director of the station, called it "the missing link in the mechanical production of cotton." With that the future was assured for someone to mass-produce a mechanical picker; by 1936 he had completed the prototype, and it was now just a matter of time. Ayres later told Rust, "I sincerely hope that you can market your machine shortly. Lincoln emancipated the Southern Negro. It remains for the cotton harvesting machine to emancipate the Southern cotton (tenant) farmer."

Rust had finally succeeded—at the height of the Depression. Already, millions of men and women were out of work. Did anyone want a machine that would quite possibly create even more unemployment? E. H. Crump, the political boss of Memphis, talked of passing a law to make it illegal to produce the machine. The *Memphis Commercial-Appeal* ran a cartoon of a black field hand with an empty sack saying, "If it does my work—whose work am I going to do?" The *Jackson (Mississippi Daily) News* suggested that the machine be thrown in the Mississippi River.

By 1940, John Rust was desperate. He had the basics of a good machine, but he still had bugs to work out. He was also broke: His home was mortgaged and he had been forced to sell his shop equipment to pay his debts. He, his wife, his brother, Mack, and his wife had all taken jobs to help pay for their very survival. "There was a long time there," said G. E. Powell, who worked with Rust, "when he and his wife and his brother and his wife lived in this tiny apartment together, and they essentially lived on starvation wages." Worst of all, it was rumored that Harvester had its machine down pat and was ready to go into production the minute the war was over. His brother, Mack, finally took off to customize cotton pickers in the Southwest, but at his wife's urging, John Rust decided to give his machine one more shot: He sat down and for three months all he did was redraw the machine. He cashed his war bonds, went to Washington, and filed his new patents. At the same time Allis-Chalmers, a large company, decided that Rust's old patents were feasible and was trying to contact him.

He sold Allis-Chalmers permission to use his patents, and the company in turn put him on contract as a consultant; during the war it built six machines for experimental use in the Delta. With the war over, Harvester was ready to go into production and by 1948 it was building a plant to manufacture the picker in Memphis, capital of the cotton belt. But Allis-Chalmers faced strikes and shortages of material after the war and was slower to go into production. When, in 1949, it finally did get going, it manufactured so few machines that it lost exclusive rights to Rust's designs.

. . .

The cotton planters were ready for the arrival of the mechanical picker—rumors of which had been floating around for some twenty years. They saw it as the answer to their growing labor shortage. During the war, many crops had not been fully picked because there were not enough hands. Now the war was over, and to the growers' shock, the manpower shortage still existed. In addition, the planters realized that they could no longer set the price of labor themselves, because of the growing number of job opportunities for blacks in the North. The cost of labor had tripled in just one decade: In 1940 the price for picking a hundred pounds of seed cotton was 62 cents; by 1945, it was $1.93, and what was worse, after the war it did not go down, as some planters had assumed it would. It kept going up, reaching $2.90 by 1948. At the same time they were suddenly competing with such synthetic fabrics as rayon, for the manufacturing of synthetics had been expedited by the wartime shortages. "COTTON PICKERS, WHERE ARE YOU?" read a headline in the *Memphis Press Scimitar* a year after the end of the war. The local director of the federal employment service was appalled because farmers were begging for pickers, even at $2.10 for a hundred pounds of cotton. "A good picker can average 300 or 400 pounds a day," said Mrs. Clara Kitts. "A whole family can bring home lots of money. The weather has been warm and beautiful. There are lots of people idle. But still nobody comes out to pick. I don't understand why." In the days before the war, she added, her office sent out some 16,000 short-term pickers every day. Now that number was down to 3,000.

Worse, and this was something the planters spoke about privately, there were now attitude problems. The war, it was said locally, had ruined many of the black people, particularly the young men. They had become uppity. There were stories about black people sassing their white bosses, or just walking off their jobs one day and never showing up again. The future lay, everyone seemed to agree, with the new machines. Some planters had actually seen demonstrations. In addition, everyone knew Harvester had built a factory in Memphis after the war—a sure sign of confidence. That showed that the company was making a commitment. By 1948 Harvester was in production, turning out 1,000 machines annually, priced at $7,600 (mounted on a tractor)—but it was tax deductible. It was the 1948 crop, more than anything, that convinced the farmers to go mechanical. That had been a particularly good crop, but almost everyone was having trouble getting it picked. By the end of the year some farmers on the Arkansas side of the Mississippi suggested that the Ben Pearson company, which made archery equipment in Pine Bluff, go into the manufacture of cotton pickers. They arranged for Carl Hahn, the head of Pearson, to attend a meeting of planters in January 1949. One of them had seen a demonstration of one of Rust's machines, and the machine was just waiting for Hahn to take a look. Would Pearson build it, they asked? Hahn thought it a good risk and promised to take it on, if the farmers could guarantee him fifty orders, noncancellable, with $1,000 of the full $3,750 price down. Everyone was enthusiastic, and he quickly raised the necessary money from the men present. By July 1949, they had their first machines out.

It was not exactly a perfect machine, and in that first year, it proved to be better picking cotton in the Southwest and California, because the cotton fields there were irrigated; that meant an easier place to work than the rich, often muddy Delta land. The stress on the machine in the Delta was far greater; in some cases the Pearson company ended up giving the $1,000 down payment back to the Arkansas farmers and selling the machine out West. Still, of the one hundred machines the Pearson company made that year, ninety-nine were sold. Within eighteen months the Pearson people, working with Rust, improved the spindle on the Rust machine so that it could work the rougher Delta farms.

. . . .

Billy Pearson grew up in Tallahatchie County and went off to the University of North Carolina, thinking perhaps he would be a lawyer. But his uncle died in 1945 when he was twenty-three, and he came back to take over the family

place: 1,500 acres of fertile alluvial soil. The Rainbow Plantation, it was called, because it was
shaped like a rainbow. Pearson had never really
intended to be a cotton planter, but in later years,
he decided that everyone in life has some form of
predestination that dictates how his or her life will
be spent, and he had been chosen to be a cotton
farmer. His mother's family, the Simpsons, had
been in the Delta since the latter part of the nineteenth century: His maternal grandfather, William Marion Simpson, had arrived without
money or land but was a shrewd businessman.
Some twenty-five years after he arrived in the
Delta, he found a partner and bought the Rainbow Plantation, then a handsome spread of 2,300
acres. Those were boom years for agriculture in
the Delta; the total price even then was $300,000
with a down payment of $75,000. Within five
years, as the price of cotton remained stable,
Simpson and his partner had wiped out their indebtedness, at which point they split the land
evenly and formed separate plantations. By the
mid-twenties, times had become very hard. The
price of cotton began an uninterrupted decline,
and each spring William Simpson would an-
nounce, "Well, the only thing I can do this year is
lose some more money." For almost a decade the
Simpsons lived well but accumulated heavy debts,
and William Simpson's considerable shrewdness
was required to keep his spread going—essentially, he traded parcels of land against its own

indebtedness. By the time cotton farming began to be viable again, at the beginning of World War Two, the plantation had shrunk considerably, from 3,500 acres down to 1,800.

As soon as Pearson returned from the war, he heard about the imminent arrival of the mechanical pickers. In fact, when he took over the family place, he believed machines were the future, and most of the other men his age felt the same way. It was only the older men who looked at the price of the machines—about eight thousand dollars in all, with the tractor—and thought they themselves were so old and had been around so long that there was no point in changing at this late date. Instead, they would do as they had always done. But the younger men thought of the future, and the future was clearly in the machines. The labor shortages were so acute there had even been some stealing of hands among planters desperate to get their cotton in—a practice so frowned on by most Delta planters that it would have been unthinkable in the past. Pearson bought his first machine, a Harvester, in 1948. He decided on a one-row machine because the spindle seemed stronger, and there was already a good deal of talk about spindle problems with the Rust machines. The problem with the Harvester was that it picked dirty cotton—that is, it pulled in more trash than either the Rust machine or hand labor did: Because the cotton gins were not yet sophisticated enough to separate the trash, Pearson and others like him had to sell their cotton at a discount price, roughly one third off.

Delta planters knew they had only a brief window of time in which to pick their cotton, from the instant it was mature, in late September, to around October 20th, when the rains always came—about four weeks. Pearson's one-row picker could pick somewhere between 150 and 175 acres in the time allotted, so eventually he went to two-row machines, which could do about 350 acres. A decade later, he had as many as three or four machines on the place. Pearson had only the vaguest sense of the great black migration that was taking place: He was so preoccupied with his cotton that he had not stopped to think about the larger social implications.

From the time that he had come back from the war, he had employed more people than he had needed, and he had watched the migration taking place as people no longer able to make an acceptable living opted to go north, often in the middle of the night without even a farewell. It was a terrible time for these men and their families, he realized; they existed on the edge of solvency and when they got behind and borrowed, as they regularly did, they could rarely climb out of debt. He thought often about one family whose journey had reflected the general hardship of black field hands caught by a dying agricultural way of life. The husband had silently gone off to Detroit one night, leaving behind a wife and seven children. A few months later the rest of the family departed. What shocked Pearson was the manner of their departure: One winter night a pickup truck had shown up and the entire family got in the open back and drove to Detroit in the cold. It was, Pearson thought later, not unlike Eliza going across the ice.

In 1991 he would read a book by a young writer named Nicholas Lemann about the great migration, and although he disagreed with some of Lemann's conclusions, he was impressed by the authority and sensitivity of the book. Billy Pearson was intrigued that he, a man who cared so much about the past and about history, and who took such pleasure reading about it, had been part of so profound a social movement and had never even been aware of it. But he had realized at the time the vulnerability of the black people, of how little they got from so much hard work, and he had been disturbed by the rising anger he had felt among the white people in the years after the *Brown* decision.

During the Till trial in 1955, his wife, Betty, and her friend Florence Mars had gone into Sumner every day to watch the trial, and they had been stunned by what they saw; Clarence Strider had not wanted them to attend, but sheriff-elect Harry Dogan had given them both press passes for the local paper, the *Summer Sentinel*. They were shocked by what had taken place. It was like watching a community you thought you knew reveal itself as something else entirely.

Much later in his life, Billy Pearson's thoughts often went back to a day during the Emmett Till trial when he had gone into town to take a look around. He had been appalled by the tension he had found in a small town he thought he knew well. Clarence Strider had hired a number of extra deputies, and they seemed to be bully-boys, young men with long sideburns and pistols who delighted in pushing people around, particularly the blacks. Pearson had gone there with Nathan Kern, who was a black employee Pearson admired greatly, and Kern had clearly been upset by what he saw: He said it was something new, this cruelty and violence toward black people. "Mr. Pearson," Kern had said. "Those of us that are still here, we're here because we chose to be here. We don't have to stay. We've all got cousins and kin up north and all we have to do is send a postcard saying save me a room, and we're gone. We stayed here because this was our home and now we wonder if it's our home anymore."

Gradually, over the years the number of black people on the Rainbow Plantation dwindled until Pearson was left with only eight full-time employees. It was, he thought, a world without easy answers—the forces of change had proved more powerful than any of them, white or black. Though his land was rich—as rich as any land in America, with the possible exception of the San Joacquin Valley, he thought—he was not a wealthy man except in the value of his land. The only way to survive was through mechanization, which of course required fewer field workers. But he had sensed the workers were probably going to leave the land anyway—the machine merely accelerated the process. The one money crop for a long time was cotton, which was a wonderful crop but heartbreaking in some ways—for there was so much that could go wrong. Yet there was a special pleasure in doing it right, in fighting and coming up with a successful crop. Cotton farming was, he liked to muse when he reached the age of seventy, a bad business but a good life. The government now set strict limits on cotton acreage. There had been talk of soybeans, but for a long time it was not a valuable crop. Then in the mid-fifties, a new variety of soybean that did not shatter was developed. Some men he knew eventually went to rice as well and some finally turned to catfish, but he remained with cotton and soybeans.

· · ·

During the fifties the race for dominance among the great farm-implement companies was on: There was the Rust machine, there was Harvester, and the John Deere people were said to be working on a machine that eventually many would consider the best of the three. By 1952 there were some ten thousand machines in use, and by 1955 there would be almost twice that number. Some estimated that by 1955, 25 percent of the cotton crop was harvested by machine, by 1960,

55 percent. In addition, it was believed that where it had taken 130 hours to pick a bale of cotton before the mechanization, it now took only 45 hours with it. In 1952 the National Cotton Council estimated that the entire operation of producing cotton, from sowing to harvesting, could be done with 15 man-hours of work per acre using machines, compared with 155 hours using hand labor and a mule.

The Pearson Company paid Rust $100,000 on the sale of the first one hundred machines, which allowed Rust to pay back his creditors at a rate of two dollars for every dollar borrowed. He died in 1954. John Rust, who had invented the cotton picker to help small farmers, did live to see the machine of his dreams roll off several assembly lines, and he did escape the grinding poverty that had dogged him for so long. His picker did not, though, become an instrument that helped small farmers; indeed, it predictably played a role in the trend that saw plantations grow ever larger as small farms fell by the wayside. His widow, Thelma, who did not share her husband's utopian dreams, managed to divert the royalties from a foundation he had established to her private estate and to buy a motel in Pine Bluff. In all, the Pearson Company paid some $3.7 million to the Rusts in royalties.

Before he died, Sheriff Clarence Strider did not come around on the issue of integration, and he left a piece of his own plantation to be used for an all-white academy, which was named after him, the Strider School. His nephew Jesse was also a big man—about six feet four inches and 250 pounds—and was known, deservedly enough, as Big Daddy Strider. Elected sheriff of nearby Grenada County, Jesse Strider changed with the laws of the land. He helped rescue his county from the Klan, and he hired black deputies. When a young black man named Mike Espy was running for Congress in that part of Mississippi, Chuck Robb came down from Virginia to speak at an Espy rally in Vicksburg. Robb suggested to Espy that he could help defuse the race question by getting a big old redneck sheriff to come out for him. Espy said, he knew just the man. So Espy's television people shot a commercial of Big Daddy Strider leaning against a tree saying that he was for Mike Espy, and it turned the election around and helped send Espy to the House.

THIRTY-ONE

THE SUPREME COURT ruling on *Brown* v. *Board of Education,* which occurred in the middle of the decade, was the first important break between the older, more staid America that existed at the start of the era and the new, fast-paced, tumultuous America that saw the decade's end. The second was Elvis Presley. In cultural terms, his coming was nothing less than the start of a revolution. Once, in the late sixties, Leonard Bernstein, the distinguished American composer and conductor, turned to a friend of his named Dick Clurman, an editor at *Time* magazine. They were by chance discussing political and social trends. "Elvis Presley," said Bernstein, "is the greatest cultural force in the twentieth century." Clurman thought of the sultry-faced young man from the South in tight clothes and an excessive haircut who wiggled his body while he sang about hound dogs. Bernstein's statement seemed a bit much. "What about Picasso?" he began, trying at the same time to think of other major cultural forces of the century. "No," Bernstein insisted, and Clurman could tell that he was deadly serious, "it's Elvis. He introduced the beat to everything and he changed everything—

music, language, clothes, it's a whole new social revolution—the Sixties comes from it. Because of him a man like me barely knows his musical grammar anymore." Or, as John Lennon, one of Elvis's admirers, once said, "Before Elvis there was nothing."

If he was a revolutionary, then he was an accidental one, an innately talented young man who arrived at the right place at the right time. He had no political interests at all, and though his music symbolized the coming together of black and white cultures into the mainstream in a way that had never happened before, that seemed to hold little interest for him. Though much of his music had its roots among blacks, he, unlike many young white musicians, seemed to have little interest in the black world and the dramatic changes then taking place there. Indeed, he often seemed to have little interest in music at all. What he really wanted from the start was to go to Hollywood and be a movie star like James Dean or Marlon Brando, a rebel up on the screen. It was almost as if the music that shook the world was incidental. Brando and Dean were his role models, and when he finally got to Hollywood and met Nicholas Ray, who had directed Dean in *Rebel Without a Cause,* he got down on his knees and started reciting whole pages from the script. He had, Ray realized, seen *Rebel* at least a dozen times and memorized every line that Dean spoke. If he would never rival Brando and Dean as a movie actor, he learned from them one critical lesson: never to smile. That was the key to their success, he was sure. He was sure he could manage the same kind of sultry good looks they had. As a teenager he spent hours in front of a mirror working on that look, and he used it to maximum effect, later, in his own appearances.

Sam Phillips, Memphis recording man, enthusiast of black music, had been looking for years for someone like Elvis—a white boy who could sing like a black boy and catch the beat of black music. Elvis, Phillips later said, "knew I was there a long time before he finally walked into my studio. I saw that Crown Electric Company truck that he was driving pull up a number of times outside the studio. He would sit in it and try to get his courage up. I saw him waiting there long before he got the nerve to come in." Elvis Presley walked into that studio in the summer of 1953. He had been sent there by another talent scout, who had not wanted anything to do with him—and those awful pegged pants, the pink and black clothes. He was an odd mixture of a hood—the haircut, the clothes, the sullen, alienated look; and a sweet little boy—curiously gentle and respectful, indeed willing and anxious to try whatever anyone wanted. Everyone was sir or ma'am. Few young Americans, before or after, have looked so rebellious and been so polite.

Sam Phillips immediately liked Presley's early greaser style. The clothes came from

Lansky's, a store more likely to be visited by flashy black men about town then by young white males. "And the sideburns, I liked that too. Everyone in town thought *I* was weird, and here was this kid and he was as weird as I was," Phillips recalled. There is some dispute as to whether Sam Phillips was in the studio the day that Elvis first walked in. Marion Kreisker, Phillips's secretary, believes he was not, and in her account she takes credit for his first recording. Phillips insisted that he *was* there, and that while Ms. Kreisker may have spoken to him first, he actually cut Presley's first disc. "It's a very expensive piece of equipment and I wasn't about to let a secretary use it," he noted. "What do you sing?" Marion Kreisker asked. "I sing all kinds," she remembered him answering. "Well, who do you sound like?" she prodded. "I don't sound like nobody," he replied. He told her he wanted to cut a record for his mother's birthday, which was still several months away.

So he sang into Sam Phillips's little record machine, getting his three dollars' worth. He sang two Ink Spots songs, "My Happiness" and "That's When Your Heartaches Begin." Presley himself was disappointed with the results. "Sounded like someone beating on a bucket lid," he said years later. Sam Phillips later said that he heard Elvis sing and thought to himself, *Oh man, that is distinctive. There is something there, something original and different.*

Sam Phillips listened to Presley a few times and was sure that Elvis had some kind of special talent, but he just wasn't sure what it was. He was not a particularly good guitar picker, but there was a sound almost buried in there that was distinctive. Part of it was Elvis's musical promiscuity: He did not really know who he was. After one frustrating session, Phillips asked him what he could do. "I can do anything," he said. He sang everything: white, black, gospel, country, crooners. If anything, thought Phillips, he seemed to see himself as a country Dean Martin. "Do you have any friends you woodshed with?" Phillips asked him. Woodshedding was a term to mean musicians going off and working together. Elvis replied, no. Phillips said he had two friends, and he called Scotty Moore at his brother's dry-cleaning shop. Moore was an electric-guitar player and Phillips suggested he and Bill Black, a bassist, work out with Elvis. They were to try to bring forth whatever it was that was there. Elvis, Moore thought—that's a science fiction name. After a few weeks of working together, the three of them went to Phillips's studio to record. Phillips by chance entered the date in his log: July 5, 1954. For a time the session did not go particularly well. Elvis's voice was good, but it was too sweet, thought Phillips. Then Elvis started picking on a piece, by a famed black bluesman named Arthur Crudup, called "I'm All Right, Mama." Crudup was a Mississippi blues singer who had made his way to Chicago with an electric guitar. He was well known within the narrow audience for black blues. He had recorded this particular song seven years earlier, and nothing had happened with it. Suddenly, Elvis Presley let go: He was playing and jumping around in the studio like all the gospel singers, black and white, he had watched onstage. Soon his two sidemen joined him. "What the hell are you doing?" Phillips asked. Scotty Moore said he didn't know. "Well, find out real quick and don't lose it. Run through it again and let's put it on tape," Phillips said. They turned it into a record. Having covered a black blues singer for one side, it seemed only fitting to use Presley's version of bluegrass singer Bill Monroe's "Blue Moon of Kentucky" on the other.

Country blended with black blues was a strain that some would come to call rock-a-billy, something so powerful that it would go right to the center of American popular culture. Crudup, one of the legendary pure black blues singers of his time, was not thrilled by the number of white singers who seemed to make so much money off work he had pioneered. "I was makin' everybody rich and I was poor," he once said. "I was born poor, I live poor, and I'm going to die poor." Bo Diddley, the great black rocker, was more philosophical. Someone later asked Diddley if he thought Presley had copied his style. "If he copied me, I don't care—more power to him," Diddley said. "I'm not starving."

Phillips was sure the record was a winner and he sent it to a local disc jockey named Dewey Phillips (no relation), who had a show called *Red, Hot and Blue,* on WHBQ. He was very big with the young white kids—Elvis himself had listened faithfully to him almost every night since he was fourteen years old. Dewey Phillips played traditional white artists all the time, but just as regularly, he played the great black singers, blues and gospel. "Dewey was not white," the black blues singer Rufus Thomas once said in the ultimate accolade. "Dewey *had* no color." Dewey and Sam, spiritually at least, were kin. If Sam was a man who subscribed to very few local conventions, then Dewey openly liked to flaunt them. He had ended up at WHBQ, as much as anything else, by being very unsuccessful at anything else he tried. He came from Adamsville, in west Tennessee. As a boy he had loved listening to black music, although he had been assured by his elders that it was the work of the devil. He had visited Memphis as a boy once when he was ten to sing in a Baptist church choir. The lady in charge had taken them to their hotel, the Gayoso, and explained to them that there were two rules: first, they were not to order from room service, since they would eat at churches; second, they were not to wander over to Beale Street. Dewey immediately took a younger boy and went to Beale Street. It had not disappointed him, with its rich black life and music. Eventually, after serving in the army, he came back home and migrated to Memphis. There he had started out working in a bakery. He was fired when he convinced the other bakers that instead of making the regular bread, they should all make loaves shaped like little gingerbread men. Baking, obviously, was not his calling. He next went to work as a stockboy for the W.T. Grant store downtown. There he managed to get himself in the store's music department and soon was beaming his department's records over loudspeakers into the street at top volume. That, of course, stopped downtown traffic. He also accompanied them with his own patter by plugging a microphone into the store's record player. He had invented himself as a disc jockey. All he needed was a radio station.

At the time Memphis had a radio show called *Red, Hot and Blue,* which consisted of fifteen minutes of popular music on WHBQ. Dewey Phillips often told friends that he would do the show for nothing if they would let him try. He went down to WHBQ, asked for a job, and miraculously got it. He was so different, so original, that the management did not know at first whether to fire him or expand the show; within a year he had three hours to himself. He was, in the words of his friend Stanley Booth, both brilliant and terrible as a disc jockey. He could not read a line of copy, and he could not put a record on without scratching it. But he had perfect taste in the music that young people wanted to hear. Soon he was the conduit that hip young white Memphis kids used to hear black music with its powerful beat. Political boss Ed Crump might keep the streets and schools and public buildings segregated, but at night Dewey Phillips integrated the airwaves. Daddy-O-Dewey, he was soon called. Phrases he tossed away casually at night on his show became part of the teenage slang of Memphis the next day. Stumble he might while doing the commercials (and he might even do commercials for people who had not bothered to buy time—he was always suggesting that his listeners go out and buy a fur-lined Lincoln, even if Lincoln was not an advertiser), but he was wildly inventive.

There were always surprises on his show. He loved having contests as well, and all three of his sons were named during radio contests. He was a man driven by a kind of wonderful madness and an almost sweet desire to provoke the existing establishment, and to turn the world gently upside down. Memphis in those days still had a powerful movie censor, Lloyd Binford, and when Binford had banned an early teen movie, Phillips had played its theme song, Bill Haley's "Rock Around the Clock," and dedicated it to Binford: "And this goes out to Lloyd Binford. . . . How you *doin',* Lloyd? . . . Anyway . . ." There he was in clean, well-ordered Memphis, tapping beneath the polite, white surface into the wildness of the city.

On one occasion he decided he wanted to find out how large his listenership was. Nothing as clumsy as demographic polls for Dewey Phillips, particularly since Memphis had just won an award for being the nation's quietest city—instead, he just told everyone listening to him to blow their horns at 9 P.M. If they were in a car they could blow it, and if they were in their homes, they should go out to their cars and blow the horns. At 9:05 the police chief called the station and told him, "Dewey, you just can't do this to us—the whole city's gone crazy, everybody out there is blowing horns." So Dewey Phillips went back on the air and told his listeners what chief had just told him. "So I can't tell you to blow your horns at 11:30." The faithful went back out and blew their horns at 11:30.

Dewey Phillips had, in his friend Sam Phillips's words, "a platinum ear" and was connected to young listeners like no other adult. Therefore, he was the first person Sam Phillips thought of when he had Elvis's first disc. Dewey agreed to play it. The night he did, Elvis was so nervous that he went to a movie by himself. The two songs were such a success that all Dewey Phillips did that night was flip the record back and forth. The switchboard started lighting up immediately. Finally the disc jockey decided he wanted to interview Elvis on the air, and he called Sam Phillips and told him to bring the boy in. The Presleys did not have a phone, but Sam called over to their neighbors and they got Elvis's mother. Gladys and Vernon Presley had to go looking for their elusive son in the movie theater. "Mama, what's happening?" he asked. "Plenty, son," she answered, "but it's all good." Off they went to the station. There he was introduced to Dewey Phillips, who was going to interview him. "Mr. Phillips," he said. "I don't know nothin' about being interviewed." "Just don't say nothing' dirty," Phillips said. So they talked. Among other things, Phillips deftly asked Elvis where he had gone to high school, and Elvis answered Humes, which proved to the entire audience that yes, he was white. At the end Phillips thanked him. "Aren't you going to interview me?" Presley asked. "I already have," Phillips said.

. . .

Elvis Aron Presley was born in the hill country of northeast Mississippi in January 1935. It was a particularly poor part of a poor region in a nation still suffering through the Depression; in contrast to other parts of Mississippi, it was poor cotton land, far from the lush Delta 150 miles further west. Yet the local farmers still resolutely tried to bring cotton from it (only when, some thirty years later, they started planting soybeans did the land become valuable), and it was largely outside the reach of the industrial revolution. Presley's parents were typical country people fighting a daily struggle for survival. Gladys Smith until her marriage and her pregnancy operated a sewing machine and did piecework for a garment company, a rare factory job in the area.

Vernon Presley—a man so poorly educated that he often misspelled his own name, signing it Virnon—was the child of a family of drifters and was employed irregularly, taking whatever work he was offered: perhaps a little farming, perhaps a little truck driving. He lived on the very fringes of the American economy; he was the kind of American who in the thirties did not show up on government employment statistics. At the time of their marriage Gladys was twenty-one, four years older than Vernon. Because they were slightly embarrassed by the fact that she was older, they switched ages on their marriage certificate. Elvis was one of twins, but his brother, Jessie Garon Presley, was stillborn, a death that weighed heavily on both mother and son.

When Gladys became pregnant, Vernon Presley borrowed $180 from Orville Bean, a dairy farmer he worked for, and bought the lumber to build his family a two-room cabin. The cabin was known as a shotgun shack—because a man could stand at the front door and fire a shotgun and the pellets would go straight out the back door. When Elvis was two years old, Vernon Presley was picked up for doctoring a check from Bean. It had been an ill-conceived, pathetic attempt to get a few more dollars, at most. Friends of Vernon's pleaded with Bean not to press charges. They would make up the difference. But Bean was nothing if not rigid, and he held firm against their pleas. Vernon Presley could not make bail, and he waited seven months in the local jail before the trial even took place. He was convicted and sent to Parchman prison in the middle of the Depression for two and a half years. It was a considerable sentence for a small crime, but those were hard times. When he came out times were still hard; he worked in a lumberyard and then for one of the New Deal aid programs for the unemployed, the WPA.

During World War Two he got a job doing defense work in Memphis, eighty miles away. That at least was steady work, even if he was away from home much of the time. After the war, returning veterans had priority for any jobs. Vernon had no skills and was soon out of work again. In the late forties the new affluence rolling quickly across much of the country barely touched people like Vernon and Gladys Presley. They were poor whites. Their possibilities had always been limited. They were people who lived on the margin. Religion was important to them, and when Elvis was nine he was baptized in the Pentecostal church. As a symbol of Christian charity, he was supposed to give away some of his prized possessions, so he gave his comic books to other children.

Because a city like Memphis held out more hope of employment, Vernon Presley moved his family to Memphis in the late forties. There he took a job in a paint factory for $38.50 a week. They had made the move, Elvis said later, because "we were broke, man, broke." The family was still so poor that it had to live in federal housing—the projects, as they were known. The Presleys paid thirty-five dollars a month for rent, the equivalent of a week's salary. To some whites, living in the projects was an unspeakable idea, for it was housing that placed them at the same level as blacks; for the Presleys, the projects were the best housing they had ever had.

Even in a high school of his peers, Elvis Presley was something of a misfit. He went to Humes, an all-white high school where he majored in shop. There was no thought of college for him. Not surprisingly, he was shy and unsure of himself. He was bothered by the way his teeth looked. He worried that he was too short. As an adult he always wore lifts in his shoes. He did, however, have a sense that his hair worked for him. Soon he started using pomade; his style, black clothes, shirt collar up in back, hair pomaded into a major wave, was an early form of American punk. His heroes—Brando and Dean—were narcissistic, so too by nature was he. His social life was so limited that he did not know how to slow-dance with a girl; rather, in the new more modern style, he knew how to dance only by himself. His peers deemed him effeminate and different. Everyone, it seemed, wanted a shot at him, particularly the football players. Years later he would tell a Las Vegas audience, "They would see me coming down the street and they'd say, 'Hot dog! Let's get him! He's a squirrel! He just come down outta the trees!' " His one friend was Red West, a more popular Humes student and a football player. West stopped about five other boys from cutting off Elvis's hair in the boys' room one day. "He looked like a frightened little animal," West said.

The one thing he had was his music. He could play a guitar and play it well. He could not read a note of music, but he had an ear that, in the words of Chet Atkins, the guitarist who supervised many of his early RCA recordings, was not only pure but had almost perfect pitch. He could imitate any other voice he chose. That was his great gift. Some of the other kids suggested he play his guitar at a school picnic, and he did, with surprising success. His homeroom teacher asked him to play it at the school variety show. He did, playing the Red Foley country favorite "Old Shep," about a boy and his dog. When the dog dies and goes to heaven, the boy does not feel too badly, for "old Shep has a wonderful friend." For the first time he gained some popularity.

On the surface, the Mississippi he grew up in was a completely segregated world. That was seemingly true even in music. Among the many musical subcultures that flowed across the Mississippi Delta were black rhythm and blues music (called race music in the trade), black gospel, white gospel, which in no small part was imitative of black gospel, and country, or hillbilly, music. Because whites were more influential and affluent than blacks, the last was the dominant strain in the region.

For Elvis Presley, living in a completely segregated world, the one thing that was not segregated was the radio dial. There was WDIA ("the Mother Station of the Negroes," run, of course, by white executives), which was the black station, on which a young white boy could listen to, among other people, the Rev. Herbert Brewster, a powerful figure in the world of Memphis black churches. A songwriter of note, he composed "Move On Up a Little Higher," the first black gospel song to sell over a million copies. What was clear about the black gospel music was that it had a power of its own, missing from the tamer white church music, and that power seemed to come as much as anything else from the beat. In addition there was the immensely popular Dewey Phillips. When Elvis listened to the black radio station at home, his family was not pleased. "Sinful music," it was called, he once noted. But even as Elvis Presley was coming on the scene, the musical world was changing. Certainly, whites had traditionally exploited the work of black musicians, taking their music, softening and sweetening it and making it theirs. The trade phrase for that was "covering" a black record. It was thievery in broad daylight, but black musicians had no power to protect themselves or their music.

As the decade began, there were signs that

young white kids were buying black rhythm and blues records; this was happening in pockets throughout the country, but no one sensed it as a trend until early 1951. In that year a man named Lee Mintz who owned a record store in Cleveland told a local disc jockey named Alan Freed about this dramatic new trend. Young white kids with more money than one might expect were coming into his store and buying what had been considered exclusively Negro music just a year or two before. Freed, something of a disc jockey and vagabond, had a late-night classical music show, and Mintz was pushing him to switch over to a new show catering exclusively to these wayward kids. Mintz told Freed he knew the reason why the taste was changing: It was all about the beat. The beat was so strong in black music, he said, that anyone could dance to it without a lesson. Mintz promised he would advertise himself on Freed's new program and that he would help find other advertisers if Freed would switch.

Alan Freed was hardly locked into classical music. He was a smart, free-spirited man, who like many of the nation's best disc jockeys, seemed to be two people: one a rather insecure, ordinary person who went angrily through everyday life and the other, a man in front of an open mike who exploded into a secret confident and audacious self before listeners he could not see. His career, at that moment, had not been exactly brilliant. Even within a profession given over to a significant excess of ego, Freed was considered difficult and abrasive by various employers. At one point he had worked for a station in Akron, had asked for a raise, and had been turned down, so he went to a competing station and offered his services. Unfortunately, his contract with the first station had not yet expired; the first station took him to court and a judge ordered him not to broadcast within seventy-five miles of Akron for a year. Such was the life of a disc jockey who had not yet found his special niche. When his period of disbarment expired he eventually showed up in Cleveland. So when Mintz suggested the new show, he was amenable.

In the summer of 1951, Freed inaugurated the *The Moondog Show* on a 50,000-watt clear channel station in Cleveland, a station so powerful it reached a vast area of the Midwest. His success was immediate. It was as if an entire generation of young white kids in that area had been waiting for someone to catch up with them. For Freed it was what he had been waiting for; he seemed to come alive as a new hip personality. He was the Moondog. He kept the beat himself in his live chamber, adding to it by hitting on a Cleveland phone book. He became one of them, the kids, on their side as opposed that of their parents, the first grown-up who understood them and what they wanted. By his choice of music alone, the Moondog had instantly earned their trust. Soon he was doing live rock shows. The response was remarkable. No one in the local music business had ever seen anything like it before: Two or three thousand kids would buy tickets, and sometimes, depending on the level of talent, thousands of others would be turned away—all for performers that adults had never even heard of.

At virtually the same time, Elvis Presley began to hang out at all-night white gospel shows. White gospel singing reflected the region's schizophrenia: It allowed white fundamentalist groups, whose members were often hard-core segregationists and who wanted nothing to do with black culture—to co-opt the black beat into their white music. Presley gradually got to know some of the gospel singers, and by the time he graduated from high school in 1953, he had decided to become one himself. He was eighteen, with extremely limited options. For a country boy with his background, the possibilities were few: He could drive a truck or hope for a job in a nearby plant—and he could dream of being a singer. Soon he was singing with a local group from his church called the Songfellows. But a few random singing dates were hardly a career, so he was also working at a small plant in Memphis where artillery shell casings were made. By the standards of the time and the region, the pay was not bad—$1.65 an hour—and he made about sixty dollars a week with overtime. Soon he left that job for another that excited him more—driving a truck for Crown Electric. Driving a truck seemed infinitely freer than working in a defense factory. It seemed at that moment he would be driving a truck for the rest of his life. In September 1956, a year after he had exploded into the consciousness of his fellow Americans, he tried to explain the secret of his success to a writer for the *Saturday Evening Post.* "I don't know what it is . . . I just fell into it, really. My daddy and I were laughing about it the other day. He looked at me and said, 'What happened, E? The last thing I can remember is I was working in a can factory and you were drivin' a truck.' . . . It just caught us up."

. . .

The Memphis of 1954 was a strictly segregated city. Its officials were white and its juries were white, and as late as 1947 there had been no black police in the city (when the first few were finally hired in 1948, they could not arrest white people). In 1947 *Annie Get Your Gun* was banned from Memphis because it included a black railroad conductor, and as the local censor Lloyd Binford said, "We don't have any Negro conductors in the South." That same year the American Heritage Foundation, which sponsored the Freedom Train, a traveling exhibition filled with historic documents about American history, took Memphis off its itinerary because local officials there insisted that the train be segregated.

Sam Phillips thought the city's segregation was absurd. He was not a liberal in the traditional sense and he was not interested in social issues, as many of the activists of the period were. He was a raw, rough man, with an eleventh-grade education, pure redneck in all outward manifestations, such as his love of used Cadillacs. A good country boy, Sam saw Cadillacs as the surest sign of status and comfort, and he would buy a used one and get a good deal and drive it for a few years and then turn it over and get a used but newer one and drive that for a few years. But he was different in one sense: his love of the blues. He had been drawn to Memphis in the first place because he *knew* it was a great center for black music, and he intended to capture some of it on record. Sam Phillips hated the hypocrisy of a city that denied the richness of its own heritage. Sam Phillips, thought his friend Stanley Booth, a talented music writer, was drawn to what he was doing not because he was a liberal and felt that the social order ought to be changed: "It wasn't a humanitarian gesture, and people like Sam weren't social activists," Booth said. "You did it because of the power of the music—you were drawn to the music. It made you hip and a little different, and in addition, in a life which was often very hard, it was the one thing which gave you a little grace." What others thought about his passion mattered little to him. He held a job as an engineer at the Peabody Hotel, working on a radio show broadcast from there; at the same time he began to record some of the region's black singers in a small studio he had created. He generally did this on the weekends, and it was great sport among his colleagues at the Peabody to tease him on Monday mornings, "Well, Sam, I guess you didn't spend the weekend recording all those niggers of yours like you usually do because you don't smell so bad today."

He never for a second doubted his own ear. Nor, for that matter, did he doubt his purpose. He wanted to be a pioneer and an explorer. "I have my faults in the world, a lot of faults, I guess," he once said, "but I have one real gift and that gift is to look another person in the eye and be able to tell if he has anything to contribute, and if he does, I have the additional gift to free him from whatever is restraining him." It was a description, his friends thought, that was remarkably accurate.

He had grown up poor in northern Alabama, aware of the tensions between blacks and whites. The whites had their music, country music, and in those years, when poor whites did not yet have radios, they would gather at someone's home on a Saturday night, put the furniture aside, and have square dances. But their music had none of the power of black music. Every Sunday Sam Phillips went to a white Baptist church in town. About a block and a half away was a black Methodist church. In those days before air-conditioning, the windows of both churches were open during the summer, and the power of the music in the black church was transcendent. "There was something there I had never heard before or since," he said years later. "Those men and women singing the *Amen.* Not the choir singing it. I mean the congregation. It was a heaven on earth to hear it. A jubilation. The Amen and the rhythm. They never missed a downbeat." There was, he thought, so much more power in their music than his own, so much more feeling and so much more love. He felt pulled toward it, and he would leave his own church and linger outside the black church to listen.

As he came to adulthood, he began to follow the music, to ever bigger cities, working as a disc jockey. He finally made it to a big, powerful station in Nashville, but he was still restless. Nashville was the capital of white country music, but that music cast no spell on him. He knew he had to go to Memphis. It seemed to be his destiny. Phillips knew that the best and richest soil was in the bend of the Tennessee River near where he grew up and that where there was rich soil, the people were also rich—in sorrow and joy and, above all, in music. Fertile land somehow produced fertile people as well, he believed. "There was going to be no stopping something as big as Memphis and the Mississippi River. I always knew that, *knew that.* I'd driven to Memphis, and the closer I'd gotten to the Mississippi, I knew that there was something rich ahead, this totally untamed place, all those people who had these hard hard lives, and the only way they could express themselves was through their music. You had to be a dunce not to know that."

He reached Memphis in 1945, and he was not disappointed. "I'd never seen such a gulf between two words. One side white, the other side black. One world all white, the other world, a few blocks away, all black. There was no street like Beale Street, no street I'd ever seen. It had a flavor all its own, entirely black. Lined with clubs and dives and pawnshops. Lord there were pawnshops! All these black people, some of them rich and some of them poor, they'd come from Mississippi and Arkansas and Tennessee, saved up all their money, determined to spend every bit of it there. No one tried to save money when they came to Beale Street. It was wonderful, all that energy, all those men and women dressed in their best, the country people from those hamlets, black hicks a lot of them trying to pretend that they're not hicks, that they're men of the street. It was amazing, there were these people who were rich, and who had saved all their money and were celebrating, and the people who had nothing, who were down and out, they were celebrating, too, and the one thing that was different from white folks was that it was impossible to tell who was rich and who was poor on Beale Street."

He built his own studio, a small storefront out at 706 Union Street. He laid the tile on the floor and on the walls himself, to maximize the acoustics, and created a raised control room so he could see the musicians who were recording, and finally installed an air conditioner, which always dripped. It cost about $1,000 to fix the place up, and he was paying about $75 a month rent.

In January 1950 he quit his job at the Peabody to record full-time himself. Almost all his white friends thought he was crazy, giving up a good solid job at the grandest hotel in the entire region to go off and record black music. "Hell, Sam," one friend told him. "You're not only recording them, you're going to shake hands with them too." As a white man recording black singers he offended local mores. Phillips himself, however, was absolutely sure of his mission. In Memphis there was all kinds of talent around: B.B. King, Phineas Newborn, Howling Wolf. B.B. King was typical of the music and the region: His real name was Riley B. King, and he came from Indianola, in the Delta. He had grown up picking cotton (he once noted that he could pick four hundred pounds a day and make as much as 35 cents a hundred pounds—no one, he thought, could pick more cotton than he could). He had driven tractors, sung spirituals, and had finally ended up in Memphis in 1947, where he had worked his way up and down Beale Street playing in different clubs. He was good, authentic; everyone knew it—no one had to be told. It was even in his nickname—Beale Street Blues Boy, which eventually was shortened to B.B. There was nothing smooth about his sound: It was raw and harsh—almost angry. Eventually, he got a job on WDIA. It was not an auspicious beginning. He started by singing commercials for Peptikon, a patent medicine guaranteed to cure all the things that ailed you and a few things that did not. Soon he got his own half-hour in the midafternoon, the "Sepia Swing Club," and his popularity began to grow. In those days B.B. King was young and shy, particularly around white people. The first time he recorded for Sam Phillips, he revealed that he could not play the guitar and sing at the same time, which made him different from most singers. "Can't you sing and play at the same time?" Phillips asked him. "Mr. Phillips, that's the only way I ever played," he answered. "Whatever you do," Phillips told him, "don't change it. Just keep it natural."

The last thing Phillips wanted was sweeteners: "I didn't build that studio to record a big band. The big bands didn't need me. I wanted to record the local talent. I knew the talent was there. I didn't have to look it up to know B.B. King was talented. And I knew what I wanted. I wanted something *ugly*. Ugly and honest. I knew that these people were disenfranchised. They were politically disenfranchised and economically disenfranchised, and to tell the truth they were musically disenfranchised. . . . The big trouble in those days, if you were recording black musicians, was that they would start changing what they were doing for you because you were white. They did it unconsciously. They were adapting to you and to the people they thought were going to be their audience. They'd look up in the recording booth and see a white man and they'd start trying to be like Billy Eckstine and Nat King Cole. I didn't want that. The things that RCA and Capitol winced at, I loved. I didn't want anyone who had ever recorded before, and I didn't want to do what other recording studios did."

So word got out that there was this slightly crazy man who had set up his own studio and was taping black people. B.B. King told Ike Turner, who was from Clarksdale, Mississippi. Phillips recorded Turner and his band, and soon Turner became a kind of one-man talent scout for Phillips, finding people throughout the region. One memorable receipt in Sam Phillips's office for the early fifties was for one hundred dollars paid out to a small town in Mississippi for bailing Ike Turner and his band out of jail for driving an overloaded auto—Ike had strapped his bass on top of the car, and that had been enough to enrage the local authorities.

It was a simple operation. He called it the Memphis Record Service. The studio was so small that Phillips did not even have a real office. His office, his friends like to point out, was the simple café next door, Miss Taylor's, third table back. That's where he'd meet someone who wanted to do a business deal. When he recorded black musicians he could not take them to Miss Taylor's, so he would take the food out himself and bring it back for them. To make enough money to survive, he also advertised that he recorded weddings, banquets, bar mitzvahs. "We Record Anything-Anytime-Anywhere," was his motto. His gear was portable, and he hustled around Memphis in those days, recording happy occasions for posterity and grieving with loved ones. He even did funerals, which cost about eighteen dollars—that is to wire it, tape it, and then transfer the tape to a disc. A wedding cost a little less.

He also hired out his studio to any person who wanted to record. It was a good way of hearing new talent and making a little money on the side. The price was three dollars a shot. He sensed, long before the major record companies located far away in New York did, that the traditional musical barriers that had always separated the musician constituencies no longer held. He often told his assistant, Marion Kreisker, "If I could find a white man with a Negro sound I could make a billion dollars." In addition, he said, "I knew that for black music to come to its rightful place in this country we had to have some white singers come over and do black music—not copy it, not change, not sweeten it. Just *do* it."

It would turn out that he would engineer an entire musical migration of whites into black music. In addition to Elvis, he discovered Johnny Cash, Carl Perkins, Roy Orbison, and Jerry Lee

Lewis, all major talents and all, in different ways, American originals.

Even as Sam Phillips was inventing himself as a producer, the musical world was changing dramatically. The old order was fragmenting. The traditional giants, RCA, Columbia, and Decca, had dominated in the past. They had the big names, the crooners. But they were hardly entrepreneurial; the bigger they were, the more conservative they inevitably were as well. They watched the world of country-and-western and rhythm-and-blues with disdain, bordering on disapproval. It was music that came from the wrong side of the tracks. Some companies in fact even referred to black music as the "sepia market." It was not an important slice of the market, obviously, because sepia people did not have very much money. Recorded music, in fact, until the fifties bore the label of class. People from the upper middle class and upper class had the money for phonographs with which they listened to classical and high pop, the crooners and the big bands. The people who liked country and black listened to the radio. But the forces of change were far more powerful than anyone at the big companies realized. Technology was democratizing the business of music—phonographs and records alike were becoming much cheaper. It was only a matter of time before the artists began to cross over on the traditionally racially segregated charts. In 1954 a white musician named Bill Haley did a version of "Shake Rattle and Roll." By February 1955 it sold 1 million copies; by the summer of 1955 it was number one on the white chart and number four on the rhythm and blues (or black) chart. In that same year Chuck Berry brought out "Maybellene," which was the first successful assault on the main chart by a black musician; "Maybellene" went to the top of the rhythm and blues chart and went to number five on the white chart. Soon there was "Tutti Frutti," by Little Richard.

After Elvis Presley's sensational debut on Dewey Phillips's show, his career skyrocketed. He was what first the region and then the nation wanted: a white boy to explode into the beat, to capture it for the whites. The success spread steadily: Deejays in Texas soon picked up on it, and soon after that Elvis was making regular appearances on the Louisiana Hayride, which was second only to the Grand Ole Opry as a showcase of country white talent. He began traveling the South with a company of country musicians, headlined by Hank Snow. But almost overnight he became the star of the touring group, something that did not escape the attention of Snow's manager, Colonel Tom Parker. Parker, it appeared, though he did not own Presley's contract, was encouraging the large companies to move in and buy it from Sam Phillips. In the beginning Phillips probably would have sold it for $5,000 or

$10,000, for he lacked the resources to promote and sustain a major success. But interest constantly escalated. Mitch Miller at Columbia called. Phillips asked $20,000. Miller replied, "Forget it. No artist is worth that kind of money." Ahmet Ertegun, the head of Atlantic, a label that was coming on quickly because of its owners' exceptional early awareness of rock and roll, was probably the one record executive who personally knew how valuable Presley was. He made an offer of $25,000, which, as Ertegun told Phillips, was everything Atlantic had, including the desk he was using. It was too low, said Phillips. By then Colonel Parker was in on the game, and the Colonel had friends at RCA, the traditional recording powerhouse. Phillips was fairly sure he ought to sell Elvis's contract, but just to be sure he was doing the right thing he had called his friend Kemmons Wilson, the local contractor who was just beginning to enjoy success in his own amazing career as the builder of America's first great motel chain, Holiday Inns. Sam Phillips had been smart enough to be an early investor, and he would eventually become a millionaire from his investments with Wilson. Phillips asked whether he should sell Elvis's contract. "I wouldn't hesitate," Wilson said. "That boy isn't even a professional." So Phillips went ahead. When the negotiations were over, Sam Phillips had $35,000 and Elvis was the property of RCA.

Presley's timing was nearly perfect. The

crossover, led by Bill Haley, Chuck Berry, and Little Richard, was in full force. Parents might disapprove of the beat and of their children listening to what they *knew* was black music. But their disapproval only added to Presley's popularity and made him more of a hero among the young. Local ministers might get up in their churches (almost always well covered by local newspapers) and attack demon rock as jungle music and threaten to lead a crusade to have this Presley boy arrested if he dared set foot in their community (generally, there was no problem, their towns were too small for him to play). It did not matter: Elvis Presley and rock music were *happening*.

A new young generation of Americans was breaking away from the habits of its parents and defining itself by its music. There was nothing the parents could do: This new generation was armed with both money and the new inexpensive appliances with which to listen to it. This was the new, wealthier America. Elvis Presley began to make it in 1955, after ten years of rare broad-based middle-class prosperity. Among the principal beneficiaries of that prosperity were the teenagers. They had almost no memory of a Depression and the great war that followed it. There was no instinct on their part to save money. In the past when American teenagers had made money, their earnings, more often than not, had gone to help support their parents or had been saved for one treasured and long-desired purchase, like a baseball glove or a bike, or it had been set aside for college.

But now, as the new middle class emerged in the country, it was creating as a byproduct a brand-new consuming class: the young. *Scholastic* magazine's Institute of Student Opinion showed that by early 1956 there were 13 million teenagers in the country, with a total income of $7 billion a year, which was 26 percent more than only three years earlier. The average teenager, the magazine said, had an income of $10.55 a week. That figure seemed remarkable at the time; it was close to what the average American family had had in disposable income, after all essential bills were paid, fifteen years earlier.

In addition, technology favored the young. The only possible family control was over a home's one radio or record player. There, parental rule and edicts could still be exercised. But the young no longer needed to depend on the family's appliances. In the early fifties a series of technological breakthroughs brought small transistorized radios that sold for $25 to $50. Soon an Elvis Presley model record player was selling for $47.-95. Teenagers were asked to put $1 down and pay only $1 a week. Credit buying had reached the young. By the late fifties, American companies sold 10 million portable record players a year.

In this new subculture of rock and roll the important figures of authority were no longer mayors and selectmen or parents; they were disc jockeys, who reaffirmed the right to youthful independence and guided teenagers to their new rock heroes. The young formed their own community. For the first time in American life they were becoming a separate, defined part of the culture: As they had money, they were a market, and as they were a market they were listened to and catered to. Elvis was the first beneficiary. In effect, he was entering millions of American homes on the sly; if the parents had had their way, he would most assuredly have been barred.

Certainly, Ed Sullivan would have liked to have kept him out. Ed Sullivan, in 1955 and 1956, hosted the most successful variety show in America on this strange new piece of turf called network television. The official title of his show was *The Toast of the Town.* Sullivan made his way to television from the world of print, where he'd worked as a Broadway gossip columnist, first on the old *New York Graphic* and eventually making his way to the *New York Daily News.* His column, in the city's largest paper, was one of considerable influence. In 1947 he had served as master of ceremonies for an annual amateur dance contest sponsored by the *News* called the "Harvest Moon Ball." Unbeknownst to Sullivan, CBS was televising the show. A CBS executive was impressed at how graciously Sullivan treated everyone he dealt with that evening and how natural his skills as an emcee were. He seemed completely comfortable with himself despite the fact that the show was being televised; the reason he was so comfortable was that he didn't realize it was going on television: He thought all those cameras around the hall were simply movie cameras. CBS was in the process of putting together a Sunday-night variety program, and Sullivan was offered the show. The show opened a year later, and much to everyone's surprise, it was a stunning success. Certainly, part of the reason was the leverage of Sullivan's column. Those who went on his show were likely to get plugs in the column, and it was for that reason that on his opening broadcast, Dean Martin and Jerry Lewis clowned, Eugene List played the piano, and Rodgers and Hammerstein happened to drop in just to say hello.

Eight years later, Ed Sullivan was the unofficial Minister of Culture in America. His was the great national variety theater where one could find the famous. Broadcast at 8 P.M. on Sundays—an hour when families were likely to have gathered together—Sullivan's show provided a pleasant, safe blend of acts, including some performers of exceptional talent. In addition there seemed to be a guarantee that nothing would happen that was at all threatening. Sullivan was, after all, involved in the most delicate business imaginable: selecting acts to perform live in millions of American living rooms, a place where no one had ever performed before. There was something there for everyone, and Sullivan made sure that there was always one act for the children. He stressed the importance of variety, and few acts got more than a couple of minutes. Mark Leddy, who did the booking for the show, once told Jim Bishop, the writer, "You want to know the day Christ died. It was on the Ed Sullivan Show and Ed gave him three minutes." Sullivan himself was shrewd enough to minimize his own appearances, since his style was widely perceived as being exceptionally wooden. He would introduce a number, get off the stage, and reappear in time to lead the applause. "Let's hear it for . . ." he would say, and then give the name of the act. Once, after Sergio Franchi had sung the Lord's Prayer, Sullivan turned to his audience and said, "Let's hear it for the Lord's Prayer." A mimic named Will Jordan once went on and did an imitation of Sullivan, the idea for which, Jordan said, came from watching mechanical ducks in a shooting gallery. Jordan walked on and said: "Tonight on our really big show we have 702 Polish dentists who will be here in a few moments doing their marvelous extractions . . ."

The popularity of Sullivan's show was remarkable because the master of ceremonies was, on the screen and in real life, a stiff—a staid, humorless, rather puritanical man. As a print journalist he once attacked Marlene Dietrich because she had appeared in a Broadway show wearing slacks. His charm was at best marginal. His body language was that of someone frozen and not yet thawed out. He was almost completely expressionless. His voice was sharp and high-pitched, with what the rest of the country judged to be a New York accent. John Crosby, the best television critic in the country, wrote as early as December 1948, "One of the small but vexing questions confronting anyone in this area with a television set is: 'Why is Ed Sullivan on it every Sunday night?' " The question, Crosby went on, "seems to baffle Mr. Sullivan as much as anyone else." Later, Jack Paar said of him, "Who can bring to a simple English sentence suspense and mystery and drama? Who but Ed Sullivan can introduce a basketball player with the reverence once reserved for Dr. (Albert) Schweitzer?" Slightly offended by all the criticism of her husband, Sylvia Sullivan once sought to write a piece answering all the criticism of his wooden manner. Unfortunately, the article was titled "I'm Married to the Great Stone Face." In it she proceeded to deny rumors that he seemed so stiff because he had a serious war wound or that he had been hit on the head by a golf club. "They're not true," she wrote in *Collier's*. "Nevertheless once in a while some kindly stranger will congratulate him on his courage in working despite his deformity!"

CBS, on whose network the show was carried and for whom he made a great deal of money, was never entirely happy with him. Yet miraculously, despite what the critics said, the show worked. Why, no one really knew. Perhaps it was the perfect hour for a variety show, 8 P.M. on Sunday.

Perhaps it was the sheer quality of the entertainers, since almost every entertainer in the world was desperate to be showcased on so prominent a platform. Perhaps it was the fact that television was still new and there was something comforting for ordinary Americans, tuning in their first television sets, to take this adventure with so stolid and careful a man. For his taste was conservative, cautious, and traditional. When some of the blacklisting groups criticized some of the performers he put on in the late forties, Sullivan backed down immediately and gave the blacklisters a veto power over any acts or performers who might have political liabilities.

In 1956, he was at the height of his power. He was making about $200,000 a year from CBS and another $50,000 from the *News*. He was most assuredly not a man to cross. His show was at the exact center of American mass culture. And he wanted no part of Elvis Presley, who was now in the process of enraging endless ministers and parent groups by dint of his onstage gyrations and the overt sexuality of his music. Nor did Sullivan like rockers in general. There had been a somewhat unpleasant incident earlier with the great black rocker Bo Diddley. Sullivan's people had heard that Diddley was hot, that his records were rising on the charts, and they booked him without knowing very much about his music or the strength of his personality. Diddley was raw and original, and there was a lot of movement in his act. When Sullivan saw it, he was not pleased. According to his biographer, Jerry Bowles, Sullivan wandered over to the orchestra area, thumbed through some sheet music, picked out "Some Enchanted Evening," and handed it to Diddley. "Sing this," he said. That night Diddley started by singing "Some Enchanted Evening," but the audience began to giggle. Suddenly, Bo Diddley switched over to his song about the heroic Bo Diddley, and he went straight to the beat. The orchestra stayed with Rodgers and Hammerstein. Sullivan was furious. Rockers, he decided, were different from other people and did not keep their word. He wanted nothing to do with them.

Earlier, as Elvis conquered the South with regional appearances, he had begun to perfect his act. Some of it was natural instinct—he had to carry a beat, and it was hard to carry a beat while standing still. So he began to gyrate as he had seen endless gospel singers gyrate. The first time he had done it, he had been driven by pure instinct and the crowd began to shout. Later he asked a friend what had happened. The friend explained that Elvis had started jumping around on the stage and using his body and the crowd had loved it. From then it became part of his act; if you were going to do a live show, he explained, you had to have an act. That's what people came to see. Otherwise, they could just as well stay at home and play records. A country singer named Bob Luman once said of an early Elvis concert: "This cat came out in a coat and a pink shirt and socks and he had this sneer on his face and he stood behind the mike for five minutes, I'll bet, before he made a move. Then he hit his guitar a lick and he broke two strings. I'd been playing for ten years and I hadn't broken a total of two strings. So there he was, these two strings dangling, and he hadn't done anything yet, and these high school girls were screaming and fainting and running up to the stage and then he started to move his hips real slow like he had a thing for his guitar . . ."

The teeny-boppers started to maul him. They did not mean him any harm, he explained. What they wanted "was pieces of you for souvenirs." By the end of 1955 RCA was ready to push his records nationally, and he had signed to do four Saturday-night shows on a show produced by Jackie Gleason called *Stage Show*. He got $1,250 a show for the Gleason appearances plus, of course, national exposure. Gleason knew exactly what was happening. "He's a guitar-playing Marlon Brando," he said. Only part of what worked for Elvis was the music, Gleason knew. Certainly, that was important, but it was more than just the music. It was also the movement and the style. And a great deal of it was the look: sultry, alienated, a little misunderstood, the rebel who wanted to rebel without ever leaving home. He was perfect because he was the safe rebel. He never intended to cause trouble: He was a classic mama's boy, and Gladys Presley had barely let him out of her sight until he was in high school; now finally on the threshold of great success, he used his royalties in that first year to buy three new homes, each larger than the last, for his parents. He also gave each of his parents a new Cadillac, though the one he gave his mother never got license plates, since she did not drive.

By 1956 he had become both a national celebrity and a national issue. His success, amplified as it was by the newfound wealth of the nation and the new technology of radio, record players and, finally, television, defied the imagination. He quickly made a three-picture deal with Hal Wallis for $450,000. "Hound Dog" sold 2 million copies and "Don't Be Cruel," sold 3 million. His singles were not merely taking off, they were defying traditional musical categories: "Heartbreak Hotel" was number one on the white chart, number one on the country chart, and number five on the rhythm-and-blues chart; "Don't Be Cruel" and "Hound Dog" became number one on all three charts. In April 1956 he already had six of RCA's all-time top twenty-five records and was selling $75,000 worth of records a day.

That month he made a rather sedate appearance on the Milton Berle Show and in June Berle had him back. This time he cut loose, causing an immense number of protests about the vulgarity of his act. Now Elvis Presley was working the American home, and suddenly the American home was a house divided. At this point Ed Sullivan lashed out against Presley. He announced that Presley's act was so suggestive that it would never go on his show. This was Sullivan as a guardian of public morals, a man born in 1902, fifty-four years old that summer. Within three weeks Sullivan had to change his mind. His competition, the Steve Allen show, immediately called Colonel Parker and booked Presley for July 1. The problem for Allen, of course, was that, like everyone else, he wanted it both ways. He wanted Elvis on board, but he did not want a big protest on the part of the traditional segment of his audience. So he and his staff compromised: They would go high Elvis rather than low Elvis. They dressed Elvis in a tux, and they got him to limit his body movement. He did a dim-witted sketch with Allen, Imogene Coca, and Andy Griffith, in which he played a cowboy named Tumbleweed, and he sang "Hound Dog" to a live basset hound. The Presley fans hated it. After the show, Dewey Phillips called Elvis long-distance in New York: "You better call home and get straight, boy. What you doing in that monkey suit? Where's your guitar?" When Elvis returned to Memphis for a concert in Phillips's honor, he cut loose with a pure rock-a-billy performance. It was Presley at his best, and when he finished, he told the audience, "I just want to tell y'all not to worry—them people in New York and Hollywood are not going to change me none."

But the Steven Allen show had worked in one

sense; it was the first time Steve Allen had beaten Ed Sullivan in the ratings. Sullivan surrendered almost immediately. His people called Colonel Parker and signed Elvis for $50,000 to do three shows. It was a figure then unheard of. It was one thing to guard public morals for the good of the nation and the good of your career; it was another thing to guard public morals at the cost of your career.

The battle was over: Ed Sullivan had conceded and the new music had entered the mainstream of American culture. Sullivan was not there for the first show; he was recuperating from an auto accident, and Charles Laughton was the host. The producers deliberately shot Elvis from the waist up. But soon he would be singing and dancing in full sweep. Sullivan was pleased; his ratings were extraordinary. He also wanted to make clear that he had not lowered America's morals. "I want to say to Elvis Presley and the country that this is a real decent, fine boy," Sullivan told his audience after the third show. "We've never had a pleasanter experience on our show with a big name than we've had with you. You're thoroughly all right." It was the deftest of surrenders; it appeared to be the generous speech of a man receiving a surrender while in fact it was the speech of a man who had just surrendered himself. Market economics had won. It augured a profound change in American taste: In the past, whites had picked up on black jazz, but that had largely been done by the elite. This was different; this was a visceral, democratic response by the masses. It was also a critical moment for the whole society: The old order had been challenged and had not held. New forces were at work, driven by technology. The young did not have to listen to their parents anymore.

. . .

Marlon Brando and Elvis Presley were only the first of the new rebels from the world of entertainment and art. Soon to come were many others. If there was a common thread, it was that they all projected the image of being misunderstood, more often than not by their parents' generation, if not their own parents themselves. There was little overt political content in their rebellion; their public personae and the characters they played were not fighting against the sinister injustices of the McCarthy era or racial injustice. Only Brando came close to politics when he confronted the mob in *On the Waterfront.*

Above all, they were young men with obvious emotional tensions—onstage, on screen, and in real life. After Brando finished in the Broadway production of *Streetcar,* he vowed that he hated Hollywood and would be back on the legitimate stage soon. In point of fact, he never returned. After a short run of remarkable films that included *Streetcar* and *On the Waterfront,* he seemed to become increasingly careless in his selection of roles and cynical about his art. If

Brando was rebelling against anything, it seemed to be against the idea of his profession, of having to pursue the career, the achievements, and the honors that everyone expected of him.

Just as Brando went from doing his best work to giving surprisingly ordinary performances in surprisingly ordinary movies, a new rebel star was ascending in Hollywood: James Dean. Brando was Dean's personal hero, and like Brando, Dean was plucked from the edges of the New York theater crowd by the perceptive and vigilant Elia Kazan. Even more than Brando, Dean was a cult figure. Brando might have had a bigger career and done more distinguished work, but Dean's legend was greater, because his life was so short. He was always remembered as young, always to be mourned—the ultimate, eternal rebel, whose promise had never been fulfilled. To serious fans of the era's theater and movies, Dean's legend would eventually surpass Brando's, and that was almost heretical, because Brando was the original and Dean the imitation. In a book that was in no small part an open letter to Brando, the critic Richard Schickel wrote: "To tell you what may be a more awful truth, later generations are more interested in James Dean. Can you imagine? The kid who copied you! Who used to annoy you by calling up and trying to make friends!" For Dean had a puppy-dog infatuation with the older Brando. Kazan knew it, so one day he invited Brando on the set. Dean "was so adoring that he seemed shrunken and twisted in misery," Kazan later wrote. On occasion Dean signed his name to letters in a way that showed he was conscious of the different influences on him: "Jimmy (Brando Clift) Dean."

Dean was typecast as the rebel, and like Brando, in real life he was rebelling against an unhappy childhood and a father he had grown to hate. Even more than Brando, he came to symbolize the belief of the youth of that era that because they were young, they were misunderstood. He was good-looking, almost delicate, with a sulky, androgynous appearance that made him seem vulnerable. He was driven by his own pain and anguish. Dean was, wrote Steven Vineberg, "the most inward of actors: His performances were always about the beautiful chaos in his own soul."

Dean's life and his art were inseparable. Unlike Brando, who had considerable professional training and considerable range, Dean basically played himself—but brilliantly. Sullen and sulky, he was still worthy of redemption if only the properly tender girlfriend could be found to mother him. Either he got a part right instinctively, Kazan believed, or he didn't get it at all. At a certain point the only way to get him to improve his performance was to get him liquored up.

His career was short. There were only three films before he met his death in a car accident. The end came at the height of his fame and in the very same year of his stunning debut in *East of Eden.*

That early death ensured him a place in the pantheon of artists who lived fast and died young. His
poster would grace the bedroom walls of future
generations of young would-be rebels. Dick
Schickel noted the advantages of dying young
(Dean) and the disadvantages of not (Brando):
"There is much to be said for dying young in
circumstances melodramatically appropriate to
your public image. There is very little to be said
for living long and burying that image in silence,
suet and apparent cynicism."

Dean was born in small-town Indiana. His
mother died of breast cancer when he was a young
boy, and his father, weighted by debt, had been
forced to sell the family car to pay for her final
operation. The burden of rearing a family alone
was too much for Winton Dean, and James was
sent to live with an aunt and uncle. Both of his
parents had let him down, he would sometimes
say, his mother by dying so young, his father by
being cold and distant. Once, when they were
both young actors, Dennis Hopper asked Dean
where his magic came from. Dean answered that
it came from his anger: "Because I hate my
mother and father. I wanted to get up onstage
. . . and I wanted to *show* them. I'll tell you what
made me want to become an actor, what gave me
the drive to want to be the best. My mother died
when I was almost nine. I used to sneak out of my
uncle's house and go to her grave, and I used to
cry and cry on her grave—Mother, why did you

leave me? I need you . . . I want you."

In 1949 he finished high school and headed for Hollywood, hoping to become an actor. His initial success was marginal, but gradually he learned to use his charm and looks to get ahead. In effect, he became a sexual hustler on both sides of the lines; he was, at once, both innocent and predatory. He was always ambitious, although his ambitions were a bit ill defined. When he was twenty he went east to study at the Actors Studio. He also tried his hand at television. His talent, especially his ability to show profound vulnerability, was obvious from the start, but unlike Brando, who was a major force at the Studio, Dean never really committed himself to the workshops and was wary of having his work critiqued by his peers: "If I let them dissect me like a rabbit in a clinical research laboratory or something, I might not be able to produce again. For chrissake, they might sterilize me!" he told a friend at the time. Still, Rod Serling, one of the foremost of the new television playwrights, thought Dean's move to New York was a critical break for so unusual a talent. Serling's *A Long Time Till Dawn* was Dean's first starring vehicle. In 1953 television's theatrical productions were still experimental. There was no powerful network bureaucracy yet to tell directors and writers what they could not write. It was a rare time, when unexpected talent flourished and was discovered on television—particularly young talent.

In those days, Serling thought television was well ahead of Hollywood in social and cultural adventerousness. Movies, he believed, were lodged in another time, in an outdated reality; and when, for example, they dealt with the young, with few exceptions they still showed teenage girls as cheerleaders and bobby-soxers, and teenage boys as high school athletic heroes in letter sweaters. Serling was convinced the young had begun to change, were significantly more alienated from the values of their parents. In *A Long Time Till Dawn,* the hero or antihero was, in the author's words, "a terribly upset, psyched-out kid, a precursor to the hooked generation of the sixties, the type that became part of the drug/rock culture . . ." Serling understood immediately that Dean was perfect for the role, and indeed he went on to play it brilliantly. To Serling, Dean was one of the first manifestations of a youth culture just surfacing and which Hollywood did not yet understand. "There was a postwar mystification of the young, a gradual erosion of confidence in their elders, in the so-called truths, in the whole litany of moral codes," Serling said. "They just didn't believe in them anymore. In television we were more aware of this and more in touch with what was happening. We could portray it immediately too—write a script one week and have it on the air the next."

For Dean, playing a rebel was effortless; being conventional was much harder. He seemed to have figured out during this period that his future lay in being the outsider. David Dalton points out a portfolio of photos taken of him in New York that reveal a young man in metamorphosis. In the early photos he appears to be eager to please, someone who might still be able to play an all-American boy; in the later photos, his face and his eyes have darkened and he is clearly a rebel.

During that period Kazan, then at the height of his fame, was in the process of turning John Steinbeck's novel *East of Eden* into a film. The script was a contemporary retelling of the Cain/Abel story from the Bible. The older actors were already lined up, Raymond Massey and Jo Van Fleet as the father and mother. But casting the two boys was critical. At first Kazan had wanted Brando and Montgomery Clift as the twins, one good, the other bad. But they could not decide on who would play the bad brother. Besides, both Brando and Clift were getting a little long in the tooth for these roles. Kazan started searching for even younger talent—something he liked to do anyway, because to his mind, young actors were hungrier and had more of an edge, something they lost with success. "They're like fighters on their way up. It's a life or death struggle for them and they give their utmost to the role. This quality disappears later," he once said. "They become civilized and normal."

A friend told Kazan about Dean, whom he

remembered from the Actors Studio as sullen and not very productive. At their first meeting Kazan, wanting to provoke Dean, deliberately kept him waiting; when he finally arrived, Kazan found Dean slouched down in his seat—rude, disrespectful, and shabbily dressed. The two of them were engaging in a certain kind of theatrical gamesmanship, Kazan decided. They did not talk much—conversation was not James Dean's strong suit, particularly with someone so powerful in the theater and whose good opinion he so desperately wanted. Dean offered Kazan a ride on his motorbike, and off they went. "He was showing off," Kazan later wrote, "a country boy not impressed with big city traffic."

Fortunately for Dean, his act worked. To Kazan, who bore his own resentments against *his* father, Dean *was* Cal Trask. "There was no point in trying to cast it better or nicer. Jimmy was it. He had a grudge against all fathers. He was vengeful; he had a sense of aloneness and of being persecuted. And he was uncommonly suspicious." Before heading west, Dean did one screen test with the young Paul Newman. Kazan asked Newman: "Paul, do you think Jimmy will appeal to the bobby-soxers?" Newman answered, "I don't know. Is he going to be a sex symbol?" Then, playing along with the director's question, Newman gave Dean a long flirtatious look: "I don't usually go out with boys. But with his looks, sure, sure, I think they'll flip over him." The technicians working on the set, though, were so unimpressed by him that they thought Dean was the stand-in for the real star.

Kazan scooped Dean up and flew him out to California for shooting. Dean had never been in a plane before. He carried his clothes in two packages wrapped in paper and tied together by string. When they got to Los Angeles, Dean asked if they could stop in at the suburban Los Angeles lab where his father worked. That delighted Kazan, who was always in search of life as art; Kazan remembered Dean's father as a "man [who] had no definition and made no impression except that he had no definition. Obviously there was a strong tension between the two, and it was not friendly. I sensed the father disliked his son." Soon Dean and Kazan drove on.

Dean was his own worst enemy, often alienating those around him. "Must I always be miserable? I try so hard to make people reject me. Why? I don't want to write this letter. It would be better to remain silent. Wow! Am I fucked up," he wrote a girlfriend when he had reached California to shoot *Eden.* He resented the older actors on the set. Raymond Massey, the veteran actor who played the father, could not stand Dean's sullen manner and his tendency to improvise with the script. Rather than try to heal the breach, Kazan aggravated the tension in order to show it on screen. Kazan kept Dean moody and resentful. There was a brief affair with Pier Angeli, the young actress, but it ended soon. That pleased Kazan: "Now I had Jimmy as I wanted him, alone and miserable."

With Ms. Angeli gone on to a romance with Vic Damone, in Kazan's words, "Narcissism took over." Dean had a camera and took endless pictures of himself standing in front of a mirror, changing his expression only slightly. "He'd show me the goddamn contact sheets and ask which one I liked best," Kazan wrote. "I thought they were all the same picture, but I said nothing." Kazan used that suffocating self-absorption to good effect in Dean's performance.

The success of *Eden* was stunning. It might have been perhaps Kazan's best film. Dean's performance was a sensation. "There is a new image in American films," wrote Pauline Kael, "the young boy as beautiful, disturbed animal, so full of love he's defenseless. Maybe the father doesn't love him, but the camera does and we're supposed to; we're thrust into upsetting angles, caught in infatuated close-ups, and prodded, 'Look at all that beautiful desperation.' " After a screening of *Eden,* Dean was interviewed by Howard Thompson of *The New York Times*. It was his first interview.

Even Kazan was surprised by Dean's impact, which surpassed that of the young Brando. Dean himself was acutely aware of the niche he occupied and of why his persona worked. On the set of *Giant* he told Dennis Hopper, who had become his friend: "Y'know, I think I've got a chance to really make it because in this hand I'm holding Marlon Brando, saying, 'Fuck you!' and in the other hand, saying, 'Please forgive me,' is Montgomery Clift. 'Please forgive me.' 'Fuck you!' 'Please forgive me.' 'Fuck you!' And somewhere in between is James Dean."

He went on quickly to do *Rebel Without a Cause*. When it had first been purchased by Warner in 1946, it was thought of as a vehicle for Brando, but Brando had not been interested, so the script was put aside. Then Nicholas Ray, the director, picked up on *Rebel* because juvenile delinquency was becoming such a hot issue. The script was written and rewritten by a seemingly endless stream of writers, but in the end it was a vehicle for Dean, who was to play the son of a weak father and a nagging, complaining mother. According to the notes in the screenplay for his part, Dean was to be "the angry victim" of insensitive, careless parents: "At seventeen he is filled with confusion about his role in life. Because of his 'nowhere' father, he does not know how to be a man. Because of his wounding mother, he anticipates destruction in all women. And yet he wants to find a girl who will be willing to receive his tenderness." Dean is, once again, the tender but misunderstood young man, not getting a fair chance, and his character muses: "If I could have just one day when I wasn't all confused . . . I wasn't ashamed of everything. If I felt I belonged some place." The screenplay is weak; what power the movie has is in the performance. If Dean's acting reputation rests on *East of Eden,* his myth is largely entwined with his role in *Rebel.* The role is the prototype for the alienated youth blaming all injustice on parents and their generation.

Years later Kazan had some doubts about the image of youthful alienation that he and Ray had fostered; Dean had cast a spell over the youth of America, he said. It was not something he approved of, though he accepted his share of the responsibility: "Its essence was that all parents were insensitive idiots, who didn't understand or appreciate their kids and weren't able to help them. Parents were the enemy. . . . In contrast to these parent figures, all youngsters were supposed to be sensitive and full of 'soul.'" The more Kazan thought about it, the less he liked the character of the self-pitying, self-dramatizing youth. Nor was he happy when an endless number of Dean fans wrote him letters thanking him for what he had done for Jimmy. In truth, he was not fond of Dean and did not think him a major talent; as far as Kazan was concerned, Dean had gotten through the movie largely because of the kindness and professionalism of Julie Harris. Kazan was convinced he had gotten Dean's best work out of him.

If Dean had learned from Brando, now others would copy Dean. Elvis Presley, for one, wanted to be known as the James Dean of rock and roll. A line was beginning to run through the generations. Suddenly, *alienation* was a word that was falling lightly from his own lips and those of his friends, noted the writer Richard Schickel in an essay on the importance of Marlon Brando as a cultural figure: "*The Lonely Crowd* was anatomized in 1950, and the fear of drifting into its clutches was lively in us. *White Collar* was on our brick and board bookshelves, and we saw how the eponymous object seemed to be choking the life out of earlier generations. *The Man in the Gray Flannel Suit* stalked our nightmares and soon enough *The Organization Man* would join him there, though of course, even as we read about these cautionary figures, many of us were talking to corporate recruiters about entry-level emulation of them."

THIRTY-TWO

No ONE AT GM could ever have dared forecast so much prosperity over such a long period of time. It was a brilliant moment, unparalleled in American corporate history. Success begat success; each year the profit expectations went higher and higher. The postwar economic boom may have benefited many Americans, but no one benefited more than General Motors. By rough estimates, 49.3 million motor vehicles were registered when the decade began, 73.8 when it ended; by some estimates, an average of 4.5 million cars, many of them that might have stayed on the road in a less prosperous economy, were scrapped annually. That means as many as 68 to 70 million cars, ever larger, ever heavier, ever more expensive, were sold, and General Motors sold virtually half of them. The average car, which had cost $1,270 at the beginning of the decade, had risen to $1,822 by the end of it; that rate, Edward Cray noted in his book *Chrome Colossus,* was twice as fast as the rest of the wholesale cost index.

There was in all of this success for General Motors a certain arrogance of power. This was not only an institution apart; it was so big, so rich, and so powerful that it was regarded in the collective psyche of the nation as something more than a mere corporation: It was like a nation unto itself, a separate entity, with laws and a culture all its own: Loyalty among employees was more important than individual brilliance. Team players were valued more highly than mavericks. It was the duty of the rare exceptional GM employee to accept the limits on his individual fame; he would be known within the company and perhaps within the larger automotive industry as a man of talent, but the rest of the country would not know his name; the corporation came first and the corporation bestowed wealth but anonymity on its most valued employees. The individual was always subordinated to the greater good of the company.

The men who ran the corporation, almost without exception, came from small towns in America and were by and large middle class, white, and Protestant or, occasionally, Catholic. If they had gone to four-year colleges they were usually land-grant colleges. They were square and proud of it, instinctively suspicious of all that was different and foreign. They were American, and above all else Americans knew cars. Everything about them reflected their confidence that they had achieved virtually all there was to achieve in life. Never knowing anyone very different from themselves when they had grown up (or certainly anyone very different from themselves worth emulating), they believed they represented what everyone else aspired to. They were sure of their

accomplishments and of their taste. Others, critics, outside Detroit, might believe that these men
were not such giants and might believe that they
did not so much create that vast postwar economic wave as they had the good fortune to ride
it; be that as it may, no one contradicted the men
of GM to their faces. As for the intellectuals, if
they wanted to drive small foreign cars, live in
small houses, and make small salaries, why even
bother to argue with them?

General Motors was Republican, not Eastern sophisticated Republican but heartland conservative Republican—insular, suspicious of
anything different. Zora Arkus-Duntov, a top
GM designer and an émigré, once complained to
a friend of the insularity of the culture and noted
that the problem in the company was that it was
run in every department by men "who believe that
the world is bordered on the East by Lake Huron,
and on the West by Lake Michigan." (In those
days, when the nation's anti-Communism was at
its height, Arkus-Duntov, the son of a White Russian engineer who had lived briefly in Belgium
before coming to the United States, was described
in GM promotional material as being of Belgian
extraction.) Arthur Summerfield, one of the largest Chevy dealers in the country, had always seen
the company, the country, and the Republican
party as one and the same thing. A leading figure
in the Michigan Republican party, Summerfield
in the late forties devised a plan by which all

Michigan GM dealers paid one dollar to the Republican party for each car they sold, upon fear of not receiving their regular shipment of cars from the company if they held back. For such loyalty Summerfield was eventually rewarded with the job of postmaster general in Eisenhower's cabinet.

As the success of the company grew, its informal rules gradually became codified. The culture was first and foremost hierarchical: An enterprising young executive tended to take all signals, share all attitudes and prejudices of the men above him, as his wife tended to play the sports and card games favored by the boss's wife, to emulate how she dressed and even to serve the same foods for dinner. The job of a junior executive was to know at all times what the senior executive desired at any given moment, what kind of snack or alcohol he wanted in his hotel room on the road, what his favorite meal at a favorite restaurant was in a given city (and to have an underling there several hours early, standing guard to make sure that nothing went wrong—that the right table was available, that the restaurant did not run out of the favorite food or wine). It was the underling's job not only to make sure that Harlow Curtice's favored hors d'oeuvre, smoked oysters, was at cocktail parties, but the underling was to stand as near as possible to Curtice, holding a tray of oysters for him as he moved through a crowd. Thus, at one of GM's famed

Motorama shows in New York, a reporter named Don Silber, from the *Cleveland Press,* once asked Paul Garrett, a high-ranking GM public relations official, what time it was. Garrett did not deign to look at his watch. Instead, he turned to his aide, a man named Ken Yewl, and said, "Ken, tell him what time it is."

The essential goodness of the corporation was never questioned. It was regarded as, of all the many places to work, the best, because it was the biggest, the most respected, made the most money and, very quietly, through bonuses and stock, rewarded its top people the most handsomely. Early in his career Harlow Curtice, while still the controller at AC Champion Spark Plugs, had ventured to New York with Albert Champion, the head of AC, to meet the top GM people, including Alfred Sloan. There Curtice had undergone something of an initiation rite as the home office checked out the new boys from the Midwest. Apparently, both men met GM's standards, for at the end Mr. Sloan offered both Champion and Curtice a chance to invest in GM's prime management investment program for up-and-coming executives. They could invest about $25,000 and would in a few years' time, as Mr. Sloan promised, each get back around $1.5 million. It was, in an age of rising income taxes, the company's pioneering method of trying to protect and reward its top executives. Suddenly, Curtice realized that in addition to being successful, he might also become truly rich. As they were heading back to Flint, Curtice turned to Champion and said, "That sounds like a pretty good deal, doesn't it—as close to a sure thing as you can get." "We're not going to do that, Red," Champion answered. "I don't believe in letting New York tell us how to run our business."

Even within the closed world of General Motors, there was a feeling that Chevrolet was a world apart, perhaps a little too smug. After all, the corporation was mighty, but at Chevrolet they felt the other divisions were just window dressing, that the heart and soul of General Motors was Chevy. It was responsible for nearly 70 to 75 percent of GM's profits in most years. Chevrolets were what healthy, stable young Americans drove. Chevy belonged on the short list of certifiably *American* things, which could not be duplicated anywhere else in the world: homemade apple pie, Coke, a World Series baseball game, a Norman Rockwell cover on the *Saturday Evening Post,* a grilled hamburger in the backyard. In those years it did a brilliant job of connecting its advertising to those other American artifacts. Chevy was not just the great American car, it was something uniquely American. If there was any fear in those years, it was that the government might break General Motors up into its component parts. If there was nervousness in the rest of GM over the implications of the splitting up of Sloan's masterpiece, there was a good deal less nervousness at Chevy; indeed they was almost cocky about it, for if the feds acted, and Chevy was broken off, it would still be the largest company in the United States.

In the early fifties, no one from the corporation had any power over Chevy; in fact, in those earlier days the corporation was comparatively weak, with a small, somewhat understaffed headquarters. Chevy was a mighty industrial masterpiece that had been put together by the founding giants of the corporation, such men as Sloan and his great enabler, Big Bill Knudsen. (In the late fifties and early sixties, the corporation shrewdly sought to limit Chevy's autonomy. Knowing that the Chevy people were resistant to any change mandated from the outside, the corporation promoted former top executives of Chevy who, knowing the vulnerabilities of the division they had once served, knew exactly how to subdue and undermine this once proud and once independent kingdom. Heading the corporation after heading Chevy was not, in the eyes of some, that much of a promotion: "When you left Chevy and took over the corporation," Tom Adams, a Detroit advertising man who worked closely with GM, once noted, "it was almost like retiring.")

Yet for all of Chevrolet's great wealth and power, if there was a potential weakness in General Motors as Curtice took over (replacing Wilson who had joined Eisenhower's cabinet), it was the car itself. The basic Chevy was becoming quite stodgy. It was GM's low-end model, and the inevitable result of the company's relentless thrust to make its models bigger and heavier and to make more profit per car had gradually undermined the traditional Chevy. General Motors' great surge to increase automotive power had begun when Bill Knudsen had upgraded Chevy to take the entry-level niche away from Ford. Now it appeared that Chevy was slipping, that its cars had become dowdy, and that entry-level leadership was swinging back to Ford. Ford had introduced an eight-cylinder engine, and not only was that helping Ford at the low end, it was lending a certain ominous success to the whole line-up. Ford's cars were now regarded as hotter and sexier, and Chevy, with only six cylinders, was now trying to play catch-up. Clearly, the company had stayed too long with the old six-cylinder engine—what was called the "blue flame six." In addition, the styling of the car was boring, and one auto writer said that it looked like it had been designed "by Herbert Hoover's haberdasher." So in late 1951 Wilson, in one of his last major decisions, told his then-assistant Curtice that he had to juice Chevy up.

Curtice envisioned a racier, sportier new Chevy; he wanted an eight-cylinder engine, and he wanted it immediately. Immediately, in this instance, meant two years: Normally, a project like this—the complete redesign of engine, transmis-

sion, and body—took at least three and sometimes up to four or five years. But Curtice knew
exactly what he had to do: He decided to take the
best engineer the company had, Ed Cole, and put
him in charge of the new Chevy.

Ed Cole was a troubleshooter and maverick
extraordinaire within the organization; he was by
normal standards far too idiosyncratic and outspoken for the corporation, probably the last true
maverick of his generation at GM. He had always
fought the bureaucracy as it got more powerful.
He was disliked and distrusted by the financial
people because he loved to spend the company's
money, but he was tolerated by other executives
because he was so driven and talented. Cole was
the rare man in so large an institution who not
only seemed able to deliver what the company
demanded but to deliver it under exceptional
pressure and crushing deadlines. He had been
something of a star at the company during World
War Two, working on GM's tanks, and had gone
from there to be a key figure at Cadillac, where he
had become chief engineer at the youthful age of
thirty-six. Then, during the Korean war, he had
taken over an old deserted plant in Cleveland,
which was literally filled with stored-up sacks of
beans, and created tanks for the Korean War.
Cole, unlike many in the company, had liked the
intense pressures of wartime, the sense of immediacy, and of course the leverage it gave him to

do things his way and ignore those above him
who told him that what he intended to do could
not be done.

Ed Cole was a farm boy from Marne, Michigan, who had hated the boredom of the farm and
had always vowed he would get out as quickly as
he could. He had intended to be a lawyer and was
on his way to a legal career, except that his great
natural ability as a tinkerer convinced him that he
probably ought to be an engineer. He had gone to
the General Motors Institute in Flint and had
done so well that he never actually graduated—
instead, he was recruited by Cadillac early and
went directly to work in its engineering department. From the start he was different, a man
apart, driven, relentless, challenging everything
around him. He made the company a great deal of
money and, in the words of his friend Tom
Adams, cost the company a great deal as well,
because he *had to try everything*. He had 150 ideas
a week and he had to make sure each actually
succeeded or failed. He might well, Adams
thought, have been the most driven man he had
ever met—in both work and at play. If you
hunted with him, he pushed himself and others so
ferociously that he was out in front of the dogs.
"Ed," Tom Adams used to tell him. "We don't
really need the dogs when you hunt." If he fished,
he fished longer and harder and had to catch not
only the biggest fish but the most fish. If he was
down in the Florida Keys and he hooked a mam-

moth tarpon on light tackle, he would fight the fish for what seemed like the entire afternoon—no matter how brutal the sun on himself, his wife, and his friends, no matter that the tarpon was sure to be released back into the water. If he took his young son, David, fishing up in northern Michigan, where there were a vast number of lakes, he did not fish only one lake every day for five or six days, getting to know it and its secrets; rather, he arranged to have a boat at a different lake every day.

Any mechanical object that was broken was a challenge to him. The idea of throwing out a broken piece of home equipment was a personal insult. If there was a coffee maker at home that did not work, Ed Cole had to fix it. If he and his pals were on a fishing trip in Canada and the motor on their generator conked out, Ed Cole stayed up all night to fix it—not because he needed to, not because they needed the generator in the morning, but because he was proving to the world that he could fix it, by working all night with a French Canadian guide holding a flash-light. If he was hunting in some farmer's field and there was a broken reaper, he had to stop and fix it. Once, when the heater in his home swimming pool went out, he did not, as others might do, call a specialty repairman. There was no need for the Yellow Pages with Ed Cole. Instead, he swam to the heater and started repairing it, until there was a small explosion and his eyebrows were singed.

He was a man utterly without sophistication. He was as good an engineer as there was, but outside of that, he had little interest or curiosity. He was not a particularly good businessman and was vulnerable to schemes—he bought, among other things, a fair number of leases from a man who claimed he was going to find vast oil fields in southern Michigan. Bud Goodman, a senior GM executive, liked to joke that he was still teaching Cole how to use a telephone.

He was not genteel or careful as most of the other men rising to power at GM were; they were a reflection of the cautiousness that comes when institutional values become enshrined by generation after generation and when cautiousness is rewarded. Cole argued too often and too loudly for doing whatever it took to build a good car, and by the mid-fifties, he was doing it in a corporation where many of the men around him were less committed to cars and to engineering every year. But they were a poor match for Ed Cole, who seemed to bring a kind of primal force to each encounter.

He was not smooth. He did un-GM things. He got divorced, which violated the then code of the company. He went out for a time with Mamie Van Doren, the flashy movie actress (if he was going to go out with an actress, as someone noted, why couldn't it be someone like Lee Remick?). He even gave her a Corvette painted a color that matched her lipstick. When he married for the second time, it was to a much younger, striking blonde, and her name was *Dolly;* Dolly Cole, most assuredly, was not a GM type of wife, content to wait her turn in the pecking order at the Bloomfield Hills Country Club. From the moment she arrived, there was a sense on the part of the other wives that she represented not just a challenge to the culture of the company but a threat to every marriage within it.

Cole's motto, a friend noted, was the very un-GM-like "Kick the hell out of the status quo." He had played a critical part in designing the V-8 engine that had reshaped the '49 Cadillac, but this new challenge at Chevy was even greater, for it required a powerful but lighter engine, which would not load the car down. Ed Cole went on a wartime footing. He scoured the company for its best engineers, offering them the challenge of working on something entirely new. He started in May 1952 and overnight the engineer pool at Chevy grew from some 850 engineers to 3,000. Ed Cole did a brilliant job on the new V-8. It was a marvelous engine, the best, his competitors thought, that the industry had ever produced at that time. His V-8 was inherently balanced—that is, unlike the four-cylinder engine and the six cylinder-engine, the two sets of four cylinders in the V-8 balanced each other and fired at the same time and made the engine smoother and the car less shaky. The power was there, and the new technology had allowed the engine to be consider-

ably lighter than V-8s in the past. Almost everything about the 1955 Chevy was new, in a way
that Detroit cars were rarely new: of 4,500 component parts used in it, all but 675 were brand-
new. It was, noted Clare MacKichan, one of its
designers, designed to exemplify "youth, speed
and lightness." Normally, it was Harley Earl who
liked his cars low and powerful, but this time it
was Ed Cole who pushed for it. Earl was excited
when he got the height down to sixty-one inches.
But even then Cole wasn't satisfied. "Hell, I
wouldn't want to make it over sixty inches," he
said. The two years creating the '55 Chevy were
probably his happiest time in the company—he
was dealing with something entirely new, and
though he was constantly fighting the financial
people, he was doing it with the top brass on his
side. As such, he lived with his car; it became a
part of the house, and there were meetings all the
time, even on weekends. There was a prototype of
it in the garage and, wrestling with a new idea, he
would get up in the middle of the night, and tinker
with the car. When the prototype V-8 engine was
completed, he put one under the hood of a '53
Chevy and blasted off. He and his son David took
it on a trip to northern Michigan. A state policeman in a Ford seemed to be tailing him, so Ed
Cole simply floored the accelerator and roared
away. Later, he stopped for a sandwich at a small
café in Baldwin and the trooper came in. He was
not angry; he was just curious. "What in God's

name do you have in that Chevy?" he asked. Cole was delighted; soon almost everyone in the café had gathered around him as he opened up the hood. From then on it became a special pleasure of his—pulling into a gas station, telling the attendant to fill the car up and check on the oil and gas, and hearing the kid, who was almost always a car nut, exclaim, "That's no Chevy." "It sure as hell is," he would always answer.

By October 1954, the '55 Chevy was finished and in the showrooms and it was a tour de force. With its lightweight 4.3-liter, 265-cubic-inch V-8 it supplied 160 horsepower. It was a car buff's delight. In the first year, the company sold 1.83 million cars, plus 393,000 trucks with the V-8.

Armed now with his powerful, completely new car, Cole set out to go after not just Ford but, semicovertly, GM's own Cadillac as well. For what Ed Cole had really intended from the time he took on the car was to create a Chevrolet that competed with Cadillac, a car almost as big as a Caddy and with just as much power. A poor man's Caddy, he liked to call it. "He wanted the average guy to feel he was driving a baby Cadillac," said Bob Cadaret, a designer. Or as Harley Earl said to Harlow Curtice in the design shop one day, "Now, *there* ... there's a car that if it had a Cadillac emblem [on it] I could sell as a Cadillac." Was there higher praise? The Chevy under Cole kept growing bigger and more powerful: The horsepower, which had once been around 90 to

100, now suddenly took off in quantum leaps: from 160 to 250 and, finally, to 325 and 410. Inside were such options as power steering, power brakes, and air-conditioning. In the end he had done what he set out to do—produced a Chevy that was the virtual automotive equivalent of a Cadillac. That was what the public wanted, he liked to say, "austere mink."

Ed Cole had stunned the corporation by putting the car together in such a short time, and not only had he successfully challenged an ever more confident Ford Company (and in the process been part of a year in which some $65 billion was spent on motor vehicles—one fifth of the national GNP), but it had set the stage for the next decade, for ever bigger more powerful cars. The next year the advertising slogan was: "The hot one's even hotter."

THIRTY-THREE

IN THE HOME it was to be a new, even easier age, the good life without sweat. "Never before so much for so few," wrote *Life* in 1954. Poppy Cannon, a food writer of that period, agreed: "Never before has so much been available to so many of us as now," she wrote in 1953, singling out as the key to the new American dream, the can opener— in her words, "that *open sesame* to wealth and freedom . . . freedom from tedium, space, work and your own inexperience." "Never has a whole people spent so much money on so many expensive things in such an easy way as Americans are doing today," reported *Fortune* in October 1956 in a glowing account of the consumer-driven economy entitled "What A Country!" It was, in fact, an astonishing age of abundance, an age of wondrous kitchen and household aids, ever bigger, but not ever more expensive as in the auto industry—the very success of the item meant that the price kept coming down: consumers were buying more for less.

Life in America, it appeared, was in all ways going to get better: A new car could replace an old one, and a larger, more modern refrigerator would take the place of one bought three years earlier, just as a new car had replaced an old one. Thus, the great fear of manufacturers, as they watched their markets reach saturation points, was that their sales would decline; this proved to be false. So did another of the retailers' fears— that people might save too much. Of the many things to be concerned about in postwar America, the idea of Americans saving too much was not one of them. The market was saturated, but people kept on buying—newer, improved products that were easier to handle, that produced cleaner laundry, washed more dishes and glasses, and housed more frozen steaks. What the leaders of the auto industry had done in autos with the annual model change, now, on a somewhat different scale, the manufacturers of home appliances and furniture were doing in their businesses. No wonder people bought more appliances. Suddenly, the old ones seemed inconvenient and outdated. That was, as much as anything else, a reflection of the new fantasy kitchen, as portrayed in endless women's magazines. Virtually every house had a refrigerator. Yet in 1955 alone, for example, *Fortune* reported, consumers had spent $1.3 billion buying 4 million new units, a significant increase over the previous year. The explanation was simple: frozen food. The old refrigerators had tiny freezers—enough space only to freeze a few trays of ice. The new refrigerators were designed for a wondrous, new world of frozen foods and TV dinners.

If there was one figure who came to symbol-ize the dazzling new American kitchen and all its astonishing appliances, as well as the revolution in selling and advertising that was taking place, it was Betty Furness—the Lady from Westing-house. In 1949 Betty Furness was thirty-three, an ingenue whose career was winding down after thirty-six films in five years (most of them B films). In those days, the people who did television com-mercials usually had come from radio, which meant they were good at reading lines but not at memorizing them, and they had no earthly idea of how to look at the camera. One poor woman who was directed to stand at a Westinghouse stove and heat some chocolate had been so terrified by the idea of talking and demonstrating at the same time that she had spilled melted chocolate all over the stove.

Furness had been doing some live television acting on *Studio One* at the time, and she had been appalled by these performers' lack of profession-alism, and she spoke out indignantly on the set about incompetent radio amateurs intruding in a visual medium. The next thing she knew, someone from the ad agency asked her to try a commercial. She gamely gave it a try, found that she was good at it, and got the job, which paid $150 a week— good money in 1949. It was, she soon discovered, hard work. On each episode of *Studio One,* where Westinghouse was the sole sponsor, she had to deliver one three-minute commercial and two one-and-a-half-minute commercials. They were live, and different each week, so the lines had to be memorized.

She soon discovered her chief asset was that she was attractive, but not in a way that made women jealous. Men liked her looks, but even more important, women, the prime targets of these commercials, liked her too. She came across, in fact, very much like the women portrayed in photos and ads in women's magazines—bright, upbeat, and confident, and modern without looking too glamorous. She was the all-American wife in the all-American kitchen. She exuded confidence that she could handle anything in this sparkling new workplace that promised to make household chores, if not downright obsolete, at least easy and glamorous. The advertising people wanted her to appear even more housewifely, and they pressured her to put on a wedding ring: There was even serious talk of having her take an assumed name under which she would in effect become the living Westinghouse logo. "We want you to be like Betty Crocker," someone from the ad agency told her. "But I'm not, I'm Betty Furness," she answered. "Well," he said. "What about wearing an apron when you do these commercials? That seems more kitcheny." "I don't want to wear an apron, and I don't want to seem more a part of the kitchen," she said. She had a strong sense of her own identity, and they were smart enough to let her alone after that.

She became a celebrity of significant proportions for the first time during the 1952 political conventions. Westinghouse had bought an immense amount of time, and she was on air constantly, almost as much as Walter Cronkite, it seemed, who also made his reputation during that campaign. There was an agreement not to put her on more than three times an hour, but she noted later, since the networks were on all day, she made as many as twenty to twenty-five appearances every day for a week. Add on an additional week for the other convention, and that was a lot more time on the air than any American politician was getting. Mercifully, the TelePrompTer had arrived by then and she did not have to spend all her spare time learning her lines.

Her clothes became something of an issue. She had to change minimally three times a day in order to stay fresh for herself and her viewers. She had an intuitive sense about her role, which was to keep as many people as possible from going to the bathroom during the commercial break. Therefore, she had to be interesting and unpredictable. If she changed her clothes constantly, housewives would be curious about what she was going to wear next. At the 1956 conventions she showed up with twenty-eight different outfits, so many that *Life* magazine later did a panel of photos showing her in each outfit. She bought all her clothes herself. There was a reason for this. If she let Westinghouse pay for the clothes, then the company would decide what she should wear and she was sure that she would have to look more like the wives of Westinghouse executives. But she knew exactly the look she wanted: modern, neat, no frills, sophisticated but modest.

Suddenly, she not only was famous, but all sorts of people she did not know seemed to think of her as a friend. Whenever she went out people recognized her and wanted to talk to her. To her surprise, she was Betty to them; they did not feel the need to use her last name, since she had been in their homes and, indeed, had helped them out in their kitchens. The sale of Westinghouse appliances boomed, and there was no doubt that there was a connection to this pleasant, attractive woman's appearances as the Westinghouse hostess. "You can be sure if it's Westinghouse," she said at the end of each commercial, and it became her trademark. One small incident alone demonstrated her power. In June 1952 she presented the American people with the Mobilair fan. In retrospect, she thought, it was a clunky machine, larger than most fans and mounted on wheels so it could be wheeled from room to room. It cost $89. It could blow air into a room or suck it out. Why anyone would have wanted one was beyond her. But the day after she went on television with one, the Mobilairs sold out in a number of major cities.

The Westinghouse people realized they had a star on their hands, and they asked her to sign a three-year, noncancellable contract to represent

Westinghouse exclusively, for $100,000 a year. With that she became the queen of American appliances, standing between a great faceless industrial company and American housewives. She knew little about the machines themselves except that they seemed well made and that the people who made them seemed like solid Americans from Ohio.

The one thing she did notice about the appliances, as she continued to promote them, was her sense that she was beginning to shrink—because the machines were getting bigger. When she started in 1950, the first refrigerators came up to her shoulders, which made them about fifty-eight inches high, on average. Gradually, they began to gain on her and became ever fancier, with enormous "frost-free" freezers. In this new wonder age, she mused at the time, people were being swallowed up by their kitchen appliances.

The only appliance she represented for Westinghouse that did not sell well was the dishwasher. For a long time the people at Westinghouse, as well as at other companies, were both surprised and disappointed by that appliance's poor showing. Persistent research with consumers finally showed that women were wary of buying dishwashers because the modern kitchen had become so automated that they feared if they stopped doing the dishes by hand, they would lose their last toehold in the kitchen and husbands would start wondering why they needed wives at all.

Furness did not take her new fame too seriously. Once, Westinghouse decided that she should do an institutional advertisement explaining how jet engines worked. She was appalled by the idea. They're going to laugh at me, she told her colleagues, but they insisted she do it. So the ad was written, and she stood there with what to her nonetheless seemed like a complicated explanation. "The way these engines work," she began and then quickly inserted her own words, "they tell me . . ."

Near the end of her eleven-year stint, there was a new president of Westinghouse who was clearly unhappy with her work—in part, she suspected, because he had not invented her. Immediately, he began casting doubts on her—and suggesting that perhaps Westinghouse needed a new and younger woman for its image. Gil Baird, the Westinghouse executive in charge of dealing with her, was told he should get a new person for the ads. Baird said he did not think it a particularly good idea. Why not? the new president asked. "Because," said Baird, "when you walk down the street no one knows who you are, but when Betty Furness walks down the street, everyone thinks Westinghouse."

· · ·

The power that Betty Furness had as a commercial symbol for Westinghouse was a reflection of the growing power of television as a vehicle for advertising and also of the growing power of ad-

vertising in American life. For the fifties was a
decade that revolutionized Madison Avenue. At
the turn of the century, the home had been a
reasonably safe haven from the purveyors of
goods (among other reasons, because there was so
little disposable income) other than the occasional
traveling salesman. Radio advertising had been
clever and deft and had greatly expanded the possibilities for reaching the consumer; but television
opened up the field even more dramatically and
offered a vast array of new techniques, from the
subtle and sophisticated to hammering away with
a brief, repetitive message. At first the television
departments of the major agencies were small,
understaffed, and lost money. That changed
quickly enough. "We discovered," said Rosser
Reeves, one of the prime architects and beneficiaries of television advertising, "that this was no
tame kitten; we had a ferocious man-eating tiger.
We could take the same advertising campaign
from print or radio and put it on TV, and even
when there were very few sets, sales would go
through the roof." The speed with which television's power ascended awed even those who
prophesied it: In 1949, Madison Avenue's total
television billings were $12.3 million; the next
year, it jumped to $40.8 million; and the year after
that, it jumped to $128 million. Television, of
course, could do what radio never could, for it
was visual. "Show the product," said Ben Duffy,
one of the men who was writing the rules even as

he learned them, "and show it in use." Many advertisers did that and more: A Remington razor shaved the fuzz off a peach, as Stephen Fox noted in *The Mirror Makers,* and a Band-Aid was used to show it was strong enough to lift an egg.

It was a salesman's dream: The nation had not only been wired to sell, but it was wired to sell through pictures, going right into the home. It was, Rosser Reeves said, like "shooting fish in a barrel." The advertising firms that adapted most readily to television tripled and quadrupled their annual billings; BBD&O, where Ben Duffy was an early booster of television, shifted 80 percent of its media buys to television, and by 1950 the television department had grown from twelve people to 150; Duffy was well ahead of the curve, and he was rewarded for his foresight: The firm went from billings of $40 million to $235 million in the fifteen-year period from 1945 to 1960.

Advertising men became the new heroes, or antiheroes, of American life. Novels and movies appeared about them. They were said to dress more stylishly than the mere businessmen they served: They lived somewhat unconventional, even racy lives and were supposedly torn between guarding the public good and using their great gifts to manipulate people for profit. In effect, it was seen to be a profession where talented young men traded their ideals for an even higher lifestyle, with luxurious suburban homes in Greenwich and Darien. In the film version of the

Frederic Wakeman novel *The Hucksters,* one of the early novels that helped give Madison Avenue its dubious reputation, Deborah Kerr tells Clark Gable that he does not have to sell out, that he can be an honorable man in advertising. "Why don't you be one of those who sells only what he believes in? Sell good things, things that people should have, and sell them with dignity—and taste. That's a career for any man, a career to be proud of."

If ad men were not more esteemed in this new era, no one doubted that they were more influential. The Yale historian David Potter noted in his book *People of Plenty* that in a culture of so many choices, as America was in the fifties, it was inevitable that advertising would come to play an increasingly important role. "Advertising," he wrote, "now compares with such long-standing institutions as the school and the church in the magnitude of its social influence. It dominates the media, it has vast power in the shaping of popular standards and it is really one of the very limited groups of institutions which exercise social control."

Rather than glamorous, it was in fact a job of long hours and high turnover that bred ulcers and heart attacks and children who barely knew their fathers. Studies comparing the health of men in advertising with that of executives in other professions showed them to be consistently in poorer health than their peers. It was an enormously stressful calling; if the rewards were great, so were the pitfalls. Advertising executives were at the beck and call of large, powerful companies whose chief executives rarely understood the market. The big companies could switch firms in a minute, and even within the advertising agencies themselves competition was extreme. "I sold my interest in Benton and Bowles when I was thirty-five," said Bill Benton, "and I'd been taking $300,000 to $400,000 a year out of it. Any business where a kid can make that kind of money is no business for old men."

As for television, it was all on-the-job training and, at first, almost everyone was getting it wrong. A handful of firms—like Ted Bates, and Young and Rubicam, Ogilvy and Mather, and Doyle Dane—were somewhat more nimble than the others in making the transition from radio to television and came to understand the obvious early on: The new medium was visual. But even at Young and Rubicam, the first instinct was to transfer people who had done radio to the television department, whereas what was needed was a miniature movie production team.

Previously advertising, like many professions, had depended on a sort of Ivy League old-boy network, in which heads of companies could be counted on to patronize their school chums. The largest and perhaps most famous agency, J. Walter Thompson, reached its zenith in the thirties and forties, largely because its account executives did most of their business at the Harvard and Yale clubs. But in the new age of television advertising, talent was everything, and by the fifties J. Walter Thompson was regarded as so stodgy by the bright young men on Madison Avenue that it was called J. Walter Tombstone.

It was a heady time. Everything was a risk. It was quite possible to do a campaign that succeeded brilliantly by mistake: It was equally possible to do a brilliant campaign and have it turn out to be a disaster. A young ad man just starting out at Young and Rubicam named David McCall was assigned in the early fifties to do a campaign for Rinso soap, a Lever Brothers product. Rinso had been one of the great brand names in the old radio days, but it had come on hard times, for two reasons: Its producers had not mastered the art of television advertising, and it was being challenged by the new more powerful detergents. In retrospect, probably nothing could have saved Rinso, McCall decided, but if it was possible for a campaign to hasten the demise of an ailing product, his campaign had done it: fifty-two weeks of full-page ads in *Life* magazine, beautifully illustrated by the top photographers in the country, including Richard Avedon. One ad alone showed sixteen different kinds of stains in full color. Everything was executed perfectly, and not even a ripple in sales resulted to show that someone out there had paid attention.

Thanks to the power of television, selling and

marketing became ever more important within companies—the sizzle was becoming as important as the steak. Some auto executives later decided that television advertising tilted the balance within their companies, making marketing and sales gradually more important than engineering and manufacturing. A kind of misguided ethic began to take root, one of great and dangerous hubris—that it did not really matter how well made the cars were; if the styling was halfway decent and the ad campaign was good enough, the marketing department could sell them.

In the case of cigarettes, Madison Avenue faced a particularly stiff challenge, though. The tobacco industry was in crisis by this time. There was growing evidence that smoking was in fact injurious to one's health. (Rosser Reeves tried to calm doubts with a particularly ingenious slogan for Tarryton: "All the tars and nicotine trapped in the filter are guaranteed not to reach your throat.") The beginnings of consumer resistance were already apparent; even though Philip Morris sponsored *I Love Lucy,* it received less of a boost in sales than the company hoped. Indeed, along Madison Avenue the general belief was that a cigarette company was the wrong sponsor for the show, that it was ill-positioned to extract maximum benefit from Lucy's success. At the height of Lucy's success, in 1952, Philip Morris's sales slipped slightly, in fact.

The dilemma grew worse in the mid-fifties as

the government began to close in on the tobacco companies. The Federal Trade Commission ordered Philip Morris to stop using the claim that its cigarettes were "recognized as being less irritating to the nose and throat by eminent nose and throat doctors." Soon after, in July 1954, the *Reader's Digest,* one of the great barometers of life in the American heartland (and, because of its lack of advertising, a magazine immune to commercial pressures), published an article on the possible connection between smoking and cancer. The industry, feeling cornered, was beginning to introduce filter-tip cigarettes. Philip Morris made its commitment with a brand called Marlboro. It was developed initially as a cigarette for women, but in the mid-fifties, the company decided to push Marlboro for men as well. The problem was that filter cigarettes were regarded at the time as effeminate. Real men didn't smoke filter cigarettes and didn't worry about lung cancer. The Philip Morris people took their problem to the Leo Burnett agency in Chicago. Burnett was a crusty old advertising hand who prided himself on keeping his agency in Chicago and away from New York. New York was too smooth and its people tended to be too highbrow. He wanted none of that. He wanted his copy simple, almost corny. In fact he kept a file in his desk, called "Corny Language," into which he placed simply folksy Americanisms. "Our sod-busting delivery, our loose-limbed stand, and our wide-eyed perspective make it easier for us to create ads that talk turkey to the majority of Americans. I like to think that we Chicago ad-makers are all working stiffs. I like to imagine that Chicago copywriters spit on their hands before picking up the big black pencils," he once said. Certainly, Burnett himself was a working stiff. He worked seven days a week and kept two full-time secretaries busy. He took only Christmas Day off. He often arrived home after his family had gone to bed. His children barely saw him: "It must be disconcerting for three highly intelligent children to see their father only if they happen to get up for a glass of water during the night," one colleague, William Tyler, said of him.

Burnett trusted his instincts and was wary of the new research departments just then springing up at various ad agencies. These featured polling, in an attempt to understand why people wanted certain goods. He was scornful of what he regarded as the pseudoscientific approach to selling. Advertising was not a science, he thought. It was a skill that took talent and experience. He was particularly accomplished at creating folklorish figures for his campaigns—the Jolly Green Giant and the Pillsbury Doughboy, for example.

Now when Philip Morris asked for a campaign to make Marlboro more masculine, he pondered the problem with his top people. They asked themselves which was the most masculine symbol in American life. The answer was the tattoo. A series of ads was drawn up with rugged men, from different walks of life, sporting prominent tattoos on their hands, readily visible when they lit up. Of the original ads, the one with the cowboy was by far the most effective, and gradually the theme became the cowboy instead of the tattoo. At a time when many Americans feared losing their individualism to the norms of suburbia, the myth of the cowboy, celebrated by Hollywood in a thousand films, was powerful stuff.

The first ad ran in January 1955. The Burnett people also suggested changing the packaging to a stronger red color. But the key to the campaign became the craggy-faced cowboy. It was an immense success, and it changed the market for filter cigarettes. The ads began to talk about "man-sized flavor," and suggested that Marlboro was, "[a] man's cigarette that women like too." Pierre Martineau, one of the pioneer market-research people and pop psychologists in advertising, praised the Marlboro ads and the macho quality of the campaign, which placed the cigarette "right in the heart of core meanings of smoking: masculinity, adulthood, vigor, and potency. Quite obviously these meanings cannot be expressed openly. The consumer would reject them quite violently. The difference between a topflight creative man and the hack is this ability to express powerful meanings indirectly . . ."

The cowboy was so successful for Marlboro that it was not long before other cigarettes tried to get in on the act. Soon there was a Chesterfield commercial that showed cowboys on a roundup smoking Chesterfields. There was a new Western song to go with it: "Chessss——ter—— fiieeelddd," it began: "Drivin' cattle/ desert sun a-blaze/ Poundin' leather/ roundin' up the strays/ Herdin' steers/ Across the range/ You'll find a man/ Who stops and takes big pleasure/ When and where he can." It was a nice try and the cowboys all looked like they ought to be riding with Gary Cooper, but it was in vain: Cowboys and the West belonged to Marlboro.

There was in all this new and seemingly instant affluence the making of a crisis of the American spirit. For this was not simple old prewar capitalism, this was something new—capitalism that was driven by a ferocious consumerism, where the impulse was not so much about what people *needed* in their lives but what they needed to consume in order to keep up with their neighbors and, of course, to drive the GNP endlessly upward. "Capitalism is dead—consumerism is king," said the president of the National Sales Executives, defining the difference between prewar America and the new America orchestrated by Madison Avenue. The people surging into the middle class were the target market, and they were supposed to buy any way they could—if necessary, indeed preferably, on credit. This was an important new development, for the country was prosperous, but it was not *that* prosperous; the new consumerism depended not merely on mercantile seduction but on credit as well, and ordinary buyers were extended levels of credit never enjoyed by such people before. The auto companies lengthened the credit period on buying new cars from twenty-four to thirty-six months. As that happened, the old puritanism was dramatically weakened: Expectations and attitudes were being rapidly changed. (Not everyone was so enthusiastic about easier access to credit; Winthrop Aldrich, then the head of the Chase bank, expressed his doubts at one meeting with younger employees who wanted to ease requirements: "I'm just not sure that we should offer the ability to borrow and to have easy credit to the kind of people who are clearly going to have serious problems paying us back," he said.)

Few others shared his wariness. For most Americans, the idea of buying luxury items was a relatively new concept, as was the idea of buying on time. Their parents and their grandparents had lived in a world in which they bought only what was essential, because they could afford little more. They did not like to buy on time, because they tended to be pessimistic rather than optimistic about economic trends, and they knew too many stories of banks foreclosing on houses and stores repossessing items that were only half paid for. It was not so much that they did not like being in debt; they *feared* being in debt. But in the new, affluent America even blue-collar jobs brought middle-class salaries. Young Americans, though, if they had one foot in the future and responded eagerly to the cornucopia of goods around them, still knew of a Calvinist past. The dilemma for them, and thus for Madison Avenue, was the question of how to balance the cautiousness of the past with the comparative opulence of the present.

Ernest Dichter, one of the first and most influential of the motivational research experts, was a pioneer in trying to explain to companies the complicated subterranean psychological reasons on which people based their choices. He picked up on this theme very quickly, deciding that one of the main tasks advertisers had to deal with in the mid-fifties was resolving what he called "the conflict between pleasure and guilt," among those now more affluent than their parents. The job for the advertiser, he said, was therefore not so much to just sell the product "as to give moral permission to have fun without guilt." This was, he believed, a major psychological crisis in American life: the conflict between American puritanism and appetites whetted by the new consumerism. Every time a company sold some item that offered a new level of gratification, he argued, it had to assuage the buyer's guilt and, in his words, "offer absolution."

No one understood that better than the people at Cadillac, and they hadn't needed motivational-research people to figure it out for them. For years in their advertising they had pushed Cadillacs not just as the top-of-the-line car, the best that money could buy but, equally important, as a reward for a life of hard work: "Here is the man who has earned the right to sit at this wheel," the ads said. Classically, the Cadillac ad pitched the Horatio Alger part of the American dream: "Let's say it was thirty-one years ago on a beautiful morning in June. A boy stood by a rack of papers on a busy street and heard the friendly horn of a Cadillac. 'Keep the change.' The driver smiled as he took his paper and rolled out into the traffic. 'There,' thought the boy as he clutched the coin, 'is the car for me!' And since this is America, where dreams make sense in the heart of a boy, he is now an industrialist. He has fought—without interruption—for the place in the world he wants his family to occupy. Few would deny him some taste of the fruits of his labor. No compromise this time!"

That ad set the tone for much of the advertising that was to follow. The head of the family had worked hard and *selflessly,* and he had earned the right to bestow these hard-earned fruits upon his loyal family. It worked for grand and expensive products like the Cadillac, and also for small and inexpensive ones like the McDonald's ten-cent hamburger. McDonald's slogans began as "Give Mom a Break" and ended with the classic "You Deserve a Break Today." America, it appeared, was slowly but surely learning to live with affluence, convincing itself that it had earned the right to its new appliances and cars. Each year seemed to take the country further from its old puritan restraints; each year, it was a little easier to sell than in the past.

THIRTY-FOUR

BY THE MID-FIFTIES television portrayed a wonderfully antiseptic world of idealized homes in an idealized, unflawed America. There were no economic crises, no class divisions or resentments, no ethnic tensions, few if any hyphenated Americans, few if any minority characters. Indeed there were no intrusions from other cultures. Nik Venet, a young record producer who grew up in a Greek-American immigrant family, remembered going to the real-life home of Ozzie and Harriet Nelson (which was strikingly like their television home) and being struck by the absence of odors. His had been a home where garlic and other powerful aromas from cooking wafted through the entire apartment; by contrast, the Nelsons' home seemed to reflect a different, cleaner culture. Invented by writers, producers, and directors, that America was the province of the television family sitcom of the mid- and late fifties. There were no Greeks, no Italians, or no Jews in this world, only Americans, with names that were obviously Anglo-Saxon and Protestant; it was a world of Andersons and Nelsons and Cleavers.

Since there were no members of ethnic groups, with the unlikely and eccentric exception of Desi Arnaz/Ricky Ricardo, whom Lucille Ball had virtually blackmailed CBS into accepting and who existed as a kind of running gag, there was no discrimination. Everyone belonged to the political and economic center, and no one doubted that American values worked and that anyone with even an iota of common sense would want to admire them. In that sense the family sitcoms reflected—and reinforced—much of the social conformity of the period. There was no divorce. There was no serious sickness, particularly mental illness. Families *liked* each other, and they tolerated each other's idiosyncracies. Dads were good dads whose worst sin was that they did not know their way around the house and could not find common household objects or that they were prone to give lectures about how much tougher things had been when they were boys. The dads were, above all else, steady and steadfast. They symbolized a secure world. Moms in the sitcoms were, if anything, more interesting; they were at once more comforting and the perfect mistresses of their household premises, although the farther they ventured from their houses the less competent they seemed. Running a house perfectly was one thing; driving a car one block from home on an errand was another. Then things went wrong, although never in a serious way. Above all else, the moms loved the dads, and vice versa, and they never questioned whether they had made the right choice. Ward Cleaver once asked June, "What type of girl would you have Wally [their older son] marry?" "Oh," answered June. "Some very sensible girl from a nice family . . . one with both feet on the ground, who's a good cook, and can keep a nice house, and see that he's happy." "Dear," answers Ward. "I got the last one of those." Parents were never unjust or unwise in the way they treated their children.

Moms and dads never raised their voices at each other in anger. Perhaps the dads thought the moms were not good drivers, and the moms thought the dads were absentminded when it came to following instructions in the kitchen, but this was a peaceable kingdom. There were no drugs. Keeping a family car out too late at night seemed to be the height of insubordination. No family difference was so irreconcilable that it could not be cleared up and straightened out within the allotted twenty-two minutes. Moms and dads never stopped loving each other. Sibling love was always greater than sibling rivalry. No child was favored, no one was stunted. None of the dads hated what they did, though it was often unclear what they actually did. Whatever it was, it was respectable and valuable; it was white-collar and it allowed them to live in the suburbs (the networks were well aware of modern demographics) and not to worry very much about money. Money was never discussed, and the dark shadow of poverty never fell over their homes, but no one made too much or they might lose their connection with the pleasantly comfortable middle-class families who watched the show and who were considered the best consumers in the country. These television families were to be not merely a reflection of their viewers but role models for them as well.

They were to be as much like their fellow citizens as possible and certainly not better than them. There was no need for even the slightest extra dimension of ambition which might put them ahead of the curve. Being ordinary was being better. Ozzie Nelson of *Ozzie and Harriet,* who had been, in an earlier incarnation, a successful radio bandleader, changed professions when he took his family to television in order to create the model all-American family. But a bandleader was a show-business person and show-business people were different: They were Hollywood, they made money and hung out with a fast crowd. Therefore, when Ozzie and Harriet, his wife and the band's singer, left radio to go on television, the band was gone. Instead, he took some kind of middle-class job.

He was pleasant and loving and also something of a bumbler, on occasion stumbling over things, often getting his children's simplest intentions wrong, when for example he decided that David, his older son, was going to elope with his girlfriend, Ozzie raced to the justice of the peace's office only to learn that David was there to pay a speeding ticket. Ozzie was clearly no genius; but then it was not his job to be smarter than the people watching him, it was his job to be just a little less smart than the average dad. He worked at a pleasant, unspecified white-collar job. In a way, Ozzie and other sitcom dads seemed to have it both ways compared to the new breed of real-life suburban dads, who had to go off every day very early to commute to work and often returned late at night, when the children were ready for bed. By contrast, Ozzie seemed to work such flexible hours that he was home all the time. He never seemed to be at work, and yet he was successful.

If sitcom parents were just like the same upbeat, optimistic people whose faces now peopled the advertisements of magazines, then it was the duty of sitcom kids to be happy and healthy, too. They were permitted to be feisty—which was better than being a goody-two-shoes—for the latter were not only distinctly unlikable to millions of young people across the nation, but they offered far too little chance for a scriptwriter to get them into the kind of minor trouble that could be solved in the last few minutes. After all, things could go wrong in a small way, but never in a way that threatened the families watching at home or cut too close to the nerve in dealing with the real issues of real American homes, where all kinds of problems lay just beneath the surface. Things in sitcoms never took a turn for the worse, into the dangerous realm of social pathology. Things went wrong because a package was delivered to the wrong house, because a child tried to help a parent but did so ineptly, because a dad ventured into a mom's terrain, or because a mom, out of the goodness of her heart, ventured into a dad's terrain. When people did things badly, they almost always did them badly with good intentions.

In this world the moms never worked. These were most decidedly one-income homes. The idea of a strike at a factory was completely alien. Equally alien was the idea that the greater world of politics might intrude. These families were living the new social contract as created by Bill Levitt and other suburban developers like him and were surrounded by new neighbors who were just like *them*. The American dream was now located in the suburbs, and for millions of Americans, still living in urban apartments, where families were crunched up against each other and where, more often than not, two or more siblings shared the same bedroom, these shows often seemed to be beamed from a foreign country, but one that the viewers longed to be part of. One young urban viewer, hearing that Beaver Cleaver was being threatened yet again with the punishment of being sent upstairs to his room, could only think to wish for a home of his own with an upstairs room to go to. But neither he nor anyone he knew had a home with an upstairs, let alone a room of his own.

These families were optimistic. There was a conviction, unstated but always there, that life was good and was going to get better. Family members might argue, but they never fought; even when they argued, voices were never raised. In the Cleaver family of *Leave It To Beaver,* the family always seemed to eat together and the pies were homemade. June Cleaver, it was noted, prepared two hot meals a day. The Cleavers were not that different from the Nelsons, who had preceded them into television suburbia: No one knew in which state or suburb they lived, and no one knew what Ward Cleaver, like Ozzie Nelson, did for a living, except that it was respectable and that it demanded a shirt, tie, and suit.

To millions of other Americans, coming from flawed homes, it often seemed hopelessly unfair to look in on families like this. Millions of kids growing up in homes filled with anger and tension often felt the failure was theirs. It was their fault that their homes were messier, their parents less human (in fact they were, of course, more human) and less understanding than the television parents in whose homes they so often longed to live. As Beaver Cleaver (a rascal, with a predilection for trouble, but harmless and engaging trouble) once told June Cleaver (who was almost always well turned out in sweater and skirts), "You know, Mom, when we're in a mess, you kind of make things seem not so messy." "Well," answered June, "isn't that sort of what mothers are for?"

The Adventures of Ozzie and Harriet was hardly the most brilliant show, hardly the best written (looking back on some of the scripts, which were always written by Ozzie Nelson, it seems amazing that the show succeeded), but it lasted the longest—fourteen years. *Leave It To Beaver,* arguably a more interesting, better written show, lasted only six years, and *Father Knows Best* lasted nine. But *Ozzie and Harriet* had the added fascination of using the Nelson family members playing themselves; therefore, ordinary viewers had the benefit of watching the Nelson boys grow up in real life in their own living rooms. Harriet was a television mom right up there with June Cleaver, a wonderful all-purpose homemaker. In truth, because she had grown up as the child of show-business parents and she herself had been an entertainer at an early age, most chores in her home had always been done by servants. If she had not always been the person portrayed on television, she gradually became that person in real life. She was genuinely nice in real life. Her family came first, and she became, particularly as her younger son reached a difficult adolescence, the stabilizing influence. If, in a prefeminist era, she had doubts about who she was and how she was presented to her fellow Americans, she never showed them or talked about them. Both on television and in real life, she accepted her life, for it was a good one, far better than what anyone who had grown up in the Depression had any right to expect. Ozzie Nelson's decision to use the family as a performing troupe did not bother her much;

for this was a show-business family that, unlike the one of her childhood, never had to go on the road. As a girl she had traveled all over the country with her show-business parents, who had not made a particularly good living and who had eventually divorced; now, without traveling, without leaving their home—all they had to do was drive a few minutes to a studio and inhabit a set that was a virtual replica of their real home—she and her husband and her children were being well paid and for a long time they seemed a family very much like the one they portrayed.

She did not seem, even in her home, as strong a personality as June Cleaver. She cooked and she cleaned. She seemed to approve of what the others did, and she might say near the end of a show that whatever had been proposed was a good idea as far as she was concerned. She was certainly a good sport, but why shouldn't she be, with a family as easy as this to deal with? Her own personality was never that clearly defined; her role was to make life better for her husband and children. When she was on the phone (her phone calls, by Ozzie's orders, were limited to thirty seconds, though of course, Ozzie always interrupted her), her calls, as Diana Meehan pointed out, were never revealing of her own personality but were always updates on what Ozzie and the boys were doing. She knew her role and accepted it gladly and without complaint. She did not challenge the accepted sexism of the time, most specifically her husband's vision of what a woman could do. At one point on a show she suggested that if she could join the local volunteer fire department, to which Ozzie already belonged, she would see a good deal more of him. "Are you kidding?" Ozzie answered. "You gals take too long to dress." "Oh, I don't know," she said. "We can be pretty quick." But Ozzie would have none of it: "By the time you got your makeup on, the fire would be out." The only housewife who fought back—but by doing so only served to prove that men were right and that women had no place in the serious world of business and commerce—was Lucy. Indeed, it was the very manic, incompetent quality of her rebellion that showed she should be at home burning the dinner and that women were somehow different than men, less steady, and less capable.

Of the Nelson sons, David was the good, steady, reliable older son, and Ricky was the younger son, more likely to get into trouble and to challenge, albeit lightly, the authority of the house. The Nelsons, were, of course, wonderfully attractive; the parents were handsome without being too sexy. Ozzie, after all, had been a star quarterback at Rutgers and later he and Harriet had been performers—theirs was an entertainment marriage. The boys seemed to embody pleasant American good looks. They looked as if they had been bred to be on a show about a typical American family: They were handsome, likable, seemingly virtuous and normal. They were the kids that ordinary American kids wanted to emulate. Popularity seemed to come easily to them, just as popularity came easily to their parents. Ricky was, if anything, better-looking and more natural than his older brother on air; it was toward his talents that the show was soon to be directed.

One reason that Americans as a people became nostalgic about the fifties more than twenty-five years later was not so much that life was better in the fifties (though in some ways it was), but because at the time it had been portrayed so idyllically on television. It was the television images of the era that remained so remarkably sharp in people's memories, often fresher than memories of real life. Television reflected a world of warm-hearted, sensitive, tolerant Americans, a world devoid of anger and meanness of spirit and, of course, failure. If Ozzie spawned imitators with the success of his rather bland family, then eventually the different families all seemed interchangeable, as if one could pluck a dad or a mom or even a child from one show and transplant him or her to another.

In February 1979 *Saturday Night Live,* reflecting the more cynical edge of a new era, did exactly that on the occasion of an appearance by Ricky Nelson. The skit turned the suburban world into a Twilight Zone, with Dan Aykroyd playing Rod Serling. Serling/Ackroyd began as the narrator: "Meet Ricky Nelson, age sixteen. A typical American kid, in a typical American kitchen in a typical American black-and-white-TV family home. But what's about to happen to Ricky is far from typical unless you happen to live in the Twilight Zone." At which point Ricky, on his way home from school, wanders into the home of the *Cleavers*. But he is treated warmly there. June offers him a brownie but warns him against spoiling his appetite. Ricky tells June his name. "Nelson," she says. "What a lovely name." But surrounded by all this warmth, he remains lost and cannot find his home. Again we hear Serling/Aykroyd: "Submitted for your approval. A sixteen-year-old teenager walking through Anytown, USA, past endless Elm Streets, Oak Streets, and Maple Streets, unable to distinguish one house from the other . . ." The next house he enters is that of the Andersons, of *Father Knows Best*. The Andersons immediately decide he is Betty's blind date. He tells them his name. Bill Anderson, the resident dad, says, "Nelson? What a nice name. Presbyterian?" Ricky answers: "My father is, sir. My mother is Episcopal." Bill says: "Well, I certainly hope you'll stay for dinner." And Jane chimes in, "You'll want to wash up and have a brownie first." On he continues through the family of *Make Room For Daddy,* and then on to the Ricardos', where he arrives just in time to see Lucy burn the turkey in the oven.

The world of the Nelsons was not, in reality,

art imitating life. The low-key Ozzie Nelson of the sitcoms had little in common with the real-life Ozzie, who was a workaholic. He wrote, produced, and directed the shows and was an authoritarian, almost dictatorial presence on the set who monitored every aspect of his children's lives. He placed both of them in the television series when they were quite young, and constantly reminded them of their obligation to the family and to all the people who worked on the show. The incomes of all these people, he kept pointing out, depended on the success of the show, and he demanded that both boys not only perform well but that they live up to their squeaky-clean images off camera. If they got in trouble, he reminded them, they might not only damage their own personal reputations but undermine the show as well. That was no small burden to place on teenagers growing up in the late fifties. Ricky, said his friend Jimmie Haskell, "had been raised to know that there were certain rules that applied to his family. They were on television. They represented the wonderful, sweet, kind, good family that lived next door, and that Ricky could not do anything that would upset that image. He knew those were the rules."

Ozzie Nelson was not merely a man who put great pressure on his children, but in contrast to the readily available Ozzie of the show, who always seemed to be around, he was gone much of the time—albeit at home, but gone. He would retire after dinner to his office and work all night writing the scripts and the directorial notes for the coming episode, sleeping late and coming downstairs around noon. The Nelsons were, therefore, for all their professional success, very different from the family depicted on the show, they lived with an immense amount of pressure and unreconciled issues. Chief among those issues was the fact that Ozzie Nelson had in effect stolen the childhood of both of his sons and used it for commercial purposes; he had taken what was most private and made it terribly public. After all, the children cast in the other family sitcoms of the era, despite the pressure of being teenage stars and celebrities, at least had a chance to get back to their own normal lives under their own different names; but in the case of the Nelsons, the show merged the identities of the children in real life with those portrayed on television.

If Ozzie Nelson was by no means a talented writer, he was nonetheless shrewd and intuitive, with a fine instinct for how the rest of the country wanted to see itself in terms of a middle-class family portrait; if he did not like and did not understand the increasingly sharp divisions beginning to separate the young from their parents in America, then he understood how to offer a comforting alternative to it. American families, he understood, did not want at that moment a weekly program to reflect (and, worse, encourage) teenage rebellion. There was too much of that already. Americans did not want to come home and watch a warring family. People were just beginning to worry about juvenile delinquency in inner cities, and the disturbing phenomenon of rock musicians like Elvis Presley was growing ever larger.

On the show, David was good and obedient, the classic firstborn, and Ricky, if written as the more contentious younger brother, was not defiant, or openly rebellious. This was a home where there was still plenty of respect for parents and Dad and Mom knew best. "Ozzie," wrote Joel Selvin in his biography of Ricky, "knew he had a gold mine in his cottage industry, fashioning a mythic American family out of a real one. If the two young boys ever felt the pressure of living up to roles created for them by an omniscient father, there was no escape. Anything the boys did could wind up on the show."

Ricky Nelson, whose identity was being shaped by scripts written by his father, found the search for his identity far more difficult than an ordinary child would. What part of him was real? What part of him was the person in the script? Did he dare be the person he thought he was, or did that go too far outside the parameters of Ozzie's scripts? The Nelsons were no more an all-American family than any other family; the generational tensions that ran through so many others ran through theirs as well, albeit they remained largely unrecognized. Moreover, the kind of mistakes that were normal, indeed mandatory, for most boys stumbling through adolescence were unacceptable in this tightly run family. The boys were always to be well groomed, they were always to be polite; they were to make no mistakes. A mishap that was minor for another child might land on the front pages of newspapers if it happened to a Nelson.

Ricky started on the television show when he was twelve, and by thirteen he was giving interviews to the *Los Angeles Times* on the role of the child actor ("I think the first requirement for a young actor, or any actor for that matter, is to lose his self-consciousness and be himself. People who are ill at ease and self-conscious are people who are thinking too much of themselves and worrying about the impression they are making on others. The best actors lose themselves in their parts and read their dialogue as naturally as possibly . . ."). What any adolescent needs is the chance to be himself, to have a childhood and stumble into adolescence; what Ricky and David had were scripts portraying them and their lives as they were supposed to be.

Ozzie Nelson had always ruled the real home with an unbending authority, one that was not to be questioned. When one of his sons displeased him, he did not exactly raise his voice, but his tone changed. Ricky might be in the room with some of his friends only to hear Ozzie's voice of displeasure: ". . . Rick . . . *son!* . . . could you come in here for a minute." Although there was no anger yet showing in his voice, there was no mistaking the measured tone, that it was a command and that something had gone wrong. Ricky seemed to change almost instantly when Ozzie's voice showed irritation, his friends thought. As Ricky moved into his middle teens, the contradictions in his life were becoming greater and greater. He was supposed to be a normal teenager, a fantasy model for millions of other teenagers, but even his mistakes had to be invented by his father and written into the script. He was making as much as $150,000 a year, but he was existing on a $5-a-week allowance. And when he took a girlfriend to a drive-in movie, he sometimes had to back in, to save the cost of the ticket. It was, thought one friend, as if Ricky longed to be his own person with his own life but Ozzie would not let him. In effect, because Ricky could not make his mistakes when he was young, he had to make them when he was an adult.

Gradually, the tensions between Ricky and Ozzie began to grow. Ricky was a naturally gifted tennis player, and Ozzie wanted him to play tennis; his way of rebelling was to give up tennis. He cruised the neighborhood in his car, a mandatory rite of California adolescence, but his parents were uneasy with it. ("I was," he later noted, "a nice greaser.") There were as he hit his mid-teens, as the first signs of the coming of a new youth culture were surfacing, frequent arguments between father and son about hair length and about smoking. "Goddamnit," Ozzie would say, "I told you to cut your hair," and Ricky would answer that he had cut it. It was a struggle for identity, and in the beginning Ozzie Nelson always won, for the obligations to the family and to the show always came first. But Ozzie and Harriet were uneasy—such tensions had never been experienced with David.

Friends who were believed to be a bad influence on him were banished. It was never done overtly—no one was ever ordered out of the house—but if Ozzie did not like someone, if he thought a friend was a bad influence, that his hair was a little long, he deftly put obstacles in the way of the friendship. As such, noted one friend, Ozzie was extremely skillful at whittling down Ricky's list of friends. Eventually, Ozzie made what may have been his critical mistake. He decided to seize on Ricky's genuine love of rock music and annex it for the show. In a way it was a success, and one could not at the time argue with the choice, for overnight he turned a young man who longed to be like Elvis Presley into a sanitized middle-class version of him. Ricky Nelson as a rock star— combining so naturally the two most powerful forces affecting the young in those days, television and rock—was an instant entertainment success.

At age sixteen, Ricky loved rock and wanted to cut a record for his girlfriend. Ozzie, understanding the commercial possibilities—after all, Ricky was good-looking, the right age, and was clean and therefore acceptable in millions of homes where parents loathed the idea of the more sinister Elvis—shrewdly arranged for him do a song on the show. Ricky was reluctant. He did not think he was ready yet—and musically, he was right. His singing and guitar-playing abilities were limited. Ozzie disagreed and simply went ahead and did it. The show was about the family going by ship on a vacation to Europe; near the end of it, Ozzie says to the bandleader, quite casually, "How about Ricky singing a rhythm and blues tune and the rest of us will give him a little moral support?" Ricky thereupon picked up an old Fats Domino song, "I'm Walkin'." The show aired on April 10, 1957.

The results were phenomenal. He was an instant sensation. He was a rock star before he was any good. Elvis Presley's success had been genuine: The young had understood that he was theirs, and television had been forced in the person of Ed Sullivan to capitulate, however reluctantly, and to accept him. In effect, the establishment had fought the coming of Elvis and fought his success; in the case of Ricky, it was the reverse. He was the artificial invention of conventional middle-class taste makers in a show that conventional Americans loved; his success therefore threatened no one. If anything, it seemed to sanitize rock. Yet music was important to Ricky in a way that his television career was not. The television show represented duty and obligation, something he did for his family because he had to and about which he had no choice. The show belonged to Ozzie, not to him; the person on the show, he felt, was not him, and he longed to escape from the shadow of cute little Ricky. But in the line dividing the generations in America, rock was the critical issue with which the young could define themselves and show that they were different from their parents. Now here was his father taking what was truly his and incorporating it into the show, giving it, in effect, an *Ozzie and Harriet* parental seal of approval. Ricky wanted to be Carl Perkins, noted Selvin, his biographer, but because his father had pushed him so quickly and made him play on the show before he was ready, he was a joke to real musicians—whose approval he desperately sought. A few years later Elvis Presley, having been away from live performances for a while, was planning his return to the stage but was worried about how he would look and how he should handle his hair. At that point, Priscilla, his wife, mentioned a billboard featuring Ricky Nelson, who looked particularly attractive. Perhaps, she suggested, Elvis could take a look at it. "Are you goddamn crazy," he told her. "After all these years Ricky Nelson and Fabian and that whole group have more or less followed in my footsteps and now I'm supposed to copy them. You gotta be out of your mind, woman."

Later in his life, as his early fame as a singer and television star began to fade and, ironically, as his music became far more interesting, Ricky

Nelson never received proper credit for it. Indeed, even those who showed up at his later concerts at the Palomino, in which he was playing an interesting and original version of California white rock-a-billy, seemed to want him to be Ricky from the television show. When he would play his latest songs, the audience would yell out for their favorites from his early days, such as "Poor Little Fool." When they did, said his friend Sharon Sheeley, he would wince. It was as if the public would not let him grow up and wanted him forever to be as he was cast as a boy.

He had gone, he once noted, from singing in the bathroom to the recording studio, with nothing in between. All the ingredients to make a star were there: He already had a huge ready-made constituency because of the television show; he was uncommonly attractive; he had a nice, if untrained voice. His first record sold 60,000 copies in three weeks, shot up the charts, and stayed there for five months. Eventually, it sold 700,000 copies. It was to be the start of a remarkable but unhappy career, in which his success outstripped his talent and his place in the pecking order of rock cast a shadow that always hung over him professionally. In 1958 he was the top-selling rock-and-roll artist in the country. He went on tours that summer, and the crowds were enormous. In those early years of rock, only Elvis Presley was selling more records and had more consistent hits. Yet his father was still master-

minding the entire operation, serving as his manager, arranging better record contracts for him,
bringing in Barney Kessel, the famed jazz guitarist, to help him with his sound, making sure his
backup group was worthy of him and thereby
using the Jordanaires, Elvis's backup, with him.
Rock, his friends thought, was his one source of
freedom, his way of escaping the public image
forced on him by the television show. Ironically,
his success as a teen musical idol lent additional
vitality to the show; it should have been slowing
down by the late fifties, but because of his new
success as a rocker, the show was renewed in 1959
for five more years. He, who had wanted to escape
it, had carried it forward with his means of escape.

He became rich (he made a lot of money
from the television show, and now he was making
much more from records and appearances—all of
which was put aside for him), successful, attractive, and incomplete. As such he grew up in a kind
of covert rebellion; he and Ozzie worked out an
unacknowledged quid pro quo, Ozzie indulged
him, offered him extra privileges, and limited
Ricky's rebellion; Ricky in turn stayed on the
show and remained dependent on Ozzie. He had
grown up as a teen idol, but he had not had a real
boyhood and now he was passing through adolescence still unsure of himself, his professional career with almost all of his major decisions still
dominated by his father.

His adult life was, not surprisingly, unhappy—a marriage that seemed perfect on paper soon went sour; excessive drug use followed. Finally, the harshest truth could not be suppressed: Ricky Nelson, the charming, handsome all-American boy was, to all intents and purposes, the unhappy product of a dysfunctional family.

THIRTY-FIVE

AMONG THOSE WHO were extremely ambivalent about their pursuit of the American dream were Tom and Betsy Rath. In 1955, when they first appeared on the scene, they should have been, by all rights, the quintessential upwardly mobile modern American family. But in this society of consumption, they were always in debt—not heavily, but consistently so; every month there was a stack of unpaid bills, which Betsy had to juggle skillfully in order not to have their credit cut off. Worse still, the house in which they had lived for seven years was too small and seemed to be disintegrating beneath them. The front door had been badly scratched by a dog; the hot-water faucet in the bathroom dripped. One of their three children had gotten ink all over a wall. Almost all of the furniture needed to be refinished, reupholstered, or cleaned. The neighbors who monitored such things whispered about the poorly kept yard and that the Raths could not afford a gardener.

For the Raths the house had come to symbolize all their frustrations and tensions. In the living room, a dent on a wall marked a bitter argument that had occurred when Betsy spent $40 on a cut-glass vase on the same day that, by chance, Tom spent $70 on a new suit he badly needed for business. Tom had dented the wall by throwing the vase against it. Even their 1939 Ford, a car they had driven for too long, marked them, if not exactly as failures, then as people who were not keeping up with the neighbors.

Tom and Betsy Rath were not real people, although there were plenty of young men and women who could readily identify with them. They were fictional characters, the heroes, or antiheroes, of Sloan Wilson's novel *The Man in the Gray Flannel Suit,* one of the most influential American novels of the fifties. Its theme was the struggle of young Americans against the pressures of conformity and imprisonment in suburban life. "Without talking about it much they both began to think of the house as a trap, and they no more enjoyed refurbishing it than a prisoner would delight in shining up the bars of his cell," Wilson wrote. For the Raths were victims of this modern malaise: What should have made them happy did not. "I don't know what's the matter with us," Betsy Rath said to Tom one night. "Your job is plenty good enough. We've got three nice kids and lots of people would be glad to have a house like this. We shouldn't be so *discontented* all the time."

They lived in a community of people very much like themselves; their neighbors, though pleasant and friendly, were, truth to tell, strangers, bonded by status and ambition rather than

true friendship. "Few people considered Greentree Avenue a permanent stop—the place was just
a crossroads where families waited until they
could afford to move on to something better. The
finances of almost every household were an open
book. Budgets were frankly discussed, and the
public celebration of increases in salary was common. The biggest parties of all were moving out
parties, given by those who finally were able to
buy a bigger house. . . . On Greentree Avenue
contentment was an object of contempt," Wilson
wrote.

It was not a bad world, Betsy Rath thought
when she pondered their situation—the people
around them were good and decent but they were
dreamers and most of their dreams seemed to be
about material progress. Sometimes she thought
their lives were too dull and then she would pon-
der their condition a bit more and decide that it
was not so much a dull world as a frantic one. But
there was, she knew, a narrowness to it. Nor were
they the only ones restless with their lives. When
the neighbors gathered for one of their instant
parties, late in the night, the dreams for the future
were revealed: "usually the men and the women
just sat talking about the modern houses they
would like to build, or the old barns they would
like to convert into dwellings. The price the small
houses on Greentree Avenue were currently
bringing and the question of how big a mortgage
the local banks were offering on larger places were

constantly discussed. As the evening wore on, the men generally fell to divulging dreams of escaping to an entirely different sort of life—to a dairy farm in Vermont, or to the management of a motel in Florida."

Tom Rath, whose biography was strikingly similar to that of Sloan Wilson, was thirty-three years old and made $7,000 a year, a seemingly substantial salary for a young man in those days, one that placed him squarely in the new middle class. He worked in Manhattan for a foundation that had been established by a millionaire for scientific research. He seemed neither satisfied nor dissatisfied with his job; to the degree that he was discontented, it was with his salary, not with what he did. His restlessness was revealed one day at lunch with some of his friends when he heard of an opening in public relations at the United Broadcasting Corporation. It paid between $8,000 and $12,000. Try for $15,000, one of his friends who worked there said: "I'd like to see somebody stick the bastards good." Ten thousand, he thought, might get them a new house. It was not a job he particularly wanted, nor was it a company he admired. When he mentioned to Betsy the possibilities of a life in public relations, she told him that she had never thought of him as a public relations man. "Would you like it?" she asked. "I'd like the money," he answered. Then she sighed. "It would be wonderful to get out of this house."

"When you come right down to it a man with three children has no damn right to say that money doesn't matter," Tom thought to himself. Naturally, he applied for the job. The last question on the application was intriguing: "The most significant thing about me is . . ." For a moment he thought of writing about his wartime stint as a paratrooper, during which time he killed seventeen men. "For four and a half years my profession was jumping out of airplanes with a gun, and now I want to go into public relations," he wanted to write. He pondered it, though. He could also have written: "The most significant fact about me is that I detest the United Broadcasting Corporation, with all its soap operas, commercials and yammering studio audiences, and the only reason I'm willing to spend my life in such a ridiculous enterprise is that I want to buy a more expensive house and a better brand of gin."

Whatever frustrations he felt with his current life were minor compared with those harbored by Betsy. She wanted a more civilized life, one where they would eat a real breakfast in the morning and talk to each other like real people, and eat, instead of hot dogs and hamburgers for dinner, something more substantial, a roast or a casserole. And above all there would be no more television. Instead, the family would read more, and perhaps they would read aloud to each other.

Eventually, in Wilson's novel, all the Raths' problems were resolved. Tom took the new job, and despite the treacherous politics of the organization, he discovered that his boss (a character based on Roy Larsen, one of the founders of Time-Life) was a superior man seriously pledged to a better world. In time Tom Rath confronted his demons (including fathering a child during World War Two with an Italian mother), simplified his life, and found that despite his earlier cynicism he could achieve both honor and a better salary in his new job (in addition, his grandmother left him a large tract of extremely valuable land, which could be developed). He and Betsy were able to hold on to their beliefs and their marriage while becoming part of the best of the new suburban world.

The novel was almost completely autobiographical. The book reflected, Sloan Wilson later said, his own frustrations with civilian life after serving as a young officer with the Coast Guard in World War Two. His wartime job had been rich, full of challenge and responsibility. He had commanded his own ship at twenty-three and dealt daily with the great danger involved in running high-octane fuel into combat areas. Every day in that exciting time of his life he had a feeling that what he did mattered. Civilian life, to his surprise, was infinitely more difficult. He had always wanted to be a reporter, and he had worked for a time on the *Providence Journal* at a job he loved. But with a wife and two children, the fifty-dollar-a-week salary was woefully inadequate.

"What we all talked about in those days was selling out," he said years later. "Selling out was doing something you did not want to do for a good deal more money than you got for doing what you loved to do." Though he wanted to write fiction, he took a job at Time-Life. Even as he joined the Luce publications, Wilson was appalled by his own decision because he hated everything Time-Life stood for—he viewed it as an institution that offered talented, liberal young men handsome salaries to dress up its own conservative politics. At first he had worked for *FYI*, the Time house organ, but that seemed beneath his dignity and he decided to quit. Somehow, his personnel file was sent to Roy Larsen, one of the company's founders and the top person on the business side. Larsen was about to head a major campaign on behalf of the nation's public schools and decided to hire Wilson as a special assistant to do publicity. The pay was good, and he would soon make $10,000 a year.

If Wilson did not like the political slant of Time-Life, he liked the internal politics among the managerial ranks even less. Another bright young man, who was his immediate superior, threw his first article on the floor with contempt. Later, the young man confessed that he always operated this way, believing that new employees did not work well unless they were frightened. But to Wilson's surprise, he had immediately liked Roy Larsen, a graceful, kind, and intelligent man, albeit a world-class workaholic. Best of all, he found that he could write short stories for *The New Yorker* on the side. But if there were advantages to the job, they still paled to his exhilarating experiences during the war. He was somehow, for all of Roy Larsen's personal kindness and the handsome paycheck, something of a glorified flunky. He decided to quit the day that he accompanied Larsen to have his photo taken along with the head of the outdoor advertising council. Their photo was to be part of the announcement at the beginning of a billboard campaign to promote the nation's public schools.

It was a rainy day, and both executives arrived wearing handsome overcoats and bowler hats. Each was respectfully accompanied by his bright, up-and-coming young assistant. No executive was worth his salt unless he had his own up-and-coming young man, Wilson thought. Wilson looked at his opposite number from the outdoor advertising council and saw how eager and sycophantish he was—and wondered if he looked that way to other people. Because of the rain, both men had kept their bowler hats on, but since the photographer could not see their faces, he asked that the hats come off. Unlike Wilson, the other bright young man seemed to have anticipated the photographer's request, and in a second he not only had his own boss's hat but Roy

Larsen's as well. Sloan Wilson realized he had been outhustled, in a competition he wanted no part of in the first place.

With that, he decided to write full-time. Eventually, he returned to New Canaan, Connecticut, and took a long, hard look at it. It was, he thought, a world he had come to hate. In fact, all the other men in publishing and advertising he knew who lived there hated it, too: three hours a day on the commuter trains; working in corporations where the internal politics seemed endless and where everyone was obsessed with playing up to his immediate superior. Talent, all too often, was pressed into service for pure commercial gain without regard to the larger consequences. Almost everyone he knew in New Canaan was trying to get out; it was a rat race, and all the participants dreamed of hitting the jackpot by writing the great American novel and selling the rights to Hollywood. If they did that, they would never have to get on a commuter train again. One friend came to symbolize this entire world to Wilson: He had only recently flown forty combat missions, and his uniform had been bedecked with World War Two medals. Now he worked for an advertising firm. One of his accounts was a cereal company and the question he was working on was whether the people who bought the cereal would prefer to find a tin frog or a rubber spider inside the box as the surprise.

Ironically, the greater one's success in this

world, the harder it was to escape. Salaries would go up, and newly minted executives would merely find themselves paying more taxes, burdened by a more expensive life-style, and inhabiting ever larger houses. "For a time," he remembered years later, "I was insatiable myself—I wanted ever bigger houses and more cars." In New Canaan, Wilson thought people changed houses the way other Americans changed cars. The worst thing was that these fancy jobs were supposed to offer some sort of security, but in fact they did not. The more successful you were, the deeper you were in debt and the more exposed and more perilous your position often became at work. The process was the reverse of what it was supposed to be: Ostensibly, a young man would work hard to gain some measure of success; the better he did, the more secure he and his family should have been. Instead, the higher you went, the more people there were who were after your job—so work became more stressful.

When *The Man in the Gray Flannel Suit* appeared in 1955, it hit a vital nerve. "I wasn't thinking about what was happening to the country when I wrote it. The only thing I was thinking about was what was happening to me," Wilson said thirty years later. It was a major best-seller and soon became a movie starring Gregory Peck—an ideal choice, with just the right amount of decency and moral ambivalence. Even the title, *The Man in the Gray Flannel Suit,* suggested someone who was sacrificing his individuality to become a part of the new more faceless middle class. As it turned out, the book was published just as a major intellectual debate was forming on the issue of conformity in American life, particularly as the modern corporation became ever bigger and became an increasingly important force in American life. The debate seemed to focus on the question of whether, despite the significant and dramatic increase in the standard of living for many Americans, the new white-collar life was turning into something of a trap and whether the greater material benefits it promised and delivered were being exchanged for freedom and individuality. Was this what the new definition of success meant? More of everything except individuality? Were we as a nation already well on our way to becoming faceless drones, performing bland tasks that demanded no real skill save managerial obedience? Was America losing its entrepreneurial class to cautious, gray managers, men afraid to make mistakes and take chances? At the center of the debate were the writings of one of the most important intellectual figures of the period: C. Wright Mills. Though he was on the faculty of Columbia University and nominally a sociologist, he cut across many disciplines—philosophy, history, economics, journalism.

A man of fierce physical and intellectual presence, Mills was remembered by his friends (who more often than not ended up as his adversaries) first and foremost for his energy and combativeness. Academics were expected to be genteel and solicitous of their colleagues; most professors at Columbia wore the academic uniform of tweed jacket, flannel slacks, and bow ties. But Mills seemed determined to provoke and antagonize his colleagues. He dressed as a lumberjack—in khaki pants, flannel shirts, and combat boots—and would arrive for class from his house in the country (which he had built himself) astride his BMW motorcycle. His style, body language, and pronouncements seemed calculated to rebuke the more polished world around him; he was from the real world, his manner seemed to say, as the others in academe were not. Brilliant and egocentric, Mills was the classic loner. He had few close friends. "I have never known," he once wrote, "what others call 'fraternity' with any group . . . neither academic nor political. With a few individuals, yes, but with groups, however small, no." His writing was as incisive a post-Marxist critique of America's new managerial capitalism as existed in the country at the time, even if on occasion he painted with too broad a brush and was prone to exaggerate. Mills's work was important, the historian Stanley Katz later noted, because it told important truths about America's new class strata and about the development of capitalism after the war and yet could not be attacked for being Marxist.

Mills eventually became the critical link between the old left, Communist and Socialist, which had flourished during the Depression, and the New Left, which sprang up in the sixties to protest the blandness of American life. He found hope not in the grim rigidity and authoritarianism of the Soviet Union and its satellite nations in Eastern Europe, but in the underdeveloped world, which had been victimized by European colonialism and American imperialism. Cuba, as Castro came to power, fascinated him as Poland and Czechoslovakia did not. The old left had been born of the injustices of capitalism during the Great Depression and thrived because the Communists' voice in Europe, and the United States had been the first to warn of the rise of Nazism. But the movement had been badly undermined by a number of things: the Ribbentrop-Molotov pact; the domestic crimes of Joseph Stalin and his concentration camps, which only the most slavish Marxist could ignore; the imperialism of the Soviet Union as it brutally crushed its satellite states and left those countries with repressive, totalitarian regimes; and of course, the stunning success of postwar capitalism in the United States. Mills's books were hailed in the Communist world as brilliant critiques of American society, but he was hardly enthusiastic about this often unwanted praise. At one point late in his career he visited the Soviet Union and was toasted at a dinner as the foremost critic of contemporary American life. When it was his turn to respond to the toast, he rose and said, "To the day when the complete works of Leon Trotsky are published in the Soviet Union!"

The combination of the grimness of Communism as it now existed in Europe and the success of American capitalism had essentially devastated the traditional left. By the mid-1950s, only J. Edgar Hoover seemed to think Marxism was a powerful force in postwar America. With the triumph of capitalism and the threat of the Cold War, traditional American politics had, if anything, narrowed; the differences between the Republican party and the Democratic party were seen as marginal by many serious social critics of the time. Yet the success of capitalism did not mean the end of alienation; it simply meant a different kind of alienation. Alienation, Mills and others were suggesting, could be just as powerful in a comfortable white-collar existence as it was in a harsh working-class one. The battlefield was shifting: Instead of criticizing capitalism for its failures, a new kind of left, far more idiosyncratic and less predictable, was essentially criticizing America for its successes, or at least for the downside of its successes.

This new threat to the human spirit came not from poverty but from affluence, bigness, and corporate indifference from bland jobs through which the corporation subtly and often unconsciously subdued and corrupted the human spirit. As they moved into white-collar jobs, more and more people felt as Sloan Wilson had when he portrayed Tom Rath—that they had less control over their lives. Here was a world where individuality seemed to be threatened and the price of success might well be ever greater conformity.

Much of the old left's agenda had been imported from Europe and had been shaped by historical and social circumstances, which did not necessarily fit the postwar American condition, where workers had become consumers and beneficiaries of the economic system and thought of themselves as capitalists. As that happened, not only did more working people enter the middle class, but there was a vast new reevaluation of what being on the left meant. By the mid-fifties one of the great new growth industries in Wall Street was investing the pension funds of labor unions. Those who had been a critical part of the left in the past were now being incorporated into the system, not merely politically but economically; as that happened, a new left was beginning to form around very different issues. Mills was the perfect radical iconoclast to examine the new American condition. He was unmistakably American, a rough, untamed son of the Southwest, where the clash of economic forces was still raw. Alienation came naturally to him: He was raised as a Catholic in a small town in Texas, whose culture was, he liked to say, "one man, one rifle." His parents forced him to sing in a Catholic choir in Waco and that had produced, as Irving Horowitz noted, "a lifelong resentment of Christianity." It also helped guarantee, given the prejudices of the region against Catholics, that he felt a "painful sense of isolation from his peers." Certainly, he had always felt like an outsider. There was no taint of Marxism to his work. He once wrote the sociologist Kurt Wolff that people always had come to him and told him that he wrote "as if I were a European about this country. . . . I am an outlander, not only regionally but down bone deep and for good. In Orwell's phrase: I am just outside the whale and always have been. I did not really earn it; I just was it without intending to be and without doing anything about it except what I had to do from day to day."

Eventually, the family moved from West Texas to Dallas, where Mills graduated from Dallas Technical High in 1934. After an unhappy start at Texas A & M (years later he told his friend Harvey Swados, the writer, that the hazing he had received as an Aggie had turned him into a rebel), he transferred to the University of Texas at Austin. The university and the city had been an oasis of intellectual and political ferment in Texas, and that was true more than ever during the Depression. Among his professors and fellow students there was a sense from the start that Mills was different from the start, a young man whose physical and intellectual force and passion were remarkable. His energy was always ferocious: Every topic, as far as he was concerned, was to be argued, and every argument was to be won. Clarence Ayres, a professor at the University of Texas, wrote of him at the time: "He isn't a pale, precocious bookworm. He is a big strapping fellow with an athlete's energy. He looks much older than he is. For several years he has been reading everything within his reach, and he really is prodigiously learned for his years and situation. He also has acumen and the result of this combination of qualities has not been altogether to his advantage." In this letter written about Mills when he was twenty-three, Ayres continued prophetically: "The prevailing legend about him is to the effect that he takes people up and pursues them furiously until they get so tired of it they rebuff him (or until he has milked them dry and drops them). There is something in it both ways. Mills is tremendously eager and incredibly energetic. If he gets the idea that somebody has something, he goes after it like the three furies. I think he may have worn his welcome to shreds in some quarters. . . . The picture which emerges . . . is of an unusually strong student who may become a headliner. I think any department would be lucky to have him among its advanced students."

Mills acknowledged his own rough edges. Indeed, he felt as if they gave him a psychological advantage. He was often tactless in dealing with colleagues and surprised when his words wounded them; he was also thin-skinned, and when others ventured even mild criticism of his work, a new feud was often born. He did graduate work at Texas in sociology but no Ph.D. program was offered there, so in the fall of 1939 he entered the graduate program in sociology at the University of Wisconsin. There he made important intellectual connections and broadened his studies. In Madison, he seemed to make much the same impression he had in Austin: Hans Gerth, an immigrant intellectual, remembered him "with Thorstein Veblen in one hand and John Dewey in the other. He was a tall burly young man of Herculean build. He was no man with a pale cast of the intellect given to self mortification . . ." (Later when they had a squabble over whether Mills had taken too much credit for some of Gerth's work, Gerth was not so enthusiastic. Mills, he said, was "an excellent operator, whippersnapper, promising young man on the make, and Texas cowboy à la ride and shoot.")

While he was at Madison, Mills failed his Army physical because of hypertension (he suffered from chronic heart and circulatory problems). If anything, this heightened his alienation from the American political mainstream, for it put him on the sidelines at what was the defining moment for most members of his generation. He was big, powerful, and robust, yet he could not join what most of his contemporaries judged to be the nation's finest hour. Inevitably, as he had not participated in that great democratic cause, he rebelled and did not accept the propaganda and rationales that were used to justify it. He saw parallels, observed by few other contemporary intellectuals, between the corporate capitalism of Germany, which had allowed Nazism to rise, and the corporate capitalism of America. In Madison he married his first wife, Freya (the first of three, each of whom had one child with him). It was becoming clear that the pull of contemporary events was at least as powerful on him as that of academia, and some of his friends worried that he would become a pamphleteer rather than a scholar. "Hold your chin up, young man," wrote one of his few friends, Eliseo Vivas, a philosopher at Wisconsin who worried over the pull of journalism on Mills. He told Mills to "stick to the major guns with the 'long range' and don't allow your ambition to do something right now with you in the field of the freelancer and journalist. Write for decades, not for the week. Concentrate on the thesis and don't look right or left until it is done."

After Madison, he moved to the University of Maryland, which brought him nearer the nation's capital. He was taking politics more seriously now, and he wrote to his mother: "You ought to see me clipping *The New York Times* now." At a time when, because of World War Two, most young men were asking fewer political questions, he was on a very different path. His attitude, as Irving Horowitz pointed out, was something like a plague on both your houses.

He seemed to be saying that the horror of modern Nazism could not be blamed merely on an odd combination of circumstances: frenzied nationalism, the post–World War One depression, and the complete collapse of existing values and German currency and the social anarchy that followed. By his lights, the excesses of Germany were the excesses of capitalism. He saw Germany as the prototype for the modern corporate garrison state. The only thing that might stop it, he wrote, was the powerful force of organized labor. Not everyone agreed: Some thought that labor was just as readily seduced by exaggerated nationalism as any other class. (Some fifteen years later, one of his political descendants in the New Left, Abbie Hoffman, was told to work on organizing blue-collar workers. "Organize the workers?" he exclaimed. "The workers want to beat the shit out of me!")

If nothing else, Mills helped reinvigorate the left, which was in decline after the war. Victory in World War Two, the growing awareness of Stalin's crimes, and the success of postwar capitalism had brought much of the intelligentsia back to the liberal center because fascist Germany and the Communist Soviet Union were so much worse than the United States. Other intellectuals found that America, in comparison with the rest of the world, now seemed less flawed; but Mills was not interested in a comparison with the rest of the world. He was a home-grown radical, bristling with his own native passions and his own very rugged, very American sense of independence.

The enemy, for him and many young leftists who came after him, was the liberalism of the era, so bland and corrupting, so comfortable, that it was essentially endorsed by both major political parties. People did not have to make difficult moral choices anymore. The liberalism of the society of abundance was "without coherent content; that in the process of its banalization, its goals have been so formalized as to provide no clear moral optic. The crisis of liberalism (and of American political reflection) is due to liberalism's success in becoming the official language for all public statement."

Maryland was not a particularly congenial place for him. He admired the exceptional group of young historians there—Frank Friedel, Kenneth Stampp, and Richard Hofstader—but he was hungry as ever for greater intellectual growth (on his terms), so he moved now into history, while writing more and more for national magazines, such as the *New Republic*. All of this helped enhance his reputation. Years later he told Dan Wakefield, a student of his at Columbia, that he had used his journalistic skills to escape the University of Maryland, which he found rather stultifying. "I wrote my way out of there!" he said. In 1944 he arrived at Columbia, where he had probably always wanted to be in the first place—a great Ivy League university in a great

city, with access to a large and influential audience. "Mills," wrote Horowitz, "was caught in a
cul-de-sac: antiprofessional in public utterances,
quite professional in private desire. He coveted
the status and glory of elite institutions while de-
spising their snobbery and style." Mills would
later say of *White Collar,* the first of his defining
books, that it was "the story of a Texas boy who
came to New York." At Columbia he managed to
remain an outsider, with a series of tenuous
friendships and shifting allegiances. Dwight Mac-
Donald, the writer, became his first great friend—
they were both, MacDonald pointed out, radicals at a time when it was not fashionable to
be so. "We were both congenital rebels, passionately contemptuous of every received idea and
established institution . . ." Mills, noted Mac-
Donald, could argue with just about anyone on
almost anything—and he could do it longer and
louder than anyone else. They both had, he noted,
a "mixture of innocence, and cynicism, optimism and skepticism. We were ever hopeful, ever
disillusioned."

On campus, he was a memorable figure. In
his office was a hot plate to warm soup and an
electric espresso machine. He was, thought Wakefield, who eventually became a prominent journalist, "an exhilarating teacher. He stalked the
room or pounded his fist on the table to emphasize a point, surprising us with ideas that seem
utopian, except that he was so convinced of their

practicality you couldn't dismiss them as mere theory." In the Columbia catalog he was listed as a sociologist, but he preferred to think of himself as a journalist—by which he meant someone like James Agee. That was real journalism—graceful and highly intellectual reportage.

He published *White Collar* in 1951 and *The Power Elite* in 1956. In these books he saw the new middle class as affluent but without purpose and cut off from its Calvinist past, from taking pride in craftsmanship. In *White Collar,* he seemed to bemoan the decline of the rugged American individualist and the growing frustration of the new America. He viewed history as a constant collision between competing forces that vied for power.

As an analyst of the stratification within the democratic society, Mills was without peer. Certainly, there were others writing about some of the same changes taking place in American society. David Riesman and Nathan Glazer published their important book *The Lonely Crowd,* about the inner-directed and the outer-directed new Americans, who increasingly seemed to take their signals, their values, and even their ambitions not from their own desires and beliefs but from a received value system around them. These people wanted to be a part of the larger community so much they would adjust their morality and ethics to those of the community almost unconsciously; in the end, they seemed to take on the coloration of their institutions and neighborhoods with frightening ease. Was it possible, Riesman and Glazer wondered, that America was producing a class whose sudden economic advancement, coming as it did within a generation, had outstripped the social and psychological preparations that might normally precede it? Had the very speed overwhelmed the capacity to enjoy and fully understand such affluence? Riesman himself clearly thought that Mills had touched on something important, but he was also dubious that the new white-collar class was as alienated as Mills suggested.

White Collar was, in general, favorably reviewed. As Horowitz noted, it hit on a powerful new theme that seemed to beguile American society: the growth of ever greater American power externally, alongside a feeling of a decrease in personal power among its citizens. Certainly, the new white-collar men in Mills's book seemed to be carried along by forces outside their control. They were voraciously ambitious without entirely knowing why. They never carefully considered their goals but simply plunged ahead to the next benchmark.

Yet Riesman felt Mills had a tendency to generalize and create pat, if convincing, stereotypes. From the outside, white-collar workers might indeed appear largely banal, frustrated with their lives as Mills might have been frustrated had he been forced to live similarly. Riesman thought there was a danger for someone like Mills in transferring his own need for intellectual stimulation into the minds and aspirations of people whose needs might be considerably different. Riesman pointed out that one should not underestimate, for example, the satisfaction generated by the pride of people who always had been blue-collar workers but who had finally moved up into the white-collar managerial world. Similar reservations were voiced in a letter that Richard Hofstader wrote to Mills about *White Collar*. There was, he said, a lot of human ugliness in the book, which he said was caught up in the jacket description of the book as a "merciless portrayal" of a whole class. There might be, Hofstader said, some people and perhaps even some classes "that may call for merciless treatment, but why be so merciless with all these little people? . . . Why no pity, no warmth? Why condemn—to paraphrase Burke—a whole class?"

In *The Power Elite* Mills went further, spotting early some of the forces that were coming together to create America the superpower. He pointed out the growing connection between the military and the industrial sectors—the military-industrial state that Eisenhower himself would warn of a few short years later. In addition, Mills had a strong intuitive sense of the dangers that might come, politically and socially, from a nation suddenly wielding so much power and affluence. But even here some critics thought he

undermined his own work by being too simplistic.
Yes, there were groups wielding considerable
power in America, but American politics was so
pluralistic that even as one group became too
powerful, others came together to limit that
power. Indeed some groups, supposedly with
common interests, might in fact be bitterly opposed to each other; others that were supposed to
be adversarial might get on well. For example,
corporations and labor unions, traditional antagonists, might well want the same thing in the
new power structure, and indeed labor unions,
which Mills had once seen as the savior from
domination of American life by the corporations,
might in fact be a willing partner in the growth of
too large a defense economy. But as Daniel Bell
pointed out, there was not a clear community of
interests in the power elite, as Mills would seem to
have it. Often there were surprising conflicts. In
Korea, Bell pointed out, the military, Wall Street,
and the federal government were often at cross-
purposes. The sands of American power shifted
constantly: As soon as any one group began to
overreach its place, it automatically came into
conflict with some other group. Bell's criticism
stung the sensitive Mills, who at one point wrote
a friend, "Dan Bell is here now with *Fortune.* I've
seen him only once or twice and don't look forward to meeting him again. He's full of gossip
about how he met Luce for lunch and what Luce
said. [Bell is a] little corkscrew drawn by power

magnets; really pretty vulgar stuff."

One of the ironies of postwar American capitalism was that most owners of companies were making more money than ever before, expanding their size constantly, but that even as their wealth and their seeming influence increased, the leaders felt themselves less powerful in terms of their control of their own factory floor. As such they became ever more resentful of the society around them. They found a largely unsympathetic view of themselves in the mainstream media, which was, of course, owned by large corporations. What made America's power structure so interesting in the years after World War Two were its contradictions, most of which defied the traditional dogma of either the left or the right. Where Mills was most effective was in his journalism; where he was least effective was in his judgments and his occasionally simplistic projections of how different groups would in fact behave.

By the end of the decade, the gap had widened between him and most of the traditional academic community. He was appalled by the way altogether too many intellectuals, including many liberals, had enlisted in the Cold War and failed to criticize their own country for its excesses. The rise of Fidel Castro and the Eisenhower administration's hostile and clumsy attempts to deal with him only convinced Mills of the rightness of his vision. If its behavior toward Cuba turned out to be an appalling stereotype of the worst of American foreign policy, it was a perfect fit for Mills's view. America, he thought, was on its way to becoming something of a garrison state with the concurrence of what he called, with great contempt, "the NATO intellectuals." More and more, as the decade ended, he was drawn to the issue of Cuba and his radicalism deepened.

Late in the decade, Mills's health began to fail him. In 1958 he suffered the first of at least three heart attacks. He continued to smoke and drink heavily; he liked to boast that he had more women in one month than Don Juan had had in a lifetime.

His work had always been passionate, but now it was downright evangelical. *Listen Yankee!* was the title of his last book—on Cuba. He wrote his parents in 1961, after one heart attack, "Lying here all these weeks and having damn near died, because this thing was pretty damned close, well it's made me much stronger, and made me think about myself which I'd not had the chance to do before. I know that I have not the slightest fear of death. I know also that I have a big responsibility to thousands of people all over the world to tell the truth as I see it and tell it exactly and with drama and quit this horsing around with sociological bullshit."

In March 1962 he died, at the age of forty-five, of a heart attack. He was at the height of his powers, his audiences steadily expanding.

"Mills," as Irving Horowitz wrote of him, "began to think of himself as the social bearer of mass beliefs; he became a movement unto himself. Armed with an Enlightenment faith that truth will out, he also became convinced that he was the bearer of the truth." When he died, he had already become something of a mythic figure to a new generation of young American radicals and it would turn out that his posthumous influence was to be even greater.

THIRTY-SIX

ON THE EVENING of December 1, 1955, Mrs. Rosa Parks's entire body ached—her feet, neck, and shoulders were especially sore. Parks was a tailor's assistant in a Montgomery, Alabama, department store. Hers was an exhausting job that paid a minimal salary; she made alterations and had to handle a large commercial steam press as well. On this particular day, she finished work and walked a few blocks as usual to the bus stop. The first bus on her route was so crowded she realized that there would be no place left to sit, and she desperately needed to get off her feet. She decided to wait for a less crowded bus. That gave her a little time to waste, so Parks walked over to a nearby drugstore to look for a heating pad, which might help ease the pain in her sore muscles. Not finding anything to her liking, she returned to the bus stop. Eventually, a bus arrived that had a fair number of seats available. She paid her ten cents, boarded the bus, and took a seat in the rear, or black, section of the bus, near the dividing line between the white and black sections. On Montgomery's public buses, the first ten rows were for white people, the last twenty-six for blacks. In many cities in the South, the line dividing sections on buses was fixed. This was not true in Montgomery; by custom, the driver had the power, if need be, to expand the white section and shrink the black section by ordering blacks to give up their seats to whites. First come, first served might have been the rule of public transportation in most of America, but it was not true in Montgomery, Alabama, in 1955. To the blacks, it was just one additional humiliation to be suffered—because the system did not even guarantee the minimal courtesies and rights of traditional segregation.

Three other blacks boarded the bus and sat next to Mrs. Parks in the same row. Parks had already recognized the driver as one of the meaner-spirited white men who worked for the bus line. He had once evicted her from his bus because she had refused, on paying her fare, to leave the bus and reenter the black section from the rear door—another quaint custom inflicted on black Montgomery bus riders. Gradually, as the bus continued on its rounds more whites got on. Finally, with the white section filled, a white man boarded. The driver, J. F. Blake, turned to look behind him at the first row of blacks and said, "You let him have those front seats." That was not a suggestion, it was an order. It meant that not only did one seat have to be freed, but the other three blacks would have to move as well, lest the white man have to sit next to a black. All four blacks knew what Blake meant, but no one moved. Blake looked behind him again and added, "You all better make it light on yourselves and let me have those seats." The three other blacks reluctantly got up and moved toward the back. Rosa Parks did not. She was frightened, but she was tired. She did not want to give up her seat, and she most certainly did not want to stand up the rest of the way. She had just spent her entire day working in a department store tailoring and pressing clothes for white people and now she was being told that she had no rights.

"Look, woman, I told you I wanted the seat. Are you going to stand up?" Blake said. Finally, Rosa Parks spoke. "No," she said. "If you don't stand up, I'm going to have you arrested," Blake warned her. She told him to go right ahead, but she was not going to move.

Blake got off the bus and went to phone the police, thereby involuntarily entering the nation's history books; his was the most ordinary example of a Southern white man fending off any threat to the system of segregation. If it had not been Blake, it would have been someone else. Some of the black riders, sensing trouble, or possibly irritated by the delay, started getting off the bus.

Parks continued to sit. In so doing she became the first prominent figure of what became the Movement. Perhaps the most interesting thing about her was how ordinary she was, at least on the surface, almost the prototype of the black women who toiled so hard and had so little to show for it. She had not, she later explained, thought about getting arrested that day. Later, the stunned white leaders of Montgomery repeatedly charged that Parks's refusal was part of a carefully orchestrated plan on the part of the local NAACP, of which she was an officer. But that was not true; what she did represented one person's exhaustion with a system that dehumanized all black people. Something inside her finally snapped. But if she had not planned to resist on that particular day, then it was also true that Rosa Parks had decided some time earlier that if she was ever asked to give up her seat for a white person, she would refuse to do so.

Rosa Parks was often described in newspaper reports as merely a seamstress, but she was more than that; she was a person of unusual dignity and uncommon strength of character. She was born in rural Alabama in 1913 (she was forty-two at the time of her famed ride). Her father was a carpenter, and her mother taught school for a time. The family moved to Montgomery county when she was a girl, and while educational opportunities for young black girls in those years in Alabama were virtually nonexistent, she had the good luck to go to a special school for black girls, called the Montgomery Industrial School for Girls (also known as Miss White's). There, New England schoolmarms, not unlike missionaries to foreign countries, taught young black girls who were barely literate the fundamentals of a primary education, as well as how to cook, sew, and run a home. Rosa was a serious reader, a quiet, strong woman much admired in the local community. She was an early member of the local chapter of the NAACP, eventually becoming secretary. She went to work for Clifford and Virginia Durr, a liberal couple in Montgomery (he was a former FCC commissioner in the Truman administration who left because he disagreed with its security process; Mrs. Durr was a formidable activist who frequently defied local racial mores).

Rosa Parks's relationship with the Durrs showed the complexity of human relationships in the South, for she was both employee and friend. The Durrs were friends of Ed Nixon, one of the most militant blacks of his generation, and Virginia Durr once asked Nixon, the head of the local NAACP, if he knew of anyone who "did good sewing." (She had three daughters, so a good deal of raising and lowering of hems went on in her home.) Yes, he said, and mentioned his fellow officer in the NAACP chapter. Soon Rosa Parks started to sew for the Durrs. The two women became good friends, and their friendship defied Southern custom. There was a certain formality to the way they addressed each other; they could not, after all, be Virginia and Rosa—since Rosa Parks was not allowed to call Mrs. Durr Virginia, then Virginia Durr could not in turn call her Rosa. That meant the seamstress was always Mrs. Parks and the employer was always Mrs.

Durr. (Once, Virginia Durr turned to her friend Ed Nixon and casually called him Ed, but he cautioned her: Since he could not yet call her Virginia, she would have to call him Mr. Nixon.) But Virginia Durr helped Parks attend the integrated Highlander Folk School, in Monteagle, Tennessee, a school loathed by segregationists because it held workshops on how to promote integration. At Highlander she not only studied the techniques of passive resistance employed by Gandhi against the British, she also met whites who treated her with respect. The experience reinforced her sense of self-esteem, and set the stage for the bus confrontation.

As the bus driver continued to shout at her, Parks thought to herself, how odd it was that you go through life making things comfortable for white people yet they don't even treat you like a human being. There was something inevitable about this confrontation—a collision of rising black expectations with growing white resistance. At that moment in Montgomery, as in most deep South cities, school integration was still an abstract concept, something that had not yet happened and was not near happening. By contrast, riding a bus was the flashpoint, the center of daily, bitterly resented abuse.

Soon two Montgomery policemen arrived. Was it true that the driver had asked her to get up? they asked. Yes, she said. Why hadn't she obeyed? She felt she shouldn't have to. "Why do you push us around?" she asked. "I don't know, but the law is the law, and you're under arrest," one of the policemen said. Only then did she get up. The police escorted her to the patrol car. The police went back to talk to Blake. Did he want to press charges? Yes, he answered. The police took Parks to jail, where she was fingerprinted and charged with violating the city's segregation laws. She was allowed one phone call, and she called her home. Her mother answered and asked instinctively, "Did they beat you?" No, she said, she was physically all right. She was the first person ever so charged—the first of many tactical mistakes on the part of city officials, for it gave the local black community what it had been seeking: the case on which to hang a lawsuit.

After her phone call home, the news of her arrest spread quickly through the black community. E. D. Nixon, Parks's friend, called the police station to find out what had happened. Nixon was a Pullman car porter, a union man, and a powerful presence in the black community. For some twenty years he had been a black leader and activist in a town that despised the idea of racial change, and he became, in the process, absolutely fearless. There might be some blacks who did not like him, but everyone respected him, including some of the white leadership. For more than a decade, he had engaged in one of the most dangerous tasks of all—trying to register blacks to vote. On occasion, he did it carrying a shotgun under his coat. When Nixon called the police station to inquire about Rosa Parks, he was told it was none of his business. So he telephoned Clifford Durr, who said he would post bond. Nixon was not displeased by what had happened: This was the case he had been looking for. Mrs. Parks was the perfect defendant: She had worked with him in the NAACP for twelve years, and he knew she was a strong, confident person. If she said she was going to do something, she did it, and no amount of pressure from the white community would deter her. Her example would most likely give strength to others nervous about challenging the white establishment.

That night Parks, her family, the Durrs, and Ed Nixon sat around to discuss the details of her case. Nixon badly wanted to use it to test the constitutionality of the bus law. Would she agree, he asked, to be a test case? The idea frightened Raymond Parks, her husband, a local barber who knew the violence that traditionally awaited those blacks foolhardy enough to challenge the system. He warned her, "Oh, the white folks will kill you, Rosa. Don't do anything to make trouble, Rosa. Don't bring a suit. The whites will kill you." She was torn. She did not want to put her family at risk, but neither did she want herself or the younger black people who came after her to face such indignities. Nor did she want to face them anymore herself. "If you think we can get anywhere with it, I'll go along with it," she told Nixon.

Nixon went home and sketched a map of Montgomery—where blacks lived and where they worked. The distances were not, he decided, insurmountable. "You know what?" he told his wife.

"What?" she asked.

"We're going to boycott the buses," he said.

"Cold as it is?" she answered skeptically.

"Yes," he said.

"I doubt it," she said.

"Well, I'll tell you one thing: If you keep 'em off when it's cold, you won't have no trouble keeping 'em off when it gets hot," he said.

In Montgomery the majority of bus riders were black, particularly black women who went across town, from a world of black poverty to white affluence, to work as domestics. Nevertheless, a black challenge to the bus company was a formidable undertaking. Despite the earlier ruling of the Supreme Court, the deep South remained totally segregated. Whites held complete political, judicial, and psychological power. In a city like Montgomery it was as if the Court had not ruled on Brown.

Before the whites would take the blacks seriously, the blacks had to take themselves seriously—that was the task facing the black leadership of Montgomery in December 1955.

The previous minister at the Dexter Avenue Baptist Church (a church that would be made famous by its young minister, Martin Luther King, Jr.) had been a forceful, articulate man named Vernon Johns. Some five years earlier, the Rev. Johns had endured a similar incident on a bus: He had misplaced his dime while trying to put it in the fare box, and the coin had dropped to the floor. Though it was an easy matter for the driver to retrieve it himself, he had ordered Johns to pick it up, in language that smacked of the plantation: "Uncle, get down and pick up that dime and put it in the box." Johns refused and asked the driver to do it. The driver again ordered him to pick it up, or he would be put off the bus. Johns turned to the other passengers, all of whom were black, and said he was leaving and asked them all to join him. No one moved. A week later he saw one of his parishioners, who had witnessed the incident and done nothing. Before he could reproach her, she told him, "You ought to knowed better." When he told the story to his close friend and fellow minister, the Rev. Ralph Abernathy, Johns had shaken his head, more, Abernathy thought, in sorrow than anger. "Even God can't free people who behave like that," the Rev. Johns had said. With that the Rev. Johns vowed never to ride the bus again and he bought a car.

For many blacks, the bus line symbolized their powerlessness: Men were powerless to protect their wives and mothers from its indignities;

women were powerless to protect their children. The Montgomery bus system, with its flexible segregation line, vested all authority in the bus driver himself, which, depending on his personality and mood, allowed humiliation to be heaped upon humiliation. There were, for instance, bus drivers who took a black customer's money and then, while the customer was walking around to enter through the back door, would roar off.

The white officials of Montgomery had decided not only to resist integration in the years after the war but not even to listen to legitimate grievances from the black community. With every challenge to white authority, the city officials simply hunkered down and blamed outside agitators. Attempts on the part of black leaders to register more voters had failed, and there were estimates by the Justice Department after an investigation of Montgomery county's voting procedures that as many as ten thousand blacks had been denied their political rights over a period of years. In the summer of 1954, a few months after the *Brown* decision, an older activist black minister named Solomon Seay took a group of black children to Lee High School to register them in the all-white school and was turned away. He subsequently went before the all-white Alabama board of education and, in words that had a biblical ring to them, protested that changes were surely coming. "There is going to be a second day of judgment," the Rev. Seay warned, "and a worst day of judgment, if we don't all do what we can peacefully. . . . There are ways in which integration can be worked out in a peaceful process, and if we don't find these ways, then we will be punished. Let me emphasize I am not threatening you, just prophesizing."

Yet the most visceral anger of Montgomery blacks was reserved for the bus system. Four days after the Supreme Court had ruled on *Brown,* a black leader named Jo Ann Robinson wrote a letter to Montgomery's mayor telling him of the growing resentment blacks felt about their treatment on the buses, reminding him that more than three quarters of the system's riders were blacks and mentioning the possibility of a boycott. For Mrs. Robinson, a professor at Alabama State, a black college in Montgomery, the issue was particularly emotional. In 1949 she had boarded a bus to take her to the airport. It was near Christmas, and her arms were filled with the packages from holiday shopping. She was on her way home to Cleveland. She had gotten on the nearly empty bus, and, without thinking, sat down in the white section. Suddenly, the white bus driver appeared, his arm drawn back as if to hit her, and shouted, "Get up from there! Get up from there!" "I felt," she later said, "like a dog." She stumbled off the bus, and, in her own words, completed the trip to Cleveland largely in tears. But later, as she replayed the events in her mind, she became angrier and angrier; she was a human being too and, if anything, a better educated one than the driver. What right did any human have to treat another this way? When she returned to Montgomery after her vacation, she mentioned the incident to some of her friends, hoping to start some kind of protest. She was surprised by their lack of response: They assured her that this was life in Montgomery, Alabama. Not forever, she thought. Six years later, at the time of Rosa Parks's protest, Mrs. Robinson had become president of the Women's Political Council, an organization of black professional women. Her group had only recently won a major victory, entitling black customers to have the titles Mr., Mrs., or Miss used with their names when they received their bills from downtown white merchants.

The bus issue became the most pressing one for Mrs. Robinson's group. A few months before Rosa Parks made her stand, a fifteen-year-old black girl had refused to give up her seat to a white and had been dragged from the bus ("She insisted she was colored and just as good as white," T. J. Ward, the arresting policeman, had noted with some surprise during the local court proceedings on her arrest). She had been charged with assault and battery for resisting arrest. For a time the black leadership thought of making hers the constitutional test case it sought, but backed off when someone learned that she was pregnant. So when Rosa Parks was arrested, the obvious response was a boycott. This was the blacks' strongest lever: They were the biggest group of riders, and without them it was not going to be a very profitable bus service.

One of their great problems was the terrible divisions within the black leadership itself—by religion, by generation, by age, by class. There was no doubt that Ed Nixon was a forceful figure, willing on many occasions to take risks that few others would; but some felt that he was too abrasive, too eager for glory, and not sensitive enough to others. At the first organizational meeting, held the day after Parks was arrested, there was quick agreement on the need for a one-day boycott, starting on Monday morning. There was also a decision to hold a meeting of the black leadership, which included many ministers, on Monday afternoon, and a large public protest meeting was set for Monday night. At the Monday afternoon meeting, one of the ministers suggested that future meetings be secret, closed to the press, so that the whites would know as little as possible about what they were doing and who their leaders were. Meetings closed to the press! Ed Nixon got up and began to taunt them. "How in hell are you going to have protest meetings without letting the white folks know?" he began. Then he reminded them that those being hurt were the black women of the city, the most powerless of the powerless, the domestics who went off every day to work for whites. These were the people who suffered the greatest pain from segregation and made up the core of every black church in town. "Let me tell you gentlemen one thing. You ministers have lived off the sweat of these washwomen all these years and you have never done anything for them," he said. His contempt seemed to fill the church. "I am just ashamed of you. You said that God has called you to lead the people and now you are just afraid and gone to pieces because the man tells you that the newspapers will be here and your picture might come out in the newspaper. Somebody has got to get hurt in this thing and if you the preachers are not the leaders then we will have to pray that God will send us more leaders." That stunning assault contained all too much truth. It was a young minister named Martin Luther King, Jr., who answered Nixon and said that he was not a coward, that they should act in the open, use their own names, and not hide behind anyone else. With that, the Rev. King had at once taken a strong position for the boycott, but he had also shown he was not completely Nixon's man. Before the meeting was over, Martin Luther King, Jr., was named president of the new group, to be called the Montgomery Improvement Association (MIA). It was not a role he sought, but he was the obvious choice—in no small part because he was relatively new on the scene and belonged to no faction of the city's black leadership. There were other reasons as well: His congregation was unusually affluent and therefore less vulnerable to white reprisals. Finally, a number of people did not want Nixon to be the leader, yet King got on relatively well with Nixon, who had heard King speak earlier that year at an NAACP meeting and had been impressed. "I don't know how I'm going to do it," Nixon told a friend of his who taught at Alabama State, "but someday I'm going' to hitch him to the stars." King himself did not necessarily want to be hitched to the stars; he was wary of taking on too much responsibility and had only recently turned down an offer to head the local NAACP. After all, he was new in town, had a young family, and wanted first and foremost to do a good job at his first church.

But with a certain inevitability the movement sought him. He was a brilliant speaker. He had the ability to make complex ideas simple: By repeating phrases, he could expand an idea, blending the rational with the emotional. That gave him the great ability to move others, blacks at first and soon, remarkably enough, whites as well. He could reach people of all classes and backgrounds; he could inspire men and women with nothing but his words. On that first day, the Holt Street Baptist Church was filled by late afternoon, and a crowd estimated at between six and ten thousand gathered in the street to hear the meeting broadcast over loudspeakers. The white police watched the crowd gather with increasing nervousness, and the officer in charge finally ordered the organizers to turn off the public address system, hoping thereby to disperse the crowd. One of the black organizers answered that if the police wanted the PA system off, they could do it themselves. The cops, looking at the size of the crowd, decided to let them have their PA broadcast after all.

That night, most of the black people of Montgomery got their first taste of Martin King's oratory. He started out by making one point clear: Their boycott was different from those of the White Citizens' Councils, which were using the threat of violence to stop black political and legal progress in the deep South. "Now, let us say that we are not here advocating violence. We have overcome that. I want it to be known throughout Montgomery and throughout the nation that we are a Christian people. The only weapon that we have in our hands this evening is the weapon of protest." They were nothing less than ordinary Americans, he was saying, seeking the most ordinary of American rights in a democracy they loved as much as white people loved it. They were, in effect, setting out to make America whole. "If we are wrong, the Constitution of the United States is wrong. If we are wrong, God Almighty is wrong. If we are wrong, Jesus of Nazareth was merely a utopian dreamer and never came down to earth! If we are wrong, justice is a lie." By then the crowd was with him, cheering each incantation. "And we are determined here in Montgomery to work and fight until justice runs down like water and righteousness like a mighty stream."

When it was over, it was clear that the right man had arrived in the right city at the right time; this would be no one-day boycott but one that would continue until the white community addressed black grievances.

That the black ministry at this moment was to produce an exceptional generation of leaders—of whom King was merely the most visible—was not surprising. It was the obvious repository for black talent at that moment. In the past, black leadership had tended to be fragmented and poorly educated. (Five years before the bus boycott, at the time of the 1950 census, the city of Montgomery had had some 40,000 black citizens, including three doctors, one dentist, two lawyers, one pharmacist, and 92 preachers.) There were not a lot of black lawyers around in those days, and the usual political avenues were blocked in the Deep South. Therefore, the new black ministry was where talented young black men went to learn how to lead their people: It was outside the reach of the white community, a rare place where a young, well-educated black man could rise by merit alone.

When the bus boycott began, Martin Luther King, Jr., was twenty-six years old; he had been in Montgomery only fifteen months. He was a black Baptist Brahmin, a symbol of the new, more confident, better educated black leaders now just beginning to appear in the postwar South. His maternal grandfather, A. D. Williams, had formally founded the Ebenezer Baptist Church in 1894, its eighth year of existence, and made it one of the most important black churches in Atlanta. The Rev. Williams had been a charter member of the local NAACP. When a local white newspaper criticized Atlanta's blacks as being "dirty and ignorant," he led the boycott that helped close the newspaper down. When an important school-bond issue failed to include any money for the city's first black high school, he started rallies, which resulted in the building of Booker T. Washington High. His son-in-law, Martin Luther King, Sr. (known as "Daddy" King), had led a voter-registration drive as a young minister in Atlanta and pushed the other black ministers to make their churches centers for voter-registration drives in the thirties, a move opposed by many on his board. But one thousand blacks had showed up at Ebenezer and marched to the city hall. Such activism made Atlanta, by the fifties, one of the great centers of black middle-class life, a place where black economic power had made black political power possible.

Daddy King was one of nine children of sharecroppers. As a boy he watched the vicious cycle of poverty and powerlessness destroy his father, who turned to alcohol and wife beating. Delia King farmed alongside her husband and worked in the home of the white owners. When Daddy King (whose real name was Michael and changed his name to Martin as a man) was twelve, he accompanied his father to town when the annual accounts were being settled up. The little boy, a good student and better at numbers than his father, was aware that his father was being swindled. "Ask him about the cotton seed money, Daddy," he said, for that was an important part of the equation, and the tenant farmer got the money. The landowner was furious, but in the end he paid; but he did not forget the incident or forgive the little boy. The next day he had arrived to tell the elder King that he had to leave his land altogether. With that James King started coming apart. Beaten down by the harshness and cruelty of the system, he took his anger out on his family, particularly his wife and this son whose moment of truth had caused him even greater humiliation and revealed his true powerlessness.

Watching the disintegration of his family, Mike King could not wait to leave. He and his father had a violent fight once after his father had beaten his mother. The youth, already powerfully built, won the fight, but he heard his father shout, "I'll kill you, kill you, I'll do it, damn you . . ." Terrified, his mother told her son to hide out for a time. "A man's anger gets the best of him," Daddy King wrote, describing the scene some seven decades later. "Violence is the only thing he's got to calm him down some, or get him killed, one day."

The only place young Mike King decided he could find any kind of peace was in the church. He would feel, he wrote later, bitterness and anger descend upon him at other times of the day, but not when he was in church. He became a licensed minister at fifteen, traveling and preaching in small rural churches. At eighteen he went to Atlanta. There, he was regarded as a hick, bright but unlettered. He wanted badly to be somebody, yet he felt the awful shame of his rural ignorance, his rustic language.

He was nothing if not ambitious, though. Encouraged by an older sister, he went back to school at the age of twenty-one. He was assigned to the fifth grade, which completely shattered his confidence; never had he felt so ignorant before. But he persevered: He spent five years at the school, always working full-time as a driver for a man who sold and repaired barber-shop chairs, and taking his books with him wherever he went and, of course, preaching on weekends. Finally, he received his high school degree. During this time he saw Alberta Williams, the daughter of one of Atlanta's foremost ministers. She was, he thought, everything he was not: sophisticated, educated, genteel. He immediately fell in love with her. When he told this to some friends who were also country boys, they teased him unmercifully. "Now, King," one of them said. "You know God doesn't love ugly and that's about the worst-looking story I've heard all year—you marrying Alberta Williams. Get on away from here!" But King pursued her relentlessly. For his first date he took his best pair of pants, put them between two boards, and then put the boards under his mattress for a few days in order to ensure a crease. He asked the lady who ran the boardinghouse to iron his best shirt. "Why, Reverend King, you must be fixin' to court some nice young lady," she had said. "No, ma'am," he answered. "I'm fixin' to get married."

Their courtship lasted six years. Driven by the need to be worthy of Alberta, he had decided to enter Morehouse and get a college degree. He was twenty-seven, and the officials at Morehouse were not enthusiastic. He took their tests. "You're just not college material," the registrar told him. He told them he didn't care how poorly he tested—he *knew* he could succeed, if it was a matter of hard work. Nonetheless, they rejected him. Pushed by Alberta, he tried again and was rejected again. Finally, he begged for a trial period as a student and was rejected again. In a rage, he charged into the office of the president of the college and told his story. Then he stomped out. But because of his assertiveness, he was at last given a chance. "Apparently," said the unsympathetic registrar, "you can begin classes at Morehouse. Don't ask me why, but you can . . ." By going to summer school, he managed to get his degree in four years. A year later, his father-in-law died of a heart attack and Mike King took over the Ebenezer Baptist Church.

Martin Luther King, Jr., the second of three

children, grew up in an environment far gentler than the one his father had known. He was a member of the black elite of Atlanta, perhaps not as wealthy as some, but even that in time might change, for Daddy King planned to have Martin marry a daughter of one of Atlanta's truly wealthy Atlanta families and come back home to Ebenezer and work with him. Then the Kings would presumably become *the* leading black family of Atlanta, the heiress's money attached now to the powerful social-political position that Daddy King had created at Ebenezer. Young Martin lived the odd duality of a black prince: He at once was exceptionally privileged within the black world yet virtually everything outside it was denied him. There were, for all the attempts to protect him, humiliations that occurred as he crossed over to the alien environment of white Atlanta, where he, like all other blacks, lost all status.

Though his birth had coincided with the coming of the Depression, which hit black Southerners hardest, the King family knew little deprivation. A black church as prosperous as Ebenezer was immune to the vagaries of national economics. Martin King remembered driving through Atlanta and seeing the long lines of black people waiting to buy bread as his parents tried to explain the harsh reality of the Depression to him. Martin King, Jr., grew up loved and secure; years later James Baldwin wrote that King lacked the self-doubts that burdened most blacks of their generation. "Martin," Baldwin wrote, "never went around fighting himself the way the rest of us did." He grew up with segregation, yet he saw his father's strength in the face of prejudice: Once when he was driving with his father, an Atlanta policeman stopped the car. "All right, boy," he had said. "Pull over and let me see your license." "I'm no boy," Daddy King said. He pointed at his son. "This is a boy. I'm a man and until you call me one I will not listen to you."

As a father Martin King, Sr., was unsparing. He beat his children for relatively minor infractions. (The father was surprised by the stoic quality of young Martin: "He was the most peculiar child whenever you whipped him. He'd stand there and the tears would run down and he'd never cry out.") He was a powerful preacher of the old school, all hellfire and brimstone. The Bible for him was a book of literal truths and stories that were not to be challenged, or to be interpreted to fit modern circumstances. He was uneasy when his son drank and danced as a young seminarian and ventured increasingly into the world of social gospel, which Daddy King thought at heart a world of leftists, which, if it threatened the white order, might threaten as well the existing black hierarchy in which he had so handsomely succeeded.

Martin Luther King, Jr.'s, earliest rebellion was not against his father's house rules but against his fundamentalist teachings. As a boy he shocked his Sunday School teacher by questioning the bodily resurrection of Christ; he was clearly embarrassed by the raw emotion of his father's preaching—the shouting, stomping, and wailing. It was only at Morehouse that more sophisticated men showed him the ministry could be socially valuable, intellectually respectable. At Morehouse, he would later note, "the shackles of fundamentalism were removed from my body."

Unlike his father, young Martin had been raised with choices in life—which schools he could go to and which profession he might choose. His was a world with far greater possibilities than the world of his father: Upon graduation from Morehouse in 1948 he had pondered a career at divinity school or a career at law school and finally chose the former, going to Crozer Seminary, in Chester, Pennsylvania. He was the first member of his family to be educated outside the South. Martin King did well at Crozer, extending himself intellectually for the first time, so much so that several members of the faculty encouraged him to go on with his studies. But Daddy King felt that seven years of higher education was enough. It was time to come back and help out at Ebenezer. Martin never said no to his father, but he accepted a fellowship at Boston University to get his Ph.D.

In Boston, as at Crozer, King was determined to undo the white stereotypes of blacks.

Were blacks supposed to be careless about time? Martin King was the most punctual young man on campus, never late to class. Were blacks supposed to be noisy and loud? King was always sedate and respectful. Were they supposed to be a little flashy about clothes? King dressed as seriously and carefully as anyone on campus—always in a suit—and his clothes were *always* pressed, his shoes shined.

Boston, a great college town, was a delight for him socially; he was a leader among the young upper-class blacks in Boston in the early fifties, with his handsome wardrobe and his new Chevy, a gift from his father. He was, for all his theological studies, something of a young man about town, a great dancer, and very much on the lookout for the best-looking women. He was soon known in the small world of Boston black academia, Coretta Scott King later noted, as "the most eligible young black man in the Boston area at that time." The first time he called Coretta Scott, at a friend's suggestion, he talked a smooth line: "Every Napoleon has his Waterloo. I'm like Napoleon. I'm at my Waterloo and I'm on my knees." Jive, she thought, but different than most jive, because it was "intellectual jive." Meeting him on a blind date, she thought him too short. It was only as he began to talk that she got interested. After their first date, he took her home and virtually proposed to her. He demanded, he told her, four qualifications in the woman he was going to marry: character, intelligence, personality, and beauty. She had all four. Could he see her again? he asked. She would, though with some reluctance, for she had her own career as a singer and she was not thrilled by the idea of being the wife of a young minister. But gradually they became more serious, despite her doubts and despite Daddy King's attempts to get her out of the picture in favor of a wealthy young black Atlanta heiress from, he said, "a fine family . . . very talented . . . wonderful personality. We love that girl."

Intellectually, it was an exciting time for him; he was seeking a gospel that would fit the needs of a modern black minister working in the American South. He wanted to escape the raw fundamentalism he knew was so much a part of the existing black church. Instead, King sought a Christianity that allowed him to love his fellow man and yet to protest the abundant inhumanities and injustices being inflicted on blacks. He studied Marxism diligently and found it formidable as a critique of capitalism but empty as theology—shamelessly materialistic in its antimaterialism, unloving and, finally, totalitarian. But he was impressed by the writings of Walter Rauschenbusch, a turn-of-the-century social critic who had blamed society's ills on the raw, unchecked capitalism of his time. He was also impressed by Reinhold Niebuhr and, more and more, by the teachings of Gandhi. Gandhi had had not merely the ability to lead but also to love, and to conquer inner darkness and rage. He felt that Niebuhr had misunderstood Gandhi's notion of passive resistance. It was not, King wrote, nonresistance to evil but rather non-violent resistance to evil. He was slowly finding a vision to fit the needs of his people and with which he was comfortable enough to devote his professional career. The faculty was impressed by him and encouraged him to become an academic. For a time he considered that: The life was pleasant and sheltered, and a young man could escape the ugly segregation of the South. But his obligations were real and immediate. The closer he came to finishing, the clearer his path became: He wanted a large Baptist church in the South. "That's where I'm needed," he told Coretta. They were married in 1953. Daddy King backed down from his opposition and advised Coretta of her good fortune. "You will not be marrying any ordinary young minister," he told her.

Martin King, Jr., began looking over several churches. One in Chattanooga was interested in him, as was the Dexter Avenue Baptist Church in Montgomery. The Dexter Avenue offer intrigued him. It was a famous church, built in the days of Reconstruction, in the center of town, right across from the Alabama Supreme Court and diagonally across from the state capitol. Many of its parishioners were college-educated; they were the black Baptist elite of the city. His father warned him about them: The Dexter congregation was highly political, snobbish, and they had a reputation for devouring their pastors. They did not like a lot of whooping and hollering in their sermons. "At First Baptist," Vernon Johns acidly told the Rev. Ralph Abernathy, "they don't mind the preacher talking about Jesus, though they would never stoop so low as to talk about Him themselves. At Dexter Avenue they would prefer that you not mention his name." King went to Montgomery and gave a guest sermon. Slightly nervous, he reminded himself, "Keep Martin Luther King in the background and God in the foreground and everything will be all right. Remember you're a channel of the gospel, not a source." The Montgomery people were so impressed they offered him their pulpit at $4,200 a year, which would make him the best-paid black minister in town. Coretta King had no great desire to return to Montgomery, which was only eighty miles from Moraine, Alabama, where she had grown up. She had seen the North and the South and her preference was for the North. But Martin believed that the South was where his future should be, so to Montgomery they went.

To the white leadership in Montgomery, Martin King was just another faceless preacher, surely ignorant. The popular caricature of a black minister was of a whooper and hollerer. Indeed, the whites kept calling him Preacher King at the beginning of the boycott, as if by denying him his proper title they could diminish him. He fought against such stereotyping with careful formality. One of the first local reporters to meet him, Tom Johnson of the *Montgomery Advertiser,* found him self-conscious, almost to the point of pomposity. He answered questions with references to Nietzsche and Kant. Johnson was amused when, in the middle of their long interview, an old friend of King's from Atlanta arrived and King broke effortlessly into what Johnson considered a kind of jive talk; then he switched back to his formal lecture again without breaking stride.

As in his university days, he was always well dressed, in a dark suit, a white shirt, and a conservative tie. "I don't want to look like an undertaker," he once said, describing his undertakerlike wardrobe, "but I do believe in conservative dress." As the bus boycott began, he would get up at 5:30 A.M. to work for three hours on his doctoral thesis and then join Coretta for breakfast before going off to his pastoral duties. (Critical parts of his thesis, it would turn out, were plagiarized, a reminder, like his womanizing, of the flaws in even the most exceptional of men.) From the start he became extremely close to the Rev. Ralph Abernathy, a far earthier figure. Like King, Abernathy was anxious to break with the narrowness of the preachers of the past. "They preached the gospel of 'otherworldliness,' of a better time in the sweet by and by," Abernathy later wrote. "Their ultimate solution to Jim Crow was death—when you died you were equal in the eyes of God. For such people the idea of desegregation was either frivolous or else threatening." Abernathy helped him overcome a tendency toward snobbishness. King was better educated and able to articulate a broad social vision; Abernathy was comfortable with a wide range of people.

.   .   .

The white community had no idea how to deal with the boycott. The city leadership thought it was dealing with the black leadership from the past—poorly educated, readily divided, lacking endurance, and without access to national publicity outlets. When the boycott proved to be remarkably successful on the first day, the mayor of Montgomery, W. A. Gayle, did not sense that something historic was taking place, nor did he move to accommodate the blacks, who were in fact not asking for integrated buses but merely a minimal level of courtesy and a fixed line between the sections. Gayle turned to a friend and said, "Comes the first rainy day and the Negroes will be back on the buses." Soon it did rain, but the boycott continued. As the movement grew stronger, the principal response of Gayle and his two commissioners was to join the White Citizens' Council. A month after the boycott began, it proved so successful that the bus-line operators were asking for permission to double the price from ten to twenty cents a ride. They were granted a five-cent raise. In late January, frustrated by the solidarity of the blacks, the white leadership went to three relatively obscure black ministers and tricked them into saying, or at least seeming to say, that they accepted the city's terms and would show up at a meeting at city hall. Then the *Montgomery Advertiser* was brought in—a disgraceful moment for a newspaper—to report on the alleged agreement and make it seem, without using the names of the three ministers, that the real black leadership had conceded. By chance the real black leadership found out, and the ploy was not successful. But it was a sign of how terrified and out of touch the white leadership was—as if it could, by means of disinformation, halt a movement as powerful as this. When the hoax was discovered, the mayor was petulant. No more Mr. Nice Guy, he threatened. "No other city in the South of our size has treated the Negroes more fairly," he said. Now he wanted his fellow whites to be made of sterner stuff and to stop helping their maids and workers to get to work by giving them transportation money and, worse, giving them rides. "The Negroes," he said, "are laughing at white people behind their backs. They think it is funny and amusing that whites who are opposed to the Negro boycott will act as chauffeurs to Negroes who are boycotting the buses."

The Montgomery authorities stopped the local black cabdrivers from ferrying people to and from work in groups of five and six for ten cents a ride (there was an old city ordinance that said the minimum fare for a ride had to be 45 cents), but money poured in from the outside to buy some fifteen new station wagons. Eventually, the MIA had some thirty cars of its own. Richard Harris, a local black pharmacist who was a crucial dispatcher in the downtown area, feared that his phone was tapped, so he spoke in comic black dialect to confuse the white authorities, and he used a code with other dispatchers—"shootin' marbles," for example, told how many people needed to be picked up.

Inevitably, the city leaders resorted to what had always worked in the past: the use of police power. The city fathers decided that it had to break the back of the carpool, and soon the police started arresting carpool drivers. On January 26, 1956, some eight weeks into the boycott, Martin Luther King, Jr., was arrested for driving 30 miles an hour in a 25-mile-an-hour zone. He was taken to the police station and fingerprinted; at first it appeared that he would be kept overnight, but because the crowd of blacks outside the station kept growing larger and noisier, the police let King go on his own recognizance. Two days later, King's house was bombed by a white extremist, the first in a series of such incidents at the homes of black leaders and at black churches.

In unity and nonviolence the blacks found new strength, particularly as the nation began to take notice. Things that had for so long terrified them—the idea of being arrested and spending the night in prison, for example—became a badge of honor. Their purpose now was greater than their terror. More, because the nation was watching, the jails were becoming safer. King was, in effect, taking a crash course in the uses of modern media and proving a fast learner. Montgomery was becoming a big story, and the longer it went on, the bigger it became. In the past it had been within the power of such papers as the *Advertiser* and its afternoon twin, the far more racist *Alabama Journal,* either to grant or not grant coverage to black protests and to slant the coverage in terms most satisfying to the whites. The power to deny coverage was a particularly important aspect of white authority, for if coverage was denied, the blacks would feel isolated and gradually lose heart (for taking such risks without anyone knowing or caring); in addition, the whites would be able to crush any protest with far fewer witnesses and far less scrutiny. But that power deserted the local newspapers now, in no small part because the Montgomery story was too important for even the most virulently segregationist newspaper to ignore completely, affecting as it did virtually every home in the city; second, because even when the local newspapers tried to control the coverage, and at the very least minimize it, the arrival of television meant that the newspapers were no longer the only potential journalistic witnesses.

The editor of the *Advertiser* was Grover Cleveland Hall, Jr., a seeming moderate, then in his mid-thirties. He was on the board of directors of the American Civil Liberties Union, a position which, with the pressure of events, he was soon to resign. Hall bore a famous name in Southern journalism: In the twenties, his father had won a Pulitzer Prize for covering the Ku Klux Klan. Grover Hall was a charming, witty man, much given to white suits, straw hats, and suspenders. He often wore a flower in his lapel, if at all possible a rose from his own prized collection. His foppish dress, arch manner, and flowery mode of speech and writing seemed calculated to recall another, more genteel, era. Visiting reporters were often much taken with him—"an almost perfect cross between Mark Twain and H. L. Mencken," said Karl Fleming, who covered the region for *Newsweek* and who took considerable pleasure in Hall's company.

He wrote archly, with a wicked bite, and no little tolerance for fools. He seemed well suited for this particular city as he might so readily have been out of place in the harder, edgier Birmingham. Though on occasion he liked to mock many of his contemporaries in the local establishment, finding that they were not quite worthy of the standards he set, he was very much a member of the country-club set himself. If anything, he seemed to see himself as the voice of a city, which he believed enlightened and gracious; he regarded himself as the journalistic embodiment not only of the city, but of a region and of an age, and he once wrote of Montgomery, "We love our city here in

the bend of a yellow river. We venerate its famous
past. We cherish the style and the individuality of
the present. And we trust not vaingloriously, the
city's sunburst future we take for granted, even
though it may mean a bit of factory soot on the
magnolia blossoms."

Prior to the bus boycott, Hall had been able
to straddle the contradictions between the pre-
industrial South he loved and the new South that
was beginning to take shape. The kindest thing
that could be said for the *Advertiser*'s coverage of
the Movement was that it was erratic and ambivalent. Hall apparently met Martin King just once,
largely by accident, when Hall had escorted Peter
Kihss, of *The New York Times,* to King's church.
The rise of King baffled him.

The last plantation intellectual, Fleming
called Hall. The way he was reared, and the way
he saw himself and his region, thought one associate, did not include a place for such proud, increasingly militant black leaders as the Rev. King.
Grover Hall could understand what King was
doing and, having met him, could appreciate his
intelligence; but nonetheless the agenda King represented remained alien to him, and he could
never bring himself to like Martin King. He spoke
more and more scathingly of him in private. King
was, in sum, a threat to everything Hall knew and
believed in.

Even though initially Hall urged an acceptance of the first-come, first-served segregated seat-

ing arrangement that the black leadership sought, he was soon to find himself allied with people he had once scorned as the implications of what was happening in Montgomery grew and as the black protest became a *movement*. For the situation did not allow a man who would be a great Southern editor to sit on the sidelines: It demanded a certain moral reckoning, as the Rev. Seay had so recently prophesized.

From the start, the *Advertiser* had been weak on the crisis. The first story, by the city editor, Joe Azbell, was written as if merely to let the white community know what the blacks were up to. He had been tipped off by E. D. Nixon. The story ran on page one by mistake. The publisher, Richard Hudson, had called in to order the story be placed inside, but it was too late. That gaffe greatly helped the black leadership publicize the boycott at first. Hudson was furious, and for a brief time Azbell's job seemed to be on the line. Azbell later said that he caught more heat for that than anything else he had ever done, including putting the death of Hank Williams, the great country singer and songwriter, on the front page (death of so exceptional a man being considered less than page-one news by Hudson). Hall had not fired Azbell, but he made it clear that from then on, there was to be a great deal of caution in how the *Advertiser* reported the boycott. Caught at once between its responsibilities to inform and its fear that honest coverage might embolden an increasingly audacious black leadership, the paper tried to ignore the story as much as possible. Its first in-depth piece on the leaders of the boycott ran some six weeks into the crisis. Its lowest moment was the attempt to trick the black public. (Some seven years later, at the height of the civil rights movement, the *Advertiser* did not even have a reporter cover the great Selma-Montgomery march in which some 25,000 people marched toward the state capitol along with representatives from almost every major journalistic institution in the country. The *Advertiser* used an AP dispatch.)

But even though the two Montgomery papers were owned by the same company, they no longer had a monopoly on news. Just a year earlier, on Christmas Day 1954, WSFA-TV had gone on the air. There had been one other local channel, but it did no local programming. From the start, it was announced, there would be active local news and weather coverage—fifteen minutes of news, and fifteen minutes of weather each evening, something almost unheard of locally in those days. Indeed, there was said to be a hot new news director arriving from Oklahoma City. The news director (and star reporter as well, of course) was a young man named Frank McGee, then in his early thirties. He was, in fact, a very good reporter, and he immediately decided that the bus boycott was a very big story. Unlike his local print counterparts, he did not take the protest as a social affront. Rather, he realized it was the kind of high drama that lent itself exceptionally well to television. Nor was McGee, like his counterparts at the two Montgomery papers, part of the town's white power establishment. He had grown up very poor in northern Louisiana and then in Oklahoma, and he sympathized with all poor people, white and black. He liked to joke that his father, who worked the oil rigs, might have risen up out of some back country swamp, "and you never know what color there might be in our family if you went back far enough." In an age when most of the nation's top journalists seemed to be the product of the nation's elite schools, Frank McGee had never gone to college and had a high school degree only because he finished a high-school equivalency course while in the service. He was not a particularly ideological man, but like most reporters of that era, he sympathized instinctively with the blacks, whose demands were so rudimentary. He was well aware of the dangers of covering the story, that the television journalists were vulnerable to attack. But although there were constant threats, both in the streets and over the phone, no one ever assaulted him. What surprised him most, he later would say, was that the local station managers never cramped his style, never told him what he could and could not put on the air. Part of the reason, he suspected, was that his bosses thought they needed all the excitement they could get in those early days in order to compete with the local newspapers. Besides, his bosses were too new to be part of the establishment.

Like many of his generation, he was aware that he was riding a very good story. That was particularly true as the whites blindly continued to resist and the story continued to escalate. The NBC network news show, also still in its infancy, started to use McGee with increasing regularity on the network, with a direct feed from Montgomery. It was not only a good story, in which ordinary Americans were asserting their demands for the most basic rights, but it was also helping McGee's career, which for a young, tough-minded, ambitious reporter was almost an unbeatable combination. (Within a year of the bus settlement, Frank McGee became one of NBC's first national network correspondents.) Events were soon beyond the ability of the *Advertiser* to control coverage. Montgomery was soon flooded with members of the national press, causing Grover Hall to comment that he was "duenna and Indian guide to more than a hundred reporters of the international press." The more coverage there was, the more witnesses there were and the harder it was for the white leadership to inflict physical violence upon the blacks. In addition, the more coverage there was, the more it gave courage to the leadership and its followers. The sacrifices and the risks were worth it, everyone sensed, because the country and the world were now taking notice. What was at stake in the *Advertiser*'s coverage of Martin King and the Montgomery bus boycott was, the editors of that paper soon learned to their surprise, not King's reputation but the *Advertiser*'s reputation.

The national press corps that had coalesced for the first time at the Emmett Till trial only a few months earlier returned in full strength, and its sympathies were not with Mayor Gayle, who appointed a committee to meet with the black ministers and added a White Citizens' Council member to it, or with police commissioner Clyde Sellers, who publicly joined the Citizens' Council in the middle of the struggle, saying, "I wouldn't trade my Southern birthright for 100 Negro votes." Rather, the national reporters were impressed with the dignity of Rosa Parks, the seriousness of the young Martin King, and the shrewd charm of Ralph Abernathy.

Ironically, it was the white leaders of Montgomery who first helped to create the singular importance of Martin King. Convinced that ordinary black people were being tricked and manipulated, they needed a villain. If they could weaken, discredit, or scare him, then their problems would be solved, they thought. Gradually, he became the focal point of the boycott. "I have the feeling," Bayard Rustin, the nation's most experienced civil rights organizer, told him at the time, "that the Lord has laid his hands on you, and that is a dangerous, dangerous thing." Still, King had no illusions about his role: "If Martin Luther King had never been born this movement would have taken place," he said early on. "I just happened to be there. You know there comes a time when time itself is ready for a change. That time has come in Montgomery and I have nothing to do with it."

For a time the role was almost too much for him. The amount of hate mail was staggering, and it was filled with threats that he had to take seriously. His father pleaded with him to leave Montgomery and return to Atlanta. "It's better to be a live dog than a dead lion," Daddy King said. The pressure on King was such that he was getting little sleep, and he was truly afraid. He realized for the first time how sheltered his existence had been, how ill prepared he was to deal with the racial violence that was waiting just beneath the surface in the South. One night, unsure of whether to continue, he thought of all his religious training and he heard the voice of Christ: "Martin Luther, stand up for righteousness. Stand up for justice. Stand up for truth' . . . the fatigue had turned into hope." (That was, Grover Hall noted acidly, Martin King's "vision in the kitchen speech.")

The boycott continued. The white leadership was paralyzed; in late February, it cited an obscure state law prohibiting boycotts and indicted eighty-nine leaders, including twenty-four ministers and all the drivers of the carpools. The real target, however, was King. He happened to be in Nashville lecturing when the indictments were announced. Back in Montgomery, many of the other leaders were giving themselves up in groups to show their defiance. King flew back to Montgomery by way of Atlanta. In Atlanta, his father pleaded with him not to go back. "They gon' to kill my boy," he told the Atlanta police chief. He brought over some of Martin's oldest friends, including Benjamin Mays, the president of Morehouse, to help talk him out of returning. But Martin Luther King, Jr., was firm now. Not to return, to desert his friends at this point, would be the height of cowardice, he told them. "I have begun the struggle," he said, "and I can't turn back. I have reached the point of no return." At that point his father broke down and began to sob. Benjamin Mays told him he was doing the right thing, and he returned to Montgomery.

. . .

On November 13, 1956, almost a year after the boycott had begun, King went to court to defend himself and the carpools against the local authorities who had declared it "a public nuisance." King was hardly optimistic about the outcome in a Montgomery court, but suddenly, during a recess, an AP reporter handed him a note that included an AP bulletin reporting that the Supreme Court had judged the Montgomery bus-segregation law to be unconstitutional. The blacks had won. King, always aware of the need to include rather than exclude people and the need to be magnanimous in victory, spoke at a mass rally to point out this should not be viewed as victory of blacks over whites but as a victory for American justice and democracy. On December 21, the city prepared to desegregate its buses. An empty bus pulled up to a corner near Dr. King's home. Martin Luther King, Jr., boarded it. The white driver smiled at him and said, "I believe you are Reverend King." "Yes, I am," Martin Luther King, Jr., said. "We are glad to have you with us this morning," the driver said.

So the battle was won. But the war was hardly over. It was a beginning rather than an end; the boycott became the Movement, with a capital *M*. The blacks might have alienated the local white leadership, but they had gained the sympathy of the white majority outside the South. In the past the whites in Montgomery had been both judge and jury: Now, as the nation responded to the events there, they became the judged.

Grover Hall, a man of considerable abilities, became with the passage of time an ever sadder figure. He turned on the Movement and become more conservative. His humor became bitter, his manner a caricature of what it had once been. The peer esteem he valued so greatly inevitably dwindled as the nation's consciousness on race changed. He was replaced in 1963 as editor of the *Advertiser* when the paper changed hands. He went for a time to Virginia, where he replaced James Jackson Kilpatrick as chief editorial writer on the *Richmond News-Leader*. That job did not last long; he did not blend in as well in Richmond as he had at home, and his health was failing. He returned to Montgomery, where he became ever more conservative, becoming extremely close to George Wallace, virtually becoming Wallace's resident intellectual during Wallace's national campaigns.

After his return to Montgomery, two old and rather more liberal colleagues, Ray Jenkins and Wayne Greenhaw, would go by to visit him occasionally. Hall, now in a wheelchair, would cry out to his black physical therapist as they approached, "Get me my chicken gun—I'm going to kill these Communists. . . . Why, hell, I thought you'd come up here with at least a regiment of niggers to capture this place."

THIRTY-SEVEN

Sнᴇ ᴡᴀꜱ ꜱᴏ ᴀʟɪᴠᴇ she seemed to jump off the screen to create a personal relationship with her growing audience. "The golden girl who was like champagne on the screen," one of her husbands, Arthur Miller, wrote of her. Even when she was a struggling starlet, photographers understood instantly that she was special and inevitably asked her to pose. She was, photographer Richard Avedon once said, more comfortable in front of the camera than away from it. The famed French photographer Henri Cartier Bresson described something vivid, fragile, and evanescent about her, something "that disappears quickly [and] that reappears again." "The first day a photographer took a picture of her, she was a genius," said the director Billy Wilder, who understood and exploited her talent better than any other director. To the studio heads she was, at first, just another dumb blonde, part of the endless stream of young women who had been voted the best-looking girls in their high school classes and who thereupon went to Hollywood and queued up at Schwab's Drug Store hoping to be discovered. Early on, she was perceived as being at once too desirable, too available, and too vulnerable. Watching the reaction of studio wives to her at an early Hollywood party, Evelyn Keyes, the actress, turned to Arthur Miller, who had only just met Miss Monroe, and said, "They'll eat her alive."

Her power to project such a luminescent personality surprised the veteran actors and actresses with whom she worked. "I thought surely she won't come over, she's so small-scale," said the great British actress Dame Sybil Thorndyke, who worked with her on *The Prince and the Showgirl,* "but when I saw her on the screen, my goodness, how it came over. She was a revelation. We theatre people tend to be so outgoing. She was the reverse. The perfect film actress, I thought. I have seen a lot of her films since then and it's always there—that perfect quality." She was a sex goddess but also so desperately needy and childlike that she aroused a powerful instinct on the part of audiences to protect her. "When you look at Marilyn on the screen, you don't want anything to happen to her. You really care that she should be all right," said Natalie Wood. She had, said Laurence Olivier, who directed her near the end of her career, a rare ability "to suggest one moment that she is the naughtiest little thing, and the next that she's perfectly innocent."

She had a keen sense of her own abilities and of men's response to them. Cast inevitably by others as the dumb blonde, she was shrewder and smarter than most directors suspected, and she often managed to deliver considerably more in a part than they had reckoned for. But only when she worked with a director as smart as Billy Wilder would she do her best work. He saw her as an uncommonly talented comedienne who mocked the sex-goddess mystique.

She was a genuine original. Her success, which looked so easy from a distance, was virtually impossible to repeat, try though Hollywood might with such pretenders as Jayne Mansfield and Mamie Van Doren. Those physically similar starlets never seemed to possess the intelligence that she had, or the vulnerability. Whereas she played the naif who somehow knew the score down deep, her imitators often tended to be hard and brittle. When she died, Wilder said later, a whole genre of comedy died with her. "People fool themselves," he said, by trying to come up with imitations and Monroe lookalikes. "They said, 'I have just bought myself a car, and it looks like a Cadillac,' but it turns out they've just bought a Pontiac."

The vulnerability she projected came from a nightmarish childhood; the naïveté, such as it was, came from shrewdly perceiving, however involuntarily, what men were like and what they really wanted from women. She operated on the edge: There was a very thin line between who she was in real life and the poignant, sexual figure she played on the screen. She took her strength as an actress from her real-life experiences; but as she became more and more successful, she always retained the fear of being abandoned, of being un-loved. She was needy on the screen because she was needy in real life.

There was a strain of emotional instability that had run through her family for several gener-ations. Her mother, Gladys Mortensen, had brought Marilyn, whose real name was Norma Jeane, into the world in 1926 in Los Angeles as an illegitimate child. Her husband seemed to have disappeared and was clearly not the father of the child. The man Marilyn believed to be her father, a co-worker of her mother's named C. Stanley Gifford, never accepted responsibility for her. That weighed heavily on her, and as an adult she put no little effort into trying to fight that rejec-tion by pursuing Gifford and trying to make con-tact with him. But even as the most successful actress in the world, she found that her phone calls to him were still not accepted.

Her mother, always mentally unstable, was institutionalized when she was not yet eight. Norma Jeane was passed around to different fam-ilies and moved in and out of orphanages. All of this was traumatic for a child. She knew she had a mother and somewhere out there was a father, so why was she being handed over to strangers? She pleaded, "But I'm not an orphan! I'm not an orphan!" Of the families paid by the state to take her in, she was abused by the head of at least one. Another was a harsh fundamentalist: "Jesus is supposed to be so forgiving, but they never mentioned that," she said later. "He was basically out to smack you in the head if you did something wrong." She was precocious physically, and given the rejections and insecurities of her childhood, it was hardly surprising that she soon decided that the world was not interested in her goodness or intelligence. That was particularly true in Hollywood, she decided: "In Hollywood a girl's virtue is much less important than her hair-do. You're judged on how you look, not by what you are."

As such she was always wary, for there were dangers everywhere, people who you thought you could count on who would let you down. "You'd catch glimpses," noted her first husband, James Dougherty, an airplane-factory worker she married at age sixteen as much to escape her life as anything else, "of someone who had been unloved for too long and unwanted for too many years."

Her dream had always been to become a movie star. Her mother had fantasized about Clark Gable and kept a photo of him by her bedside; Norma Jeane/Marilyn had even fantasized that Gable was her father. She wended her way inevitably toward the studios and was noticed by a variety of people on the fringes of Hollywood. She made friends with a number of photographers who worked for the seedy, sex-oriented magazines of the time. She was well aware that the men who said they would help her might or might not: There was no doubt in her mind, she later told writer Jaik Rosenstein, that trading off physical favors was part of her early career requirements. "When I started modelling, it was like part of the job. . . . They weren't shooting all those sexy pictures just to sell peanut butter in an ad or get a layout in some picture magazine. They wanted to sample the merchandise, and if you didn't go along, there were 25 girls who would. It wasn't any big dramatic tragedy."

In 1949 she agreed to do a nude shoot for a photographer friend named Tom Kelley. He paid only fifty dollars, but she was living hand to mouth and she owed him a favor—he had lent her five dollars on an earlier occasion for cab fare. Besides, fifty dollars was precisely the amount of money she needed for the monthly payment on her secondhand car. She was not nervous about the nudity, only its potential effect on her career, and she signed the model release with the name Mona Monroe. In fact, Kelley noted that once she took her clothes off, she seemed more comfortable than before—in his words, "graceful as an otter, turning sinuously with utter naturalness. All her constraints vanished as soon as her clothes were off." Not long after, she was finally given a screen test and it was considered a stunning success by those who looked at the results. But she was also stereotyped: starlet; dumb-blonde category; keep her speaking lines to a minimum.

Later there were those who believed that the studio had invented her. Certainly, with studio help, her hair became blonder, and plastic surgery was used to make her more photogenic. Her teeth were straightened, some work was done on her nose to slim it down, and additional work was done to refinish the contours of her chin. But the studios did that with hundreds of other young women and lightning did not strike them. Her success was completely hers.

By the late forties, she began to appear in the background in a number of films. Her first lines were spoken in a film with Groucho Marx called *Love Happy,* released in April 1950. Groucho played a private eye and Miss Monroe was cast as a dumb blonde who sashayed into his office (a move that later became something of a trademark): "Some men are following me," she said. Groucho did a full eye roll. "I can't imagine why," he answered. ("You have," he told her off camera, "the prettiest ass in the business.")

When she got a part in an old-fashioned crime film called *The Asphalt Jungle,* she was initially not even listed in the credits. But the early screening audiences responded so enthusiastically to her on the comment cards that the studio executives took notice and somewhat reluctantly included her name. She was the girlfriend of a corrupt lawyer, played by Louis Calhern. Her presence was electric. There she was, sexual, defenseless, with her potent body and her little-girl voice. "Some sweet kid," Calhern says about her early in the film, telling her to go to bed. "Some sweet kid."

With *The Asphalt Jungle* her career exploded. She made thirteen films in the next two years, few of them memorable. The studios seemed to have no real idea who she was, only that somehow there was something that worked. She was becoming, almost without anyone knowing exactly how, the first female superstar of the postwar years. It was Billy Wilder who once said of her, "She never flattens out on the screen. . . . She never gets lost up there. . . . You can't watch any other performer when she's playing a scene with somebody else." Her image was perfect for Hollywood, fighting new competition from television, which now offered free home entertainment. Hollywood was responding to the challenge by gradually allowing greater latitude in showing sexual matters on the screen. Her sexuality, so overt it might previously have been doomed by the censors (in such scenes as the famous blowing up of her skirt in *The Seven-Year Itch,* for example) was now not only permissible, it was desirable.

"The truth," she once said, "is that I've never fooled anyone. I've let men fool themselves. Men sometimes didn't bother to find out who I was, and what I was. Instead they would invent a character for me. I wouldn't argue with them. They were obviously loving someone I wasn't. When they found this out they would blame me for disillusioning them and fooling them."

Even as professional success came, her personal life remained in turmoil. Relationships began well but ended badly. In 1952 she was introduced by a friend to Joe DiMaggio, the greatest baseball player of his era, who had just retired. They went out intermittently, starting in March 1952, and in January 1954 they were finally married in the San Francisco city hall. The relationship thrilled the tabloid soul of America: the greatest athlete-hero of the nation going out with the greatest sex symbol. They were both shy; both had risen by dint of talent to social spheres in which they were often uncomfortable. DiMaggio was attractive but not particularly verbal. Friends noted their powerful mutual attraction but also his inability to talk to her. Her career was just taking off; his career (but not his fame) was to all intents and purposes finished. He saw her as a good and sweet girl and hated the idea that Hollywood perpetually cast her (to his mind) as a slut.

It was to be an uneasy marriage. For their honeymoon they went to Japan, where DiMaggio was doing a celebrity tour. Her passport read Norma Jean DiMaggio. On the way, though, she was asked by American military officers to entertain the troops still serving in Korea, a year after the war had finally ended. She did, though DiMaggio declined to accompany her. There were some 100,000 soldiers gathered enthusiastically in an outdoor instant amphitheater to hear her perform. Later, as Gay Talese wrote in a brilliant piece in *Esquire,* when she rejoined DiMaggio, she reported to him breathlessly, "Joe, you've never heard such cheering." "Yes I have," he answered.

Within months it was clear that the marriage was in trouble. She went to New York to film *The Seven Year Itch.* DiMaggio decided reluctantly to go with her. They shot the scene of the air blowing her skirt up at 2 A.M. to avoid a crowd, but the word got out and several thousand people showed up. She stood over the subway grating, the wind blowing her skirt above her panties, the crowd cheering, applauding and shouting, "*Higher, higher.*" DiMaggio, the child of Italian immigrants, a man who perhaps more than any athlete of his generation valued his *dignity,* watched from the corner, stone-faced and silent. That the movie was a marvelous celebration of her innocence did not matter; instead he saw it as an exposing of her in *public* for financial exploitation. They had a bitter fight that night. The next day he flew back to California alone. The marriage was effectively over. In late 1954 they were divorced; the marriage had lasted a scant year. As DiMaggio packed his things and moved out of the house, a crowd of newspapermen gathered. Someone asked him where he was going. "Back to San Francisco. That's my home."

But they remained close friends; there was no doubt of his devotion. Years later as her third marriage, to playwright Arthur Miller, began to disintegrate, she talked wistfully to her maid about DiMaggio as the great love of her life, and she kept a large poster of him in her bedroom closet.

Her life eventually became so troubled that it began to have a serious impact on her career. Unsure of her abilities, needing reassurance, she moved to New York to be near Arthur Miller, with whom she had begun a burgeoning romance, and to be a part of the Actors Studio. She longed to be respected as a serious actress, but her work habits were becoming shakier and shakier. Miller was both father figure and intellectual legitimizer. But it wasn't long before he found that he too was failing her. In July 1956, she married Miller, but there was no peace or respite. "Nobody cares," she told her maid as her marriage to Miller was coming apart. "Nobody even knows me anymore. What good is it being Marilyn Monroe? Why can't I just be an ordinary woman. . . . Oh why do things have to work out so rotten?" By 1957, her mental health was deteriorating ever more quickly: She was using even more sleeping pills and starting the day with a Bloody Mary.

More than most actors and actresses, she was exploited by the studios and was significantly underpaid at the height of her career. The studio heads always seemed to resent her success and continued to see her as essentially the dumb blonde. When she shot *Gentlemen Prefer Blondes,* the studio executives thought she was being too demanding and one of them angrily told her,

"You're not a star." "Well, gentlemen," she answered. "Whatever I am, the name of the picture is *Gentlemen Prefer Blondes* and whatever I am, I *am* the blonde."

In February 1952, just as her career was taking off, there was an anonymous phone call to Twentieth Century-Fox. The naked girl in a nude calendar, said the male caller, was its newest star, Marilyn Monroe. The caller demanded ten thousand dollars. Otherwise, he said, he would take his proof to the newspapers. The studio people were terrified by the call but decided not to pay, which, they decided, would only lead to more blackmail. But they did pressure her to deny that she was the girl. It was a terrible moment for her: She was sure that her career was over. But she also decided to tell the truth and to take the initiative by leaking the story herself to a friendly writer. It *was* her on the calendar, she said, and there was no sense lying about it. "Sure, I posed," she said. "I was hungry." The public rallied to support her.

The photo Tom Kelley had shot was soon hanging on the walls of thousands of barbershops, bars, and gas stations. It also helped launch a sexual empire. For in the fall of 1953 a young man named Hugh Hefner, anxious to start his own magazine, read in an advertising trade magazine that a local Midwestern company had the rights to the photo. Hefner drove out to suburban Chicago and bought the rights for five hundred dollars (along with a number of photos of other nudes). It was a brilliant purchase for a magazine just being born—America's newest star caught lushly in the nude, posing coyly on a red velvet drape. Her body was angled to hide her pubic area; her breasts were fully exposed.

Fittingly, given the relationships between men and women in those days, Miss Monroe got nothing additional for the use of the photograph. There was no small irony here—that Hefner's multimillion-dollar kingdom was launched by this photo. In time, Hefner, the grandson of Midwestern puritans would become a committed convert to more open sexuality, and a crusader for greater sexual freedom and honesty. He took up this cause humorlessly, with the passion of the old-time religious zealot. There was, thought some of those who knew him well, a certain grimness to his pursuit of both truth and pleasure. By contrast, Miss Monroe, the object of so much unwanted admiration, treated all the fuss with a pleasant self-deprecating humor. She seemed to be puzzled that men made such a big deal out of her body and was therefore willing to go along, more to keep them from being cranky than anything else. Asked whether she had anything on during the Tom Kelley shoot, she answered yes, the radio.

Hefner was only twenty-seven when he started his magazine on a shoestring in the fall of 1953. He had been so uncertain of his chances of success that he did not even bother to put his name on the masthead; nor for that matter did he bother to put a date on the first issue—he hoped that if the initial sale was not high enough, he might be able to keep it on the newsstand for another month. All of his limited savings were tied up in the magazine, and he was extremely nervous about the possibility of failure and bankruptcy. If the magazine failed, he would owe several thousand dollars to close friends and his family. The new magazine was to be called *Playboy,* which was not Hefner's original choice; he had wanted to give it the much cruder title of *Stag Party.* Others had tried to dissuade him, with little success, but what *had* finally changed his mind was a letter from the lawyers of a hunting magazine in New York called *Stag,* suggesting that he look elsewhere and threatening legal action if he did not.

Hefner printed 70,000 copies of the first issue, hoping it would sell at least 30,000 copies, at 50 cents an issue. Instead, bolstered in no small part by the word of mouth on the Monroe photos, it sold 53,000, a huge success. Still, in the early weeks of its appearance Hefner was like a nervous parent, casing newsstands and checking sales, making sure that his magazine got proper display, covertly rearranging it in front of the other magazines. He did, it should be noted, know something about the magazine business as he put out his first issue. For the last few years he had worked on the promotional side of magazines, and he knew a good deal about magazine distribution. He had become expert in the kind of hearty exaggerated promotional letters that magazines then favored.

With the success of the first issue he was in business. Confident as he prepared his second issue, he went out and bought himself a new Studebaker, and he also put his name on the masthead as editor and publisher. Within a year, by December 1954, *Playboy*'s circulation had reached 100,000. By early 1955, less than a year and a half after the first issue was so timidly cast forth, *Playboy* had $250,000 in the bank and Hefner turned down an offer of $1 million from a group in Chicago for the magazine. Some of its stunning initial success was in part due to Hefner's native shrewdness, his perfect pitch for what his readers—often sexually insecure young men—wanted. His instinct to package ever more glossy photos and use what he considered up-scale writing would make the magazine ever more legitimate.

Hefner had come from a financially comfortable, if emotionally arid, family. His home was largely devoid of warmth and openness, and it was against that Calvinist ethic that he would fight in the pages of *Playboy*. Their Christianity seemed to him a cold, emotionally sterile one, separated from all pleasures of life. His grandparents were pious Nebraska farmers, and theirs remained a God-fearing home: There was no drinking, no swearing, no smoking. Sunday was for church. Hefner's first wife, Millie, later noted that she never saw any sign of affection or anger displayed by either of his parents.

Hefner was a bright, somewhat dreamy child: In terms of social skills and popularity he was always on the outside looking in. He graduated from high school in 1944, went into the army and caught the last months of the war, although he saw no combat. When he came home he drifted for a time, unsure of his future, drawing 52–20 from the government—twenty dollars a week for fifty-two weeks. He entered the University of Illinois to be with his high school girlfriend, Millie Williams. He had been dating Millie for several years, but they still had not consummated their relationship. After they were married in 1949, Hefner continued to drift, supported by Millie, who was teaching school.

The one thing he loved was cartooning, at which he was, unfortunately, not particularly gifted; for the next two or three years he went back and forth between jobs, usually in the promotion department of different magazines. For much of the time, he and Millie lived with his parents in order to save money. At one point in his drive to become a cartoonist, he quit work and stayed at home to draw. The results tended to be pornographic reworkings of then-popular comic strips. Millie Hefner was convinced that his erotic sketching was a rebellion of sorts against his family's Calvinist roots and the emotional and sexual coldness of that household.

As a convert to the cause of more open sexuality, he crusaded for it with the passion his puritanical grandparents had espoused in their religion; it was as if one crusade had simply replaced another. The Calvinists, Hefner believed, thought sex was dark and furtive, and the other girlie magazines of the period were so cheap and crude they seemed to confirm that judgment. It was Hefner's particular genius to know that it was now, in this new era, going to be permissible to have an upscale, slick magazine of male sexual fantasies that customers might not be embarrassed to be seen buying—or even to leave out on their coffee tables.

As far as Hefner was concerned, he was a direct lineal descendant of Alfred Kinsey, whom he regarded as a hero, the man who had more than anyone else pointed out the hypocrisy in daily American life, the differences between what Americans said about sex and what they actually did. As a student he had quite favorably reviewed the Kinsey study for the University of Illinois humor magazine, and in truth the Kinsey studies were critically important for him. Before they appeared, he had felt himself essentially alone in his belief that sex was important and that society was duplicitous and punitive in its attitude toward sex. Kinsey had showed him that he was not alone, that there were millions of others who felt much the same way he did. Kinsey, as far as he was concerned, had opened the debate on sexual attitudes. Soon, in his own mind, at least, he was the person who took up Kinsey's banner. He also believed that he could become a role model for young men of his generation, not just in his sexual practices but for his life-style, as well.

In his first issue, Hefner wrote, "We like our apartment. We enjoy mixing up cocktails and an hors d'oeuvre or two, putting a little mood music on the phonograph, and inviting in a female for a quiet discussion on Picasso, Nietzsche, jazz, sex." There it was, the *Playboy* ethic: sex as not only legitimate but as a sophisticated life-style. By the end of 1956, still operating with a skeleton staff, *Playboy* was a phenomenon. Circulation was 600,000. "A lot of it," said Ray Russell, a writer and editor who was one of Hefner's first hires, "was good luck, random choice, being carried on the tides of the times rather than the leader of the times. It was a matter of being the right magazine able to take advantage of a rising economy, more than any degree of conscious planning."

Perhaps Hefner's great strength was his lack of sophistication. If he was square, he still longed to share the better world, which was now increasingly available around him; in that he mirrored the longings of millions of other young men of similar background, more affluent than their parents, wanting a better and freer life. His connection to his readers was immediate. It was not by chance that *Playboy* was born in the Midwest, not

New York, like most magazines. Its most successful editors were sons of the Midwest, not Easterners and not graduates of Ivy League schools. Hefner understood his readers' lives; his squareness was their squareness; his magazine answered the right questions because they were his questions. "That magazine," said Jack Kessie, an early editor, "was written and edited for Hugh M. Hefner."

As the magazine became enormously successful, he was to all intents and purposes living in his offices. He became increasingly distant and remote, a kind of latter-day Gatsby, who opened his increasingly plush residences to an endless stream of people whom he did not know (and who did not know him). In some ways he was still an outsider looking in, partaking of the new sybaritic life-style but detached from it. "Hefner," said Don Gold, an editor at *Playboy* in the early days, "is not a very complicated man. He thinks Poe is the best writer in the world. When he buys a pipe, he buys two dozen of the same pipe. He likes his mashed potatoes to have a dimple of gravy on them. He is mid-America personified. The Marquis de Sade would have told him to wait in a corner, though he is, in a healthy way, by sex possessed." Some saw Hefner not so much liberator as exploiter of American puritanism. Frank Gibney, a former *Time* magazine writer and editor who worked briefly and unhappily for him, once compared him to the Methodist missionaries who traded firewater to the Indians. To Gibney, the more he tried to be hip, the more he failed.

In June 1957, Hefner wrote of himself for that month's issue: "His dress is conservative and casual. He always wears loafers. . . . There is an electronic entertainment wall in his office, very much like the one featured in *Playboy*'s Penthouse apartment, that includes hi-fi, AM-FM radio, tape, and television, and will store up to 2000 LPs. Brubeck, Kenton or Sinatra is usually on the turntable when Hefner is working. He is essentially an indoors man, though he discovered the pleasures of the ski slope last winter. He likes jazz, foreign films, Ivy League clothes, gin and tonic and pretty girls—the same sort of things that *Playboy* readers like—and his approach to life is as fresh, sophisticated, and yet admittedly sentimental as is the magazine."

Not everyone who knew Hugh Hefner in those days, would have accepted his own self-portrait. He was, they might agree, smart, albeit more shrewd than cerebral, an easy man for his more sophisticated Eastern colleagues to underestimate, but he was not exactly hip or cool, no matter how hard he worked at it. It didn't matter. For *Playboy* would play a critical role in the coming sexual revolution; it helped, among other things, to sell the idea that sex was pleasure, to be enjoyed, not something dark to be sought illicitly and clandestinely.

The women his magazine came to feature,

seminude (and then, with the more relaxed censorship laws, completely nude) were young, preferably innocent-looking girls, more fresh-faced
and bubbly than erotic or sophisticated. They
seemed to have stopped off to do a *Playboy* shoot
on their way to cheerleading practice or to the
sorority house. That was deliberate policy, for
over the years Hefner often seemed uninterested
in much of the magazine's verbiage, but he monitored carefully the choices of the Playmates who
would grace the magazine's centerfold; he was
confident that what stirred his fantasies would stir
the fantasies of his readers. This, thought those
who knew him well, was when he was most alive
and most engaged—when he sat in his bedroom,
armed with the photographer's loop with which
he could magnify thousands of contact sheets of
film of beautiful, nude women, as the ultimate
arbiter of American sexual fantasy. Nor did his
interest in these young women extend merely to
displaying explicit photos of them to millions of
the opposite sex. Rather, they were the kind of
women whom he sought for companionship. In
the late sixties, Hefner, by then in his forties, met
a young woman named Barbie Benton, who was
to be one of his longest-running girlfriends. Ms.
Benton, then only eighteen, was pleased but a
little uneasy with the attention of this older man.
"You're a nice person, but I've never dated anyone over twenty-four." "That's okay," he answered. "Neither have I."

The success of his magazines and his personal success reflected a powerful new chord in postwar American life: the changing attitudes about sex and a steadily more candid view of sexuality. Hefner was fighting that part of the Puritan ethic that condemned pleasure. He thought hard work and sexual freedom were not incompatible in this ever richer society. In the broader sense as well, *Playboy* shepherded a generation of young men to the good life. It helped explain how to buy a sportscar, what kind of hi-fi set to buy, how to order in a restaurant, what kind of wine to drink with what kind of meal. For men whose parents had not gone to college, *Playboy* served a valuable function: It provided an early and elementary tutorial on the new American lifestyle. For those fearful of headwaiters in fancy restaurants, wary of slick salesmen in stores and of foreign-car dealers who seemed to speak a language never heard in Detroit, *Playboy* provided a valuable consumer service: It midwifed the reader into a world of increasing plenty. "Hefner," said Arthur Kretchmer, his longtime executive editor, "helped the world to discover toys. He said 'Play, it's okay to play.'" Americans, particularly younger Americans, lived in a world of more and more toys; that was the good life, and it was fun. "We are," Kretchmer added, "more about indulgence and the celebration of frivolity than we are about envy and greed." Hefner's central message, Kretchmer said, was "Celebrate your life. Free it up. Your sexuality can be as good as anybody else's if you take the inhibitions out, if you don't destroy yourself internally."

The spectacular rise of *Playboy* reflected the postwar decline of Calvinism and puritanism in America, due as much as anything else to the very affluence of the society. Ordinary Americans could afford to live better than they ever had before, and they now wanted the things that had previously been the possessions of only the very wealthy; and they wanted the personal freedoms the rich had traditionally enjoyed too. In the onslaught, old restraints were loosened. If religion existed only as a negative force, Hefner was saying, if it spoke only of the denial of pleasure and made people feel furtive about what was natural, then it was in trouble. He preached pleasure. He touched the right chord at precisely the right moment.

Dwight Eisenhower's popularity was immediate and visceral, here at a 1952 appearance in Manhasset, Long Island. UPI/BETTMANN

Network television was still something relatively new in 1952 but the political process had made the television set a mandatory household item. Here a large crowd gathers outside a New York store to watch the election results in November 1952. EVE ARNOLD, MAGNUM PHOTOS, INC.

Pat Nixon, never comfortable or happy with her public role, smiles determinedly at a 1956 meeting of Republican women. She dutifully went through the motions of being a public person, but in truth she longed for a simpler life with greater privacy. CORNELL CAPA, MAGNUM PHOTOS, INC.

(*Left*) John Foster Dulles, U.S. secretary of state, at a news conference in 1956 rejecting suggestions by Russia and India that the United States suspend further H-bomb tests. UPI/BETTMANN   (*Right*) Allen W. Dulles, director of the Central Intelligence Agency, after appearing at an executive session of the Joint Congressional Atomic Energy Committee in 1958. UPI/BETTMANN

J. Edgar Hoover (right) and his friend Clyde Tolson cheering on the FBI baseball team during a 1955 game. The closeness of their friendship and their constant companionship amused observers aware of Hoover's intense homophobia. UPI/BETTMANN

Dwight D. Eisenhower in the official photograph for his presidency. UPI/BETTMANN

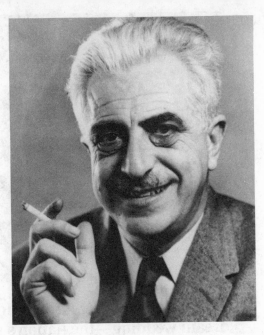

(*Left*) Alfred Kinsey, shown here in 1953, was pilloried by many for trying to bring scientific standards to the study of America's sexual habits. UPI/BETTMANN (*Right*) Gregory Pincus, the driving scientific force behind the invention of the birth-control pill, was wary of attempts to entrap him by those seeking advice on abortions. UPI/BETTMANN

(*Left*) Margaret Sanger was one of the great crusaders of the era for greater sexual freedom for women. THE BETTMANN ARCHIVE (*Right*) Katharine Dexter McCormick supplied the badly needed money for the revolution in contraceptives. THE MIT MUSEUM

Joe DiMaggio and Marilyn Monroe: It was the tabloids' dream wedding—the nation's greatest baseball player marrying its sexiest actress. UPI/BETTMANN

Marilyn Monroe in a scene from *The Seven Year Itch*; DiMaggio was enraged, and a bitter domestic fight followed. UPI/BETTMANN

(*Left*) Hugh Hefner, sensing that his own sexual obsessions were similar to those of other males of his generation, founded a magazine empire in the fifties. THE BETTMANN ARCHIVE (*Right*) Grace Metalious's accurate portrait of small-town New England life made her a bestselling author, but she had problems dealing with her newfound success. UPI/BETTMANN

Betty Friedan, assigned to do a magazine article on her fifteenth college reunion, found that she was hardly alone in her career disappointments. She is pictured here with her daughter Emily. THE SCHLESINGER LIBRARY, RADCLIFFE COLLEGE

American-backed supporters of the shah of Iran ride through Teheran aboard a tank, holding up a portrait of their leader. A 1953 CIA coup toppled the government of Prime Minister Mohammed Mossadegh and installed the shah as Iran's sole ruler. UPI/BETTMANN

Mohammed Mossadegh being led into Iranian court in 1953 for a session of his trial for treason.
UPI/BETTMANN

A soldier stands guard while supporters of Colonel Carlos Castillo Armas make broadcasts outside of his headquarters in Chiquimulilla, Guatemala. Armas was installed by a CIA coup after American authorities decided the government of Jacobo Arbenz was too left-wing. UPI/BETTMANN

Earl Warren posing for the first time in his black silk judicial robe after being sworn in as the fourteenth chief justice of the United States in 1953. He immediately set out to make the Supreme Court's decision on the landmark Brown case a unanimous one. UPI/BETTMANN

Emmett Till was fourteen years old when he allegedly whistled at a white woman in Money, Mississippi. He was beaten and then killed, his body thrown into the Tallahatchie River weighted down by a heavy cotton-gin fan. UPI/BETTMANN

His was a powerful voice in a powerful cause: Martin Luther King, Jr., scion of one of Atlanta's most prominent black families, became the symbol for a generation.
DON UHRBROCK/*LIFE*/TIME WARNER, INC.

Mrs. Rosa Parks sits in the front seat of a Montgomery, Alabama, bus, more than a year after she was arrested for violating the city's segregation laws. In December 1956, the Supreme Court ruled the laws unconstitutional.
UPI/BETTMANN

Little Rock became the first great battleground of the civil rights struggle when Arkansas governor Orval Faubus defied a court order to integrate Little Rock Central High (some of whose students are shown here). Riots provoked by Faubus and his allies followed, and President Eisenhower reluctantly sent in elite airborne troops and federalized the Arkansas National Guard. BURT GLINN, MAGNUM PHOTOS, INC.

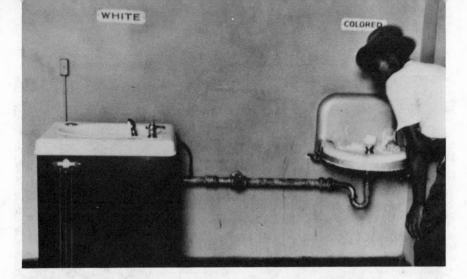

In the rising affluence of America in the fifties, it was sometimes easy to forget that the society's blessings did not extend to everyone. The South was still segregated by law and custom (as shown here at drinking fountains in North Carolina in 1950), though a series of Supreme Court rulings undermined the idea of separate but equal facilities. ELLIOTT ERWITT, MAGNUM PHOTOS, INC.

Supporters of Faubus rallied behind their man in 1958 and the lines were drawn at Little Rock. Federal officials had to push integration almost at gunpoint, helping the governor politically. Faubus, whose chances of reelection had once seemed slim, now presented himself to white voters as a victim of integrationists and was reelected several times. COSTA MANOS, MAGNUM PHOTOS, INC.

Nothing captivated the nation like the quiz shows of the late fifties, and no one was a bigger hero than Charles Van Doren, a graceful, charming young Columbia English instructor from a famed literary family. Here he beats Herb Stempel, right, in *Twenty-One*. Millions of Americans were later shocked to find that Van Doren had been given the answers. *TIME*

Van Doren and *Twenty-One* M.C. Jack Barry show their pleasure as Barry adds up Van Doren's record-breaking winnings. THE BETTMANN ARCHIVE

Though the striking success of Elvis Presley produced many imitators, there was nothing artificial about Presley. His success was immediate and powerful. The night that a Memphis radio station played his songs for the first time, its switchboard lit up; the deejay sent for Presley and interviewed him that night; he also made sure that the singer gave the name of his high school so listeners would know he was white. FRED WARD, BLACK STAR

To many Americans the successful launch of a Soviet space satellite seemed to show that the United States was behind the Russians in both pure science and advanced weaponry. The reverse was actually true. Shown here is a model of the first Russian satellite, *Sputnik*. UPI/BETTMANN

Powers, released after serving time in a Russian prison, holds up a model of the U-2 as he testifies before the Senate Armed Services Committee. UPI/BETTMANN

Russian peasants survey the wreckage of Francis Gary Powers' U-2 spy plane. More than the plane was shot down, for the U-2 incident damaged any hopes for a greater American-Soviet détente, and undermined Nikita Khrushchev's ability to hold power. UPI/BETTMANN

In 1959, Nikita Khrushchev barnstormed Hollywood during the first visit of a Soviet premier to the United States. Khrushchev's prudish side showed when he met a number of Hollywood actresses—here Shirley MacLaine—in skimpy outfits. BOB HENRIQUES, MAGNUM PHOTOS, INC.

During his 1959 march on Havana, Fidel Castro became leader of all forces opposed to the hated Batista regime and his movement's strength greatly increased.
UPI/BETTMANN

THIRTY-EIGHT

Indian summer is like a woman. Ripe, hotly passionate but fickle, she comes and goes as she pleases so one is never sure whether she will come at all, nor how long she will stay."

It began in prose that threatened neither John Cheever nor John O'Hara as the most famous chroniclers of American social mores. "In Northern New England, Indian summer puts up a scarlet-tipped hand to hold winter back for a little while. She brings with her the time of the last warm spell, an unchanged season which lives until winter moves in with its backbone of ice and accoutrements of leafless trees and hard frozen ground. Those grown old, who have had the youth bled from them by the jagged edged winds of winter, know sorrowfully, that Indian summer is a sham to be met with hard-eyed cynicism . . ."

In 1956, the most surprising book on the best-seller list was *Peyton Place,* by Grace Metalious, a young woman who had never published a word before. It was brought out in hardcover by Julian Messner, a small publisher, and went on to become the third best-selling hardcover novel of the year. Allan Barnard, an editor at the paperback house Dell, read the manuscript just before it was published and told his boss, Frank Taylor: "I have something I want to buy [to reprint as a mass softcover edition], but I don't want you to read it." Taylor gave Barnard permission to go ahead and he bought the softcover rights for $11,-000 in an auction with other publishing houses. It turned out to be one of the great bargains of all time. A few years later, Taylor asked Barnard why he had asked him not to read it. "Because you wouldn't have let me buy it," Barnard answered, referring to the ambivalence many paperback editors felt about the commercial quality of the books they published.

Peyton Place was considered a hot book in the vernacular of the time, although Metalious was far less explicit than other, more serious writers who were then struggling with the oppressive censorship laws of the era. But *Peyton Place* was such a phenomenon that the title entered the language as a generic term for all the small towns that appeared placid on the surface but underneath were filled with dark secrets, most of them sexual. In her book, Metalious tore away the staid facade of Peyton Place/Gilmanton, New Hampshire, to reveal a hotbed of lust and sexual intrigue. "To a tourist these towns look as peaceful as a postcard," Ms. Metalious told Hal Boyle of the Associated Press in an early interview. "But if you go beneath that picture, it's like turning over a rock with your foot—all kinds of strange things crawl out. Everybody who lives in town knows what's going on—there are no secrets—but they don't want outsiders to know."

Indeed, the principal occupation of *Peyton Place* seemed not so much farming or the town's textile factory but gossip; people there not only led secret lives, they devoted most of their waking hours to sitting around and talking about them— at least about everyone else's. To wit: of Kenny Stearns, a local handyman with a green thumb whose wife runs around on him, the locals say, "Too bad Kenny don't have the same good luck with his wife as he has with his plants. Mebbe Kenny'd be better off with a green pecker."

It was a small town of some 3,700 people, still largely cut off from the rest of the society. A certain sense of loneliness pervaded it. A teacher lamented the waste of time teaching the children of this sad little town: "What sense was there in memorizing the date of the rise and fall of the Roman Empire, when the boy, grown, would milk cows for a living as had his father and grandfather before him? What logic was there in pounding decimal fractions into the head of a girl who would eventually need only to count the numbers of months of each pregnancy?" Class lines ran through the middle of Peyton Place; a handful of powerful men—the town's factory owner, the lawyer, the editor of the newspaper, and the doctor—played poker once a week and decided what was going to happen in the town. When Betty

Anderson, a local girl from the wrong side of the tracks whose father worked for Leslie Harrington (the mill owner), became pregnant after a fling with Harrington's son, the senior Harrington handed his employee a check for $500. A furious Betty charged in to see Harrington in his office and announced that she planned to marry the son. But Harrington told her that it would require only six men to say that they also had had relations with her to make her legally a prostitute. He then tore up the check for $500 and gave her one for $250, promising that it would be $125 if she came by him again.

Mostly, the town's secrets stayed secret with much less fuss. Constance MacKenzie, the prim, attractive young widow who ran the town's dress shop, dreaded the idea that people might learn that in her brief time in New York she had an affair with a married man, who was the father of her daughter; another local girl was sexually assaulted and impregnated by her sinister stepfather, and the kindly local doctor decided to save the young girl's reputation by disguising an abortion as an emergency appendectomy.

If there ever was a book that reflected the changing nature of American book business as it changed to the new high-powered world of paperbacks from the more genteel old-fashioned world of hardcover publishing, it was *Peyton Place*. It was not so much a book as an event, with a force all its own. Published as a paperback in the fall of

1957, it quickly sold 3 million copies and it kept right on selling. By the middle of 1958 its sales were over 6 million. By 1966 there were some 10 million copies in print. In years to come, as the paperback industry grew and as the capacity to promote books became an ever more sophisticated industry, there were best-sellers whose path up the best-seller list was achieved with several hundred thousand dollars in promotion costs. *Peyton Place,* by contrast, was a true popular success.

At the time of publication Ms. Metalious's novel was perceived as being successful for the most basic of reasons: It told the blunt truth about the sexuality of a small town at a time when that was still sensational. Gradually, however, as the society evolved into the sixties and seventies, there was a revisionist view of that success, a sense that at least some of it had been due to Ms. Metalious's powerful and visceral comprehension of the problems faced by women in the modern world. Metalious did not exactly become a heroine or a role model to the generation of young women who emerged in the seventies determined to lead lives more independent than those of their mothers. Nonetheless, cultural detectives tracking the evolution of the feminist movement could find in her pages the emergence of independent women who dissented from the proscribed lives and limited opportunities reserved for women. Metalious, they suspected—for there was little evidence of this in the initial reviews of the book—had touched a nerve without anyone realizing it. Kenneth Davis noted in his book on the paperback revolution, *Two-Bit Culture,* that the women in *Peyton Place* "were on the cutting edge of a movement that had not yet arrived and still had no voice. They wanted more than to simply find the right man, settle down and begin breeding and keeping house."

Rather, Davis pointed out, Metalious's characters might have come right out of the Kinsey Report on women. They had sexual feelings and appetites that contrasted starkly with the attitudes women were then supposed to have, as set down in endless books written by men. Nor were Metalious's women nearly as admiring of men as they were supposed to be. In fact, they often considered men unreliable and childish. They did not want to be controlled by men; they wanted to be independent and to have careers in places like New York or, even if they remained in towns like Peyton Place, to have some control over their lives and their bodies. "For perhaps the first time in popular fiction a writer was saying that women wanted sex and enjoyed it but they wanted it on their terms," wrote Davis. "They were not passive receptacles for dominant men. To a generation fed on Mickey Spillane, for whom women counted as little more than animals, or Erskine Caldwell, whose Southern women were for the most part sluttish trash, the women of Peyton

Place presented a new image. Independent, self-fulfilling, strong yet capable of love and desire, they were far from the perfect exemplars of the shining new woman that eventually followed with the onset of the feminist movement, but they were a breakthrough, a first faint glimmering that women were preparing to break out of the mold carefully prepared for them by centuries of male domination."

As Emily Toth pointed out in her book *Inside Peyton Place,* a serious feminist reappraisal of Metalious and her work, *Peyton Place* brought very different attitudes to sexual politics than the seemingly similar books that preceded it. It described rape not as an act of sexual pleasure but as violence; the doctor who performs an abortion is described as saving a life. In *Peyton Place,* Toth pointed out, the women who depend too greatly on men lose out, while the women who are independent are winners. Therefore, she noted, *Peyton Place* was a book before its time.

Metalious was, at first glance, an unlikely feminist hero. She never fully articulated her own vision and probably would have been surprised to find some thirty years later women at colleges reading her book not so much as literature but as part of the change in the politics of gender. With a few rare exceptions, she was not close to other women, and as her literary career progressed and her own life began to unravel, she wrote of the frustrations of women with less skill and perception than she had in her first book.

Metalious had written as she did—roughly, simply, but powerfully—because it could have been her own story. She was, by instinct, angrier and more rebellious than she herself realized, although she had always shown contempt for conventional female roles. Women were expected to be good housekeepers; Grace Metalious's home was littered with garbage, dirty dishes, and beer cans. Women were supposed to be good mothers, putting their children above their own ambitions; Grace Metalious loved her three children in her own erratic way, but she let them do pretty much as they wished; any real supervision tended to come from neighbors. Women were supposed to be dutiful handmaidens to their husbands' careers; Metalious made little effort in that direction. She dressed in a way that jarred small-town sensibilities—in blue jeans, checked shirts, and sneakers. She stayed home and wrote a book instead of attending polite dinner parties. She never fully articulated her own feminist vision and probably would have been surprised had someone told her that one day she would be a heroine of the women's movement. But she was not slick and she did not know how to romanticize her own story.

She was a lower-middle-class French Canadian girl who grew up in small towns in New Hampshire, living always involuntarily in a matriarchy. The men in her family were bit players;

her own father deserted the family when she was young, and she was raised by her grandmother. Her mother fantasized a better life but slipped into alcoholism at a relatively early age. Grace loved to read and fancied that she would be a writer one day; at age thirteen she had already begun a historical novel.

In high school Grace was bright and different, and teachers noticed her. Nonetheless, a literary future seemed out of reach. It seemed dimmer still when in February 1943, at the age of eighteen, she married George Metalious, a high school friend, because she was pregnant. When George Metalious enlisted and went off to war, Grace was stunned by his decision—she was not caught up in the patriotic cause, and remembering her father, she saw her husband's desire to serve as an escape from family responsibility. She worked at different jobs and raised her daughter Marsha. When George Metalious came back from the war, sure that his army salary had been salted away for the down payment on a dream house, he was stunned to find that she had saved none of it. Rather, she had been supporting her extended family with his allotment checks. "How could you be so stupid!" he shouted at her.

They were not unlike many couples trying to make their way after the war. George had come back to a child and a wife he barely knew. They struggled for a time, had a second child, both of them held jobs, and yet they could save very little.

Finally, it was decided that the only way to succeed was for George to go to the University of New Hampshire on the GI bill. His family would follow and his wife would take a job to support him—so common an arrangement in those days that there was even a phrase for it: PHTS, Putting Hubbies Through School. But Metalious was different; for above all she wanted to write; it was the one way she could escape the dreary world that seemed to be closing in around her.

If other young couples were caught up in the excitement of those years, living in cramped housing with young children, eating cheap meals thrown together from cans, always sure that their current sacrifice would be rewarded eventually, when the husband got his degree, Grace Metalious was having none of it. She hated being a poor student's wife. "I am trapped, I screamed silently," she later said of those years. "I am trapped in a cage of poverty and mediocrity, and if I don't get out, I'll die."

She was already writing, absolutely sure that she was going to be a novelist. Her work habits were excellent. She wrote every day. The odds against her must have seemed hopeless. She had no college education. She knew no one in the literary world. She was utterly without literary connections. She had no immediate literary role models. Her chances of success seemed ever slimmer, particularly after 1950 when their third child arrived, when by all rights she should have stopped writing and been crushed by the terrible odds against her. Yet she kept writing, feeling the loneliness of someone virtually without friends and without a support system. But she had several qualities that kept her going—a fierce drive, a belief that in writing and publishing there was liberation, an innate talent and shrewdness that were not to be underestimated, and finally a love of books.

In 1950 their third child had arrived. When George graduated, they were so poor that they had to borrow $300 to pay his debts so the university would release his degree. His first job, as a teacher at a tiny school in Belmont, paid $2,500, with an additional $1,100 thrown in for coaching the baseball team.

By 1953, she began to send manuscripts to publishers and began the search for a literary agent. She surveyed various writers' magazines and finally came up with a name, Jacques Chambrun, an agent with a good deal of charm and a most unfortunate reputation for siphoning off the earnings of his writers. By early 1955 she had sent him her first novel, a rather routine semiautobiographical story about a young couple struggling through GI-bill life at a New England college.

Entitled *The Quiet Place,* it was rejected everywhere it was sent. Around the same time, she sent off her second novel, entitled *The Tree and the Blossom.* She had read *King's Row,* an extremely popular novel of the forties that dealt with the incestuous relationship of an adolescent girl and her father. By chance a similar incident had occurred in the small town where Metalious lived: A young girl had shot her father to protect herself and the rest of her family. In that, Metalious seized on a sensational incident that would give her novel a special darkness. The novel, which was renamed *Peyton Place,* was mailed to publishers in May 1955.

It was turned down at several houses, but a young woman named Leona Nevler, who had a good eye, read it while she was working as a freelance manuscript reader at Lippincott. It was impressive, Ms. Nevler thought: There was something poignant, vital, and authentic about the book. But it was not right for Lippincott, an unusually staid house. A few days later, Ms. Nevler was interviewed for a full-time job by Kitty Messner, the head of Julian Messner. She had founded the small publishing house with her husband, Julian Messner, and had divorced him, but she had continued to work with him. When he died she took over the company; so when Ms. Nevler mentioned the book, Kitty Messner, one of the first women to head a publishing company, was unusually receptive to the theme, which dealt with a young woman's desire for a better life. Ms. Messner, a formidable woman of very considerable independence, made a note of it, called Chambrun, got a copy, and stayed up all night reading it. She understood immediately the force of the book and made Chambrun an offer. "I know this is a big book," she told him. "I have to have it." Chambrun cabled Metalious, who was so excited that she forgot to ask how much her advance was—the answer was $1,500. He told her to come to New York as soon as she could to sign the contracts, which she did. She was awed by the fashionably elegant Kitty Messner, who wore jackets and pants—not, as one friend noted, off the rack, but beautifully tailored by a man's tailor for her. She seemed, particularly to this vulnerable young women from a small New England town, to be the epitome of a New York career woman. It was mid-August and Metalious felt wilted by New York's steamy heat; by contrast, Messner "looked as if she had never had a hot uncomfortable moment in her life. As for me, my armpits itched, I stuck to my chair, and my hair had gone all limp."

The early editing did not go well. Nevler had made a number of notes on how she thought it could be improved and tightened, but the relationship did not work out well. Metalious took the editing as a sign that Nevler had really never liked the book. Nevler had a series of lunches and dinners where they tried to work together but where Ms. Metalious ended up drinking and not eating. Later she decided that what she had encountered was the first sign of an increasingly serious problem with alcohol. Soon Ms. Messner took over the book herself.

Messner thought the book might sell 3,000 copies—standard for a first novel—but Howard Goodkind, who handled the publicity, thought it could be promoted into a best-seller; he suggested spending an additional $5,000 to get a publicist to create a special promotion campaign for the book. That sum was a considerable risk in those days, but Messner agreed. A man named Bud Brandt was hired and he in turn got the AP's veteran reporter Hal Boyle to go up to Gilmanton to do a prepublication story on the author.

In the course of his visit, Metalious casually predicted to Boyle that her husband would be let go as the local school principal (as he soon was) and perhaps the reason was that a number of powerful people in town disapproved of her—she behaved differently, she dressed differently, and she was said to be writing a book. In Boyle's subsequent article, the story had been mutated sufficiently to eliminate any doubt: George Metalious had been fired from his job as a principal because of his wife's book, which tore the veneer off the respectability of this small town. The publicity machine was ready to roll. The ads for the book employed a series of headlines reflecting the controversial nature of the book. By the time it was published in late September, it shot up some best-seller lists and a number of studios were bidding for the film rights. It sold 60,000 copies in the first ten days. The reviews were generally respectful. Carlos Baker, the distinguished

Hemingway scholar, placed Metalious in the tradition of American writers who had helped expose the underside of small-town American life. Interestingly enough, a critic named Sterling North, writing in the *New York World Telegram* who had earlier praised blunt language when used by male writers, was appalled by Metalious's use of the same words: "Never before in my memory has a young mother published a book in language approximately that of a longshoreman on a bellicose binge."

Fame and success were sweet at first. The people in New York were touched by the contrast between her sweetness, and indeed vulnerability, and the harsh quality of her life as depicted in the book. All her dreams seemed to be coming true. She sold the book to the movies for $250,000, and the first check was for $75,000. She seemed to take particular pleasure in taking it to various stores in Gilmanton asking the owners to cash it for her. But if she had been well prepared to overcome the adversities of her life, she proved significantly less able to deal with the pressures of success. "This book business," she wrote friends in November 1956, "is some evil form of insanity." Everyone suddenly seemed to want something from her and wanted her to play the role of a sexy writer.

The writer of *Peyton Place* was supposed to be both sexy and glamorous, after all, and Grace Metalious was a rather plain young woman. (She would tell the makeup men and women in television studios to make her look beautiful.) She was uneasy about the press and television appearances that were a part of the book's promotion and she particularly disliked it when someone asked whether or not the book was autobiographical. She made an appearance on an early television talk show called *Night Beat,* hosted by a young man named Mike Wallace, then gaining a reputation for himself as a tough interviewer. She thought she had been assured he would not ask the autobiography question. Almost as soon as the interview began, Wallace asked her, "Grace, tell me, is *Peyton Place* your autobiography?" She struck back by calling him Myron, his real name, which she had been told beforehand he did not like to be called, and by asking him how many times he had been married, another sensitive point.

Even before the book's publication, her marriage had started falling apart. There had been an affair with a local farmer. Liberated by her success and her changed financial position, she ended her marriage, took up with a disc jockey, and married him. She began to spend money freely; at the same time she stopped writing. Years later George Metalious referred to that period in her life as "the tinsel years." Driven mostly by Hollywood producer Jerry Wald, she eventually wrote a listless sequel she was not proud of, called *Return to Peyton Place*. At the last minute a writer named Warren Miller was brought in to doctor it into a readable book. Nonetheless *Return* also sold well, though not as well as its predecessor.

For all of her fame and the attention, Metalious's emotional needs did not abate. "Our mother had to be told with the consistency of a flowing brook that echoes, 'I love you, I love you, I love you,'" her daughter Marsha remembered. "We did love her strongly, but after a while 'I love you' became a ludicrous expression—worn to its nap like a rug traveled on day after day, night after night."

Her work habits continued to deteriorate. When T. J. Martin, the disc jockey whom she had married, tried to get her to work, she would yell at him, "Who the hell are you? Who appointed you my guiding light?" Soon she was always seen with a glass in her hand, usually with Canadian Club and Seven-Up in it.

By 1960, George Metalious had come back into her life, and she published *The Tight White Collar,* which became her favorite book. It sold well, but not nearly as well as *Peyton Place.* To shrewd editors, it was obvious that her audience was beginning to slip away. Soon she had serious financial problems. When *Peyton Place* had been a success, she had worked out an agreement with her lawyer to place her and her family on a budget of $18,000 a year, a good deal of money then. But she never lived by the agreement and had paid almost nothing in taxes; she was said to owe the government $163,400, plus 6 percent interest.

Now, ever more fearful of the government, she tried to return to writing. She finished *No Adam in Eden,* a book about her French Canadian family, which was published in September 1963. Messner passed on it, albeit selling the rights to Pocket Books for $50,000, and the movie rights went for $150,000. Her unhappiness, indeed her increasing lack of self-esteem, one shrewd critic noted, now showed in her work. "It would seem that the writer hates women, individually and en masse. If she had anything kind or understanding to say about them, I confess to having forgotten what it was, so weighed down are all the female characters under a load of sin, lechery, selfishness and cruelty." The remaining year of her life was sad. Metalious left her again in the fall of 1963, and a few months later, in February 1964, she died of chronic liver disease.

THIRTY-NINE

IT WAS ALL PART of a vast national phenomenon. The number of families moving into the middle class—that is, families with more than five thousand dollars in annual earnings after taxes—was increasing at the rate of 1.1 million a year, *Fortune* noted. By the end of 1956 there were 16.6 million such families in the country, and by 1959, in the rather cautious projections of *Fortune*'s editors, there would be 20 million such families—virtually half the families in America. *Fortune* hailed "an economy of abundance" never seen before in any country in the world. It reflected a world of "optimistic philoprogenitive [the word means that Americans were having a lot of children] high spending, debt-happy, bargainconscious, upgrading, American consumers."

In all of this no one was paying very close attention to what the new home-oriented, seemingly drudgery-free life was doing to the psyche and outlook of American women. The pictures of them in magazines showed them as relentlessly happy, liberated from endless household tasks by wondrous new machines they had just bought. Since the photos showed them happy, and since there was no doubt that there were more and better household appliances every year, it was presumed that they were in fact happy. That was one of the more interesting questions of the era, for the great migration to the suburbs reflected a number of profound trends taking place in the society, not the least important of which was the changing role of women, particularly middle-class women. Up until then during this century women had made fairly constant progress in the spheres of politics, education, and employment opportunities. Much of their early struggle focused on the right of married women to work (and therefore to take jobs away from men who might be the heads of families). In the thirties a majority of states, twenty-six of forty-eight, still had laws prohibiting the employment of married women. In addition, a majority of the nation's public schools, 43 percent of its public utilities, and 13 percent of its department stores enforced rules on not hiring of wives. A poll of both men and women in the thirties that asked "Do you approve of a married woman earning money in business or industry if she has a husband capable of supporting her?" showed that 82 percent of the men and women polled disapproved.

During the Depression, large numbers of women went to work because their homes needed every bit of cash they could bring home. In addition women were always welcome in those parts of industry that offered poorer-paying jobs. At the beginning of the New Deal in the garment district of New York, where traditionally workers were the wives of immigrants, women worked forty-eight hours a week for 15 cents an hour, which meant that after a long, exhausting work week they brought home $7.20.

But in general there was an assumption that as society began to change and more and more women were better educated, there would be more women working in the professions for better wages. World War Two dramatically (if only temporarily) changed how the nation regarded the employment of women. Overnight, that which had been perceived as distinctly unfeminine—holding heavy-duty industrial jobs—became a patriotic necessity. Four million additional workers were needed in industry and in the armed forces and a great many of them had to be women. The *Ladies' Home Journal* even put a woman combat pilot on its cover. Suddenly, where women had not gone before they were very welcome indeed; some 8 million women entered the work force during the war.

That trend came to a stunning halt in the years after the war. Part of it was the traditional tilt of the society toward men—if there were good, well-paying jobs, then the jobs obviously belonged to men as they came home from the war to head families. Within two months after the end of the war, some 800,000 women had been fired from jobs in the aircraft industry; the same thing was happening in the auto industry and elsewhere. In the two years after the war, some 2 million women had lost their jobs.

In the postwar years the sheer affluence of the country meant that many families could now live a middle-class existence on only one income. In addition, the migration to the suburbs physically separated women from the workplace. The new culture of consumerism told women they should be homemakers and saw them merely as potential buyers for all the new washers and dryers, freezers, floor waxers, pressure cookers, and blenders.

There was in all this a retreat from the earlier part of the century. Now, there was little encouragement for women seeking professional careers, and in fact there was a good deal of quite deliberate discouraging of it. Not only were women now reared in homes where their mothers had no careers, but male siblings were from the start put on a very different track: The boys in the family were to learn the skills critical to supporting a family, while daughters were to be educated to get married. If they went to college at all they might spend a junior year abroad studying art or literature. Upon graduation, if they still had ideas of a professional career, the real world did not give them much to be optimistic about.

The laws about married women working might have changed, but the cultural attitudes had not. The range of what women were allowed to do professionally in those days was limited, and even in those professions where they were welcome, they were put on a lower, slower track. Gender, not talent, was the most important qualification. Men and women who graduated at the same time from the same colleges and who had received the same grades (in many cases the women received better grades), then arrived at the same publishing or journalistic companies only to be treated very differently.

Men were taken seriously. Women, by contrast, were doomed to serve as support troops. Often they worked harder and longer for less pay with lesser titles, usually with the unspoken assumption that if they were at all attractive, they would soon get married, become pregnant, and leave the company. Only someone a bit off-center emotionally would stay the course. It was a vicious circle: Because young women were well aware of this situation, there was little incentive to commit an entire life to fighting it and becoming what was then perceived of as a hard and brittle career woman. ("Nearly Half the Women in Who's Who Are Single," went one magazine title in that period trying to warn young women of the pitfalls of careerism.) If there were short stories in womens' magazines about career women, then it turned out they, by and large, portrayed women who were unhappy and felt themselves emotionally empty. Instead, the magazines and the new television sitcoms glorified dutiful mothers and wives.

Even allegedly serious books of the era (for

instance, an influential book of pop sociology by a man named Ferdinand Lundberg and his psychoanalyst collaborator Marynia Farnham, entitled *Modern Woman: The Lost Sex*) attacked the idea of women with careers. "The independent woman is a contradiction in terms," Lundberg and Farnham had written. Feminism itself, in their words, "was a deep illness." "The psychosocial rule that takes form, then, is this: the more educated a woman is, the greater chance there is of sexual disorder, more or less severe. The greater the disordered sexuality in a given group of women, the fewer children they have," they wrote. They also suggested that the federal government give rewards to women for each child they bore after the first.

A postwar definition of femininity evolved. To be feminine, the American woman first and foremost did not work. If she did, that made her competitive with men, which made her hard and aggressive and almost surely doomed to loneliness. Instead, she devotedly raised her family, supported her husband, kept her house spotless and efficient, got dinner ready on time, and remained attractive and optimistic; each hair was in place. According to studies, she was prettier than her mother, she was slimmer, and she even smelled better than her mother.

At this particular moment, it was impossible to underestimate the importance and influence of the women's magazines—the *Ladies' Home Jour-*

nal, Redbook, McCall's, and *Mademoiselle*—on middle-class young woman. Isolated in the suburbs they felt uneasy and lonely and largely without guidance. More often than not, they were newly separated from their original families and the people they had grown up with. They were living new lives, different from those of their parents, with new and quite different expectations on the part of their husbands. Everything had to be learned.

In an age before the coming of midday television talk shows largely designed for housewives, womens' magazines comprised the core reading material for the new young suburban wives. If the magazines' staffs at the lower rungs were comprised mostly of women, the magazines were almost always edited by men; in addition, editorial content much more than in most general-circulation magazines, echoed the thrust of the advertising. Research showed, or seemed to show, that husbands made the critical decisions in terms of which political candidate a family might support, but the wives made the decisions on which refrigerator and which clothes washer to buy. If the advertising was designed to let women know what the newest appliances were and how to use them, then the accompanying articles were designed to show they could not live up to their destinies without them.

This was not done deliberately. There were no editorial meetings where male editors sat around and killed ideas that showed the brave new suburban world as populated with a significant percentage of tense, anxious female college graduates who wondered if they were squandering the best years of their lives. But there was an instinctive bias about what women needed to hear and that it should all be upbeat, and that any larger doubts were unworthy.

The magazines explained their new lives to them: how to live, how to dress, what to eat, why they should feel good about themselves and their husbands and their children. Their sacrifices, the women's magazines emphasized, were not really sacrifices, they were about fulfillment. All doubts were to be conquered.

The ideal fifties women were to strive for was articulated by *McCall's* in 1954: togetherness. A family was as one, its ambitions were twined. The husband was designated leader and hero, out there every day braving the treacherous corporate world to win a better life for his family; the wife was his mainstay on the domestic side, duly appreciative of the immense sacrifices being made for her and her children. There was no divergence within. A family was a single perfect universe— instead of a complicated, fragile mechanism of conflicting political and emotional pulls. Families portrayed in women's magazines exhibited no conflicts or contradictions or unfulfilled ambitions. Thanks, probably, to the drive for togetherness, the new homes all seemed to have what was

called a family room. Here the family came together, ate, watched television, and possibly even
talked. "When Jim comes home," said a wife in a
1954 advertisement for prefabricated homes, "our
family room seems to draw us closer together."
And who was responsible ultimately for togetherness if not the wife?

"The two big steps that women must take are
to help their husbands decide where they are
going and use their pretty heads to help them get
there," wrote Mrs. Dale Carnegie, wife of one of
the nation's leading experts on how to be likable,
in the April 1955 *Better Homes and Gardens.*
"Let's face it, girls. That wonderful guy in your
house—and in mine—is building your house,
your happiness and the opportunities that will
come to your children." Split-level houses, Mrs.
Carnegie added, were fine for the family, "but
there is simply no room for split-level thinking—
or doing—when Mr. and Mrs. set their sights on
a happy home, a host of friends and a bright
future through success in HIS job."

Those women who were not happy and did
not feel fulfilled were encouraged to think that the
fault was theirs and that they were the exception
to blissful normality. That being the case, women
of the period rarely shared their doubts, even with
each other. If anything, they tended to feel guilty
about any qualms they had: Here they were living
better than ever—their husbands were making
more money than ever, and there were ever big-

ger, more beautiful cars in the garage and appliances in the kitchen. Who were they to be unhappy?

. . .

One of the first women to challenge the fallacy of universal contentment among young suburban wives was a young woman from the heartland of the country. Born and reared in Peoria, Illinois, she did well enough in school to be admitted to an elite Eastern women's college, one of the Seven Sister schools. She entered Smith College in 1939, finding everything that she had longed for as a small-town girl in Peoria: a world where women were rewarded for being smart and different instead of being punished for it. She graduated in 1942, summa cum laude, full of optimism about the future even though the war was still going on. Several scholarships were offered her. Ambitious, admired by her classmates, Betty Goldstein was certain that she would lead a life dramatically different from her mother's. Miriam Goldstein had been a society-page writer for the Peoria, Illinois, paper, before marrying a local storeowner and becoming a housewife. In her daughter's eyes, she took out her own frustrated ambitions by pushing her children to achieve. But at graduation time, Betty Goldstein turned down the fellowships because she was interested in a young man; since he had not been offered a comparable scholarship, she was afraid it would tear their relationship apart if she accepted hers. That decision, she later wrote, turned her instantly into a cliché. Looking back on her life, Betty Goldstein Friedan, one of the first voices of the feminist movement, noted the young man's face was more quickly forgotten than the terms of the scholarship itself.

Instead of getting married, she moved to the exciting intellectual world of Greenwich Village and became part of a group of liberal young people involved in labor issues and civil rights before it was fashionable. The women all seemed to be graduates of Smith, Vassar, and Radcliffe; they were bright and optimistic, eager to take on a static society. Betty Goldstein worked as a reporter for a left-wing labor paper. As a journalist, she had got a reputation of knowing her way around and having lots of contacts. She became the person designated to arrange illegal abortions for involuntarily pregnant friends. This, she found, she was able to do with a few discreet phone calls. The going price was a thousand dollars. Once it was also her job to find a minister for two Protestant friends who wanted to marry. Because the groom was a divorced man, she noted with some irony, it was harder to find a willing minister than an abortionist.

When the war was over, the men returned from Europe and the South Pacific, and the women were gradually squeezed out of their jobs. Betty Goldstein, unsure of her role and her future, not liking the idea of a life alone (she had, she noted, "a pathological fear of being alone"), met a young veteran named Carl Friedan, who seemed funny and charming, and in 1947, two years after the war had ended, they were married. In 1949 they had their first child. When she was pregnant with her second child she was fired from the labor paper, whose radicalism, it appeared, did not yet extend to women's rights. When she took her grievance to the newspaper guild, she was told that the second pregnancy, which had cost her job, was her fault. There was, she later realized, no union term for sex discrimination.

Ms. Friedan soon found herself part of the great suburban migration as she moved further and further away from the Village, which had been the center of her professional and intellectual world. There, ideas had always seemed important. As she and her husband moved to larger and larger living quarters, first to Queens, where the Friedans lived in a pleasant apartment, and then to houses in the suburbs, her time was gradually more and more taken by children and family. As that happened, she was cut off, first physically, from what she had been, and then increasingly intellectually and socially as well. Betty Friedan now poured her energy into being a housewife and mother, into furnishing the apartment and houses and shopping, cooking, and cleaning for her family.

The Friedan family, she later realized, had been almost unconsciously caught up in the postwar migration to the suburbs. It was an ascent to an ever better style of living; but she also began to see it as a retreat as well from her earlier ambitions and standards. She liked doing the domestic things that Americans now did in their new, ever more informal social lives—grilling hamburgers on the outdoor barbecue, attending spur-of-the-moment cocktail parties, sharing summer rentals on Fire Island with friends. Finally, the Friedans bought an old house, worthy of Charles Addams, in Rockland County for $25,000 (with $2,500 down), where Betty Friedan, Smith summa cum laude and future feminist leader, spent her time, scraping eight layers of paint off a fireplace ("I quite liked it"), chauffeuring children to and from school, helping to run the PTA, and coming as close as someone as fiercely independent as she was could to being a good housewife, as portrayed in the women's magazines of that day. In some ways her life was full, she would later decide, and in some ways it was quite empty. She liked being a mother, and she liked her friends, but she missed the world of social and political involvement back in New York. She also worried that she had not lived up to her potential. By the time they were living in Rockland County, she had begun to write free-lance for various women's magazines. It was a clear sign, she realized later, that while the domestic side of her life was rich, it was not rich enough.

The deal she made with herself then was a

revealing one. It was her job as a writer to make more money than she and Carl spent on a maid—otherwise her writing would be considered counterproductive and would be viewed as subtracting from rather than adding to the greater good of the family. Her early articles, "Millionaire's Wife" (*Cosmopolitan,* September 1956); "Now They're Proud of Peoria" (*Reader's Digest,* August 1955); "Two Are an Island" *Mademoiselle*) July 1955; and "Day Camp in the Driveways" (*Parents'* Magazine, May 1957) were not exactly the achievements she had had in mind when she left Smith.

She was also very quickly finding out the limits of what could be done in writing for women's magazines at that time. In 1956, when she was pregnant with her third child, she read in a newspaper about Julie Harris, the actress, then starring in a play called *The Lark*. Ms. Harris had had natural childbirth, something that Betty Friedan, who had undergone two cesareans, admired and even envied. She decided, with the ready agreement of the magazines, to do a piece on Ms. Harris and her childbirth. She had a glorious time interviewing the actress and was completely captivated by her. She wrote what she thought was one of her best articles on the joys of natural childbirth. To her surprise, the article was turned down at first because it was too graphic.

That was hardly her only defeat with the

magazines. When she suggested an article about Beverly Pepper, just beginning to experience considerable success as a painter and sculptor, and who was also raising a family, the editors of one magazine were scornful. American women, they told her, were not interested in someone like this and would not identify with her. Their market research, of which they were extremely confident, showed that women would only read articles that explained their own roles as wives and mothers. Not many American women out there had families and were successful as artists—therefore it would have no appeal. Perhaps, one editor said, they might do the article with a photograph of Mrs. Pepper painting the family crib.

At the time one of her children was in a play group with the child of a neighboring woman scientist. Ms. Friedan and the woman talked on occasion and her friend said she believed that a new ice age was approaching. The subject had interested Friedan, not normally a science writer, and she had suggested an article for *Harper's*. The resulting article, "The Coming Ice Age" was a considerable success and won a number of prizes. In New York George Brockway, a book editor at Norton, saw the piece and liked it. He called to ask if she was interested in writing a book. She was excited by his interest but had no desire to expand the piece into a book; the scientific work was not really hers, in the sense that it did not reflect her true interests and feelings. It was, she later said, as if she had served as a ghostwriter for another person on it.

Then something happened that changed her life. She and two friends were asked to do a report on what had happened to the members of the Smith class of '42 as they returned for their fifteenth reunion in 1957. She made up a questionnaire and got an assignment from *McCall's* to pay for her time. The piece was supposed to be called "The Togetherness Woman." The questions were: "What difficulties have you found in working out your role as a woman?" "What are the chief satisfactions and frustrations of your life today?" "How do you feel about getting older?" "How have you changed inside?" "What do you wish you had done differently?" The answers stunned her: She had tapped into a great reservoir of doubt, frustration, anxiety, and resentment. The women felt unfulfilled and isolated with their children; they often viewed their husbands as visitors from a far more exciting world.

The project also emphasized Friedan's own frustrations. All those years trying to be a good wife and mother suddenly seemed wasted; it had been wrong to suppress her feelings rather than to deal with them. The surprise was that there were thousands of women like her out there. As she wrote later in *The Feminine Mystique:* "It was a strange stirring, a sense of dissatisfaction, a yearning that women suffered in the middle of the twentieth century in the United States. Each suburban wife struggled with it alone. As she made the beds, shopped for groceries, matched slip cover materials, ate peanut butter sandwiches with her children, chauffeured Cub Scouts and Brownies, lay beside her husband at night, she was afraid to ask of herself the silent question—'Is this all?' "

As she had walked around the Smith campus during her reunion, she was struck by the passivity of the young women of the class of 1957. Upon graduation, her generation had been filled with excitement about the issues of the day: When Ms. Friedan asked these young women about their futures, they regarded her with blank looks. They were going to get engaged and married and have children, of course. She thought: This is happening at Smith, a place where I found nothing but intellectual excitement when I was their age. Something had gotten deep into the bloodstream of this generation, she decided.

She left and started to write the piece for *McCall's,* but it turned out very different from the one that she had intended to write. It reflected the despair and depression she had found among her contemporaries, and it was critical of women who lived through their husbands and children. *McCall's,* the inventor of "togetherness"—not surprisingly—turned it down. She heard that all the women editors there wanted to run it but that they had been overruled by their male superiors. That did not entirely surprise her, but she was sure someone else would want it. So she sent it to the *Ladies' Home Journal,* where it was accepted. There, to her amazement, it was rewritten so completely that it seemed to make the opposite points, so she pulled it. That left *Redbook,* where Bob Stein, an old friend, worked. He suggested that she do more interviews, particularly with younger women. She did, and sent the piece back to him. He was stunned by it. How could Betty Friedan write a piece so out of sync with what his magazine wanted? Why was she so angry? What in God's name had come over her? he wondered. He turned it down and called her agent. "Look," he said over the phone. "Only the most neurotic housewife would identify with this."

She was, she realized later, challenging the magazines themselves. She was saying that it was wrong to mislead women to think they should feel one way when in fact they often felt quite differently. She had discovered a crisis of considerable proportions, and these magazines would only deny it.

She was angry. It was censorship, she believed. Women's magazines had a single purpose, she decided—to sell a vast array of new products to American housewives—and anything that worked against that, that cast doubt about the happiness of the housewives using such products, was not going to be printed. No one from the advertising department sat in on editorial meetings saying which articles could run and which could not, she knew, but the very purpose of the magazine was to see women first and foremost as consumers, not as people.

At about that time she went to New York to attend a speech by Vance Packard, the writer. He had just finished his book *The Hidden Persuaders,* about subliminal tactics in advertising. His efforts to write about this phenomenon in magazines had been completely unsuccessful, he said, so he turned it into a book, which had become a major best-seller. The parallels between his problems and hers were obvious. Suddenly, she envisioned "The Togetherness Woman" as a book. She called George Brockway at Norton, and he seemed delighted with the idea.

The economics of publishing were significantly different from those of magazines. Books were not dependent upon ads, they were dependent upon ideas, and the more provocative the idea, the more attention and, often, the better the sales. Brockway knew there had already been a number of attacks on conformity in American society, particularly as it affected men. Here was an attack that would talk about its effect on women, who were, of course, the principal buyers of books. He was impressed by Ms. Friedan. She was focused and, to his mind, wildly ambitious.

She told Brockway she would finish it in a year; instead, it took five years. Later she wrote that no one, not her husband, her editor, or anyone who knew her, thought she would ever finish it. She did so while taking care of three children. She later described herself as being like all the other mothers in suburbia, where she "hid, like secret drinking in the morning, the book I was writing when my suburban neighbors came for coffee . . ."

Her research was prodigious. Three days a week she went to the New York City Public Library for research. The chief villains, she decided, were the women's magazines. What stunned her was the fact that this had not always been true. In the same magazines in the late thirties and forties, there had been a sense of women moving steadily into the male professional world; then women's magazines had created a very different kind of role model, of a career woman who knew how to take care of herself and who could make it on her own.

But starting around 1949, these magazines changed dramatically. It was as if someone had thrown a giant switch. The new woman did not exist on her own. She was seen only in the light of supporting her husband and his career and taking care of the children.

The more Ms. Friedan investigated, the more she found that the world created in the magazines and the television sitcoms was, for many women at least, a fantasy world. Despite all the confidence and happiness among women portrayed in the magazines, there was underneath it all a crisis in the suburbs. It was the crisis of a generation of women who had left college with high idealism and who had come to feel increasingly frustrated and who had less and less a sense of self-esteem.

Nor, she found, did all the marvelous new appliances truly lighten the load of the housewife. If anything they seemed to extend it—there was some kind of Gresham's law at work here: The more time-saving machines there were, the more things there were to do with them. She had stumbled across something that a number of others, primarily psychiatrists, had noticed: a certain emotional malaise, bordering on depression, among many women of the era. One psychiatrist called it "the housewife's syndrome," another referred to it as "the housewife's blight." No one wrote about it in popular magazines, certainly not in the monthly women's magazines.

So, gathering material over several years, she began to write a book that would come out in 1963, not as *The Togetherness Woman,* but as *The Feminine Mystique.* She was approaching forty as she began, but she was regenerated by the importance of the project; it seemed to give her her own life back. The result was a seminal book on what had happened to women in America. It started selling slowly but word of it grew and grew, and eventually, with 3 million copies in print, it became a handbook for the new feminist movement that was gradually beginning to come together.

FORTY

AT THE Worcester Foundation, the search for an oral contraceptive pill was beginning to go surprisingly well. The breakthrough of synthetic progesterone had given them all an immense lift. Word of how well they were doing spread throughout the scientific community and eventually reached the general public; an article had even appeared in *Look* predicting that Pincus would soon succeed in his quest.

The next stage was reached when Searle passed on to Worcester a progesterone steroid called norethynodrel, which, Chang reported back to Pincus, was more powerful than natural progesterone by a factor of at least ten to one. Goody Pincus knew at that point that it was time to bring on board a distinguished medical doctor as a collaborator—for soon the Pill would have to be tried on human subjects. At first he considered Alan Guttmacher and Abraham Stone, both doctors and leaders in the birth-control movement. But Pincus worried that their affiliation might diminish their legitimacy for the project, and in addition, both were Jewish. This might prove to be a liability, for opposition to birth control came primarily from Catholics and fundamentalist

Christians. (For all its freedom from administrative control and political pressure, the Worcester people remained cautious in publicly discussing what they were doing. The 1955 annual report was more than a little disingenuous; it spoke of work with animals to control ovulation; the 1956 report detailed the use of steroids to help control painful menstruation.)

Finally, Pincus turned to an old colleague and friend, Dr. John Rock. Rock was a distinguished doctor, chief of gynecology and obstetrics at Harvard Medical School. He was also a devout Catholic, father of five children, and grandfather of fourteen. Rock and Pincus had known each other since the thirties by dint of their common interest in hormones. Rock, however, was trying to use them to cure infertility in women. He believed progesterone and estrogen might stimulate the womb, and he sent one of his assistants to work with Pincus to learn from his experience in retrieving mammalian eggs. Gradually, their work brought Rock and Pincus closer together.

In 1953 Pincus suggested to Sanger that Planned Parenthood get Rock to do a study on the use of progesterone as a contraceptive device. Rock, whose attitudes toward contraception had been slowly changing, was finally ready to participate. Margaret Sanger was wary of Rock at first because he was a Catholic ("He would not," she said, "dare advance the cause of contraceptive research and remain a Catholic"). But Pincus convinced her that Rock's attitudes were flexible, and that he was increasingly sympathetic to the idea of birth control. Besides, he was an imposing figure—strikingly handsome, charming, and graceful—and he was also a representative of one of America's great universities. Kate McCormick agreed with Pincus; Rock, she explained to Sanger, was a "reformed Catholic." His position, she told her friend, "is that religion has nothing to do with medicine or the practice of it, and that if the Church does not interfere with him, he will not interfere with it—whatever that may mean." Eventually, Margaret Sanger finally came around on Rock because it seemed he would be able to win support from those who had rejected Sanger and her causes in the past. "Being a good R.C. and as handsome as a god, he can get away with anything," she noted. In 1954 he began experiments using the new synthetic hormone from Searle on three women.

Later, some critics claimed that Rock was no more than a front man. In fact he was a good deal more than that. He was the perfect choice, as a doctor, to take the experiment from the lab and move it into the real world of people. His was a powerful presence, a doctor of great distinction and originality whose own work and social ideas were taking him ever closer to the work of Pincus and his team. "If you went to doctors in New England in those days," said Oscar Hechter, "and asked who was the best obstetrician in the region, you would almost surely be told that it was John Rock—he was a formidable figure." He was also a man of singular independence. Rock's courage was admired by both Hoagland and Pincus, but they knew he was a brilliant clinician as well, not merely a theorist as they were. When they had created the Worcester Foundation, they had wanted more than anything else to make it a *relevant* institution (after all, they spent much of the war studying the biological aspects of fighter-pilot fatigue, and they had also done advanced work on the biochemistry of schizophrenia), so Rock was a man whom they would have invented had he not lived, a bridge from their world of the abstract to a world of real people with real medical problems.

Rock was the son of a small-town businessman in Marlborough, Massachusetts: His ancestors were Irish Catholics. He finished Harvard College in three years, went on to Harvard Medical School, and soon became a prominent professor of gynecology. When he married Anne Thorndike in 1925, the cardinal of Boston himself performed the ceremony, something he had done only once before, for Joe and Rose Kennedy. But the Catholic Church almost stopped the ceremony. The day before his wedding, Rock performed a cesarean section, an operation then forbidden by the Catholic Church. At confession, a local priest refused to absolve him and thus it was impossible for him to receive the sacrament of marriage. But William Cardinal O'Connell overruled the priest.

Rock was in many ways a very conservative man. He argued against the admission of women to Harvard Medical School and often told his own daughters that he did not think women were capable of being doctors. But his views on birth control evolved steadily. In 1943, when he was fifty-three years old, he had come out for the repeal of legal restrictions on physicians to give advice on medical birth control. But he added at the time: "I hold no brief for those young or even older husbands and wives who for no good reason refuse to bear as many children as they can properly rear and as society can properly engross." In the mid-forties, although scrupulous about not offering contraceptives to his own patients, he began to teach his young students at Harvard Medical School how to prescribe them. Years later he would pinpoint the late forties as the time when he became aware of what he called "the alarming danger of the population explosion." He began to fit some of his patients with diaphragms, which so enraged some of his Catholic colleagues that they tried to have him excommunicated. In 1949 he wrote a book with David Loth called *Voluntary Parenthood,* which was a comprehensive survey of birth-control methods available for the general public. His colleagues admired him because he so seriously wrestled with questions of morality. In many ways the transformation of his own values reflected those taking place among many in the middle class. Although he remained a serious Catholic who regularly attended mass, he became even blunter about his changing views on population control. Indeed, after the introduction of the Pill, he said, "I think it's shocking to see the big family glorified." When the Pill first came out, he received an angry letter from a Catholic woman who excoriated him for his role in its development. She told him, "You should be afraid to meet your maker." "Dear Madam," he wrote back. "In my faith we are taught that the Lord is with us always. When my time comes, there will be no need for introductions." Still, Rock's primary motivation in joining with Pincus was for the opposite problem that Pincus and his team were working to solve. He wanted to help couples who, despite all physiological evidence to the contrary, were unable to have children. In the past he had had some success injecting the women with natural progesterone.

He gave the progestin steroids to a group of fifty childless women at his clinic, starting in December 1954. The dosage was 10–40 milligrams for twenty successive days for each menstrual cycle. When the women came off the progestin, seven of the fifty, or 14 percent, were able to get pregnant. That was wonderful news for Rock. In addition, there was among the fifty a virtual 100 percent postponement of ovulation. That was wonderful news for Pincus and Chang. Pincus became so confident that he had begun to refer to "the Pill."

So these three very different men began to work together. Each of the three had his own private doubts. Rock, the good Catholic, still worried about the morality of what he was doing; Chang was wary of capitalist exploitation, uneasy about placing his scientific skills in the service of drug companies (Pincus had to reassure him constantly that what he was doing was for the good of the society and that the drug companies did not matter); and Pincus himself, constantly racing against the clock, wondered if what they were doing was safe. But even as they were making rapid progress, Kate McCormick remained impatient. On one occasion, after John Rock returned from a brief vacation, she wrote Margaret Sanger, "I was able to get hold of Dr. Rock today. . . . I did not want to leave him for fear that he would escape!" To term what seemed a speedy process was terribly slow to McCormick.

By the fall of 1955 Pincus was so optimistic that he decided to go and talk publicly about his research at the International Planned Parenthood meeting in Tokyo. He asked Rock to join him, but Rock was uneasy about it; he felt that the results while so far very positive, were not yet adequately conclusive and that Pincus was on shakier ground than he realized. He was also sensitive about making the announcement at what he considered a politicized event—a meeting of birth-control advocates. It was the closest the two men came to a break. Pincus and Chang desperately wanted Rock to add his name and considerable prestige to the announcements they intended to make in Tokyo. At the time, a disappointed Pincus felt that Rock was being too timid. Rock, by contrast, felt his colleagues were going too fast for the evidence. "He [Pincus] was a little scary," Rock told Paul Vaughan years later. "He was not a physician and he knew very little about the endometrium, though he knew a good deal about ovulation." If anything, noted Mahlon Hoagland, the son of the director, who himself later became the Worcester Foundation's director, Rock was right, and Pincus and Chang probably did exceed their evidence, by talking not just about what they had accomplished with animals, but dwelling on the implications for humans. "They did it," the young Hoagland noted, "because they were restless, talented mavericks, cocky and arrogant, very good and aware of being very good—it was what made Worcester such a wonderful place to work." Rock did not go, and in fact urged Pincus not to go.

What they all needed now were more patients and a broader selection of them: It was one thing to succeed with middle-class, college-educated women, who would be disciplined about taking the Pill, but what about poorer, less well educated women? Would they be as careful? Puerto Rico and Haiti were chosen as locales for mass testing. These places were perfect for their needs—poor and overcrowded. Public officials were more than ready for a serious study of birth control. (There was no small irony in the choice of Puerto Rico. At that time the primary birth control was for a woman to go to the hospital and demand the *operación,* which was a sterilization procedure. As Puerto Ricans migrated to New York, they went to New York's hospitals with the same request, but under New York law, not every woman who wanted to be sterilized had that right. Under pressure from this growing new Hispanic population, the law was changed.)

In April 1956, the tests began on one hundred women in a poor suburb of San Juan. It had been exceptionally easy to get volunteers; the problem was keeping other women out. The pill used was Enovid, made by Searle, whose officials were nervous about being associated with Pincus in the program and whose top public relations officials warned that this activity might destroy their good name. (A few years later, as they were preparing to market Enovid publicly in America and their research showed overwhelming public acceptance, they swung around 180 degrees and considered calling it The Pill. "After all, if you could patent the word Coke for Coca-Cola why not 'The Pill' for the oral contraceptive? So we kicked the idea around. But we never took any action," said James Irwin, a Searle public relations executive.) The early returns from Puerto Rico were very good: In the first eight months, 221 patients took the Pill without a single pregnancy. There were some side effects, primarily nausea, but Pincus was able to reduce them, by adding an anti-acid. Soon the tests were being expanded to other areas in Puerto Rico, and to Haiti as well.

Pincus's daughter, Laura, took some time off from her studies at Radcliffe to help with the tests in Puerto Rico. Upon her return to Boston she was sent to brief Kate McCormick, who lived in a grand mansion in Back Bay, a foreboding house that seemed to have neither lights nor life to it. Laura Pincus was, in her own words, rather naive about sex and she got a little flustered talking to this old woman about the experiments then taking place. But Kate McCormick did not become unsettled: She talked openly and frankly. The sex drive in humans was so strong, she kept insisting, that it was critical that it be separated from reproductive functions. She followed that with a brief discussion of the pleasures of sex and then added rather casually that sex between women might be more meaningful. This was spoken dispassionately, not suggestively. Nonetheless, young Ms. Pincus was stunned. Here she was in this nineteenth-century setting hearing words that seemed to come from the twenty-first century. Then, knowing that her visitor had to take the subway back to college, Mrs. McCormick summoned her butler, who brought her a silver tray with coins. She reached down and picked out two dimes and handed them to her visitor. Later, after she left, Laura Pincus looked down at the coins and noticed they were minted in 1929.

But if the breakthrough was near, Margaret Sanger remained on a wartime footing. In 1957 she made her first television appearance, on the Mike Wallace show, and the reaction stunned even Sanger. There was so much hostile mail that for the first time in her life, she was wary of reading it. "The R.C. Church," she wrote in her diary at the time, "is getting more defiant and arrogant. I'm disgusted and worried. No one who was a worker in defense of our Protestant rights has got to accept the Black Hand from Catholic influence. Young Kennedy from Boston is on the Stage for President in 1960. God help America if his father's millions can push him into the White House."

. . .

It was an extraordinary triumph for Pincus. Pincus, claimed Oscar Hechter, was the prototype of a new kind of biologist, the engineer of "a conscious use of science to effect social change in the interests of man and civilization." By so doing he was able to "liberate humanity from an immediate social threat and to remove restraints from the full development of uniqueness of men and women alike." Pincus began to travel around the world, talking with great enthusiasm of the coming breakthrough in contraception. He would tell his audiences "how a few precious facts obscurely come to in the laboratory may resonate into the lives of men everywhere, bring order to disorder, hope to the hopeless, life to the dying. That this is the magic and mystery of our time is sometimes grasped and often missed, but to expound it is inevitable." It was, his friends thought, the great validating moment of his professional life.

Some people in Planned Parenthood still thought Pincus was too optimistic and precipitous, but his optimism was now shared by Rock. They were both now pushing for acceptances of the Pill, and they were getting results: In 1957, the U.S. Food and Drug Administration authorized the marketing of the Pill for treatment of miscarriages and some menstrual disorders. By 1959 both Pincus and Rock were convinced that Enovid was safe for long-term use by women. In 1959 Pincus completed a paper on the uses of Enovid for oral contraception and sent it to Margaret Sanger. "To Margaret Sanger," he wrote, "with affectionate greetings—this product of her pioneering resoluteness."

In May 1960, the FDA approved Enovid as a contraceptive device. By the end of 1961 some 408,000 American women were taking the Pill, by the end of 1962 the figure was 1,187,000, and by the end of 1963 it was 2.3 million and still rising. Of it, Clare Boothe Luce said, "Modern woman is at last free as a man is free, to dispose of her own body, to earn her living, to pursue the improvement of her mind, to try a successful career."

The discovery made Searle a very rich company. To Chang's great regret, the Worcester Foundation never took any royalty. Nor, in the eyes of the Worcester people, was Searle generous in later years. Despite several representations on behalf of Pincus's family and of the Worcester people, Searle paid only three hundred dollars a month in benefits to his widow. When the Worcester people suggested repeatedly to Searle that the company might like to endow a chair at the Worcester Foundation in Pincus's honor, Searle not only declined but soon afterward donated $500,000 to Harvard to endow a chair in reproductive studies. It was the supreme indignity—rewarding the institution that had once denied Pincus tenure with a chair in his own specialty. To Pincus's colleagues in Worcester, it appeared that no good deed went unpunished. Nor were the Searle people very generous with Chang. Years after the Pill's development, Hudson Hoagland suggested that Searle (which was making millions) might give some financial aid to Chang, who was by the standards of science making very little. "Who the hell is M. C. Chang? We've never heard of him," a Searle executive asked. When that story was related to Chang, he quoted Confucius: "Do not get upset when people do not recognize you." "I hope," he added with a sardonic touch, "Chairman Mao will say the same."

Margaret Sanger's fears about a Catholic President turned out to be ill-founded. After a century of American Presidents who refused to deal with the issue of overpopulation, Kennedy expressed cautious approval of federal support for contraceptive research. In 1966, a year before Mrs. Sanger's death, Dwight Eisenhower and Harry Truman, neither of whom had been helpful to her while in office, became co-chairmen of Planned Parenthood's world-population committee.

FORTY-ONE

IN 1955, in a quiet ceremony in Huntsville, Alabama, Wernher von Braun, at the age of forty-three, became an American citizen. This was not a particularly good time for von Braun and his German colleagues in the American space program at Huntsville. To a nation trying on the uncomfortable new role of international power, space seemed, if anything, a futuristic fantasy—and an expensive one at that. That was particularly true for the President and most of his chief advisers, men born in the previous century. But for von Braun, who believed the space age was already here (thanks in no small part to his own V-2 rockets, used by the Germans in World War Two), this was unusually frustrating. When he had first come to America he had even written a novel called *Mars Project,* a book based not on idle fancies but on real data. It envisioned a major national effort to make manned space trips a reality. He sent the book off to a publisher, who replied that "it sounds too fantastic." Eighteen other publishers turned it down. He could hardly believe no one was interested.

Von Braun was probably at the moment the leading rocket scientist in the world. His V-2 was the first successful ballistic missile, and in the last year of the war, thirteen hundred of them had been fired at London with mounting success. Had German technology been on a slightly more accelerated schedule, Eisenhower mused later, the V-2s might have threatened his capacity to land at Normandy and thereby altered the outcome of the war. At the end of World War Two, von Braun and his team of German rocket scientists chose America as their future home as the Red Army pushed toward Peenemünde, where they were headquartered. In January 1945, von Braun called his team together and told them, "Germany has lost the war, but let us not forget that it was our team which first succeeded in reaching outer space. We have never stopped believing in satellite voyages to the Moon and interplanetary travel . . ." To which of the victorious countries, he then asked, "should we entrust our heritage?" That was an interesting choice of words—skills were practical knowledge, whereas heritage was more like one's lifeblood. They voted to stay together and to offer themselves to the Americans. The choice was relatively easy. "We despise the French; we are mortally afraid of the Soviets; we do not believe the British can afford us; so that leaves the Americans," one team member said later. Richard Lewis, writing in *Appointment on the Moon,* noted of Dieter Huzel, ("perhaps the most articulate of the émigrés") ". . . [he saw] their role as Promethean bearers of a great technological skill for mankind, forged in the fires of war, but of greater import as a means of exploring space than as a weapon. In the chaos of Germany's collapse, Huzel saw himself and his colleagues as men with a mission to perpetuate the engineering science they had created. These men, Huzel believes, tend to think of themselves as a group apart from the Nazi war machine, with ambitions transcending its military and political objectives."

The team slipped out of Peenemünde, burying most of their important papers in a deserted mine, and with the aid of faked papers, reached Bavaria and the American forces. Wernher's brother, Magnus von Braun, who spoke relatively good English, went out to hunt for an American soldier to whom they could surrender. In time one was found, and Magnus announced to a rather startled private: "My name is Magnus von Braun. My brother invented the V-2. We want to surrender." When Wernher himself appeared soon after, there was considerable doubt that he could actually be the father of the V-2. He was, said one American, "too young, too fat, too jovial." Then he began to talk. The American scientists were dazzled; his knowledge was so complete and he easily blended the practical with the visionary. Colonel John Keck, one of the debriefing officers, told reporters later, "This will make Buck Rogers seem as if he had lived in the Gay Nineties." Had anyone else spoken like this he would have seemed a dreamer, but when von Braun spoke listeners paid attention. "We were," said Keck, "impressed with their practical engineering minds and their distaste for the fantastic." So the deal was done, and the entire German team of over a hundred scientists came over. In addition, von Braun led his captors to several V-2s and gave the Americans important documents. The capture of the Germans was known as Operation Paperclip, and it was one of the great coups of the war, since the V-2 was not so much the last weapon of the old war as the first new weapon of the war that might come next. The Russians were furious. Stalin was a major promoter of the uses of science and technology, and he was well aware of the importance of Peenemünde. He had pushed his generals to the north rather than straight to Berlin.

When his troops reached the rocket camp, they found almost everything of value gone and Stalin was reportedly furious. "This is absolutely intolerable," he said, according to reliable defectors. "We defeated Nazi armies; we occupied Berlin and Peenemünde, but the Americans got the rocket engineers. What could be more revolting and more inexcusable? How and why was this allowed to happen?" In a way, the Red Army's race toward Peenemünde was symbolic: It was, without anyone knowing it, the beginning of the race for outer space, or what Winston Churchill once called "the wizard war."

Later, any number of American conserva-
tives raged against the Soviet successes in Eastern
Europe, but for all the territory swept up by the
Red Army, the Americans, by getting the German
scientists, had pulled off a major coup. In 1945,
the Germans were far ahead of other nations in
rocket developments, the Soviets were second,
with a significant pool of talent, and the Americans, having diverted much of their scientific resources to developing nuclear weapons, were a
poor third. But getting von Braun and his colleagues instantly made the Americans competitive. Rocketry was his life.

"For my confirmation," von Braun once
noted, "I didn't get a watch and my first pair of
long pants like most Lutheran boys. I got a telescope." His father was a large landowner and
served in the Weimar government as minister of
agriculture. Young Wernher was always fascinated by the stars and outer space. As a boy he
tied six firework skyrockets to his child's wagon,
lit them, and was delighted when the wagon went
surging forth. "I was ecstatic. The wagon was
totally out of control and trailing a comet's tail of
fire, but my rockets were performing beyond my
wildest dreams. Finally they burned themselves
out with a magnificent thunderclap and the vehicle rolled to a halt. The police took me into cus-
tody very quickly," he noted. At prep school, he
neglected his math courses until he was informed
they were critical to the study of space. Soon he

was doubling as a math teacher. In Berlin he enrolled at the Charlottenburg Institute of Technology and apprenticed at a local metal shop. At the shop he was ordered to make a perfect cube. He was furious. "Why waste time filing a chunk of iron?" But he submitted. The foreman measured it. His angles were off. Try again, he was told. So he did. His angles were still off. Again he tried; again his cube was imperfect. Finally, five weeks later, when his cube had shrunk from the size of a child's head to that of a walnut, the foreman said, *"Gut!"* It was an important lesson: Even dreamers have to perfect their practical skills.

At the age of eighteen, he and his friends experimented in an abandoned lot in Berlin, which they decided to call the Raketenflugplatz, or the Rocket Flight Field. Two years later, he was part of the embryonic German rocket team, under Dr. Hermann Oberth. Senior colleagues were already in awe of his extraordinary theoretical knowledge. Perhaps the Treaty of Versailles had limited German efforts in traditional weaponry, but it had said nothing about rockets and so the Germans began to undertake a major effort in this area. Von Braun soon became the leader of the team. In 1934, when it was decided a better place for testing than Berlin was needed, von Braun's mother suggested a little-known area on the Baltic coast called Peenemünde, where her father had often duck-hunted.

When the war began they were just finishing

work on the V-1, a twenty-seven-foot-long sub-
sonic rocket, which flew just low enough and
slowly enough to be intercepted. At first Hitler did
not seem particularly interested in their research.
During his first visit in 1939, he looked around,
listened to the briefings, and said nothing—to the
scientists' bitter disappointment. Germany's stunning early successes in the war had seemed to
eliminate the need for a secret weapon. Who
needed a weapon of the future when the weapons
of the present—the Panzer divisions and the
Wehrmacht—were so effective. Still, von Braun
and his team pushed ahead with the V-2. It was to
have a range of about 160 miles and had to be
small enough to be able to go through Germany's
railroad tunnels. The first V-2, fired in July 1942,
reached an altitude of one yard and blew up; the
first successful launch was on October 3, 1942. It
broke the sound barrier and reached an altitude
of some 55 miles and a range of 120 miles. Walter
Dornberger, the military commander of the
rocket team, turned to von Braun and said: "Do
you realize what we accomplished today? Today
the space ship is born!" It was now merely a matter of more thrust from bigger payloads, and gaining greater reliability and accuracy. "Our main
objective for a long time was to make it more
dangerous to be in the target area than to be with
the launch crew," von Braun once noted.

Then, just on the edge of success, the Peenemünde team received a message in March 1943,

which seemed to doom its work. The Führer had had one of his psychic dreams, this one about the V-2. In his dream it had failed to reach London. Three months later, with continuing bad news from the eastern front, Hitler reversed himself. He granted an audience to Dornberger and von Braun, who made a brilliant presentation and showed dramatic film footage of their successes. Hitler was galvanized, and Dornberger later said he seemed almost to scold himself for not having been a believer earlier. "Europe and the world will be too small from now on to contain a war," he had said. "With such weapons humanity will be unable to endure it." He immediately began giving military orders, and the Peenemünde scientists were relieved of whatever illusions they may have had that they were creating vehicles for space travel. These were to be *weapons*. Hitler demanded that the payload be increased from one ton to ten tons. "What I want," he told Dornberg, "is annihilation." Dornberg answered, "When we started our development work we were not thinking of an all-annihilating effect. We—" Hitler interrupted him in a rage: "You! No, *you* didn't think of it. But *I* did!" One incident, though, convinced Dornberg of Hitler's military genius. Hitler asked how the V-2 would explode. Von Braun said that the explosive would have extra destructive power because it would hit the earth with such velocity. Hitler said he thought that the high speed would cause the V-2 to bury itself as it was exploding and thus throw up a great deal of earth. He suggested a supersensitive fuse that would explode on impact. Von Braun checked it out—to his surprise, Hitler was right.

The situation was not without a terrible irony as these brilliant men, working with one eye on the world of the future, were hounded by the very system they worked for. Von Braun was briefly arrested in 1944 by Himmler because he had been overheard saying that he was not really interested in weaponry but rather in space travel. Visionaries they might be, but they were working in Nazi Germany, and the rockets were manufactured at a nearby site by slave laborers, most of them from Russia. By some estimates, 150 of them a day died of malnutrition.

By the spring of 1944, they were producing three hundred V-2s a month (eventually, the figure would reach nine hundred). Production took place in underground facilities because RAF bombing strikes were so effective. On September 8, 1944, they launched their first V-2 (for Vengeance Weapon Two, by Goebbels's decree) against London. Forty-six feet long and five and a half feet in diameter, it weighed 28,000 pounds, most of which was fuel and a fuel tank. Its rocket engine had a thrust of 56,000 pounds, and it was launched vertically. It took about six minutes to hit London. It flew faster than a rifle bullet, and there was no defense against it, no possibility of interception. Because it flew faster than the speed of sound, it gave no warning until after it landed—the sound of it arrived after the rocket itself. Thus, the casualties were very high. One V-2, for example, landed at a market in London and killed a hundred people. According to Dornberger, some 3,745 rockets were fired between September 1944 and March 27, 1945, when Peenemünde closed down. Seventy-four percent landed within eighteen miles of the target, and 44 percent within six miles. They were surprisingly accurate, in retrospect, for this was still an experimental weapon. At the end of the war, von Braun and his team were working on both the A-9 and the A-10 rockets—"the America" rockets. The A-9 was, in effect, a jet airplane with wings that would glide for long periods above the atmosphere when its fuel was exhausted; the A-10 was to have 440,000 pounds of thrust and launch the A-9. These were the forerunners of intercontinental ballistic missiles. Launched from sites on the French coast, they were supposed to hit New York. The future was closing in even as the war was winding down.

After surrendering, von Braun and his people first ended up at the White Sands, New Mexico, testing grounds. Von Braun was, he liked to say later, not a POW but a prisoner of peace. The early days at White Sands were hardly easy ones. They were men between countries in terms of loyalty; Germany was gone, but they were not yet Americans. Actually, their real loyalty was not to any nation but to science, and their special vision was little understood by others. They were paid six dollars a day. They were not even allowed to send packages back to Germany. But by 1947 many of the families had arrived, and that year von Braun was allowed to go back to Germany to marry his eighteen-year-old first cousin.

Von Braun quickly found that Germany had been far ahead of the Americans in rocket development. The first American rocket they worked with was a WAC Corporal. It was much smaller than the V-2 and much slower. By 1950, the German team was transferred to the Army rocket center at Huntsville, Alabama. By this time it was clear that their new country would welcome them as citizens. At the same time, they continued to make steady progress. Von Braun dreamed of placing a satellite in space, but that demanded multiple-stage rockets—that is, rockets that launched other rockets to gain even higher altitude and greater speed. In 1949, he and his colleagues used a V-2 to boost a WAC to an altitude of 250 miles.

Von Braun was not merely a brilliant rocket scientist, but a kind of space poet who envisioned manned space flights to the moon and Mars. His most practical thoughts always seemed to others like dreams and fantasies. Years later, in July 1969, on the eve of the Apollo 11 launch of a manned trip to the moon, a news conference was held at which several NASA officials answered questions. Reporters repeatedly asked the officials what the true historic significance of the moon landing was. None of the officials had an answer except von Braun. For him the moon shot was one more major step in human evolution. It was comparable, he said, to the moment when life emerged from the sea and established itself on land.

He liked to tell friends of the excitement he had felt when he looked through his first telescope and saw the moon: "It filled me with a romantic urge. Interplanetary travel! Here was a task worth dedicating one's life to. Not just to stare through a telescope at the moon and the planets, but to soar through the heavens and actually explore the mysterious universe. I knew how Columbus had felt." Much later in his life, after a successful rocket launch, he walked away from the press center at Cape Canaveral and quoted Jules Verne to a friend, for it was Verne who had originally written in some detail about men flying to the moon: "Anything one man can imagine, other men can make real." His vision of what the moon would be like was very clear. Long before man landed there, he described to his biographer, Erik Bergaus, what it would be like: "Shadows and images in the strange nightly sunshine will seem haunted by a sense of loneliness . . ."

There was ambivalence among Americans about men like von Braun, once enemies who now were at the core of our rocket program. At Huntsville there were certain euphemisms with which the German scientists were described: They were called "first-generation Americans" or "former German scientists who are now American citizens." When people seemed to push the issue, General John Medaris liked to emphasize that the Germans were here, "of their own volition." Nonetheless, in the earlier part of the fifties, some of the doubts were still there, and when a movie was made about von Braun's life, *I Aim at the Stars,* Mort Sahl, the comedian, added the line "But sometimes I hit London." Von Braun became in time not merely an American citizen but an enthusiastic American—a fan of the barbecue, a delighted deep-sea diver, a believer in the process of democracy—who added his voice to those advancing the cause of integration in the Huntsville, Alabama, schools.

Von Braun would talk about the period of 1945 through 1951 as a time when we lost six years and had no ballistic missile program to speak of. In 1956, he liked to note, we had gone to a crash ballistic missile. Only as the Russians started working on a missile did our program begin to move ahead. But it was no small irony, as Walter McDougall pointed out, that a team of scientists who had chosen America because of its limitless financial resources was almost from the start saddled with limitations that were primarily financial.

There was no delay in the Soviet missile program. At first, the Soviets had planned to base their nuclear strike force on bombers rather than rockets. But it became clear after the war that the U.S. had allies in Europe on whose territory they could base their bombers, but the Soviets had no such base in the Americas. So Stalin moved to develop missiles and Khrushchev continued the program after Stalin's death in 1953.

In theory at least, the Soviets were not far behind the Germans. They quickly picked up the second tier of German rocket scientists, nuts-and-bolts-men who had the capacity to reproduce the V-2 but lacked theoretical skills. Still the Russians thought space vitally important.

The Russians very soon had their own version of the V-2, though it did not, in the beginning, dramatically change their geopolitical situation. As Georgi Malenkov told Grigory Tokady, a rocket expert and one day a defector, ". . . the point is that the V-2 is good for 400 kilometers and no more. And after all, we have no intention of making war on Poland. Our vital need is for machines which can fly across oceans!" They were not about to waste time: By 1949 they had the T-1, with a range of about five hundred miles, and by 1952 they were working on the T-2. What they wanted was nothing less than an intercontinental ballistic missile.

If the Americans had von Braun, then the Russians had their own great rocket scientist: Sergei Korolev. Korolev was considered by other rocket experts a brilliant designer. He had been born in the Ukraine, and was three years older than von Braun. He had eventually turned to designing, first as an airplane designer in the thirties, when the Soviets seemed to have little interest in space. Gradually, he moved toward missiles and shifted from winged rockets to pure ballistic missiles. He was a protégé of Mikhail Tukhachevsky, who was the leader in Soviet airplane and rocket design. Korolev was arrested in 1937 by Stalin, who was ambivalent about modern weaponry: He was in awe of it, and yet he feared the political ambitions of these unpredictable geniuses who were its architects. With that, Korolev vanished from view. But not from work. He was in a gulag, but a work gulag, a *sharashka.*

There he worked first on airplanes; only later was he transferred to another *sharashka,* where he could work on space. To a Westerner the anomaly of this—a man under a life sentence for treason working in a prison on the most secret scientific developments—is almost too much to comprehend. In the Soviet Union it was an accepted practice. Korolev was immensely valuable, but because he was so valuable, he was also dangerous. He consented to work because this way, at least, he got some rations, he was with his colleagues, and he was doing what he loved most of all. After the war Korolev, still technically a prisoner, was placed in charge of the shipment of what little remained in Peenemünde of the V-2 back to the Soviet Union. He supervised the interviews with the German rocket scientists the Americans had left behind. In 1953, after Stalin's death, he was allowed to join the Party, which he did in order to expedite his work.

If Korolev had to have a title, it would be "chief designer"; if he had to publish, it would be under the pseudonym of Sergeyev. If there were international conferences on space, he was never allowed to attend. By the time he was finally acknowledged as the towering figure of Soviet space, as James Oberg noted, in one of those endless ironies of Russian life, all achievements under Khrushchev were deleted from the history books. He was, not surprisingly, something of a cynical and pessimistic man. His motto, Oberg noted, was, "We will all vanish without a trace."

His vision had dazzled his political superiors. Khrushchev later wrote, "I don't want to exaggerate, but I'd say we gawked at what he showed us as if we were sheep seeing a new gate for the first time. When he showed us one of his rockets, we thought it looked like nothing but a cigar-shaped tube, and we didn't believe it would fly. Korolev took us on a tour of the launching pad and tried to explain how a rocket worked. We were like peasants in a marketplace . . ."

By the mid-fifties the Russians were far advanced on what was their basic rocket of the decade, the R-7. There was nothing very stylish about the R-7. It was, by the standards of rockets, short and fat. Because the Soviet metallurgists had had considerable difficulty developing a metal that could withstand the heat from a giant rocket engine, the R-7 was made up of clusters of smaller engines. There were twenty separate engines in the central cone and four great skirts, but they could bring together a total thrust of 1.1 million pounds. It would be able to carry a primitive atomic weapon of the period all the way to the United States. By 1955, the work toward completing the R-7 was going well enough that Soviet officials began to talk openly about launching an earth satellite during the International Geophysical Year, in 1957–58.

In America our rocket scientists were still working on what was effectively the back burner. It was indicative of how little weight missiles carried in the minds of the policymakers of the Truman administration that K. T. Keller, the president of Chrysler, was appointed Truman's special adviser on missiles; as Walter McDougall points out, he held the job for eleven months, never gave up his job at Chrysler, and never briefed the President on missiles. In the early budget struggles, the B-36 bomber won out over long-range-missile development, and money was poured into the strategic A-Command (SAC).

Years later, when Ike gave his farewell speech warning against the power of a military-industrial complex, he was much heralded; but the truth was that such views were always the bedrock of his philosophy. He was the second

President who had to make difficult choices about complex and expensive weapons systems. He worried about the potential drain on the economy, and he believed that the Joint Chiefs cared little or nothing about the dangers of inflation. He spoke often in private about the danger of spending so much on weaponry and defense and in the process destroying the economy and thus weakening the country these weapons were going to protect. The federal budget, he liked to say, had risen from $4 billion a year in 1932 to $85.5 billion in 1952—with some 57 percent of that increase going to the Pentagon. "This country," he once noted, "can choke itself to death piling up expenditures just as surely as it can defeat itself by not spending enough for protection." Defense spending, he believed quite passionately, was dead weight; it was inflationary and subtracted from the nation's vitality rather than added to it.

. . .

The great American fear in the fifties was of Soviet intentions and capabilities. As Michael Beschloss pointed out, even the Moscow phone book was classified. Hitler's military build-up in the thirties had, because of the nature of armaments and of Germany's physical location, been self-evident, but the Soviet Union was something else. It was both secretive and vast; much of its territory had no possibility of being inspected; it was a veritable black hole for the new uncertain world power across the Atlantic that felt so threatened. We had made our great investment in SAC, the bomber attack fleet that was on constant alert, but the men around Eisenhower still feared a surprise Soviet attack.

. . .

Early photo-reconnaissance attempts to penetrate Soviet airspace with balloons were ineffective. The CIA became particularly worried about missile testing at Kapustin Yar, seventy-five miles east of Stalingrad, far out of the range of aerial surveillance. The need became obvious for some kind of new reconnaissance plane, one that would fly above Soviet air defenses. The photographic technology was already available; by the summer of 1955, the Air Force had the capacity to take a picture from 55,000 feet of Ike's golf ball on a putting green. The great American photographic genius Ed Land, who had invented the Polaroid camera, was absolutely sure the technology was there. In 1954 Philip Strong, a retired Marine general, went out to Burbank, California, to talk with America's most talented airplane designer, Kelly Johnson. "Kelly," he asked. "What would you do if all you were trying to do was get up as high as you could—get moderate speed but not great speed and just sit above their air defense?"

Johnson immediately responded to the challenge. "Jesus," he answered. "I've got just the thing for you—I'd take a Lockheed F-104. I'd give it wings like a tent. It's a cinch!" Johnson drew up plans that called for the plane to fly at an altitude of seventy thousand feet and have a range of some four thousand miles. James Killian, the president of MIT and a principal scientific adviser to the President, and Land went to see the President to convince him of the project's importance. The great question in Eisenhower's mind was whether the intelligence benefits of the flights outweighed the risks of violating Soviet airspace. Otherwise, Eisenhower was interested: Photo reconnaissance had been vital in World War Two, and he had been readily convinced of its tactical value. He was immensely frustrated by how Soviet secrecy fed anxiety in America, causing ever greater pressure on him to spend more and more on potentially useless weapons. To Killian's and Land's surprise, Ike gave tentative approval at the first meeting. His one restriction was that he did not want uniformed Air Force fliers violating Soviet airspace. That meant it would be the CIA's project.

That December Johnson flew to Washington for one more session, to go over cover stories and security. Richard Bissell, deputy director of the CIA, told Johnson that he did not care what the plane looked like as long as they could produce it quickly. That made things easier, for the Air Force traditionally cared about the cosmetic lines of its planes. What we want, said Bissell, is function. "Good," said Johnson. "That will save you a good deal of money. On the other hand I'm going to put my top force on it, and that's going to cost you money." So they bartered with each other, this man of the secret government and this brilliant designer, and in the end they struck a deal—$22 million for twenty planes, with Lockheed permitted to come back for more money if needed.

Each plane was built by hand at the Skunk Works, a secret area of the Lockheed grounds, named after the place in the comic strip "L'il Abner," where Kickapoo Joy Juice was brewed. This particular project was so secret that no janitors were cleared to enter the huge hangar with blacked-out windows where the planes were being built, and therefore the men in charge had to clean up after themselves and worked in constant litter. The code name was Aquatone, although the members of the team generally referred to it as Kelly's plane. Others called it simply The Angel.

Step by step, Johnson argued away the doubts of others. At such high altitudes might the pilot explode or pass out? Johnson said he would invent a pressurized suit to protect the pilot. Wouldn't the fuel evaporate quickly at that height? Johnson was confident a successful fuel could be created. Wouldn't the jet engines fail? Wait and see, he suggested. He was absolutely sure it could be done. The real problem was that the plane needed to stay in the air for perhaps ten hours at a time. This demanded immense amounts of fuel, which in turn created a huge burden of weight. It became, therefore, in the words of one of its early pilots, a young man named Francis Gary Powers, a hybrid, "a jet with the body of a glider." The final product was light, made of titanium and other lightweight metals. It could stay in the air for eleven hours, or 4,750 miles. The only thing ordinary about it was its name; fighters were designated by the letter *F,* bombers had the prefix *B;* but for reasons of secrecy this was called utility plane number two, or as it entered history, the U-2.

For plane aficionados it was a thing of beauty. Its lines were those of a jet, except they were wildly exaggerated; it was so low-slung that when it sat on the runway, its nose was at the height of a man. The fuselage was forty feet long, the wingspan eighty feet. In landing, the pilots had to be extremely careful, for it balanced more like a bicycle than a tricycle. In order to meet Washington's specifications, much had to be sacrificed, and in the case of the spy plane, as Francis Gary noted, "it was strength." "Each piece of structure," he wrote, "was a little thinner than a pilot would have liked. Where there was usually extra support, such as joints and junctures, in the U-2 there was none." It had, Powers said, "a beautiful symmetry all its own but [it was] not built to last." Some of the pilots talked at first about whether it was the world's first disposable plane, a sort of aeronautical Kleenex.

But it could fly at 70,000 feet (soon 80,000) and its cameras could capture the tiniest of objects on the ground some fourteen miles below. Land had created a camera that could swing from horizon to horizon and cover an arc of 750 miles. Most remarkable of all, Kelly Johnson and his people built the prototype from start to finish in only eighty-eight days. The pilots loved it instantly. Every day they were able to break the existing records for altitude: The only problem, Powers later noted, was that they could not boast about it.

Even Charlie Wilson, the great doubter of all things scientific and experimental, was an enthusiast. Generally, Wilson had no interest in the new science of weaponry. He was dubious about missiles and moon shots (he did not need to know if the moon was made of cheese, he liked to say) and he was not worried, as some of the science people around Eisenhower were, about Soviet missile developments. "You'll never convince me that the Russians are ten feet tall," he liked to say when anyone worried aloud about Russian missile progress. But Kelly Johnson took him to the training ground in Nevada and let him watch one of the planes in action. He was put on a radio phone with a pilot who had already been in the air for some eight hours and assured Wilson that he could stay aloft another hour and a half. With that, Wilson came aboard. As they decided to go from prototype to production, the cost of building some thirty planes was placed at $35 million—a bit bulky for the CIA's budget, Allen

Dulles noted. Wilson volunteered to carry a significant part of the costs at Defense, though; money was elaborately laundered so there would be no financial tracks. When Johnson sent in his first two vouchers, the checks, for $1,256,000, were sent not to Lockheed but to Johnson personally at his Encino home.

The pilots had to be very good, but they were not to be flashy and colorful, like the great fighter jockeys of the past; rather they were men of endurance who worked in the shadows, the more anonymous the better. Gary Powers was typical of the pilots recruited for the program. He was not an ace, had not flown in Korea, and it took him more than two years to earn his officer's wings.

He was twenty-six when he was approached with an offer that would more than triple his salary as an Air Force first lieutenant. He was the son of an Appalachian miner who worked as a shoe repairman at night to make enough money to send his one son to a small religious college. Oliver Powers had made one vow: His son would never work in a mine. It was the son's idea to become a pilot instead of the doctor his father wanted him to be. He married Barbara Gay Moore when she was eighteen, the prettiest girl around Turner Air Force Base, in Albany, Georgia. A graduate of a local business college for girls, she was the daughter of the cashier at the PX.

Powers was not political or questioning, and he had no doubts about the mission as it was explained. But because of its secret nature, there was little he could tell his family about this exciting new assignment. Just before he went overseas, his father took him aside and said, "I've figured out what you're doing." "What do you mean?" Powers said. "I've told you what I'm doing." (There was a cover story about flying high-altitude weather reconnaissance.) "No, I've figured it out," his father said. "You're working for the FBI." Powers loved that his plane was his own, a single-seater. The hard part was the pressurization suit: "Once on," he noted, "it felt exactly like a too-tight tie over a badly shrunk collar." Because you couldn't go to the bathroom in it, the pilots could eat little food and drink no coffee while flying.

The suit was so heavy that it made them sweat heavily, and at the end of a long flight, they would wring the water out of their long johns. The job was, as much as anything else, about endurance. Because of the high altitude, before each flight they had to put on their suits and helmets and endure a two-hour denitrogenization process—in which they were given pure oxygen. It left the pilots with fierce headaches and earaches. The one tricky skill required was keeping the plane at just the right speed. At maximum altitude, if you went too slowly the plane stalled, and if you went too quickly, it began to buffet and become unmanageable. There was an automatic pilot, but it was considered unreliable.

In September 1956, Powers made his first flight, along the Soviet border, and by November of that year he was flying deep into Soviet territory. There was an ejector seat in the plane, but Powers, like the other pilots, was wary of it. It was, he wrote, like "sitting on a loaded shotgun." Not only were the pilots uncertain the device would work as designed, they did not entirely trust their sponsors; they suspected that the CIA might have designed it to blow them up so there would be no trace in case of a mishap. Though in fact it was not designed to blow them up, the pilots were well advised to be nervous. The last thing in the world the Agency wanted was that a U-2 pilot be shot down and then survive. Indeed, responding to questions from Eisenhower, Allen Dulles assured the President that a pilot could not survive a crash.

There had been some hope on the part of planners that the planes would fly above Soviet radar, but that proved wrong. From the beginning the Soviets were able to track the flights and they were furious both with the American violation of their airspace and at their own impotence, for they were powerless to shoot the planes down. On July 10, 1957, the Soviets made a formal protest, which contained a rather accurate description of what the U-2 had done and where it had gone. The State Department flatly denied it. John

Foster Dulles himself wrote a letter saying that no *military* plane had violated Soviet space. He called his brother Allen and read it to him, and Allen Dulles told him, "Fine-perfect-good luck!" At the same time the Soviet officials could not go public with what they knew about the U-2 flights, for they could not admit to their own people that they were powerless in the face of such audacious American violations.

The photos from the first flights stunned Eisenhower. Not only could the U-2 take a clear photograph of a parking lot fourteen miles down, but you could even, he said, see "the lines marking the parking areas for individual cars." In terms of intelligence work, it was a breakthrough of gigantic proportion. The photos were better, fuller, and more accurate than anything they had ever seen before. "Photography," said Ray Cline, a senior CIA official, "became to the fifties what code breaking was to the forties." Now Ike could know what the Russians were up to in terms of bomber and missile construction. That ability would allow him to make informed choices about the American defense budget and not get caught up in a useless and unnecessary military buildup.

"I was able to get a look at every blade of grass in the Soviet Union," Allen Dulles boasted later, after it was all over. But the general public did not know it. The U-2 was a classic invention of the secret government and pointed up the problems of a two-tiered government in general. The

intelligence provided by the U-2 was crucial information for the President as he formulated foreign
policy, but he could never reveal it to the voters.
Thus, at a moment when the U-2 was proving just
how limited the Soviet military build up was,
there was no public appreciation of it.

Indeed, one of the first things the U-2 proved
was that there was no bomber gap, as some critics
of the administration had claimed. There had
been a nervousness since Russia's Aviation Day
in 1955, when a squadron of Bison bombers had
flown over the parade, followed by several other
squadrons. The U-2 revealed that what the Soviets had almost surely done that day was flown the
same few squadrons in repeated sorties. As for the
missile gap, the U-2 showed that though the Soviets were working on their missiles, they had yet to
launch an ICBM.

. . .

By the summer of 1956, von Braun was absolutely certain that the Soviets were planning to
launch a satellite. Von Braun was completely confident that he and his colleagues could do it, too,
if they could only get the go-ahead from Washington. But if von Braun dreamed of men in space,
his nemesis, Charlie Wilson, dreamed of orderly
figures and balanced budgets and of tidy weapons
systems that he already understood. In early 1956
Wilson had arrived in Huntsville to look over the
Army rocket program, and he had seemed a great
deal less interested in that than in the old farm-

house near the base that officials had turned into a guesthouse. How much had this cost? Why had they painted these logs? (The logs, Major General John Medaris, the local commander, noted, were cedar logs and had not been painted.) Wilson clearly believed that Medaris and his rocket scientists were living the high life. From then on there was not, as Medaris hoped, greater interest in what von Braun and his team were doing, but merely more intense harassment by Army controllers. We had, Medaris believed quite rightly, the greatest space engineers and scientists in the world and we were doing almost nothing with them; to pay so little attention to the work of someone like von Braun was almost sinful.

For most of the decade, von Braun and his colleagues worked on the most important American rocket of the decade—the Redstone. It was not unlike the old V-2, only larger and more powerful—fifty-six feet long, and seventy inches in diameter. If it was more a hybrid than thoroughbred, that was a reflection that its architects were working with less money and fewer resources than they should have. Still, it was a rocket that von Braun and his people were proud of: It could, von Braun believed, readily launch the first of several of his dream projects—an earth satellite—by 1956. A report he prepared in 1954, entitled "A Minimum Satellite Vehicle," requested only $100,000 for the satellite program, pointing out, "It is only logical to assume that other countries could do the same. *It would be a blow to U.S. Prestige if we did not do it first"* (italics in the original).

Suddenly now, with the International Geophysical Year coming up, there was renewed interest in the missile program. The Americans planned to launch a satellite as part of it. Nor were they alone. The Soviets were beginning to talk ever more confidently about a satellite as well. For the race into space was now on. The Soviets, weak in other areas of modern weaponry, were working at a fever pitch and the Soviet leadership understood, as the more confident American leadership did not, the psychological nature of the race. Asked in 1954 whether he worried over whether the Russians might win the race to place a satellite in orbit, Charlie Wilson said, "I wouldn't care if they did."

But now Eisenhower understood the real value of getting a satellite up: photo reconnaissance. Predictably, the various branches of the military began to jockey for the honor of launching the satellite, even though there was no doubt that von Braun and his Army team were far ahead of everyone else. The Navy offered its Viking project—a generous description was that it was in the experimental stage. But for reasons that were absurd to the detached observer, a civilian team under the auspices of the Secretary of Defense chose the Navy. Thus did the United States pin its hopes, as historian Walter McDougall noted, "on a slim experimental first-stage rocket and three entirely new upper stages, expected to coax a grapefruit-sized satellite to orbital velocity before the end of 1958." "In retrospect," added McDougall, "the decision seems disastrous." Dr. Homer Stewart, the head of the committee and a physicist at Caltech, told von Braun immediately after the vote: "We have pulled a real boner." Von Braun was absolutely appalled by the decision.

The Army people protested bitterly, but to no avail. If anything, von Braun's superiors set out to hinder him. He launched his Jupiter C on September 20, 1956. It was to be a four-stage rocket, but the fourth stage, to von Braun's bitter disappointment, could not, under orders, be a live satellite. The Army, wary that von Braun might pull some sort of trick, made sure that the fourth stage was filled with sand. The launch was a stunning success. It reached a record altitude of 682 miles and a speed of 13,000 miles per hour, which probably would have been sufficient to hurl a satellite into space. The next morning von Braun confided, "We knew with a little bit of luck we could put a satellite in space. Unfortunately, no one asked us to do it."

At the same time the Navy program was running into serious problems, just as von Braun had suspected it would. It was no small thing, von Braun knew, to design a rocket from scratch. The Viking's guidance system kept gaining weight, despite the plans on the drawing board. Meanwhile, to anyone paying attention, there was growing confidence, indeed audaciousness, in the Soviet press. In May 1957 an announcement from the Soviet Academy of Science told Soviet citizens to prepare to track the satellite. A month later a trade publication gave ham radio operators detailed instructions on the course the satellite would take. On August 3, 1957, an R-7 was successfully launched. It did not carry a satellite, but the Soviets were clearly on the verge of a major success. On August 26, 1957, Khrushchev announced that "a super long-distance intercontinental multistage ballistic missile was launched a few days ago."

By the first week in October 1957, Walter Sullivan, *The New York Times* science reporter, had heard enough to go to the paper's Washington bureau and file a notice that he would write a story for the Saturday paper reporting that the Russians would launch a satellite at any moment. His story was never published, for it was overtaken by events. On the morning of October 4, the Soviets launched an intercontinental ballistic missile. By chance that evening, Sullivan attended a cocktail party at the Russian embassy in Washington for some fifty international scientists at the IGY conference. Sullivan was called to the phone and his office told him there was a wire-service report from Moscow that the Russians had placed a satellite in space. Sullivan whispered the news to American scientist Lloyd Berkner, who called for attention. "I am informed by *The New York Times* that a satellite is in orbit at an elevation of 900 kilometers. I wish to congratulate our Soviet colleagues on their achievement." Applause broke out in the room. The Soviet satellite was a relatively small aluminum alloy sphere that weighed 184 pounds and was 22.8 inches in diameter. It had two radio transmitters. The Russians called it *Sputnik,* which means "fellow traveler" in Russian.

No one in the Eisenhower administration, despite all the warnings, was prepared. Even worse, and this was almost surely generational, none of the senior men even saw at first what a psychological victory it was for the Soviets. Defense secretary Engine Charlie Wilson, who had an almost perfect instinct to say the wrong thing at the wrong time, called *Sputnik* "a useless hunk of iron." Sherman Adams, Ike's closest personal assistant in the White House, said that America was not interested in getting caught up "in an outerspace basketball game." Clarence Randall, who was a White House adviser, called it "a silly bauble in the sky." Eisenhower himself was pounded with questions at his next press conference, on October 9. Merriman Smith began by asking, "Russia has launched an earth satellite. They also claim to have had a successful firing of an intercontinental ballistic missile, none of which this country has done. I ask you, sir, what are we going to do about it?" Eisenhower answered that there was no link between having *Sputnik* and an ICBM, although the Soviet success certainly showed that they could hurl an object a great distance. Moreover, he added, there had never been a race to get into space first. Nor did *Sputnik* prove that an ICBM could hit a target. But the questions kept coming. Finally, Hazel Markel of NBC asked, "Mr. President, in light of the great faith which the American people have in your military knowledge and leadership, are you saying that at this time with the Russian satellite whirling around the world, you are not more concerned nor overly concerned about our nation's security?" The President sought to calm such fears: "As far as the satellite is concerned, that does not raise my apprehensions, not one iota. I can see nothing at this moment, at this stage of development, that is significant in that development as far as security is concerned," he said. Thanks to the U-2 photographs, he had good reason for confidence; unfortunately, he could not share the evidence with the country.

But the younger men in the administration—Nixon, Cabot Lodge, Nelson Rockefeller—understood immediately the propaganda value of *Sputnik*. They knew that in the age of atomic weapons, any kind of scientific breakthrough on the part of the Soviets was seen as a threat. Percival Brundage, the director of the budget, went to a dinner party and said that *Sputnik* would be forgotten in six months. "Yes, dear," answered his dinner companion, the famed hostess Perle Mesta. "And in six months we may all be dead."

The success of *Sputnik* seemed to herald a kind of technological Pearl Harbor, which in fact was exactly what Edward Teller called it. A Democratic legislative aide wrote a paper for Lyndon Johnson showing him that this issue could take him to the White House. (He was wrong.) Some saw it as a rebuke to America's material self-indulgence. Johnson seized on a metaphor of Detroit and American affluence and complacency: "It is not very reassuring to be told that next year we will put a better satellite in the air. Perhaps it will even have chrome trim and automatic windshield wipers." Suddenly, it seemed as if America were undergoing a national crisis of confidence. Admiral Hyman Rickover criticized the American school system. A book called *Why Johnny Can't Read—and What You Can Do About It,* which had appeared two years earlier to little attention, suddenly became a smash best-seller. The president of Harvard, Nathan Pusey, was moved to declare that a greater percentage of the GNP should go to education.

It was a shattering moment. *Life* magazine printed an article called "Arguing the Case for Being Panicky." John Foster Dulles, defying logic and the facts, noted that the Soviets had had an advantage because of their capture of German scientists. *Sputnik* jokes abounded: A *Sputnik* cocktail was two parts vodka, one part sour grapes. One critic noted that as *Sputnik* went over the White House, it said, "Beep, beep, I like Ike, I like Ike."

The Soviets could not resist the temptation to gloat. Their leaders saw it as a victory over American materialism. At an international conference in Barcelona, Soviet space scientist Leonid Sedov told an American: "You Americans have a better standard of living than we have. But the American loves his car, his refrigerator, his house. He does not, as we Russians do, love his country." Khrushchev had a visceral sense of the impact of *Sputnik* on ordinary people, how terrifying and awesome it seemed. The Soviets, he boasted, could do this anytime. They would produce rockets like this by the dozens—"like sausages." When the Americans finally launched a satellite, he belittled it (although in scientific terms it was considerably more impressive than the Soviets'). The American satellites were small, like oranges, he said. The Americans would have to hurl many oranges into space to catch up with the Soviet people. Space became Khrushchev's newest propaganda weapon. In public he glorified not the scientists but the cosmonauts. They were his space children, "celestial brothers" of the Soviet people; he was their "space father."

The day *Sputnik* was launched, Neil McElroy, who was soon to replace Wilson as secretary of defense, was visiting Huntsville by chance with some of his top aides. They were touring the facilities when they heard the news. All von Braun's frustrations exploded: "We knew they were going to do it!" Then he added, "Vanguard will never make it. We have the hardware on the shelf. We can put a satellite up in sixty days." When McElroy left, von Braun, for the first time in months, seemed confident about the future of his program again. "They'll call me soon," he thought. "McElroy will give me the green light soon. He doesn't have any alternative." It took a month. On November 8, McElroy sent a telegram asking them to launch two satellites.

Soon there was *Sputnik II*. Launched on November 3, 1957, it weighed 1,120.29 pounds, some six times more than its predecessor, its orbit was even higher, and it carried a small dog, Laika. Clearly, the Soviets intended to put a man in space soon. It was another psychological triumph. But the worst was still to come. Jim Hagerty, Ike's press secretary, had announced right after *Sputnik* that the Navy team planned to put a satellite in orbit very soon. Hagerty's announcement stunned the Navy.

But the Navy team speeded up its schedule. Smarting from the Soviet success, the White House not only announced the launch but in effect showcased it as a major media event. On the day of the launch, there was talk of delaying because of high winds, but gradually they died down and the decision was made to go ahead. The countdown finished, and in the words of Kurt

Stehling, a German engineer, "It seemed as if the gates of hell had opened up. Brilliant stiletto flames shot out from the side of the rocket near the engine. The vehicle agonizingly hesitated for a moment, quivered again, and in front of our un-believing, shocked eyes, began to topple. It sank like a great flaming sword into scabbard down into the blast tube. It toppled slowly, breaking apart, hitting part of the test guard and ground with a tremendous roar that could be felt and heard even behind the two-foot concrete wall of the blockhouse and the six-inch bulletproof glass. For a moment or two there was complete disbe-lief. I could see it in the faces. I could feel it myself. This just couldn't be. . . . The fire died down and we saw America's supposed response to the 200-pound Soviet satellite—our four-pound grape-fruit—lying amid the scattered glowing debris, still beeping away, unharmed."

"U.S. Calls It Kaputnik," chuckled the *London Daily Express.* "Oh, What a Flopnik!" head-lined the *Daily Herald.* "Phut Goes U.S. Satellite," said the *Daily Mail.* It was a "Stayput-nik," said another paper. Again the Soviets gloated. A prominent Soviet clown named Karan-dash (the Pencil) went into the arena with a small balloon. The balloon exploded. His assistant asked what it was. "That was *Sputnik,*" he said. The audience gasped. "The American *Sputnik,*" he added to great cheers.

So von Braun's team was left to recoup

American prestige. Hopes were pinned on Missile #29. The date chosen for the launch was January 29, 1958. There was to be no premature publicity. The rocket was checked out at night so that newsmen would not catch on. The early part of the countdown went well, but the weather report was bad. They decided to delay the launch. Kurt Debus began to worry that the fuel in the rocket might start corroding the tanks. By January 31 he was pleading to launch.

Finally, everything seemed to come together. With some one hundred reporters in the grandstand, the launch took place at 10:47:56 P.M. They knew immediately it was a good one. Everything seemed to work perfectly. At six minutes and fifty seconds into the flight, the final rocket, or kick stage, ignited and burned for six seconds and hurled the satellite into space. Von Braun was at the Pentagon with Army officials, including Wilbur Brucker, secretary of the Army, and William Pickering, the head of the Jet Propulsion Laboratory. The minutes seemed interminable as they waited for some hard confirmation of the orbit. No one wanted to call the President until it was a sure thing. The satellite was, by von Braun's calculations, supposed to pass the Pasadena tracking station at 12:41 Eastern time. At 12:40 they queried Pasadena. Had it heard anything? Nothing yet. At 12:43, the tension ever greater, they queried Pasadena again. Had it heard anything. "Negative," came back the answer. "Well, why the hell don't you hear anything?" asked Pickering. Brucker was nervous. "Wernher," he asked von Braun. "What happened?" Von Braun was sweating. Pickering, on the phone to Pasadena, yelled out, "They hear her, Wernher, they hear her." Von Braun looked at his watch. "She is eight minutes late," he said. "Interesting." Finally, Hagerty was allowed to call Eisenhower and tell him. "That's wonderful," he said. "I surely feel a lot better now." Then he paused and considered things. "Let's not make too great a hullabaloo about this," he added. America, after some significant and quite unnecessary humiliations, was finally in the space race.

FORTY-TWO

T ELEVISION WAS turning out to be a magic machine for selling products, and the awareness of that was still dawning on Madison Avenue in the late 1950s. Yet the ad men had already discovered that television favored certain products and could sell them more readily: beer, cigarettes, various patent medicines and, above all, such big-ticket items as cars. No company spent more money on advertising or advertised its products better, as the country was riding the crest of that great economic wave, than GM.

Kensinger Jones, a young man in the advertising department of the Leo Burnett Company in Chicago, saw an ad in the industry journal *Advertising Age* around the middle of 1957—an unidentified company was looking for a television creative director to handle the world's largest account. Jones was immediately interested. He had worked at the Burnett company for some five years and had done well there, but he felt that it, like most advertising companies of the period, was still too print-oriented. As far as Jones could tell, it was a generational thing. He believed all the top people at all the top agencies had made their reputations by handling words—words were what they understood and responded to. Television made them uneasy. Some of them looked down on it; some of them feared it. Few of them seemed to realize the extent to which it had already changed their own industry. Even when they used it and thought they were using it well, Ken Jones thought, they didn't fully exploit its greatest strength: images. Instead, they did what they knew how to do best—employ words. As far as Jones was concerned, television was the dog and print was the tail, and the generation that dominated the ad agencies was letting the tail wag the dog. Leo Burnett himself seemed to realize he had to adapt to television, but he couldn't quite force himself to do it fully.

Jones especially liked the freedom offered in the early days of television commercials, when budgets were small and almost everything was done live. There were no rules and no one could tell you what you were not allowed to do. He had done one set of live commercials for a new pop-cap bottle for Pabst Blue Ribbon. It was seemingly simple: a flick of the thumb, and the cap was supposed to come flying off—except that it did not always work. Jones learned how to cut away quickly to something else—the continuation of the program, or another commercial—and then to come back when the cap was off. For the Green Giant vegetables, a major Burnett account, Jones helped create a huge puppet of the Jolly Green Giant. It was about two and a half feet tall, and he thought it was going to charm hundreds of thousands of young children. Jones was very pleased with himself and thought he had taken a giant step forward for the visual arts. But when the puppet Giant premiered, it was an absolute disaster. It lurched at the camera, like a Frankensteinian monster, frightening thousands of children. There were endless phone calls to the studio that day demanding that they get that awful thing off the air. Jones had learned a great deal in his experimental period, and he was confident he knew, as few others did, how to sell a product visually. In particular, he was pleased with a commercial he had done for Campbell's tomato juice in which he had used time-lapse photography to show the life of a tomato as it grew into one of the lucky vegetables chosen for the honor of being in Campbell's tomato juice.

Intrigued by the notice in *Ad Age,* Jones responded. The world's largest account had to be Chevy, he was certain. He was right: It was Chevy, and it was handled by the Detroit firm of Campbell Ewald. He was called in for an interview, and the Ewald and General Motors people liked what they saw in him. He might be a television man, a relatively unpredictable breed as far as they were concerned, but he was a good son of the Midwest—born in St. Louis, educated at Washington University of St. Louis, and currently working in Chicago at Burnett, which fancied itself a bastion of Midwestern values in a profession dominated by Eastern and Californian elitism and snobbery. As such, he was not a man likely to look down on either cars or Detroit. Jones was thrilled when the job was offered to him; he liked the big budget—around $1 million. It was an amazing figure for the time; it meant that on a given commercial he could spend as much as $70,000 in production costs. In addition, Chevy's commitment to television advertising was imposing. Jones was soon in charge of spending some $90 million annually, and there were times when Chevy sponsored three major network shows—*My Three Sons* on ABC; *Route 66* on CBS; and *Bonanza* on NBC.

If Jones had thought people were a little slow to pick up on the uses of television at Burnett, that was no longer a problem at Chevy. In addition, he liked the openness and directness of the top professional people at Chevrolet, especially Ed Cole. Ed Cole, he thought, would not dream of telling him how to make a commercial. Instead, Cole's only marching orders were to make good commercials. Cole thought Chevy was making the best cars in its history, and he thought if the advertising men made commercials that were as good as his cars, the company would sell even more cars.

What Ken Jones wanted to do was use this new medium to tell stories visually and to minimize words. If there was to be storytelling, then let the camera do it. By coincidence, at almost the same time he went to Campbell Ewald, a friend of his named Bob Lawrence, who ran a small production company in New York, sent him some experimental films. They had been made independently by a cinematographer in Los Angeles named Gerry Schnitzer. When Ken Jones saw the films he was stunned: What Schnitzer had been doing on his own, with very little money, was exactly what he was looking for. Schnitzer's stories were short and arresting, and in some way they reflected the essence of American life. They were the work of an original and very gifted man. One of them showed a mailman making his rounds, coming upon a hopscotch board and, when he thought no one was looking, playing a secret game of hopscotch. In another, Schnitzer had waited by a drawbridge and caught the idle moments of people in their cars as the bridge was up and their lives were momentarily interrupted. In another film, he had quietly staked out a scene in Los Angeles where an older and obviously quite poor Mexican-American man was trying to sell a cocker spaniel puppy with a rope around its neck. A father, mother, and young daughter drove up and negotiated with the man, but they failed to make a deal and drove off. Then a little while later, obviously in response to the pleas of the child, the family came back and completed the deal. The simplicity of the scene was powerful.

Ken Jones saw those small stories and knew he had found his man—someone who could tell a story with a camera, used no narration, and had a vision of America that reminded Jones of Norman Rockwell's. He got in touch with Gerry Schnitzer immediately. Schnitzer had grown up in Brooklyn and gone to Dartmouth intending to be a writer, but had found much to his surprise that he liked using a camera better than a typewriter. He had written and directed some of the early *Bowery Boys* films and made some small films about the Canadian fishing and lumber industries for the Canadian Film Board. Eventually, he moved to California and continued making small, highly original films that contained no dialogue. Commercial success had largely eluded him, in no small part because he had not actively sought it. Someone had used his films for children in remedial reading and writing classes. Here, children who were nominally loath to express themselves verbally, saw his films and were encouraged, perhaps by the lack of narration, to talk about what they had just seen. At the very least, that was a sign that he was touching an audience normally resistant to most traditional forms of communication. Schnitzer, in those days, was getting by on a very small amount of money, and no one on Madison Avenue seemed to have any interest in his work. Someone had sent him to meet Max Wylie, the creative director at one of the major New York firms, and Wylie, Schnitzer thought, had not only rejected his work but treated him with great contempt. In fact, Wylie had told Schnitzer he knew nothing about storytelling. "They're very pretty," Wylie had said, "but they're not really stories, are they? I mean, where are the words? Where is the story line? I'm afraid we can't sell tobacco with work like this." Then Schnitzer got a call from Ken Jones, who proposed they work together.

Schnitzer agreed, but he knew that he was going to be walking a very fine line between his art on one hand and commerce on the other. That meant he had to be very tight in his storytelling. There could be no ambiguities. The theme had to be very sharply focused, and there was to be no doubt when the commercial was over what the point of it was: to sell cars. Years later, he noted, though, that he and Jones were not selling cars but dreams.

The first commercial Schnitzer shot with Jones was for the 1958 Chevrolet. Jones deferred to Schnitzer's instinct for the right story. Schnitzer had thought about it. He wanted something that was basic to ordinary American life, something that touched every home and reflected a rite of passage to which Chevy could be connected. In the end he came up with a very simple idea. "How about a family at graduation time?" Schnitzer asked Jones. That was it, they agreed. So the commercial was shot at two minutes in length—then, and now, a lifetime as far as commercials were concerned.

It featured an unbelievably wholesome

young blond teenager, a Tab Hunter lookalike, clearly soon to leave high school and go on to college and the right fraternity. It is prom night, and as the commercial begins, he is a little disorganized and running behind time. As he rushed out in his white dinner jacket, his family gathers at the door. They are immediately recognizable: a likeable, wise, and good-natured dad; a pleasant (but somewhat more severe) mom; and a younger sister, with the obvious look of a tomboy. There is a sense that they are sharing a secret, but it is a little hard to tell at first. This is all done deftly in mime, as Schnitzer wanted, with no sales pitch. The music in the background is the Chevy fight song of the period: "See the U.S.A. in Your Chevrolet," and it is played in a Les Paul/Mary Ford style, to show that Chevy is hip. The boy leaves the house and heads to his jalopy, which is an American classic of the period, painted with folksy teenage mottos: ENTRANCE, it says on the front door, and GO ƧLOW on top, clearly an all-American car. As the boy heads toward his car, we see his eyes catch something else—another car parked in front of the house. We see his surprise. It is a brand-new Chevy convertible, with the top down. For the first time, the announcer speaks: "If it's happened once, it's happened a thousand times." The boy stops, looks at the new car, and then turns and looks back at the front door of his house, where the rest of his family is standing. The audience senses that there is a secret between Dad and Sis. Back and forth go the looks—boy to family, boy to new convertible. Finally, Dad smiles and reaches into his pocket for a set of keys. The boy rushes to get them, races to the convertible, and is about to drive off when he realizes he has forgotten something. The corsage is in the old jalopy. He gets the corsage and picks up his girlfriend, one well worthy of the car (the actress Shirley Knight, in one of her first roles). It is all clear: This is a great kid, a great family, a great car. Just to be sure, lest we may not have gotten it, the announcer says: "What a gal! What a night! What a car! The new Chevrolet!" When Jones and Schnitzer screened it for the first time, Jones knew he had a winner when the advertising manager of Chevy broke into tears and said, "It's perfect—it makes me think of my oldest son."

Among other things, the commercial signaled that a new, more affluent era was coming, even for teenagers. The age of the jalopy was over, it seemed to say, the age of tinkering and patching done with it. Dads from now on had better give their sons and daughters something worthwhile, *something brand-new,* when they graduated from high school. A new era was being announced and sold in a very new way.

The next major commercial the two men did together took place in the fall of 1958 and was known as the "Family Shopping Tour." It was very specifically designed to attack the almost un-American idea of not trading in for a new car and instead trying to squeeze an additional year or two out of an old model. The economy had hit a soft patch that year; people were perhaps thinking of keeping their cars a little longer than in the past. The selling theme addressed this problem. It begins with a shot of a father and a son passing a Chevrolet window. Inside the showroom, a salesman is showing a 1959 station wagon to another family. The camera closes to a little girl hanging out the rear window of the new station wagon. She makes a face and sticks her tongue out at the boy, who is watching from the street. The salesman sees her and does a double-take, then smiles. The boy and the father keep looking at the station wagon. The camera picks up the byplay between the boy and the girl. Then the camera picks up the boy's mother (and the man's wife) carrying a load of groceries to an old car. She puts the groceries in the front seat and closes the door with considerable difficulty—she has to slam it three times before it catches. Then she casts a disapproving look at her husband's interest in the auto showroom. He makes things worse by pointing to the new Chevy wagon. She is not pleased. Clearly, they have had arguments about a new car before, and she has held the line against spending. Just then the door of the old car slips open and the groceries tumble out, including a bunch of oranges. The camera closes on one orange as it tumbles down the street, follows it, and by the time the orange finishes its roll, it has turned into the mother, father, and little boy, now inside the showroom, where the salesman is working on them. Mom gets into the station wagon and slams the door. It catches immediately. She smiles. The next shot is of the family on the road, all of them smiling heartily. The announcer says: "Fun to see. Fun to drive. Fun to buy. The new Chevrolet." There were others to come—a driverless Chevy going through the streets of Paris as the style-conscious Parisians gape at it; a Chevy on the top of a mountain in southern Utah; and an airline pilot saying "My God, there's a car on that rock."

A few years later, after a string of remarkable successes, Jones and Schnitzer found that the Chevrolet management started to interfere, calling for more narration extolling the cars' virtues. Schnitzer thought it was because the corporate people "understood everything but the dreams." Some thirty years later, he pondered the reasons for the success of his early Chevy commercials and decided that it had to do with capturing the dreams and ambitions of ordinary families—*always,* he noted, *a family.*

· · ·

As the cars were becoming more powerful all the time, the men running the company were becoming blander and the power of the financial men was growing. Ed Cole was becoming very much the exception. Central headquarters was growing ever more powerful at the expense of the divisions. For many GM people the critical moment came in 1958, when Frederic Donner became president. Donner's roots were in accounting but, unlike Harlow Curtice, who had also been an accountant, Donner was a man who gave off a sense of being interested only in numbers. When he traveled around the company, he was known to ask of the younger GM employees, "How much are we paying that young man?" His general reputation was for being shy and extremely private. He denied that: "I am not taciturn. I am not shy. I am not afraid of people and I don't even own a slide rule." His efforts at public relations, both inside and outside the company, were marginal: When Bob Dietch, the business editor of the Scripps-Howard chain asked for an interview with Donner as part of a series he was doing on the ten most influential businessmen in America, Donner at first refused. Dietch then said he would simply leave Donner off the list, and the latter changed his mind. The interview did not get off to a good start. "It's very nice of you to give me the time," Dietch said at the beginning. "Yes, I agree with that," said Donner, quite deadpan. "I think it's very nice of me too."

His ascent was a reflection of the changes at the company. At the daily meeting with the heads of the divisions, Fred Donner kept talking about the stock, about what the stock analysts in New York said about it. For Bunkie Knudsen, then the head of the Pontiac division, talk like this was downright sacrilegious. There had *never* been talk of the stock price at these meetings in the past. It was perfectly proper for the head of a company to talk about the need for profits, even the need to maximize profits, but to talk about driving the stock up and to talk about what Wall Street analysts thought of the company, he believed, was unthinkable. In the old days there had been a simple concept: The people in Detroit had to make good cars, and if they did, the people in New York would take care of the stock.

Donner's talk signaled something ominous to Knudsen: a profound change in the purpose of the corporation. It meant that profit, rather than the quality of the product, was now the objective of the corporation, and it meant, though few realized it at the time, that there would be an inevitable decline in the power of the engineering and manufacturing departments. It also signaled an even greater decline in the willingness of the corporation to experiment with new technology (each new development added costs to a car), and finally, it would lead to an unswerving drive to make the divisions as homogenous as possible, so that the same pins and screws and nuts and bolts and body shells could be used in each division. For a profound metamorphosis was taking place in America's largest and biggest industrial companies: the rise of financial experts over product men. It was a sure sign that these companies, unconsciously at least, believed that they were de facto monopolies and faced no real competitive challenges anymore. Rather, their only real concern was to maximize the profits that now seemed to be permanently theirs and to drive the stock up.

Bunkie Knudsen did not understand all of the ramifications of this, but he knew that something was terribly wrong. What begot greater performance on Wall Street did not necessarily mean greater performance in terms of autos; what was good for Wall Street was not, regrettably, always good for General Motors. When the meetings with Donner were over, Bunkie Knudsen could not go off and have lunch with any of his colleagues. Instead, he would go down to the Detroit Athletic Club and work out furiously to burn off his anger. Knudsen couldn't have seen it then, but the issue he was so upset about was nothing less than the entire purpose of American industry, whether it was to make the best product possible or whether it was merely to make the maximum profit possible each year. The two, it turned out, were not mutually compatible—not by a long shot. All of this placed the corporation in jeopardy.

The first shot across GM's bow was a small import whose makers rejected all the norms that were regarded as sacred in Detroit. It was smaller than most American cars—*much* smaller. It did not offer more power, more options, more luxury; it offered decidedly less. The "Bug," or "Beetle," as it was dubbed almost immediately, did not promise that next year's model would be hotter and sexier; in fact just the opposite was true—next year's model would be very much the same as this year's. This last was a basic repudiation of Mr. Sloan's philosophy, based as it was on the annual model change. In fact, the Volkswagen was so different from anything Detroit offered that it seemed to be immune to criticism. And there were advantages: It was cheap; it was reliable; it was fun; and because there were no model changes, repairmen always had an excellent inventory of parts and knew exactly what to do with them to fix the car should anything go wrong.

Volkswagen had placed a high priority on creating a strong service department and had sent its best mechanics to teach the American mechanics how to service a car whose problems were, given the nature of the car, quite simple. As such it got high marks from the start from customers for service, an area in which Detroit was just beginning to slip. Lack of spare parts had signaled the death knell for many other foreign imports. It was a no-frills approach; Volkswagen did not even do any serious advertising until 1959, because its executives in America believed in word-of-mouth advertising. Therefore, they felt that whatever extra money the car generated could be better spent on good service rather than on something as frivolous as advertising.

The Beetle was the dream of Ferdinand Porsche, the great German automotive genius who wanted to create a German version of the

Model T, a car for ordinary workers. Porsche had been a great admirer of the first Henry Ford, and he had made a trip to America in 1937 to tour American factories. He was greatly impressed by the production lines and the confidence and life-styles of the workers. He had met with his hero Ford, and they spoke at great length of his desire to produce a comparable car in Germany. Did that bother Ford? he asked. No, answered the great industrialist. "If anyone can build a car better or cheaper than I can, that serves me right."

For a time before the war, Hitler had backed Porsche in his idea of a people's car—a "Volksauto" in German. But the car and its prospective buyers were overtaken by events, and the company never put the car into production. At the end of the war, no one knew quite what to do with the Volksauto plant; it was offered to various major auto companies, none of which was interested. In March 1948, it was offered to the Ford Company at a meeting attended by the young and inexperienced Henry Ford II, who had just taken over a nearly bankrupt company, and the actual head of the company, Ernie Breech, then chairman of the board. Ford, who still deferred to Breech, asked his chairman what he thought of it. "Mr. Ford, I don't think what we're being offered here is worth a damn," Breech answered. With that the Wolfsburg plant was turned over to an exceptional man named Heinz Nordhoff, who not only rescued it but made it the premier symbol of Germany's industrial rebirth. His car, remarkably like Porsche's original design, was the perfect vehicle for a nation struggling to rebuild itself after a cataclysmic war. When Porsche eventually saw the production line, at that point producing 90,000 vehicles a year, he said, "Yes, Herr Nordhoff, that's how I always imagined it."

Nordhoff was a brilliant businessman. He knew immediately that he had to cut production time from 400 man-hours per car to 100, which he did, and he knew he needed better materials. He understood that the pride and commitment of his workers was of paramount importance, and he got rid of a sign in the parking lot that said BRITISH OFFICERS ONLY. What Nordoff needed was hard currency so that he could improve both his workplace and the quality of his cars. The only way to get it was to sell in the United States.

The Beetle's first venture to the land of the automotive giants was a good deal less than a complete success. Sensitive to postwar anti-German feelings, the company sent its first car to America in 1949 in the care of a Dutch salesman named Ben Pon. He had won the honor of bringing the Beetle to America by dint of his considerable success in selling it in Holland, where anti-German feeling was still very powerful. Pon brought one car to the States with him in January 1949 and ran into complete rejection. No American dealer would take him seriously. Pon did not get a lot of media attention and in the stories he did receive, the car tended to be referred to as Hitler's car. In the end he was forced to sell his one model to a dealer for $800 to cover his hotel bill. It was not, however, a permanent defeat. The next year, 1950, some 330 Volkswagens were sold in America. They seeped into the country, brought back by returning servicemen, who had picked them up in Europe. Gradually, a fragile dealer network was being created. But very quietly, relying as much as anything on word of mouth, the Beetle became a success. It happened because the car was everything it was said to be. By 1955 it was selling some 30,000 vehicles; by 1957, some 79,000.

Detroit from the start quite predictably treated the phenomenon of the Beetle with contempt. It was in the immortal words of Henry Ford II, "a little shit box." It lacked power, it lacked size, and it lacked style. It was two feet shorter than the smallest Chevy of its time, and its 1300cc engine seemed an insult to the colossal engines Detroit was producing. The car was not particularly comfortable and the early models lacked even a gas gauge. It was a work of minimalist but very sound engineering. Some of Detroit's engineers, however, were impressed from the start, because it is in the nature of engineers to be minimalists, to seek the most production for the least amount of input. That most basic of engineering values had become virtual heresy in Detroit after Kettering's high-octane gas had created the idea of power as an end in itself, accompanied by the waste of power and fuel. In 1956, Arthur Railton, writing in *Popular Mechanics,* said of the VW: "The Volkswagen sells because it is, more than anything else, an honest car. It doesn't pretend to be anything it is not. Being an honest piece of machinery, it is one the owner can be proud of. Wherever he looks, he sees honest design and workmanship. There are no places where parts don't fit, where paint is thin, where the trim is shoddy. There are no body rattles, no water leaks. Neither, of course, is there overstuff, false luxury either. There is nothing about the car that is not sincere. One cannot imagine, for instance, a Volkswagen with a fake air scoop or tail fins to make it look like an airplane in flight."

To the degree that Detroit took the VW seriously, it was pleased because it ended the pressure to build a small low-performance car, which industry critics had been demanding since the end of the war. Detroit, therefore, for a surprisingly long time, was happy to have the VW at the low end of the line, costing only $1,280, to take care of people it regarded as cranks—all those college professors, rocket engineers, and architects who could afford to pay more but were content to pay less. It was, after all, good basic transportation, the perfect second car, particularly for Americans who took their self-definition from something other than their cars. There was on the part of Detroit's top people a certain amount of irritation with those who could easily have afforded larger, more expensive cars and were shirking their civic duty as Americans by buying the Beetle. "Gray flannel non-conformists," one Detroit executive called them. Because it took up little space, it was easy to park in increasingly crowded urban environments. That its owners represented a more significant part of the market than their sheer numbers indicated, that the people themselves were tastemakers, that by their education and self-confidence they were making decisions more independently than average American consumers, did not register quickly in Detroit. But when it did, Detroit sat up and took notice.

The growing success of the Volkswagen eventually convinced General Motors that it would have to offer something competitive to protect the low end of the market. Somewhat reluctantly, GM gave the go-ahead on a small rear-end-engine car to the one person who truly hungered to do it: Ed Cole. By 1956, he was the general manager of Chevrolet, and what he envisioned was nothing less than a car that was totally new in its engineering and styling—in effect a faster, more high-powered, thoroughly Americanized Volkswagen. Almost as soon as he became general manager of Chevy, Cole set out to plan his small car. This time, however, unlike the earlier crash programs when he created the '55 Chevy, he did not have the full force of the corporation behind him. Quite the contrary. From the

start Cole encountered the old wariness about
doing a small car, particularly a new car that
would have to be completely retooled. It soon
became obvious that he was fighting a powerful
corporate undertow of opposition. Some people
in the company did not want to do small cars
because they might not be successful, and some
did not want to do them because they *might* be
successful. To say that the company's more senior
executives were ambivalent about the project is an
understatement. At one point in 1958, Harlow
Curtice visited the design room where Cole was
preparing his model. He got inside the prototype
Corvair and reportedly said, with some degree of
irritation, "This is amazing—there's as much
head room here as in a Buick." Then he paused
and thought for a moment. "Take some of the
headroom out. We can't have a little car like this
with as much room as a big car." With that, Cole
was more isolated within the ever more conservative corporation than he realized. Sure of his own
vision, confident, indeed overly confident, of his
strengths, he did not entirely understand his new
marching orders. In reality, they went like this:
We'll do your small car at GM, though it goes
against our grain, but only on our terms. If there
is a conflict between what you want and what we
want, we, not you, will make the final decision.
Energized by the excitement of a new challenge,
Cole poured his energy into the Corvair. It would
have a rear-engine drive and an air-cooled six-

cylinder aluminum engine.

Three years in the essential design and creation, the Corvair debuted in the showrooms in September 1959. As far as Detroit executives were concerned, it was just in time, for the low end of the market had been consistently growing over the past decade and could no longer be ignored. In 1958, some 379,000 imported cars were sold in America; added to the growing sales of the little American Nash Rambler, the compacts now accounted for about 12 percent of the market. The Corvair had a chance, some automotive people thought, to be a superb small car. There was, on the part of its creator, a receptivity toward new ideas and new technology. But from the start it was always an orphaned car—the institution itself never really approved of it and the sales department at Chevy hated it. Arguments that Cole might have won when he was working on the '55 Chevy he now lost or had to compromise on, because he was fighting the culture of the company, and he could not prove that what he wanted was cost-effective. The Corvair's small size worked against it. Because it was a small car and not likely to make a large profit margin for the company, Harlow Curtice was able to set very strict limits on what it would cost. It had to sell for under $2,000, he said, which was Volkswagen's list price in 1959.

Cole's car, in comparison with the Volkswagen, was sporty—indeed, the name Corvair was meant to imply a kinship with the Corvette. It was 1,300 pounds lighter than the smaller Chevys of the time, but it was filled with compromises that bothered some of the engineers working on the program, and apparently bothered Cole, too. The tires were smaller than they should have been. The engine became a half-breed—part aluminum, part cast iron. Because of the size of the tires, the car had a tendency to swing out or, in the vernacular of auto engineers, to jack on corners, the rear tires losing traction if the driver did not have a particularly good feel for the car. A seasoned, experienced race driver soon realized that one of the keys to safe handling of the car was to keep the tire pressure at different levels for the front and rear tires, but few ordinary drivers paid attention to their tire pressure. Because its weight was differently aligned and the engine was in the rear, no one had much of a natural feel for driving it. The early tests reflected serious problems in handling. Cole's desire to add stability to the rear end through a stabilizing mechanism was lost in cost cutting. It was estimated that a better stabilizing system, such as a stabilizing bar, would have cost only about $14 or $15 more per car. Some of the Corvair engineers protested that the safety bar was necessary, but their protests were lost in the rush to get to market. There was, thought Cole's opposite number at Ford, Don Frey, who watched the birth of the Corvair and was aware of the fierce intramural struggle going on, a certain hubris to Ed Cole, and it showed here more than anywhere else. "We tested two of them," said Frey, who was generally an admirer of Cole's, "and we were appalled." Cole was so strong-willed that on occasion no one could stop him; this was one of the times he should have been stopped, Frey thought.

On sharp corners, particularly with neophyte drivers at the wheel, the car had a tendency to flip at high speeds. Perhaps a race driver could handle the car, but what about ordinary Americans, many of them younger and anxious to go for higher speeds than the car was able to negotiate safely? What made this different was not that the Corvair was that much less safe than the Volkswagen, which was, if anything, less safe, a number of engineers thought. But there was less of a tendency on the part of its owners to drive the Beetle at high speed.

In addition, General Motors was about to come under a new and different kind of political and social scrutiny than in the past. By the time the stabilizing bar was added, in 1963, the number of lawsuits against Chevy on the Corvair was mounting and within a year would reach a hundred. Once the stabilizing bar was added and the tendency to swing out was eliminated, *Car and Driver* wrote a harsh epitaph for the early cost-conscious Corvair. It was, said the magazine, a bible of auto enthusiasts, "one of the nastiest-handling cars ever built. The tail gave little warning that it was about to let go, and when it did, it let go with a vengeance few drivers could deal with. The rear wheels would lose traction, tuck under and with the tail end jacked up in the air, the car would swing around like a 3-pound hammer on a 30-foot string. This is not to say that the car was unstable within the limits of everyday fair-weather driving—just that those limits were none too clearly posted, and once transgressed, you were in pretty hairy territory, indeed."

Among those following the flaws of the Corvair and the crippling accidents left in its wake was a young man named Ralph Nader. He had already set out on a lonely path as a kind of one-man consumer critic of Detroit and what he considered its lack of concern for the greater good of its consumers, including on the issue of safety. GM, in turn, would lash out at Nader and would be caught in the act. Humiliating Senate hearings would follow in which General Motors was forced to apologize for its arrogance. For the first time, the government began to pay attention to the auto industry and the impact of its decisions on the people of the nation. The legacy of the Corvair was that it connected the fifties to the sixties. At the same time, top executives at General Motors were convinced that their great mistake had not been in trying to do the car too cheaply, thereby making it a dangerous vehicle, but in bothering to produce a small car in the first place.

FORTY-THREE

THE RADIO QUIZ SHOWS had been, in retrospect, small potatoes, with prizes to match. On *Take It Or Leave It,* the ultimate challenge was the "$64 question"—a phrase that even worked itself into the American vernacular by 1945. In the new age of television, though, everything had to be bigger and better. Americans were not going to sit home, glued to their television sets, wondering whether some electronic stranger, who had briefly entered their living rooms, was going to be able to double his winnings from $32 to $64. In the postwar era that was pocket money.

Such was the dilemma facing Lou Cowan in early 1955. Cowan, one of the most inventive figures in the early days of television, needed a gimmick for a game show worthy of television, one so compelling that millions of Americans would faithfully tune in. He needed high drama, and what better way to achieve that than a *very* large prize? Six hundred and forty dollars? Not so terribly exciting. Nor, for that matter, was $6,400. "But $64,000 gets into the realm of the almost impossible," he thought. Cowan liked the double-or-nothing format—so he envisioned a contestant who had answered a series of questions correctly and won the dizzying sum of $32,000. At that point it would be time to play double or nothing, for $64,000. With one answer to one question, an ordinary American could be wealthy beyond his or her wildest dreams.

The concept depended on the belief that seemingly unexceptional Americans did indeed have secret talents and secret knowledge. That appealed greatly to Cowan, who, with his Eastern European Jewish background, had a highly idealized view of his fellow citizens' potential to reach beyond the apparent limits life had dealt them. His was an idealistic, almost innocent belief in the ordinary people of the country. Cowan's wife, Polly, daughter of a successful Chicago businessman and a graduate of Sarah Lawrence College, most decidedly did not like the idea for the show. She thought it essentially a corruption of the real uses of learning—glorifying trivial memorization rather than true thought and analysis. She believed that the rewards for knowledge should not be huge amounts of cash, doled out in front of millions of cheering strangers, ultimately to benefit commercial hucksters; instead, it should be the joy of knowledge itself. She did not hesitate to make her feelings known to her husband and in a way the debate in the Cowan household reflected the schizophrenic nature of the program itself—a compelling mix of achievement, purity and, of course, avarice.

Polly's doubts did not deter her husband.

With his generous and optimistic nature, he saw the show as emblematic of the American dream; it offered everyone not only a chance to become rich overnight but to win the esteem of his fellow citizens. It proved every American had the potential to be extraordinary. It reflected, one of his sons said years later, a "White Christmas" vision of America, in which the immediate descendants of the immigrants, caught up in their optimism about the new world and the nobility of the American experiment, romanticized America and saw it as they wanted it to be.

Cowan was an independent television packager, a familiar figure in the early days of television; he and others like him came up with ideas, found sponsors, and then sold the entire package to the then rather passive networks. He sold this idea to Revlon, which was so enthusiastic that Walter Craig, an executive of the advertising agency that worked for Revlon, locked the door at Cowan's initial presentation and said, "Nobody leaves this room until we have a signed contract."

The name of the program was *The $64,000 Question.* It aired for the first time from 10:00 to 10:30 P.M. in June 1955, on CBS. It was an immediate hit. Millions of people identified with the contestants—who were very much like neighbors. The program showed a CBS psychologist named Gerhart Wiebe who said, "We're all pretty much alike, and we're all smart." The show contained all kinds of dramatic touches attesting to its integrity. The questions sat all week in a locked vault at a bank, and when they finally arrived on the set, they were transported by an executive from Manufacturers Trust, who was accompanied by two armed guards. An IBM machine shuffled the questions on the set. Ed Murrow, the most distinguished American broadcaster of two generations, a man who had pioneered the socially conscious documentary and who was becoming increasingly skeptical about the future of prime-time television, watched the first broadcast and turned to his partner, Fred Friendly. "Any bets on how long we'll keep this time period now?" he asked. He was prophetic in his wariness.

Eight thousand dollars was the maximum a contestant could win on one show; then he or she had to come back next week. Suspense would start building. At the eight thousand-dollar level, the contestant had to enter an isolation booth, presumably so no one in the studio audience could whisper an answer. The speed with which the program enthralled the entire country was breathtaking. Its success surprised even Lou Cowan. The show offered hope of an overnight fortune, and it proved that ordinary people were not in fact necessarily ordinary. As such there was a powerful chord of populism to it. But more than anything else, it appealed to the viewers' sense of greed. Five weeks after its premiere, *The $64,000 Question* was the top-rated show on television.

Studies showed that approximately 47.5 million people were watching. The sales of Revlon ("the greatest name in cosmetics") skyrocketed. Some Revlon products sold out overnight, and the show's master of ceremonies had to beg the public to be more patient until more Revlon Living Lipstick was available. The head of Hazel Bishop, a rival cosmetics company, subsequently blamed his company's disappointing year on the fact that "a new television program sponsored by your company's principal competitor captured the imagination of the public." It was the most primal lesson yet on the commercial power of television.

The contestants became the forerunners of Andy Warhol's idea of instant fame: people plucked out of total anonymity and beamed into the homes of millions of their fellow Americans. Between ten and twenty thousand people a week wrote letters, volunteering themselves or their friends to be contestants. After only a few appearances on the show, audiences began to regard the contestants as old and familiar friends. Perhaps, in retrospect, the most important thing illuminated by the show was how easily television conferred fame and established an image. Virtual strangers could become familiar to millions of their fellow citizens.

One of the first contestants, Redmond O'Hanlon, a New York City policeman, whose category was Shakespeare, reached the $16,000 plateau. At that point he decided to stop and, in his words, put "the conservatism of a father of five children" over "the egotism of the scholar." Soon Catherine Kreitzer, a fifty-four-year-old grandmother whose category was the Bible, reached $32,000. She was confident, Mrs. Kreitzer said, that she could win the full amount, but she stopped, quoting from the Bible: "Let your moderation be known unto all men." Perhaps the most engaging of all the early contestants was Gino Prato, a New York shoe repairman, whose category was opera. He easily reached the $32,000 plateau, whereupon his ninety-two-year-old father in Italy cabled him to stop at once. Prato, in time, became roving ambassador for a rubber-heel company, was given season tickets to the Metropolitan Opera, and went on to other television shows as well. If the producers faced a dilemma in the beginning, it was the hesitance of the top contestants to go for the ultimate question. Some of it was the fear of losing everything and some was the nation's then extremely harsh income tax schedules. As Kent Anderson pointed out in his book *Television Fraud,* a contestant who went for the whole thing was risking almost $20,000 in order to win only $12,000 more.

A Marine captain named Richard McCutcheon became the first contestant to go all the way. Bookies kept odds on whether or not he could get the right answer. His field was cooking, not military history. With an audience estimated at 55 million watching, on September 13, 1955, he became the first contestant to climb the television Mt. Everest. For $64,000 he was asked to name the five dishes and two wines from the menu served by King George VI of England for French president Albert Lebrun in 1939. He did: consommé quenelles, filet de truite saumonée, petits pois à la françaises, sauce maltaise, and corbeille. The wines were Château d'Yquem and Madera Sercial. The nation was ecstatic—it had a winner. "If you're symbolic of the Marine Corps, Dick," said Hal March, the emcee, "I don't see how we'll ever lose any battles."

Everyone involved seemed to profit from the show: Lou Cowan soon became president of CBS; the bank official who was in charge of the questions became a vice-president at Manufacturers Trust. But no one profited more than Revlon. The impact of the show upon its revenues was a startling reflection of changes that were taking place every day in more subtle ways because of the ferocious commercial drive of television and its effect upon both consumers and industry.

Revlon, at the time, was the leading cosmetic company in the nation, but Coty, Max Factor, and Helena Rubinstein were relatively close behind in net sales. In 1953, for example Revlon had net sales of $28.4 million; Helena Rubinstein had $20.4 million; Coty had $19.6; Max Factor, $19 million; and Hazel Bishop, $9.9. All in all, it was a fairly evenly divided pie, and Revlon's sales increased on average about 15 percent annually in the years just before 1955. But sponsoring the quiz show changed all that. In the first six-month season, Revlon increased its sale from $33.6 million to $51.6—a stunning 54 percent increase. The stock jumped from 12 to 20. The following year saw sales increase to $85.7 million. By 1958 Revlon completely dominated its field. (Asked later by a staff member of a House subcommittee whether sponsoring *The $64,000 Question* had had anything to do with Revlon's amazing surge to the top, a somewhat disingenuous Martin Revson answered, "It helped. It helped.")

Not surprisingly, *The $64,000 Question* produced a Pavlovian response to its success. Suddenly the networks were flooded with imitations, all of them for big prize money. The people in Cowan's old organization came up with *The $64,000 Challenge.* Others produced *Tic Tac Dough, Twenty-One, The Big Moment, Beat the Jackpot,* and *The Big Board.* There was even talk of *Twenty Steps to a Million.*

By 1956, the appeal of these shows appeared to be limitless; then subtly, and soon not so subtly, there was the inevitable pressure that television especially seemed to inspire: to improve the show by manipulation, to *cast* it—that is, to ensure each contestant would find some special resonance with the millions of people watching at home. The process began naturally enough at first, with the preference to choose a contestant possessed of considerable charm over a contestant without it. Soon the producers, by pretesting, were able to tell where a candidate's strengths lay and what his weaknesses were, without the contestants themselves even knowing what was happening: Prato knew Italian opera but little about the German opera; McCutcheon knew French cuisine rather than Italian or British. "We wrote the questions into the matrices of their existence," Mert Koplin, one of the men who worked on *The $64,000 Question,* later said. As the pressure built for ratings, the manipulations grew more serious. Some guests would be put through dry runs only to find that when they appeared on the live shows, the questions were remarkably similar to the ones they had answered correctly in the rehearsal. (McCutcheon, it turned out, was deeply bothered by this and thought seriously of getting out; he was encouraged to remain a contestant by his family. Later he told Joe Stone, the prosecutor from the New York District Attorney's office, that he thought the shows were fraudulent and immoral, and he disagreed violently with the claim of the various producers that the rigging had hurt no one.)

The Revlon executives from the start were extremely outspoken about the guests on the two shows they sponsored, *The $64,000 Question* and *The $64,000 Challenge.* Starting in the fall of 1955, there was a weekly meeting in Martin Revson's (Charles Revson's brother) office, where he and his top advertising people critiqued the previous week's shows and contestants. Revson was not shy about telling what he wanted to happen and who he wanted to win. He posted a chart in the meeting room with the ratings on it; if the ratings were down, it was the fault of the contestants. Were the contestants too old? Too young? Were they attractive enough? The criticism was often brutal. (The Revsons apparently did not like a young psychologist named Joyce Brothers, who appeared as an expert on boxing. Thus the questions given her were exceptionally hard—they even asked her the names of referees—in the desire to get her off the show; their strategy had no effect: She became the second person to win $64,000.)

More and more, with so many different shows vying for public approval, the producers found it was the quality of the contestants themselves—and the degree to which the nation identified with them—that made the difference. When the Barry and Enright company, one of the big hitters in the world of game shows, introduced its new game in March 1956, called *Twenty-One,* loosely based on the card game of the same name, Dan Enright was confident it would be an immediate success. Two contestants would answer questions for points, without knowing how many points their opponent had. Enright thought it was a sure bet for unbearable dramatic excitement, especially since the audience would know more about the competition than the contestants themselves. He was dead wrong. The premiere was, he said later, a dismal failure, "just plain dull." The day after, Marty Rosenhouse, the sponsor, made an irate call to say he did not intend to own a turkey. "Do whatever you have to do," he told Enright, "and you know what I'm talking about." Those were the marching orders for Enright and his staff.

Fixing the show did not particularly bother Enright; the quiz shows had never been about intelligence or integrity as far as he was concerned; they were about drama and entertainment. "You cannot ask random questions of people and have a show," one game-show producer later said. "You simply have failure, failure, failure, and that does not make entertainment." That made it a predatory world, and Enright excelled in it. He was not, Dan Enright reflected years later, a very nice man in those days. He was totally compelled by work, wildly ambitious, and utterly self-involved. "I was determined to be successful no matter what it cost," he said, "and I was greedy, greedy, not for money, but for authority, power, prestige and respect." The end, he believed at the time, always justified the means. People were to be used; if you did not use them, he believed, they in turn would use you. Soon— with considerable fixing—*Twenty-One* became a huge success; at a relatively young age, Enright had already exceeded his own expectations, and he was wealthy and powerful. People coveted his attention and gave him respect. Thus he was able to rationalize everything he was doing.

From then on, *Twenty-One* became the prototype of the completely crooked show. Enright cast it as he might a musical comedy. He wanted not just winners and losers but heroes and villains. He tried for his first hero with a young writer named Richard Jackman, who appeared on the show on October 3, 1956. Before Jackman's appearance, Enright went over a vast number of questions with Jackman. At the end of the session, Enright told him, "You are in a position to destroy my career." Jackman had no idea what he was talking about, although he figured it out the next day, when the questions put before him were the very same questions used in the dry run. Jackman easily won $24,500, but then told Enright he wanted no part of being on a fixed program and withdrew. A worried Enright pleaded with him to continue, offering up all kinds of rationales. Finally, he got Jackman to accept a $15,000 check for his first appearance and convinced him to appear on one additional program, in order to bow out gracefully rather than just disappear mysteriously.

That left Enright with all that money to give out and no cast of characters. His first break had come a little earlier, when a young man named Herb Stempel wrote asking for a chance to be a candidate. Stempel had seen the debut of *Twenty-One* and had thought the questions rather simple.

He had, he had always been told, a photographic memory. "The walking encyclopedia," one uncle called him. He had watched all the other shows and invariably got the right answers. "I have thousands of odd and obscure facts and many facets of general information at my fingertips," he wrote the producers. At the time, Stempel was an impoverished graduate student at City University, and his wife's moderately wealthy parents felt that their daughter had married beneath herself. Stempel was immediately invited to the offices of Barry and Enright, where he was given an exam consisting of 363 questions, of which he got 251 correct—the highest score anyone had gotten so far on the entrance exam. He was perfect for the show, except for one thing—he was short, stocky, and not particularly appealing on television.

He was, Enright decided, unlikeable. Because of that, Enright decided to exploit that and emphasize his unattractive side. Stempel had grown up in a poor section of the Bronx. His father, who had been a postal clerk, died when he was seven, and his mother suffered from high blood pressure and was on welfare from the time of her husband's death to when she died. There had seemed to Stempel an unfairness about his childhood from the start—other kids had fathers, he did not; other kids had some money, he did not. But his photographic memory was remarkable. For all the knowledge stored in his head, Enright thought, he was socially limited, and almost unable to sustain a conversation. To talk with him you had to ask a very specific question, and when you did, you got a specific answer and nothing more. "If you saw him," Enright said years later, "you had no choice but to root for him to lose."

A few days after the first meeting, Enright came by to see Stempel at the latter's home in Queens. Enright opened an attaché case and pulled out a bunch of cards similar to the ones used on *Twenty-One*. With that he began going over the questions in a dry run with Herb Stempel. Stempel got most of the answers right, and for the ones he didn't get, Enright supplied the answer. It was, Stempel began to realize, a rehearsal for *Twenty-One*. "How would you like to win $25,000?" Enright asked Stempel. "Who wouldn't," he answered. With that Enright had made him a co-conspirator, demolishing any leverage he might have if qualms arose in the future.

While he was at Stempel's Queens apartment Enright checked out his new contestant's wardrobe. Since he was to be portrayed as a penniless ex-GI working his way through school, he was to wear his worst clothes: an ill-fitting double-breasted blue suit that had belonged to Stempel's father-in-law. He also selected a blue shirt with a frayed collar to go with it. Enright made Stempel get a marine-style haircut, which made him look somewhat like a Nazi soldier, Enright thought, and thereby increased the audience's antipathy. Stempel was even told to wear a cheap watch, which, in Stempel's words, ticked like an alarm clock, the better to make a loud sound during the tense moments in the isolation booth. He was never to answer too quickly. He had to pause, to show some doubt and conflict, perhaps even stumble on an answer. Questions should look like cliffhangers. He was to carry a handkerchief and pat, not wipe, his brow. He was not to call Barry, the emcee, Jack on the air as everyone else did; rather he was to refer to him obsequiously as *Mr. Barry.*

Nor was he to deviate from his instructions. At one point, when he changed suits and wore a single-breasted one and got a better haircut, Enright warned him, "You're not paying attention to your lessons—you are not cooperating." Stempel realized the role he was to play was the nerd, the square, the human computer. It was a cruel thing to do, Enright reflected years later, to make a man who obviously had considerable emotional problems go before the American people in as unattractive an incarnation as possible.

If Stempel resented such treatment, it was still his one moment of glory. Suddenly, he was a hero on the CCNY campus. He could sense, as he walked across the campus, that other students were pointing him out and talking about him. Sitting one day in the cafeteria, he heard another student boast to a colleague, "Herb Stempel's in one of my classes." Another student, whom he had never met before, came up and told him that he and all his friends were all proud that Herb Stempel went to CCNY. There were covertly admiring glances from girls. It was heady stuff.

Good soldier that he was, Stempel was not a satisfactory winner for *Twenty-One*. His only real value was as a loser. The show needed a hero in a white hat—a handsome young gladiator to defeat him. In October the producers found him in the person of a young English instructor at Columbia University named Charles Van Doren. Al Freedman, Enright's deputy, met him at a cocktail party and was impressed by his intelligence and manner. "I think I've got the right person to beat Stempel with," Freedman told Enright, "someone very smart, who I think is going to come over very well on the show." Will he do it? Enright asked. "Yes," Freedman answered. "I think he'll do it, because his appearance will make erudition and education more popular."

Of all the people associated with the quiz-show scandals, the one who remains most indelibly burned on most people's memory is Charles Van Doren. He was the bearer of one of the most illustrious names in American intellectual life and he captivated the audience as no one else ever did. His manner—shy, gentle, somewhat self-deprecating, like a young, more intellectual Jimmy Stewart—was immensely attractive, for he was smart enough to win yet modest enough to seem just a little uneasy with his success. His father was the celebrated Columbia professor Mark Van Doren. His uncle Carl was just as famous a man of letters. He seemed to Freedman almost perfect for this particular show: He had a rare intellectual curiosity—apparently he was a speed reader and he read two or three books a day—and was informed on a broad range of subjects. Then, in addition to all else, there was the charm: Van Doren was someone whom the audience would see as an aristocrat, and yet there was nothing snobbish about him. He would appeal to ordinary people in every region of the country. Since it was a time when Stempel was, in the view of the producers, destroying the show, swallowing up more likable contestants, Van Doren's appeal was all the more attractive, and Freedman set out to get him on board.

That was not an easy process, though. A series of lunches followed, to seduce Van Doren, who remained largely unresponsive. Van Doren pointed out that he liked teaching very much, thank you; there was nothing else he coveted, and he was not interested in a career in television, not even as a lark. "It's not my world," he answered. "My world is academe and I like it very much." But the more he resisted, the more Freedman was impressed; his very reserve was tantalizing, and so Freedman continued to see him. One thing that both Enright and Freedman had mastered by this time was the art of discovering a potential contestant's vulnerability. Every man, they thought, had, if not his price, his special vanity, which was the weakness they could exploit. So Freedman, sensing that Van Doren's love of teaching was critical to turning him, began to emphasize how much he might help the world of education and the teachers of America by coming on board. Teachers all over the country would get a boost from his appearances; he would be able to show that teachers were role models, worthy of the respect of their fellow citizens. "You can be erudite and learned but show that you don't have to be an intellectual snob," Freedman said. At first Van Doren seemed rather amused by this transparent ploy.

Then it began to change. Van Doren asked Freedman what made him so sure that he, Van Doren, would actually win on the show. At that point Freedman gave him a brief but somewhat sanitized history of radio and television game shows, explaining that they were all controlled in some way, because the producers had to hold the interest of the audience as well as educate it. It was not a question of truth, or documentaries; rather, it was show business. Why, look at Eisenhower, he said. A book came out under his name, but it was most likely produced by a ghostwriter. Or a movie might show Gregory Peck parachuting behind the lines in Nazi Germany, but the person in the parachute was not Peck, but a double.

They kept in touch, and the seduction continued. "How much do you make as an instructor?" Freedman asked at one point. "About four thousand dollars a year," Van Doren answered. Freedman wondered aloud whether a young man could support a family on that salary. For the first time Van Doren asked how much money he might make as a contestant. Freedman explained that he might make as much as $50,000, or even $100,000. Van Doren asked Freedman how much the most recent contestant had won. Sixty thousand dollars, Freedman answered. Van Doren walked down some steps to leave, got to the bottom, and thought to himself, *Sixty thousand dollars! Sixty thousand dollars!* It took his breath away.

The next time they talked, Van Doren asked, "Who would have to know about it?" Freedman sensed that he had him. Just Enright and me, he answered. Freedman pledged to Van Doren that he would never turn him in. There were more talks; the seduction went on for several weeks. Finally, he agreed to go on; at first he asked to play it straight, but then it was explained to him that no one on *Twenty-One* played it straight.

It was a masterful stroke of casting: Van Doren turned out to be a superb performer. In contrast to the unattractive Stempel, he was, in Enright's phrase, the kind of young man "you'd love to have your daughter marry." He never seemed to lose his boyish innocence, which in fact he had lost from the start. At the height of his success, Van Doren seemed oddly immune to all the fuss. "Charlie," Freedman would say. "Do you know that somewhere between 25 and 30 million people watched you last night? Isn't that amazing?" Van Doren would simply shake his head: "It's hard for me to picture." Even more amazed than Charles was his father. Mark Van Doren wrote to his friend and former student Thomas Merton, the poet and Trappist monk, "About fifteen million people have fallen in love with him—and I don't use the word lightly."

Perhaps it was the contrast between Charles Van Doren's innate modesty and the hyped-up atmosphere of the quiz show, but there was no doubt about it—Charles Van Doren, not yet a Columbia Ph.D., merely a $4,000-a-year instructor, was one of television's first stars, and arguably its first intellectual star. Ironically, even his inner doubts worked for the show: The longer he stayed on the show, the more he hated what he was doing and the more he wanted to get off; and some of that conflict must have shown through and made him an even more winning contestant.

The Van Dorens were an old American family, dating back to the eighteenth century. Because their name was Dutch and had the prefix Van, many assumed they were aristocrats; instead the family was one of hardworking salt-of-the-earth Midwesterners. Mark Van Doren's grandfather, William Henry Van Doren, had been a farmer, blacksmith, and preacher (and, noted Mark in his autobiography, "not much of a businessman"). But he stressed education and his son became a doctor and two of his grandsons, Carl and Mark, got Ph.D.s. As a young graduate student Carl wrote his mother of the hardships of student life: "Some days I grow a despicable coward and am nearly tempted to turn my back upon all the bright ideal to which I have been true now for nearly a third of my life, and drop my energies to a slighter task where there is a chance of wealth and ease after a time. I know I could be rich—but I don't care to be . . ."

Mark Van Doren was not only a professor— he had won a Pulitzer Prize in poetry and had written a distinguished biography of Hawthorne. His wife, Dorothy (and Charles's mother), was a former editor of *The Nation* and a novelist; his brother, Carl, won a Pulitzer Prize for biography in 1939, and Carl's wife, Irita, was book editor of *The Herald Tribune,* a position of considerable influence in those days. It was her affair with Wendell Willkie, during which she encouraged him to run for the Presidency, that inspired Howard Lindsay and Russell Crouse to write their hit musical *State of the Union.*

The Van Dorens were, in sum, a family that seemed to reflect the best of the liberal, humanist values of the era; Mark and Dorothy Van Doren had a town house in the Village and country house in northwestern Connecticut. If anything, Mark was the most blessed of them all, a successful and gifted poet and a truly beloved teacher, absolutely in command of his work, gentle, generous to, and tolerant of his students, even if their work was different from his (as in the case of Allen Ginsburg even before he emerged as an early Beat poet). One student later wrote that he had the gift of making "the difficult attainable through lightness." Another of his students, Alfred Kazin, later one of America's most distinguished critics, remembered the pleasure of Van Doren's lectures in a course on "the long poem." The sun would go down just as Van Doren was finishing the lecture, Kazin remembered, and then he would leave the campus and take the Seventh Avenue subway to his house in the Village, often accompanied by students, who used the subway ride to expand the classroom hour and who were often invited in for a drink or for tea.

Family friends included James Thurber (the Van Doren family cat was named Walter, after Thurber's character Walter Mitty), John Berryman ("Charlie, by the way," Mark Van Doren had written Berryman when his son was young, "values your letters if only for their stamps"), Joseph Wood Krutch, Franklin P. Adams, Jacques Barzun, Thomas Merton, Lionel Trilling, and Rex Stout.

The Van Dorens were not wealthy; money was always secondary to teaching and writing. As Mark Van Doren wrote Charles in the fall of 1952, in a letter filled with a father's pride that his son would soon be asked to teach English at Columbia at a salary of $3,600 a year: "Really Cha, I'm not advising you to say Yes. You would have to love it to do it at all, and the rewards, I don't need to tell you, are scandalously slight; they have always been for teachers, and they always will be. I have enjoyed it, even though I am quitting soon; but the enjoyment was the greater part of my pay . . ." (Indeed, one of the first things that Charles Van Doren did when he became successful on *Twenty-One* was to buy his parents a television set.)

Charles Van Doren reflected both the strengths and the weaknesses of so privileged and protected a background. He developed into an erudite classicist and gifted musician. But it was always there, the fact that he was a *Van Doren.* When he first went on the show, Jack Barry coyly asked him, "Just out of curiosity, Mr. Van Doren, are you in any way related to Mark Van Doren, up at Columbia University, the famous writer?" Van Doren: "Yes. I am. He is my father." Barry: "He is your father!" Van Doren: "Yes." Barry: "The name Van Doren is a very well known name. Are you related to any of the other well-known Van Dorens?" Van Doren: "Well, Dorothy Van Doren, the novelist and author of the recent 'The Country Wife' is my mother, and Carl Van Doren, the biographer of Benjamin Franklin, was my uncle." Barry: "Well, you have every reason in the world to be might proud of your name and your family, Van Doren . . ."

Coached by Freedman on how to answer, Charles Van Doren became very good at the theatrics of the show. He learned to stutter, to seem to grope toward answers he had already been given. He was good at the game, but not too good; the questions were answerable, his struggling implied, but they were not easy. (When Jack Barry, talking about the cast of *On The Waterfront*, asked him, among other things, for the name of the Best Supporting Actress, Van Doren had answered, "Uh well, the only woman I can remember in that picture was the one who played opposite Brando, but I would have thought that she would have got the Best Actress award. But if she's the only one I remember—let's see—she was that lovely frail girl—Eva Saint—uh, Eva Marie Saint." Later, he noted, on the occasions when he had been given an answer, a curious pride made him go and look it up.

What Stempel, who hated him, and millions of others who were rooting for him could not understand about Van Doren was that coming from a family that accomplished was not without its burdens. What in life really belonged to Charles Van Doren independent of his family? Van Doren's life was not as enviable as it seemed. He was dealing with an age-old dilemma, made no easier by its familiarity—being the son of a famous and successful father and/or mother in the same profession. Charles had reluctantly decided to seek a career as an English professor. As a young man he had gone to Paris and tried to write a novel about patricide, although as he told Dick Goodwin, a House investigator, he had also asked for his father's help in editing it. There was a quality about his life that was oddly airless. As Van Doren himself said a few weeks after he finally came forward to admit that he had been part of the scam, "I've been acting a part, a role, not just the last few years—I've been acting a role for ten or fifteen years, maybe all my life. It's a role of thinking that I've done far more than I've done, accomplished more than I've accomplished, produced more than I've produced. It has in a way something to do with my family, I suppose. I don't mean just my father, there are other people in my family. But I've been running." Burdened and conflicted, uncertain about what was his and what was his family's, desperately needing successes and an identity of his own, Van Doren had been a perfect catch for someone like Enright. By going on the quiz shows, perhaps Charles Van Doren was seeking fame of his own; and for a brief time he became far more famous than his illustrious relatives; they were known only to a small elite; he was known to millions—his face was even on the cover of *Time*.

To Stempel, Van Doren was the enemy and the epitome of all the injustices he had suffered in terms of privilege and looks. "I felt here was a guy, Van Doren, that had a fancy name, Ivy

League education, parents all his life, and I had just the opposite, the hard way up," he once told Enright. That Stempel, because of the deal he had made with the devil, would now have to give up his television celebrity, pretend that he was dumber than he was, and lose to someone he was sure he could beat was the unkindest cut of all.

When Enright first told Stempel it was his turn to lose, he angrily balked. The fame had proved to be addictive; he was in no hurry to give up his appearances on television. No, he said, he wouldn't do it. But Enright knew he was a street kid, and street kids kept their word. "Herbie, when this started, you gave me your word," Enright said. So Stempel agreed to take the fall, but he was bitter about it. He begged Enright to revoke the deal, to let him play Van Doren fair and square.

All of this was done under the sponsorship (but without the direct knowledge of) Pharmaceuticals Inc., a maker of patent medicines. So there was the bizarre spectacle of Jack Barry challenging these two intelligent young men with extremely serious questions and then switching back to his pitches for Geritol: "I guess I've asked thousands of questions at one time or another here on television. I haven't got enough used to it yet, but there is one simple question that I think almost everybody asks everybody else—I think you know the question—what's the weather gonna be like. . . . So, remember, if tired blood is your problem, especially in this rough weather after those colds or flu or sore throats or a virus, take either the good-tasting liquid Geritol or the handy Geritol tablets . . ." Pharmaceuticals Inc., like Revlon, reaped huge benefits from sponsoring the quiz shows; in the first year, its sales went from $10.4 million to $13.9.

The denouement for Herb Stempel came on the night of December 5, 1956. According to Enright's script, he was to lose by answering incorrectly a question the answer to which he knew perfectly well: which movie had won the Academy Award for Best Picture in 1955. The answer was *Marty,* and Stempel had seen the movie three times. He loved it because he could identify with its principal character, an unattractive but sensitive man who has as many feelings as someone who is handsome. That it was a movie he cared about made it all the harder. On the day just before he was to lose, he became so frustrated that he told a few of his friends that he was going to take a dive on the show. On the day of the program, NBC hyped the confrontation all day long: "Is Herb Stempel going to win over $111,000 on *Twenty-One* tonight?" an announcer would say over and over again as the day wore on. Stempel would talk back to the television set in his room: "No, he's not going to win over $111,000, he's going to take a dive."

Once the program began, he came perilously close to answering the *Marty* question correctly, breaking Enright's rules and just going for it. Years later he pondered how history might have been different: He would have won, he would not have proceeded to help blow the whistle on Enright, and Charles Van Doren would have lost and been able to go back gracefully to Columbia and to his real love, teaching. But he played by the rules, and Van Doren ended up riding a tiger. Van Doren, in time, became a national hero, with a record fifteen appearances on the show. He had greatly underestimated the power of television. Something that had begun as a lark turned into the young academic's nightmare. Hundreds of letters came in each day telling him how he represented America's hope for a more serious, cerebral future, particularly after the dark years of McCarthy had poisoned the minds of the American public about the value of education. Other universities offered him tenured professorships. There were offers to star in movies. NBC signed him to a three-year contract that included regular stints on the *Today* show, where he was to be the resident intellectual. His salary from the network was a staggering $50,000 a year. "I felt like a bullfighter in a bull ring with thousands and thousands of people cheering me on and all I wanted to do was get out of there," he later told Dick Goodwin. In the end his total winnings came to $129,000; but given the draconian taxes of the period, he actually took home only about $28,000. Stempel asked to challenge Van Doren one more time but was told that Van Doren would not take him on. Perhaps Vivienne Nearing, Van Doren's then opponent, might; when Stempel heard this, he understood immediately that in the forthcoming contest between Ms. Nearing and Van Doren, Van Doren was scripted to lose, so Stempel, nothing if not shrewd, took $5,000 of his savings and bet it two-to-one on Nearing.

Stempel won $10,000 but quickly squandered that and his prize money in a series of bad investments. His bitterness festered. He began to bug Enright, demanding a chance to play Van Doren ("that son of a bitch") in a clean, unfixed game. Enright became increasingly aware that Stempel was a live hand grenade. There was some talk about a place on another show. Stempel pledged to lose weight, " 'cause when I go on I want to look like a gentleman, not a little short, squat guy, like I looked on *Twenty-One*." At one point, Enright even secretly taped Stempel to show that the latter was blackmailing him and then skillfully cajoled him into signing a piece of paper that said there had been no fixing on *Twenty-One*. But none of this could stem Stempel's growing rage.

The one thing that neither Enright nor Freedman had counted on was the impact of all this on Stempel's psyche. It had all been traumatic, and they were now about to pay the price for what they had done. The key for fixing the show had been the ability to co-opt all the players; common sense decreed that those who had been part of the scam would keep quiet rather than hurt themselves. But Stempel was beyond the point of caring. What he wanted was revenge.

Stempel began to look for reporters who might write about the scandal. At first the press was wary of picking up the story because there was no way of corroborating it. Later Enright realized he had done an unspeakable thing: He had exploited a man who was emotionally vulnerable. Of all the things he had done during the quiz-show rigging, that was the thing that, many years later, Enright was most ashamed of. He was not nearly as bothered by what he had done to Van Doren, who, he decided, was an intelligent adult with a fully workable moral compass and who knew exactly what he was doing.

In the district attorney's office there was a strong belief that the program had been rigged. But it was a hard case to break, for Enright and his deputy, Albert Freedman, had been careful fixers. The fixing had been done one-on-one, with no witnesses. Deniability was critical. In case a contestant changed his mind and wanted to talk, it was to be his word against that of a program executive; thus, charges of fraud against the program could be neutralized. There was to be as little overlapping as possible: Enright had fixed Stempel; Freedman had fixed Van Doren. They liked to co-opt the contestants even before they set foot on the show. That way they were less likely to turn on the men who had fixed them.

When the story of Stempel's charges finally broke in a New York newspaper, Enright received a call from an uncle. "Dan," his uncle said. "I hope this teaches you one thing." "What's that?" Enright asked. "Never bet on any animal that can talk," his uncle said. Enright soon discovered he had seriously underestimated the sheer power of the show. In his own mind he had done nothing that violated the moral code of the world of entertainment as he knew it. But the show had transcended mere entertainment: It had become the property of an entire nation. Enright had crossed over, without knowing it, into another sphere, with another set of ethics and standards. He was playing with this new instrument of television without knowing its true power.

Their phenomenal success, Freedman realized, had also stirred powerful resentment in other segments of the media. As evidence of the fixing began to surface, the ferocity with which the newspapers picked up the story stunned him. It was not covered as a minor scandal in the minor world of entertainment but as a threat to the republic—something on the order of the press coverage of Watergate, he later thought. He had greatly underestimated the dimensions of celebrity that the game shows conferred. The press, especially the city's more vulnerable newspapers, particularly those already suffering financially from television's ever more powerful reach—the *World Telegram,* the *Journal American,* and even the *Post*—feasted on the story as a means of showing that their prime competitor was not to be trusted.

It was a phenomenon of the fifties, Freedman thought. They were playing with this new instrument without knowing its real power: They had toyed with it as if it were merely an extension of radio, and they did not know that, in those days at least, it overwhelmed the people sitting at home watching and consumed those who went on the programs. A decade later, Freedman believed, the show might have been a success, but a much smaller one as the nation would have become far more immunized to the immediacy of television.

In 1957, Barry and Enright had sold the rights to the show to an eager NBC for $2 million. As the deal was being completed, Enright wondered whether they should tell the network that it was buying a rigged show. He called his agent, Sonny Werblin, an astute New York wheeler-dealer, and asked his advice. "Dan, have I ever asked you whether the show was rigged?" Werblin responded. No, Enright said. "And has NBC ever asked you whether the show was rigged?" Again Enright said no. "Well, the reason that none of us has asked," Werblin continued, summing up the morality of the networks on the issue in those days, "is because we don't want to know."

But Stempel refused to go away, and was becoming increasingly obsessive. In his own mind, he had carried the show, had made it what it was, and would get no long-term benefit. Enright had promised him a job when he'd agreed to take the fall, but—and it seemed typical to Stempel—he was now hedging on it. By contrast, Van Doren was being given a steady job at $50,000 a year from NBC. There was simply no justice, he felt. He kept calling reporters, trying to give his story to them, but libel laws were tougher then and there was no corroborating evidence.

Inevitably, the whole scam unraveled. A young woman who had been coached left her notebook in the outer office of one show. Another contestant saw the notebook, which contained many of the answers the woman was asked to give as a contestant, and complained. Others came forward. One contestant mailed a registered letter to himself in which he placed an exact description of the process and including the answers themselves—powerful evidence for the courts. Finally, the district attorney's office launched a broad investigation of the quiz shows. The evidence of rigging was overwhelming, but for reasons never quite clear, the judge in the case impounded all the evidence. With that, the quiz show scandal was passed to a congressional committee.

Gradually, the congressional investigation kept coming back to focus on Charles Van Doren, the young man who had charmed the entire nation. Van Doren steadfastly maintained his innocence and claimed that he had received no help.

That meant he continued to lie to the prosecutors, to the New York grand jury investigating the quiz shows, to the media, to his employers, to his family, and to his own lawyer. In 1959 Richard N. Goodwin, a young investigator for the congressional committee looking into the quiz-show scandals, had to deal with Stempel, Van Doren, and the others. Goodwin's roots were not that different from Stempel's, but he empathized with Van Doren; if he, like Stempel, was Jewish and came from a rather simple background, then his innate talent as a member of the new generation of the meritocracy was already manifesting itself. He had gone to Tufts and then to Harvard Law School, where he had been first in his class and gained the ultimate accolade: He had been chosen as a Felix Frankfurter law clerk. Goodwin found Stempel's hatred of Van Doren distasteful; by contrast, Goodwin was charmed by Van Doren. Soon they became not hunter and hunted but almost pals, Dick and Charlie. Clearly, Van Doren was intrigued by Goodwin's exceptional intelligence, by the fact that in addition to being a brilliant young lawyer, he loved American literature; Goodwin in turn had never met anyone like Van Doren, so intelligent, so graceful, from an old family, utterly devoid of snobbishness. The evidence, Goodwin thought, overwhelmingly showed that Van Doren had to be part of a fix, but he *wanted* to believe Van Doren, and for a time Goodwin lacked the final piece of evidence to implicate him: Freedman, Van Doren's handler, had conveniently left the country for Mexico. Finally, under threat of the loss of his citizenship, he reluctantly returned.

When Goodwin had Freedman's testimony, he called Van Doren to let him know where the case stood, that the committee now had a lock on it. For the first time, Van Doren seemed to pause. The next time they met, there was a lawyer at Van Doren's side. Still, Van Doren protested his innocence. "Dick, someday I hope I'll be able to tell you why he [Freedman] is lying," Van Doren said. "Charlie, isn't it interesting that the only people not telling the truth are from the best families?" Goodwin answered, mentioning one other quiz contestant with an exceptional background. At this point Goodwin felt himself in a bind: He was absolutely sure Van Doren was lying, but he also saw no purpose in having the committee destroy him in public. It was, after all, not long after the McCarthy hearings and Goodwin still had vivid images of people whose lives had been ruined by their appearances before investigating committees. As far as Goodwin was concerned, the principal villains were the networks, which had averted their eyes from what was happening despite a number of warnings, the sponsors, who were the real beneficiaries, and the producers. Goodwin's lack of zeal in going after Van Doren did not please Stempel. There were endless phone calls from him: "Are you calling Van Doren [to go before the committee]? Are you calling Van Doren?" Stempel would ask. Finally, Goodwin asked, "Herb, why do you hate him so much?" "I don't hate him," Stempel protested. "Come on," Goodwin said. "You've been on my case since the beginning for one thing and one thing alone—to get him." At that point Stempel told of an incident in which he had gone over to shake Van Doren's hand at a charity benefit but Van Doren, according to Stempel, had turned away from him. That, thought Goodwin, sounded unlikely, because there was not a trace of snobbishness to Van Doren. But in some way he understood that even if it hadn't happened in reality, it had happened in Herb Stempel's mind.

Goodwin went to the committee members in closed session, said that he had more than enough information to show that the programs were rigged, but that he saw no need to destroy Van Doren in public before the committee. The committee members agreed, and the decision was made not to call him. With that, Goodwin told Van Doren, "Charlie, I know you're lying to me," he said. "Dick, I'm sorry you feel that way," Van Doren answered. The committee, Goodwin continued, had decided not to call him. But don't, he warned Van Doren, say anything publicly or do anything the committee might view as a challenge and which might force it to change its mind. With that, it seemed that Van Doren was home free. But then NBC told Van Doren that he had to send

a telegram to the committee declaring his innocence or lose his job on the *Today* show. The
obvious decision, Goodwin thought, was for Van
Doren to tell NBC to stuff it and quit. Instead,
pushed by his own pride, Van Doren took a fateful step and sent the telegram. It was a wildly
self-destructive thing to do, Goodwin thought.
Inevitably, he was subpoenaed. Goodwin, bothered by the coming confrontation, went to see his
mentor, Justice Felix Frankfurter. Frankfurter
had no personal connection with Van Doren and
took a more objective view of what was happening: "A quiz-show investigation without Van
Doren," he said, "is like *Hamlet* without anyone
playing Hamlet." Besides, Frankfurter added,
Van Doren was not exactly innocent. He had been
a willing participant. The fact that others in the
scandal had done things worse did not exactly
exonerate him.

. . .

On November 1, 1959, the night before Van
Doren's appearance before the committee, Dick
Goodwin invited him and his father to dinner.
Goodwin remembered being touched by the mutual affection between the two and Mark Van
Doren's self-evident relief that his son was going
to be able to free himself of his terrible weight.
The irony of all this—that the father and son who
were so graceful and charming and who could,
even in this most terrible hour, come to dinner
and make a simple evening so rich with literate yet

unpretentious conversation—did not escape Goodwin, who found himself torn by the entire experience.

The next day, a crush of journalists and photographers recorded Van Doren on the witness stand, beginning, "I would give almost anything I have to reverse the course of my life in the last three years. I cannot take back one word or action. The past does not change for anyone. But at least I can learn from the past. I have learned a lot in the last three weeks. I've learned a lot about life. I've learned a lot about myself, and about the responsibilities any man has to his fellow men. I've learned a lot about good and evil. They are not always what they appear to be. I was involved, deeply involved, in a deception. The fact that I, too, was very much deceived cannot keep me from being the principal victim of that deception, because I was its principal symbol. There may be a kind of justice in that . . ." Aware of Van Doren's great popularity, the committee members handled him gently and repeatedly praised him for his candor. Only Congressman Steve Derounian announced that he saw no particular point in praising someone of Van Doren's exceptional talents and intelligence for simply telling the truth. With that, the room suddenly exploded with applause, and Goodwin knew at that moment ordinary people would not so easily forgive Van Doren.

Stempel had taken a train to Washington,

paying for the trip with his own money, to see Van Doren's appearance. In the crowded congressional hearing room, he wanted some kind of vindication. And although in the beginning his seat was far in the back, he had steadily edged forward so he could look in Van Doren's face: He wanted to see and hear the members of the Congress of the United States scolding this privileged young man for breaking faith with the American people, but he was bitterly disappointed by what happened. "I felt terribly hurt by the way they praised him," he said years later. Afterward, Stempel grabbed Joseph Stone, the New York assistant DA who had done much of the early work on the case, and started to complain about the professors at CCNY who had turned down his proposal for a Ph.D. thesis. Even at what might have been a moment of triumph, it still seemed that he regarded himself a victim.

When it was over, a reporter asked Mark Van Doren if he was proud of his son and the old man said yes, he was. Are you proud of what he did on the quiz shows? another reporter asked, and Mark wavered for a moment and said no, he was not, but at least Charles could get back to what he ought to be doing—teaching. That was something, he added, that he was very good at. At that point one of the reporters told Mark Van Doren what he did not yet know: that the board of trustees at Columbia had voted that day to fire Charles Van Doren as an instructor. A friend noted that the decision must have been like an arrow through the heart of the old man.

Charles Van Doren wrote Dick Goodwin a poignant note the next day, thanking him for his kindnesses during the preceding few weeks. "The dinner was superb, the accommodations splendid, and the conversation even at times uncharged with passion and danger. What an extraordinary evening it was. I will of course never forget it. . . . Hunters," he continued, "used to say that the stag loved the hunter who killed it . . . thus the tears, which were the tears of gratitude and affection. Something like that *does* happen, I know. And Raskolnikov felt the same. Thus Gerry [his wife] and I do extend an invitation to you to come and wish you would come. There are a number of things I'd like to talk to you about—none of them having to do with quiz shows. I made the mistake of reading the papers. I should have taken your advice. I wish the next six months were already over. There have been many hard things. But I am trying to tell you that we will live and thrive, I think—I mean I know we will live and I think we will thrive—and that you must never, in any way, feel any regret for your part in this. Perhaps it is nonsense to say that, but I thought it might just be possible that you would. Charlie."

It was a traumatic moment for the country as well. Charles Van Doren had become the symbol of the best America had to offer. Some commentators wrote of the quiz shows as the end of American innocence. Starting with World War Two, they said, America had been on the right side: Its politicians and generals did not lie, and the Americans had trusted what was written in their newspapers and, later, broadcast over the airwaves. That it all ended abruptly because one unusually attractive young man was caught up in something seedy and outside his control was dubious. But some saw the beginning of the disintegration of the moral tissue of America, in all of this. Certainly, many Americans who would have rejected a role in being part of a rigged quiz show if the price was $64 would have had to think a long time if the price was $125,000. John Steinbeck was so outraged that he wrote an angry letter to Adlai Stevenson that was reprinted in *The New Republic* and caused a considerable stir at the time. Under the title "Have We Gone Soft?" he raged, "If I wanted to destroy a nation I would give it too much and I would have it on its knees, miserable, greedy, and sick . . . on all levels, American society is rigged. . . . I am troubled by the cynical immorality of my country. It cannot survive on this basis."

The scandal illuminated some things about television in addition to its growing, addictive power: The first was the capacity of a virtual stranger, with the right manner, to project a kind of pseudo-intimacy and to become an old and trusted friend in a stunningly short time. That would have profound ramifications, as television increasingly became the prime instrument of politics. The other thing it showed, and this was to be perhaps its most powerful lesson, was that television *cast* everything it touched: politics, news shows, and sitcoms. The demands of entertainment and theater were at least as powerful as substance. Among the first to benefit from that new casting requirement was a young junior senator from Massachusetts, who, like Charles Van Doren, was young, attractive, upper-class, and diffident because he was cool on a medium that was hot. If Charles Van Doren was the major new star of television in the late fifties, then he was to be replaced by John Kennedy as the new decade started.

As for Charles Van Doren, he quickly dropped out of the public arena. He moved to Chicago with his young family and, drawing on a family connection with Mortimer Adler, the editor of the Great Books series, he worked for the Encyclopedia Britannica as an editor. His life in Chicago was largely private, and he was not often seen in that city's journalistic and literary circles. He and his wife, Geraldine Bernstein Van Doren, whom he had first met when she had a job answering the mail prompted by his early success on *Twenty-One,* reared two children there. He never wrote or spoke about the quiz-show events. When, on different occasions, journalists telephoned, suggesting that they were working on an article about that period and asked to speak with him, they were told that Mr. Van Doren was living a very happy life and did not need or want to get involved in their project. He was the editor of a number of important collections, including *The Great Treasury of Western Thought,* and *The Joy of Reading,* but his ability to promote the books, and thereby enhance both their sales and his own reputation, was limited by his wariness of going on television. He was aware that if he made a book tour, he was not likely to be asked about the history of Western thought, or about the relative influence of Plato, Aristotle, and St. Thomas Aquinas on our lives, but rather about Freedman, Enright, and Revson.

In the late 1980s, a distinguished television documentary maker named Julian Krainan was looking for a narrator-editor for a thirteen-part public television series on the history of philosophy. Krainan had read Van Doren's work, had loved *The Joy of Reading,* and was impressed by the powerful sweep of his intellect. Krainan, some fifteen years younger than Van Doren, had only the vaguest memory of the quiz-show scandals some thirty years after they had taken place. He contacted Van Doren, and gradually they began to agree on the outline of a public television series. They seemed to like each other and liked dealing with each other. Then Krainan's project hit a wall. The top people at PBS were wary about dealing with Van Doren until he himself dealt publicly with the quiz-show issue. At that point

Krainan suggested doing a documentary on the quiz-show scandals. It would clear the air, lance the boil, and prepare the way for the multipart show on philosophy. Krainan also pointed out that Van Doren himself, on a number of occasions when the subject came up, always said that he had nothing to hide and nothing to apologize for.

Van Doren and Krainan went back and forth about doing a quiz-show documentary matter a number of times until one day Van Doren suddenly announced, "I'm going to do it. I should have done this a long time ago." But a few days later he called to say that he'd reconsidered. Krainan went ahead with his documentary, which was exceptionally well received and much praised for its fairness and sensitivity. Of the important players still living, only Charles Van Doren refused to participate.

FORTY-FOUR

THE MOST INDELIBLE images of America that fall came from Little Rock, scenes captured by still photographers and, far more significantly, by movie cameramen working for network television news shows. The first and most jarring of these images was of angry mobs of white rednecks, pure hatred contorting their faces, as they assaulted the nine young black students who dared to integrate Little Rock Central High. The second and almost equally chilling image came a few weeks later, showing the same black children entering the same school under the protection of elite U.S. Army paratroopers. The anger and hatred that had been smoldering just beneath the surface in the South since the enactment of *Brown* v. *Board of Education* had finally exploded, and now because of television, the whole nation and soon the whole world could watch America at war with itself.

It was bound to happen sooner or later, but no one thought it would happen in Little Rock. Arkansas was a moderate state, as much a Southwestern state as it was truly Southern. Its medical and law schools had been integrated a decade earlier, without even a court order. Orval Faubus, the governor, was considered a moderate and there was no feverish quality to his voice when he spoke about issues of race. He seemed to lack the terrible hatred that infected so many Southern politicians. In 1955, when *Brown II* was handed down, Faubus had said: "It appears that the Court left some degree of decision in these matters to the Federal District courts. I believe this will guarantee against any sudden dislocation. . . . Our reliance must be upon the good will that exists between the races—the good will that has long made Arkansas a model for other Southern states in all matters affecting the relationship between the races."

In his successful 1956 campaign for reelection, Faubus barely mentioned the race issue, and the Little Rock plan for integration was so gradual that initially only nine black students were to attend a white school. The plan called for integrating at the high school level and working downward, one grade, one year at a time. Originally, Virgil Blossom, the school superintendent, wanted to do just the opposite—beginning at the lower levels and working upward, on the theory that younger children would have less learned prejudice. But he found that white parental fear in the lower grades was more intense: parents were less nervous about their teenagers than their first-graders.

Blossom wanted only the ablest and most

mature black students. A list of eighty at the old Horace Mann School who were interested in transferring was drawn up. School officials quickly whittled the number down to thirty-two. That was easy: As Blossom explained to parents and children the pressures they would surely be subjected to, many dropped out. Blossom and his staff met with all thirty-two families—both parents and children. Some students were told they were not ready for either the social pressure or the schoolwork. A few good athletes were told they might be better off staying at Horace Man because at a white school they would have to face the possibility that other schools might cancel games as a result of their being on the teams. The list shrank to seventeen names, and then, as rumors and doubts continued, only nine. That pleased the white leadership. The entire process had been designed to minimize the emotional impact of integration on the whites. If the local black leadership was not entirely thrilled with the cautious approach, it had accepted it as law, for the Blossom plan clearly met the test of the Supreme Court and had been approved by the federal district court. Virgil Blossom was an affable man, whom Harry Ashmore, the executive editor of the liberal *Arkansas Gazette,* thought of as a "natural-born Rotarian." He was named Little Rock's man of the year in 1955, and both newspapers, the *Gazette* and the *Democrat,* as well as the city council and the chamber of commerce, backed his plan. Everybody in the local establishment seemed to be on board.

Harry Ashmore was the liberal working editor of the liberal *Arkansas Gazette,* one of the South's best newspapers and, as far as he was concerned, Little Rock reflected the gradual evolution taking place in much of the urban postwar South, with the ascendance of a more moderate generation of white leadership. These younger men, most of whom had fought in World War Two, and who had in some way been broadened by that experience, did not welcome integration, Ashmore thought. Most of them, in fact, probably preferred things the way they were. But unlike their parents, they were not violently opposed to integration. It was not as emotional an issue with them as it had once been. They were businessmen first and foremost, and they understood that the world had changed and that to fight to maintain white supremacy would be self-defeating—it was probably a lost cause. They accepted the idea of "social justice"—that is, a fairer legal and political deal for blacks—but they remained wary of what they considered "social equality"—which implied an integrated dance at a country club, for instance. That went against everything in their upbringing. At the heart of their position was a desire to do business as usual and an acceptance that when it came to the crunch, the presence of a white redneck mob in the street was a greater threat to tranquility and daily commerce than was the integration of a school system or other public facilities. Thus they accepted the law of the land because they saw it, in long-range business terms, as the path of least resistance.

A few days before the schools were to open, Benjamin Fine, the education editor of *The New York Times,* came to town to cover the event, and years later Ashmore was amused by Fine's initial purpose: to find out why Little Rock was handling so sensitive a matter with such exceptional ease. Fine visited Ashmore in his office, and the local editor predicted that there would be little more than routine verbal protests at the coming desegregation. In fact, just about everyone locally expected a rather peaceful transition. But Orval Faubus had started playing his cards ever closer to his vest, Ashmore noted. Still, the worst he expected was that Faubus would refuse to back the local police officials, thereby preserving his ties to the segregationists without overtly blocking the law of the land as mandated by the district court.

Little Rock authorities felt particularly comfortable with the Blossom plan because the nine black students were chosen not merely for their exceptional educational abilities but for their strength of character as well. They came from middle-class families, black middle-class to be sure, which meant smaller incomes than that of white middle-class families, but they all had a strong sense of home and family. Religion played an important part in most of their homes. Typical was Terrance Roberts, fifteen, the second of seven children. His father was a Navy veteran who worked as a dietician at the veterans' hospital in north Little Rock, and his mother ran a catering service out of their home. Though it was part of the white mythology that the NAACP in New York pushed unwilling parents to sacrifice their children to its subversive aims, the real drive to integrate usually came from the children themselves. The parents were nervous about a possible confrontation, but the children felt it was time to get on with integration. The *Brown* decision had been handed down three years previously, when they were twelve or thirteen, and with the idealism of the young, they trusted in their country and its laws. As Terrance Roberts told a reporter who asked him in the early days whether he was doing this at the urging of the NAACP, "Nobody urged me to go. The school board asked if I wanted to go. I thought if I got in, some of the other children would be able to go . . . and have more opportunities."

One thing few outsiders noticed was that the integration was scheduled for Little Rock Central, a school for working-class whites, while a new suburban high school, designed to serve the city's upper middle class, was not involved. The city establishment, which came from the world of upper-middle-class Little Rock, was, of course, absolutely unaware that there was a double standard here and accepted all too readily its right to make the decisions on matters like this. They did not understand that others, less powerful, less successful, and less influential, would have to live with their decisions and might resent them. Daisy Bates, the head of the local NAACP, was aware of the class tensions that ran through the crisis, the rage on the part of the poor whites because they had to bear the burden of integration while the upper-class whites would be largely unaffected by it. At one point Mrs. Bates, referring to the deep class tensions that lay just beneath the surface in the white community, told one of the town leaders, "You may deserve Orval Faubus, but by God I don't!"

As the first day of school drew closer, Faubus's political position began to change. He was no longer Faubus, friend of moderates. He became evasive in dealing with school-board officials and other civic leaders. Those who thought they could count on him at least to remain neutral found that they either could not reach him or that if they did, he was ambivalent, in the opinion of some, or out and out slippery, in the opinion of others. "Governor, just what *are* you going to do in regard to the Little Rock integration plan?" Blossom asked him. Faubus paused and then answered: "When you tell me what the federals are going to do, I will tell you what I am going to do." Blossom thought that meant Faubus wanted the federal government to act decisively and thus remove any responsibility for integrating the schools from local officials, particularly from the governor. What was foremost in Orval Faubus's mind at that moment was not the education of the nine black children or the 2,000 white children whom they would join at Central High but rather his own political future in a state where, in the three years since *Brown,* race was beginning to dominate local political discourse. In Arkansas, the governor had to run for reelection every two years, and Arkansas voters were notoriously ungenerous about handing out third terms. Faubus was not a lawyer, he had no family wealth to fall back on, and he did not look forward to going back to being a rural postmaster. Other governors, their term of office over, could make a lateral move to a powerful Little Rock law firm and earn more than they ever had while in office. But that was not true of Faubus.

As the day for Little Rock's school integration approached, other politicians from the Deep South began applying pressure on Faubus to make him toe the line—to them he was the weak link in the chain of resistance. Mississippi senator James Eastland attacked him as being among the "weak-kneed politicians at the state capitols. . . . If the Southern states are picked off one by one under the damnable doctrine of gradualism I don't know if we can hold out or not." Faubus began to feel that he might, if he was not careful, become a politician who had obeyed the law only to find his political career ended overnight for his good deed. At the same time feelings were steadily becoming more raw, and Faubus could tell he was losing much of his room to maneuver. In the spring he had pushed a package of four segregationist bills through the Arkansas legislature. They had passed by votes of 81 to 1. That vote told him something. The governor knew the laws were pointless, that in a legal confrontation with the feds the state's powers were invalid, but he was beginning to respond to growing pressure around him and creating, if nothing else, a paper record. He was torn, as the deadline approached, between doing the right thing, and taking on the federal government to make himself a symbol of Southern white resistance.

Elsewhere in the Deep South segregationists were forming Citizens' Councils, local committees of white leaders pledged to stop integration. Regarding Faubus as something of a major liability, they decided to hold a major rally in Little Rock on August 22 and to bring in Marvin Griffin, the racist Georgia governor, and Roy Harris, the overall head of the Citizens' Councils, to speak at a ten-dollar-a-plate dinner. Faubus was not pleased by their visit; he knew they were trying to stoke the fires of racial resistance and to corner him. He complained about Griffin's visit to Virgil Blossom. "Why don't you telephone him and ask him to stay away?" Blossom suggested, somewhat innocently to the governor. "I'll think about it," Faubus answered. But Griffin and Harris came, stayed at the governor's mansion, and had breakfast with Faubus. From then on, Blossom noted, it became extremely difficult to reach Faubus.

Ironically, Faubus was not much of a racist. His roots were populist, but not racist populist. He was shrewd and earthy, from the Snopes school of politics, and was more intelligent and politically skilled than most of his critics suspected. His resentments were directed toward the upper class and business establishment of Little Rock, which he (rightly) suspected of looking down on him. His father, Sam Faubus, said later that Orval hated to be looked down on even as a little boy. There was, Harry Ashmore thought, something of a contradiction to Faubus's attitude toward the elite of Little Rock—he liked to put them on by pretending to be nothing but a good old country boy, as if he were still wearing his first store-bought suit, but when they believed him in that role, he resented it. He was, Ashmore liked to say, like an Airedale dog—a lot smarter than he looked. Later, after Little Rock had been torn apart by Faubus's decision to block integration, Ashmore noted that there had been plenty of earlier signs of which way he might go, since in the past whenever there had been any kind of crunch, Faubus had always followed his sense of what the preponderant feeling was among the poor whites, whom he knew so well and with whom he could so readily identify. His politics were the politics of class.

Faubus came from poor rural stock; he never even saw a black man until he was fully grown, when he went to Missouri to pick strawberries, his father later said. Sam Faubus was an old-fashioned, back-country radical who greatly admired Eugene Debs and was later appalled by his son's decision to block integration. (Sam Faubus was not a man to criticize his own flesh and blood openly, but he wrote a series of critical letters to the *Arkansas Gazette* under the pen name Jimmy Higgins.) Orval's childhood was poor: The water came from a nearby spring, the house was made of unfinished sawmill lumber, and the kitchen was completely unfinished. Orval graduated from grammar school in a one-room schoolhouse at the age of eighteen. He then became one of fifty people taking an exam for a third grade teacher's license, and he had gotten the highest marks. The certificate allowed him to teach school in Huntsville and attend high school at the same time. He got his high school diploma at the age of twenty-seven. By that time, he had been married for six years and he and his wife regularly spent their summers as migrant fruit-and-vegetable pickers. It was hard to find white people much poorer than they were and, Virgil Blossom noted, it was hard to find people that poor with so much ambition. In World War Two, he rose to the rank of major, came back, and bought a weekly paper in Huntsville; that brought him into the orbit of Sid McMath, the patrician liberal governor who was his first statewide sponsor and in whose cabinet he had served. (Later, McMath, appalled by the direction his protégé had taken, said, "I brought Orval down out of the hills and every night I pray for forgiveness.") He had helped McMath with the poor white vote, and he intended to run himself.

In 1954 Faubus ran for governor; he was so much the outsider in Little Rock that when he wrote his check for the $1,500 qualifying fee, it was not accepted until a friend who was a former state legislator endorsed it on the back. Because of his connection to McMath, he did reasonably well with blacks and upper-middle-class whites; as for poor rural whites, he was one of them. The one thing he remembered about that race was that it was one of the hottest summers in Arkansas history and all the other major candidates were traveling around in air-conditioned cars, but he made it, stop after stop, in the brutal heat, without any air-conditioning. He won even though, ironically enough, he had been red-baited for having briefly attended a small college with radical roots. As governor he appointed more blacks to state positions than any predecessor. Later, the liberal-moderate camp, including such men as Blossom, Ashmore, and Brooks Hays, the well-connected Little Rock congressman, cited the visit of Griffin and Harris as the turning point, the moment when Faubus looked at his political future, saw no middle ground, and made his choice.

Monday, September 2, fell on Labor Day; school was scheduled to start on Tuesday, September 3. By the beginning of the previous weekend, Faubus decided to call out the Arkansas National Guard—on the pretext of preventing violence, but in reality to block integration. Blossom found out about this only late on Monday night. According to Faubus, there were caravans of white racists heading for Central High. There would be bloodshed in the streets of Little Rock if the blacks tried to enter the school.

On the Sunday before school opening, Winthrop Rockefeller, the member of the famed Rockefeller family who had chosen to live in Arkansas, got wind of Faubus's plan to call out the National Guard and he rushed to the statehouse. There Rockefeller, the leader in trying to bring industry to a state desperately short of good jobs, pleaded with Faubus not to block integration. The governor told him he was too late: "I'm sorry but I'm already committed. I'm going to run for a third term, and if I don't do this, Jim Johnson and Bruce Bennett [the two leading Arkansas segregationists] will tear me to shreds."

What he did was very simple: He announced that he was unable to maintain the peace (thereby encouraging a mob to go into the streets), and then he placed the Arkansas National Guard on the side of the mob: Its orders, despite the specific mandate of the district court, were to keep the blacks out of the schools. The Guard encircled the school; meanwhile, the mob grew larger. The police force of the city was inadequate to deal with the mob, and the fire chief refused to permit the hoses of his fire wagons to be used against it. The black children were suddenly very much at risk. Daisy Bates, the leader of the local NAACP, asked black and white ministers to accompany them on Wednesday, September 4. She arranged for a police car to protect them. But as they approached the school, they were abused and threatened; when they finally reached the school, they were turned away by a National Guard captain, who said he was acting under the orders of Governor Faubus. What are your orders? someone asked one of the soldiers. "Keep the niggers out!" he answered. The confidence of the mob grew greater by the minute as it found that the law-enforcement forces were on its side. Sensing this, the ministers and children quickly retreated.

They were the lucky ones. One child, fifteen-year-old Elizabeth Eckford, had not gotten the message the night before about how they were to assemble together. Her father was a railroad-car maintenance worker who worked nights; her mother taught at a school for black children who were deaf or blind. The family did not have a phone. In the morning, an exhausted Daisy Bates completely forgot that she had not advised Elizabeth about the new arrangements. Elizabeth, like most of the other children involved in the early integration cases, had made the decision to go to Central very much on her own. Elizabeth wanted to be a lawyer, and she had heard that Central offered a speech course that might help her prepare for law school, while Horace Man did not. Her mother, Birdie Eckford, was unhappy about her choice, and when Elizabeth had suggested during the summer that they go to the school board office and get the requisite transfer forms for Central, Mrs. Eckford gently and vaguely agreed to do it some other time, hoping Elizabeth would forget about it. Two weeks later Elizabeth brought it up again. Again her mother tried to delay. Finally, near the end of August, Elizabeth demanded that her mother take her that very day to get the transfer. With that it was obtained. That first day of school she got up early and pressed her new black-and-white dress, one she had made herself to wear for her new experience in an integrated school. At breakfast the family television set was on and some commentator was talking about the size of the mob gathering in front of the school and wondering aloud whether the black children would show up. "Turn that TV off!" said Mrs. Eckford. Birdie was so nervous that Elizabeth tried to comfort her mother by saying that everything would be all right. Her father, she noted, was just as nervous, holding a cigar in one hand and a pipe in his mouth, neither of them lit. Before Elizabeth left, her mother called the family together and they all prayed.

Alone and unprotected, Elizabeth approached the school, and the crowd started to scream at her: "Here she comes! Here comes one of the niggers!" But she saw the National Guard troopers and was not scared, because she thought the soldiers would protect her. She tried to walk into the school, but a guard thrust his rifle at her and blocked her way. She walked a few feet further down to get by the guard but was blocked again by two other soldiers. Some white students were being let in at the same time, she noticed. Other soldiers moved toward her and raised their bayonets to make the barrier more complete. She was terrified now, blocked in her attempt to get to the school, aware that the mob was closing in behind her. Someone was yelling, "Lynch her! Lynch her!" Someone else yelled: "Go home, you bastard of a black bitch!" She tried to steady her legs as she turned away, the school now at her back. The mob pressed closer. "No nigger bitch is going to get in our school!" someone shouted. She was blocked in all directions. She looked down the street and saw a bench by a bus stop. If she could just make it to the bench, she thought. When she finally got there, she felt she would collapse.

A man she had never known, Ben Fine, the education reporter for *The New York Times,* who was there to write his story on how Little Rock had stayed so calm, came over and put his arm around her and tried to comfort her. "Don't let them see you cry," he said. An elderly white woman (the wife of a white professor at a black college) came over and also offered her solace and tried to face the crowd down. The woman, despite the howls of the mob, managed to get Elizabeth on a bus and out of the combat zone.

Among those who had been there and caught all of it—the virulence of the white mob, its rage and madness mounting as it closed in, the lone young black girl who seemed to be bearing herself with amazing calm and dignity—was John Chancellor, a young reporter with NBC. He had watched Elizabeth Eckford's perilous journey with growing fear: one child, alone, entrapped by this mob. He was not sure she was going to make it out alive. He had wanted a story, a good story, but this was something beyond a good story, a potential tragedy so terrible that he had hoped it wasn't really happening. He was terribly frightened for her, frightened for himself, and frightened about what this told him about his country. He could not believe that someone had so carelessly allowed this child to come to school alone, with no escort. The mob gathered there in the street was uglier than anything he had ever seen before in his life. It was a mob of fellow Americans, people who under other conditions might be perfectly decent people, but there they were completely out of control. Chancellor wondered briefly where this young girl found her strength. It was almost as if he was praying: *Please, stop all of this; please, there's got to be a better way.* He watched in agony and captured it all for NBC.

Chancellor was a relatively junior reporter for NBC in the summer of 1957. He was thirty years old and based in Chicago. After working for the *Chicago Sun Times,* he had been hired by the local NBC station in Chicago in 1950, ostensibly as a news writer; but the real reason was that his superiors thought he could cover so-called street stories—fires and accidents. On the early *Camel News Caravan* with John Cameron Swayze, he would go out in the field with a cameraman and a sound man. He doubled as film editor, for the show's producer had asked him what he knew about editing film. Nothing at all, he answered. Well, buy a book, and read and find out about it, the producer had said, which Chancellor did. As a result he had become surprisingly expert in editing film, which in those days was 35mm and, in the vernacular of the trade, went through the gate at ninety feet a minute. He became in the process something of a film nut, and he came to understand, as few others of his generation did, the journalistic power of images. Years later he thought his tour as reporter-film editor taught him how to write for film, a process he might otherwise not have understood.

Most of the big-name journalists at the networks were still doing radio reporting when he had joined NBC. Some of the early television figures, such as John Cameron Swayze, the NBC anchorman ("Let's hopscotch the world for headlines," he would say every night), held their positions because they had been sufficiently low down in the radio pecking order that they had nothing to lose by going over to this new medium. Many others, like Chancellor, had roots in print and were learning television the hard way, since the rules were still being set every day as they worked.

On that Labor Day weekend in 1957, Chancellor had been poised to go to Nashville to report on school integration in the South, but his superior in New York, Reuven Frank, told him that according to the AP wire, Orval Faubus was going to call out the Arkansas National Guard to prevent court-ordered integration. That sounded like a bigger story than Nashville, so without stopping to pack, Chancellor raced to catch the last plane to Little Rock. He was relatively new to what was now becoming known as the Southern, or race, beat. His introduction to it had come back in 1955 with the Emmett Till case, still primarily a print story. But there had been a brief harbinger of the future the day after the acquittal of the two men accused of murdering Till. Chancellor happened to be in Memphis at the time and he was sent down to Sumner to do a radio report for *Monitor,* the lively NBC radio show of that period. Chancellor grabbed a primitive early-model tape recorder and drove over in the company of a man from the Jackson radio station.

From the instant he arrived, Sumner had scared him: He had an eerie feeling that something terrible was going to happen as he walked up the street, interviewing blacks and whites alike on their opinion of the trial. Suddenly, a sixth sense told him that he was in trouble and he slowly turned to look behind him. There coming directly at him was a phalanx of eight or nine men in overalls and work shirts. Rage was etched in their faces. His car was ten feet away, and the Jackson radio man was in it, honking the horn. Chancellor was terrified, for he knew the men wanted to hurt him. For a split second he thought of running to the car, but the men were too close. He did the only thing he could think of. He took the microphone and pointed it at the first white man. "Okay," he said, "you can do what you want with me, but the whole world is going to hear about it and see it." The men stopped, he later speculated, because they had mistaken his tape recorder for a camera. It had been, he decided, like holding up a talisman to some primitive tribal chief, but it worked. With that, he walked to the car and drove away.

If print reporters and still photographers had been witnesses to their stories, then television correspondents, armed as they were with cameras and crews, were something more: They were not merely witnesses, but something more, a part of the story. Television reporters, far more than their print predecessors, contributed to the speeding up of social change in America. Little Rock became the prime example of that, the first all-out confrontation between the force of the law and the force of the mob, played out with television cameras whirring away in black and white for a nation that was by now largely wired.

Reuven Frank, the most powerful and cerebral figure in the NBC newsroom at the time, who more than anyone else created the standards of that network's journalism, understood immediately that the world of television was different. The cameramen he had inherited had a newsreel vision of shooting film—their ideal was two heads of state meeting and shaking hands. Frank wanted something different, something more subtle and more real. He believed if you were creative enough, you could create a mosaic of the country—its humanity, its diversity, and its tension points. He had a supple sense of the medium, and Chancellor remembered his own pleasure when Frank called to tell him after one report that his piece had "a lovely Mozartian unity to it." Frank emphasized constantly to his reporters that their role was to be, in some ways, minimal. Film was so powerful that a reporter was well advised to get out of the way and let the pictures do the talking. Certainly, that was true in Little Rock. The images were so forceful that they told their own truths and needed virtually no narration. It was hard for people watching at home not to take sides: There they were, sitting in their living rooms in front of their own television sets watching orderly black children behaving with great dignity, trying to obtain nothing more than a decent education, the most elemental of American birthrights, yet being assaulted by a vicious mob of poor whites. What was happening now in the country was politically potent: The legal power of the United States Supreme Court had now been cast in moral terms for the American conscience, and that was driven as much as anything else by the footage from the networks from Little Rock. The President, uneasy with the course of events, had failed to give any kind of moral leadership, and he had deliberately refused to define the issue in moral terms; now, almost unconsciously, the media was doing it instead, for the ugliness and the cruelty of it all, the white mob encouraged by a local governor tormenting young children, carried its own indictment. The nation watched, hypnotized, from its living rooms every night, what, in the words of television reporter Dan Schorr, was "a national evening seance." Every clip of film diminished the room to maneuver of each of the major players. With television every bit of action, Chancellor decided, seemed larger, more immediate; the action seemed to be moving at an ever faster rate.

On his arrival there, Chancellor thought, Little Rock had seemed a sleepy town, as yet unconnected to the ever greater bustle of modern American life. The pace of living seemed almost languid. Chancellor remembered a vivid symbol of the older America that still existed when he arrived. The bellboy who took him to his room at the old Sam Peck Hotel brought him a pitcher of iced water and then suggested that if he wanted any female companionship later in the evening, he need only call. One night, early in October, after the 101st had momentarily stabilized the situation, Chancellor had gone out to dinner with Harry Ashmore at Hank's Doghouse in North Little Rock. It happened to be the night that *Sputnik* went up, and the two of them had watched the news reports of this most remarkable achievement in the new space age. "Can you believe this?" Chancellor had said. "This means that men are really going to go to the moon." "Yes," said Ashmore. "And here we are in Little Rock fighting the Civil War again." It seemed to symbolize the time warp they were in.

At the beginning of the story, Chancellor could not broadcast live because there was still no AT&T equipment available. He had to race to the airport each afternoon for a chartered plane to take him to Oklahoma City, where he could do his broadcast live. The NBC show was on for fifteen minutes, which meant it contained twelve minutes of news. Network news was just coming of age. The previous fall, Swayze had been replaced by a new team of anchors: Chet Huntley, sturdy and steadfast, his reliability vouched for by his strong face, was electronically married to David Brinkley, mischievous and waspish, a perfect foil for the overpowering immediacy of television. It, along with the other two network shows was creating a new electronic media grid binding the nation.

Chancellor now became their first star in the field. Every night NBC led with his story, in part, Chancellor suspected, because Reuven Frank understood what was happening—not only on the streets of Little Rock, but in the American psyche. It was perhaps the first time a television reporter rather than a print reporter had put his signature on so critical a running story. Chancellor not only worked hard but, to his credit, he never thought himself a star. An anchorman, he liked to say years later, was someone who ran the last leg of a relay race; and some fifteen years later, when he did in fact become the anchorman of the *NBC Nightly News,* he took the additional title not of managing editor, but of principal reporter.

Little Rock made him famous, and the unique aspect to television fame was that his face became his byline. People came to associate him with the story he was covering, and they began to feel they already knew him. Because of this, they were quicker to confide in him than in print reporters. Being a television reporter, he realized, meant instant access and instant connection, and in no small part because of his electronic fame, he soon obtained a secret mole inside the school. His mole, Chancellor discovered later, was a sixteen-year-old Little Rock boy named Ira Lipman, just starting his senior year. Ernest Green, one of the Little Rock nine, had been a locker-room attendant at the Jewish country club in Little Rock, where Lipman's parents had a membership. On a number of occasions Lipman had ended up driving Ernest Green home after work, and the two had struck up a friendship. Lipman thought Ernest Green pleasant and intelligent, with a rare gentleness about him. Their relationship had in his mind underlined the madness of segregation, the fact that the two of them could not have a normal friendship and that he had only managed to know him through a club where his parents were privileged members and Ernest Green was an attendant.

Lipman worked a few nights a week at the *Arkansas Gazette* and had once met another NBC reporter, Frank McGee. Now he decided to help Chancellor, because he felt he had a connection to NBC and also because he had seen Chancellor on television and thought him decent and fair-minded, a man who was trying to tell the truth about a difficult situation. He would gather information and then call Chancellor anonymously from a pay phone just outside the school. The first of his calls took place at the very beginning of the crisis. Chancellor did not have time to check out the information before he filed that day, but late that night, upon his return from Oklahoma City, he found the information to be accurate.

The next day Chancellor's youthful anony-

mous source called to chide him: "I'm very disappointed in you," he said. "I have all this terrific
information and you didn't use it." Chancellor
apologized, but promised to take the information
more seriously in the future. Not knowing his
source's name, Chancellor comprehended in some
way the background and the motivation of this
young boy. Lipman always had to whisper lest
another student discover what he was doing and
tell someone. The boy was placing himself in great
danger. But having this source gave Chancellor a
terrific edge on the story, and he was able to move
ahead of his print rivals.

Wallace Westfeldt, a reporter for the *Nashville Tennessean,* was amused by the spectacle of
this reporter from the upstart institution of television news, who was gaining every day the grudg-
ing admiration of his older print colleagues.
Westfeldt's own sources were excellent, since he
had visited Little Rock several times before the
crisis. Each night he would file his own story for
the early edition of his paper and then sit in the
Little Rock press club having a sandwich and a
drink with the other reporters. As he ate, the *NBC
Nightly News* would come on, and Chancellor
would often have something that few, if any, of
the print reporters had. Westfeldt could see them
cursing under their breath, and when the news
show was over, there would be a quiet exodus
from the press club as reporters went to the
phones to call their offices and update their own

stories. Television, Westfeldt thought, was quickly catching up with print: If anything, in this story the new medium might have exceeded the old for the first time.

As Little Rock developed, the national media force focusing on civil rights crystallized. It had its own pecking order and rules. Johnny Popham, and soon his successor Claude Sitton, of the *Times* set the tone. There were also the legendary Homer Bigart, also of the *Times,* Bob Bird of the *Tribune,* Bob Baker of *The Washington Post,* and soon Karl Fleming of *Newsweek.* The older men in this brigade had often been war correspondents in World War Two and Korea, which helped— because the situation was not unlike a war on native soil; the younger men, by and large, were Southerners, because a Southern accent was considered helpful.

They were at risk all the time, for the mobs perceived them as liberals, Jews, and Communists. Several *Life* magazine reporters were beaten badly by the mob early in the crisis, and then the reporters were arrested by local officials for having been beaten up. The network people, because of their high visibility, the familiarity of their faces, and the obvious presence of their cameramen, were particularly vulnerable. Chancellor soon found that when he walked down the street, he would often be followed by cars full of segregationists, hate contorting their faces as they stared at him. At first he would panic. *Should I run?* he would ask himself, but he soon learned merely to keep walking. The locals became angrier and angrier—for television, in particular, was holding up a mirror of these people for the outside world to look at it, and the image in the mirror was not pretty. If you went to the sheriff's office to do an interview, Chancellor remembered, you gave your name and organization to the deputy, who would holler back so the entire office could hear, "Sheriff, there's some son of a bitch out here from the Nigger Broadcasting Company who says he wants to see you."

Because of the dangers, there were certain rules—a reporter never carried a notebook that he could not hide in a pocket. Popham's first rule of coverage was: Never take notes in front of the crowd. It was better to dress casual than sharp. A reporter never went out on a story alone. One did not argue with the segregationists or provoke them. Whatever moral abhorrence a reporter felt about the events taking place in front of him, it was to be kept bottled up. Ben Fine of the *Times,* an indoor man in the vernacular, had lost his cool when he comforted Elizabeth Eckford. He had started to argue with the mob and the *Times* had been forced to bring him back to New York.

Watching these journalists in Little Rock, as he had watched them almost two years earlier in Montgomery, Alabama, was a man named Will Campbell. A native of a tiny town called Liberty in south Mississippi, he had earned a bachelor's

degree from Wake Forest and a master's from the
Yale Divinity School: He was technically the Rev.
Will Campbell, though for most of his life he
never had a church. He liked to describe himself
as "a Baptist preacher, but never on Sunday."
The contradiction between his own liberalism and
the conservatism of his church amused him, and
he liked to say that he "was a Baptist preacher of
the South, but not a Southern Baptist preacher."
During the early days of the civil rights movement, he became an important but anonymous
player. Sometimes his face would appear in the
back of a photograph taken during some particular confrontation, but he would almost never be
identified, just as his name would never appear in
the news stories themselves, by agreement with
the journalists for whom he had already become
a valuable source. He was quoted hundreds of
times in newspapers but never by name, instead,
always as an anonymous reliable source, which he
in fact was. He was a shrewd recorder and inter-
preter not only of the facts but of the intentions of
the many different players involved, and he had
important friends on all sides in these confronta-
tions. His first job after school had been to serve
as the chaplain at the University of Mississippi,
but his liberal views on integration had almost
immediately gotten him fired. Although violence
had never been directed at him at Ole Miss, at one
reception he had given, a turd had been discovered in the punch bowl. That had convinced him

his days at Ole Miss were numbered. In 1956 he took a job as a kind of roving field agent for the National Council of Churches based in Nashville. Acting as a friend and adviser to those blacks threatened or in trouble, and connecting them to sympathetic people and agencies in the North, he was a ubiquitous figure, always on the move. The national reporters discovered he was able to move back and forth between different groups, bringing them information and making quiet, astute suggestions about what was likely to happen next.

Will Campbell, then thirty-three, understood as much as anyone the growing power of the media and what it meant to the Movement. Earlier in Montgomery, he had gained a sense of how it could define this story in moral terms. But one day early in the crisis at Little Rock, he had an epiphany about the importance of the media. He had been out in the streets watching the mob when a friend nudged him and pointed to a slim young man who seemed to be talking into the air. "That's John Chancellor of NBC," the friend noted. Campbell had never seen Chancellor in the flesh before, though he had heard of him. There seemed nothing remarkable about his appearance, nor did he seem to know anything more than Will Campbell himself about the violent situation playing itself out in front of them. But a few hours later, back in his hotel room, Campbell happened to turn on his television set and there was the very scene he had witnessed earlier in the day: Chancellor, shrunk now to about three inches on his screen, was calmly giving a summary of what was happening as the mob jostled and jeered behind him. The commentary, for most Americans, was chilling, and it struck Campbell in that instant that these modern journalists, both print and television, were the new prophets of our society. Moreover, they had, because of television, what the prophets of old had lacked—a mass audience to which they could transmit with stunning immediacy the events they witnessed. It was in their power, as it had been in the power of the prophets before them, the tent and brush-arbor revivalists, to define sin, and they were doing it not to a select few of the chosen but to the entire citizenry. They did not think of themselves as modern prophets and they did not think they were actually defining sin, but what they were doing, in Will Campbell's view, was just that, for there was no way that an ordinary citizen could watch these events through their eyes and words and pictures and not be offended and moved. What John Chancellor might as well have been doing, thought Campbell, was letting the film roll and repeating again and again, "This is a sin . . . this is a sin . . . this is a sin . . ."

Locally, Harry Ashmore had never had any doubt what he intended to do with his paper once Faubus drew the line, but he warned the paper's elderly owner, J. N. Heiskell, what the price of telling the truth and upholding the law would be.

Heiskell brushed Ashmore's warnings aside. He had no desire to accommodate such demagoguery even if it meant losing subscribers and advertising (which, in a subsequent boycott of the *Gazette,* it did). "I'm an old man," Heiskell answered, "and I've lived too long to let people like that [Faubus] take over my city." Most editors at American newspapers of the era were not so brave. More often than not, they put their own survival first and tried not to offend local sensibilities. Often, in moments of crisis, their instinct would be to protect the community against its critics, to soften accounts of its failings and, above all, to blame outsiders. Harry Ashmore was having none of that. This was the moment, he was sure, when he would be judged with a finality.

Ashmore was fearless not only in how he covered the crisis in his own paper but also in opening up its resources to visiting reporters. That was true not only at the beginning of the crisis, when most of the Little Rock establishment supported the integration plan, but in the months to follow as well, as people (including, most notably, his competitors on the rival *Arkansas Democrat*) who once praised the plan began to falter and switch sides. Relatively early on, a top Justice Department official called Ashmore to get a reading on what was happening: "I'll give it to you in one sentence," he answered. "The police have been routed, the mob is in the streets and we're close to a reign of terror."

His paper became the general press head-quarters. Visiting reporters would head over there every day, in effect to be briefed by Ashmore and his reporters on the day's events. Then, if they wanted to, they could go out for dinner with him as he talked on into the night, regaling them with stories of Arkansas politics. Orval Faubus might have been able momentarily to block the school integration, orchestrate the mob, and confuse the President of the United States as to his true aims, but he had met his match in Harry Ashmore. (Some thirty years later, at a conference at Fayetteville where panelists looked at the events of Little Rock in retrospect, Faubus began to sanitize his version of what had happened. His view by then, created to tidy up his place in history, was that through his actions he had only been trying to push President Eisenhower to act. Some one thousand people, almost all of them pro-integration, were attending the symposium, and one morning just before Faubus spoke, he and his old antagonist Ashmore had breakfast together. Faubus gave his version of what he was going to say, and Ashmore wished him well in getting away with it. "But remember, Orval," he said as the latter had gotten up from the table to give his speech. "This time I've got the mob on *my* side.")

Both the nation and the world watched with horror and fascination as Faubus steadily moved into the vacuum created by the Eisenhower administration. Largely unsympathetic to the idea of integration, the President had given little thought to the question of what might happen if the Southern states rebelled. Despite the constant rumblings about the possibility of serious Southern resistance, Eisenhower seemed ambivalent about the events unfolding so dramatically in the month after the *Brown* decision. Meanwhile, the job grew steadily more difficult, until in Little Rock the governor seemed to be openly defying the law of the land. A few men around Eisenhower, more committed to civil rights—Herbert Brownell, Richard Nixon, and Bill Rogers— thought that the President had underestimated Faubus from the start and that Faubus was aiming for a major constitutional confrontation for his own political gain.

Soon after the *Brown* decision, Attorney General Brownell, as the chief law enforcement officer of the country, had met with the attorneys general of the Southern states and spoke informally about what they could all do together to expedite the process of integration. He had asked for suggestions on how federal and state forces could make the transition as easy as possible. When he finished he was met by thunderous silence. Afterward one state attorney general took him aside and pointed out that each man in this room intended one day to become governor of his state. None therefore wanted to be seen as partners of the U.S. government in carrying out local integration. In fact, the state attorney general added, Brownell should expect significant opposition rather than assistance.

Ike was very much in conflict within himself over whether integration was right or wrong; his essential sympathies were with neither the nine children nor the mob in the street but primarily with his new and extremely wealthy and conservative Southern golfing and hunting friends, those old-fashioned Southern traditionalists who found integration objectionable. As such the President remained silent on the issue and continued to dally. This was alien and extremely uncomfortable territory for him. Conservative by nature, he saw even the smallest change in the existing racial order as radical and upsetting. In the brief period while he was president of Columbia University it had been decided (but not by him) to give Ralph Bunche an honorary degree. Bunche was then at the peak of his career at the UN, and possibly the most honored and least controversial black man in the country. But Ike was uneasy with the choice, because it meant Bunche and his wife would have to join the other recipients for drinks and dinner. It wasn't that Ike was against Bunche receiving the degree, he confided, but he wondered if *the other* recipients would object to socializing with the Bunches. To his considerable surprise, the evening went off smoothly and several of the other recipients went out of their way to seek out the Bunches. The man to whom Eisenhower told this story, his friend Cy Sulzberger, was quite shocked; it showed, he thought, not only how biased Ike was about black people but how little he understood his own bias. Now, in the midst of a major constitutional crisis, to aides who suggested that he speak in favor of integration on the basis of moral and religious principles if nothing else, he answered somewhat disingenuously that he did not believe you could force people to change what was in their hearts. To those who suggested he meet with black leaders to talk about the nation's growing racial tensions and the threat of increased white Southern resistance, he answered, in a particularly telling moment, that if he did, he would have to meet as well with the leaders of the Ku Klux Klan.

Eisenhower did finally meet with Faubus in Newport, Rhode Island, much against Brownell's wishes. The attorney general warned the President repeatedly that the governor was thinking only of his reelection campaign. Faubus at first played Eisenhower extremely well: He had come not to exploit the issue, he claimed, but as an anguished moderate who wished only for a little more time. Ike, it seemed, was amenable to that: a little more time to do something that he himself could not readily understand. He began to speak of a compromise solution. Faubus later wrote that Eisenhower turned to Brownell in one of their sessions and asked, "Herb, can't you go down there [to Little Rock] and ask the Court to postpone this thing for a few days?" Brownell answered, "No, we can't do that. It isn't possible. It isn't legally possible. It can't be done." Brownell explained that the case was in the jurisdiction of the courts. Ike still seemed uncertain. Faubus noted: "I got the impression at the time that he was attempting to recall just what he was supposed to say to me, as if he were trying to remember instructions on a subject on which he was not completely assured in his own mind." Eisenhower, with no moderate solution available, finally turned up the heat and believed that he had gotten Faubus to agree to back down. But then as soon as Faubus returned to Little Rock, he reneged on his promise. When asked if he hadn't backed off his promise made at Newport, he answered, "Just because I said it doesn't make it so."

That did it as far as the President was concerned. "Well, you were right, Herb," he angrily told Brownell. "He did just what you said he'd do—he double-crossed me." If Eisenhower did not entirely comprehend the moral issue at stake, or for that matter the legal one, he certainly understood a personal challenge. A man who had been a five-star general did not look kindly on frontal challenges by junior officers. After vacillating for so long, he came down hard, seeing the issue not as a question of integration so much as one of insurrection. He sent in troops of the 101st Airborne to protect the nine children and he federalized the Arkansas National Guard. For the first time since Reconstruction days, federal troops were sent into the South to preserve order. Little Rock, Dean Acheson wrote Harry Truman at the time, terrified him, "a weak President who fiddled along ineffectually until a personal affront drives him to unexpectedly drastic action. A Little Rock with Moscow and the SAC in the place of the paratroopers could blow us all apart."

. . .

More than thirty years later, John Chancellor could still talk about the day the 101st Airborne came to Little Rock as if it had happened yesterday: The soldiers marched into the area and set up their perimeter. Their faces were immobile and, unlike the Guardsmen's, betrayed no politics, just duty. As they marched in, the clear, sharp sound of their boots clacking on the street was a reminder of their professionalism. Chancellor had never thought much about the Constitution before; if anything, he had somehow taken it for granted. But he realized that day that he was watching the Constitution in action. There was something majestic about the scene: it was a moment at once thrilling and somehow frightening as well.

With the arrival of the 101st, the nation yet again witnessed a stunning spectacle on television: armed soldiers of one of the most honored divisions in the United States Army escorting young black children where once there had been a mob. When the segregationists in the street protested, the paratroopers turned out to be very different from the National Guard soldiers who had so recently been their pals. The men of the 101st fixed their bayonets and placed them right at the throats of the protestors, quickly moving them out of the school area. That first morning, an Army officer came to Daisy Bates's house, where the children had gathered, and saluted her. "Mrs. Bates," he said. "We're ready for the children. We will return them to your home at three-thirty." It was, said Minniejean Brown, one of the nine, an exhilarating moment. "For the first time in my life I felt like an American citizen," she later told Mrs. Bates.

For the moment, the law of the nation had been upheld against the will of the mob and the whims of a segregationist politician. The black children were escorted to and from school every day by the soldiers. Little Rock seemed to calm down. Faubus screamed about the encroachment of states' rights by the federal government and bemoaned the fact that Arkansas was occupied territory. Why, he himself, he said, had helped rescue the 101st when it was pinned down at Bastogne during the Battle of the Bulge (which was untrue—by the time his outfit had arrived, the 101st had already stopped the last German drive).

After a few weeks, with the situation seemingly under control, the government pulled out the 101st and put the federalized Arkansas National Guard in charge. With that, the situation began to deteriorate. The mob was no longer a problem, but inside the school there was a systematic and extremely well organized assault upon the nine children by high-school-age segregationists. They not only harassed the black children but, more effectively, any white child who was courteous or friendly to them.

It was a calculated campaign (organized, school officials suspected, right out of the governor's mansion). The school bullies, behaving like youthful Klansmen, knew they had behind them the full power of the state government and the increasingly defiant Arkansas population. That meant the job of protecting the nine fell on a handful of teachers and administrators in the school. The nine students were in for a very hard and ugly year. There was a relentless assault upon them—kicking, tripping, hitting them from behind, harassing them with verbal epithets as they walked down the hall, pouring hot soup on them in the cafeteria. Their lockers were broken into regularly, their books stolen. The school administrators knew exactly who the ringleaders were but found them boastfully proud. One girl told Elizabeth Huckaby, the vice-principal, that she was entirely within her rights. All she had done, the girl said, was to use the word *nigger*. It was as if her rights included harassing others for racial reasons.

How, in retrospect, the nine children stood all of this is amazing, but they did, showing remarkable inner strength and character, again and again turning the other cheek. On many occasions they seemed ready to break, and one or two would show up in Ms. Huckaby's office in tears, exhausted by the cruelty and on the verge of quitting. It was the job of Ms. Huckaby and others to plead with them to keep going and to remind them that if they faltered, it would merely be harder on the next group, because the segregationists would be bolder with success. Only one of the nine did not finish the first year: Minniejean Brown. Perhaps the most enthusiastic and emotional of the nine, she seemed to be the one least able to turn away from the harassment. Soon, the segregationists realized that she was the weak link and turned their full force on her. Minniejean on occasion fought back. Tormented in the cafeteria one day by her enemies, she dumped a soup bowl on the head of a student and was suspended. She tried desperately to control herself but in time responded once too often and was expelled. Immediately, cards were printed up that said, ONE DOWN. EIGHT TO GO.

Some of the black children's parents wanted them to pull out at various times during the year, fearing the price was simply too high. But Daisy Bates was strong: She reminded the children again and again that they were doing this not for themselves but for others, some as yet unborn. They were now, like it or not, leaders in a moral struggle. That year Ernest Green graduated, and twenty years later, he was perhaps the most successful member of the graduating class: As an assistant secretary of labor in the cabinet of Jimmy Carter, he was the featured speaker at the twentieth reunion of his classmates.

In a way, everyone seemed to have gotten something out of Little Rock. The civil rights leaders learned how to challenge the forces of segregation in front of the modern media, most notably television cameras. The networks, new and unsure of their role, had found a running story composed of almost nothing but images, which would not only prove compelling to viewers but which would legitimize its early reporters for their courage and decency (just as the broadcasts of Ed Murrow and his CBS colleagues had been legitimized by radio during World War Two). In the months after the quiz-show scandals rocked the networks, there was a calculated attempt to address the resulting loss of prestige by giving the news shows ever greater freedom to cover such important events as Little Rock. Not just the news shows but the networks themselves were suddenly in the business of building respectability. John Chancellor in time would go on to one of the most distinguished careers in American journalism and public life, as anchor of the *Today* show, as head of the Voice of America and, finally, as anchorman of the NBC news.

No one, of course, gained more than Orval Faubus. He portrayed himself as the victim of massive federal intervention, the lonely man who believed in states' rights and the will of his own people. No longer could any good (white) citizen of Arkansas be for segregation and against Faubus. A third term, which had seemed unlikely before Little Rock, was guaranteed. With two moderate candidates running against him in 1958, he beat their combined total of votes by more than two to one. A fourth term followed. And a fifth term. And finally a sixth. On occasion there was talk of retirement, but he had, wrote the *Arkansas Gazette,* ridden off into more sunsets than Tom Mix. His decision to block integration set the stage for a generation of Southern politicians, most notably George Wallace, who had learned from Little Rock how to manipulate the anger within the South, how to divide a state by class and race, and how to make the enemy seem to be the media. The moderate position had been badly undermined at Little Rock, and an era of confrontation was to follow, Harry Ashmore wrote prophetically in *Life* in 1958.

A year after Little Rock, Daisy Bates suggested that she come to the White House with the nine children. It would be a wonderful thing, she suggested, for the children, who had endured so much hatred and violence, to be received by the President of the United States. The idea terrified Eisenhower's White House staff. In truth, it was a hard thing to say no to. Sherman Adams, the White House chief of staff and the boss of Frederick Morrow, the one black man on Ike's staff, shrewdly put the ball in Morrow's court. Adams asked Morrow: Was Mrs. Bates's request a wise one? No, said Morrow, because it was not a question of whether the President sympathized with the nine children. Rather, if he met with them, it would so enrage Southern leaders that it would diminish his role as a leader on such issues in the future. In addition, he added, the meeting would only subject the students "to more abuse than ever before, and certainly the President does not want to be a party to this kind of affair." "You are absolutely correct," Adams told Morrow. "That was my thinking on the meeting." Adams had one more move left. Would Morrow please call Mrs. Bates to tell her? It was, Morrow noted, a call he dreaded making, but he knew the rules and he knew what he was there to do. He was a team player, so he did it. He suggested that if she and the children came to Washington, he would set up a specially conducted tour of the White House.

No aspect of the crisis, particularly the role played by Orval Faubus, escaped the notice of Martin Luther King, Jr. He was nothing if not political, and he understood the emerging politics of protest brilliantly. King knew from his experience in Montgomery, where television news was making its earliest inroads, that what he was doing was no longer merely local, that because of television, for the first time the nation was convening each evening around 6 or 7 P.M.

King and his people were conducting the most perilous undertaking imaginable, for they knew that the more skillfully they provoked their enemies, the more dramatic the footage they would reap, and also the more likely they were to capture the moral high ground. King was appealing to the national electorate at the expense of the regional power structure, which he considered hostile anyway. He needed some measure of white backlash, and he needed, among other things, proper villains. He wanted ordinary white people to sit in their homes and watch blacks acting with great dignity while Southern officials, moved by the need to preserve a system he hated, assaulted them. As such he was the dramatist of a national morality play: The blacks were in white hats; the whites, much to their surprise, would find themselves in the black hats. A play required good casting and Martin King soon learned to pick not just his venues carefully, but also his villains.

Montgomery, for all its successes, had lacked villains. Certainly, the local officials in Montgomery had mistreated the black protestors, but there was no one brutal figure who had come to symbolize the evils of segregation and who could be counted on, when provoked, to play into the hands of the Movement. But Orval Faubus was a different matter, a man who made ordinary Americans recoil. As the Movement grew, King was offered various cities as platforms for his protests, but he was always careful to select those with the ugliest and crudest segregationists—such men as Bull Connor, in Birmingham, and Sheriff Jim Clark, in Selma. In the past, segregation had been enforced more subtly, often through economic threats. Blacks would lose their jobs if they signed petitions asking schools to desegregate, for example. Racial prejudice had been like a giant beast that never came out in the daytime; now King and others like him were exposing it to bright light, fresh air, and the eye of the television camera and the beast was dying.

The timing of King's protest was critical: 1955 and 1956 marked the years when the networks were just becoming networks in the true sense, thanks in large part to the network news shows. Along with John Kennedy, King was one of the first people who understood how to provide action for film, how, in effect, to script the story for the executive producers (so that the executive producers thought they were scripting it themselves). It was an ongoing tour de force for King: a great story, great action, constant confrontation, great film, plenty of moral and spiritual tension. There was a hypnotic effect in watching it all unfold; King treated the television reporters assigned to him well. He never wanted a confrontation that the network newsmen could not capture on film and feed to New York, nor did he, if at all possible, want the action too late in the day that it missed the deadlines of the network news shows. So it was that the Movement began and so it was that television amplified and speeded up the process of political and social change in America.

. . .

One of the most powerful currents taking place and changing in American life in this decade—taking place even as few recognized it—was the increasing impact and importance of black culture on daily American life. This was particularly true in the fifties in two areas critically important to young Americans: music and sports. In popular music the influence of black culture was profound, much to the irritation of a generation of parents of white teenagers. While Elvis was the first white country artist to use the beat, he was merely part of a larger revolution in which not only were many of the features of black music being used by white musicians, but black musicians were increasingly accepted by white audiences as well. Chuck Berry, Little Richard, Sam Cooke, Ike Turner, and Fats Domino were now integrated into the white hit-charts. The other evolution, equally important, was taking place in sports, and it had a significant impact on the society. With the coming of television, professional sports, particularly football and basketball, had a far greater national impact than they had ever had before. What had once happened before relatively small crowds now happened simultaneously in millions of American homes; in effect, it was going from the periphery to the very center of the culture.

In terms of the coming of technology and the coming of the gifted black athletes, a dual revolution was sweeping across the country: in the quality of athletic ability of those able to play, and in the number of people now able to watch. Professional football, which, in comparison with professional baseball, had been virtually a minor sport before the arrival of television, now flowered under the sympathetic eye of the camera, its importance growing even as the nation was being wired city by city and house by house for television. Suddenly, professional football had become a new super sport, the first true rival to Major League baseball for the nation's affection.

In baseball, the coming of Jackie Robinson had been quickly followed by the coming of several other magnificent black players—Willie Mays, Monte Irvin, Ernie Banks, and Henry Aaron. From the start, because Brooklyn had signed the first black players, the other National League teams had been forced to go to the same extraordinary talent pile, while the American League, holding on to the prejudices of the past, lagged far behind in its acquisition of great black players. NL, the traditional newspaper abbreviation for the National League, the black players liked to joke, now had come to stand for Negro League. Willie Mays seemed to be the model for the new supremely gifted black athlete, making plays that had never been made before, playing gracefully and aggressively, with an exuberant style all his own. As much as anything, he showed that the new-age black athlete had both power and speed: In 1955 he had hit fifty-one home runs and stolen twenty-four bases. A new kind of athlete was being showcased, a player who, in contrast to most white superstars of the past, was both powerful *and* fast. Sociologists, physiologists, and historians might soon debate the reasons for this—why black athletes seemed so much faster and athletically more gifted than white athletes of seemingly comparable size—but the changes wrought in all of America's national sports were dramatic. And the black athletes themselves laughed about the difference, saying of a particular black player who had neither speed nor leaping ability that he had the white man's disease, which meant that he could not jump very high or that he was not very fast.

Clearly, a social revolution wrought by great athletes was taking place, and it was in many ways outstripping the revolution engineered by the Supreme Court of the United States and by Martin Luther King, Jr., in the streets of the nation's Southern cities. If the face of America, at its highest business, legal, and financial level, was still almost exclusively white, then the soul of America, as manifested in its music and its sports, was changing quickly. In sport after sport, blacks became the dominating figures, first in baseball, and then in professional football in 1957, when Jim Brown, the great running back, was drafted by

Cleveland after playing at Syracuse. Brown, so superior an athlete that he was also considered the greatest lacrosse player of his era, had had professional offers in baseball and basketball as well as football, but it was in football that he made his reputation. As a pro player he was not unlike Mays in that he combined both speed and power. In the past, great running backs either were swift and ran to the outside or were big and powerful and ran inside, but Jim Brown was something new, he almost alone could do both.

But it was in basketball that the revolution most quickly took place and was most quickly completed. Basketball soon became the professional sport with the highest percentage of black players; yet as recently as 1947, John Gunther had written that although blacks could play college football in the Big Ten, they could not compete in basketball. "This is an indoor sport and taboos are strong (though not so strong as in the South) against any contact between half-clad, perspiring bodies, even on the floor of a gym," he had noted.

The basketball revolution began in 1956, when Arnold (Red) Auerbach, the coach of the Boston Celtics, made a complicated deal at draft time in order to get the rights to a young man who had starred at the University of San Francisco. The young man was named William F. Russell, Jr. Russell was part of the great black migration to the North and the West; he was born in Louisiana but had gone to California as a boy. His father was a proud man who had ended up working in a small trucking business in California. (Later, in 1965, when Bill Russell, by far the most valuable player in professional basketball, signed a contract for $100,001 a year, that extra dollar being there to put him ahead of Wilt Chamberlain, his great rival, he had suggested that his father never work again. "Of course I'm going to work," said Charlie Russell. "I've given that place eighteen good years out of my life. Now I'll give them a couple of bad years.")

Before the signing of Russell, Auerbach already had the reputation as the smartest coach in the league. Now his reputation, because of this particular trade, was going to grow considerably in the years to come. No mind that Russell had been the key player on the University of San Francisco teams that had won two national championships and had lost only one college game in which he played. Though Russell's defensive skills were something of a given, some professional scouts worried because he was not a good shooter. Certainly, few experts thought Russell's play would completely transform the game. He was six feet nine and a half inches which was tall (although others were taller), and he was quick, but quickness was not yet considered as important as heft and muscle, and doubts remained about his professional ability—and particularly about his strength, since he was to play regularly against men not only as tall as he, but twenty-five pounds heavier. Auerbach had been asking around the college ranks whether Russell had the guts to play in the rough and physical pro game.

At that time the Celtics, in an eight-team league, were good, but not quite good enough: They had good shooters and a supremely gifted ball handler and passer in Bob Cousy, but they were not champions and they lacked a dominating big man. At the end of the '55–'56 season Auerbach had promised his frustrated players that he would somehow manage to get them a big man in the draft. That he did. He drafted Russell, whose ability to dominate the college game was so complete that by the end of the 1955 season, the NCAA had put into effect what was called "the Russell rule," which widened the foul lanes from six to twelve feet in a flawed attempt to limit his dominance as an inside scorer and rebounder.

On draft day Rochester, which had the first chance at Russell, passed and took Sihugo Green, in large part because Russell was so good that he had other options, such as playing for the all-black road-storming Harlem Globetrotters. Russell was said to want a salary of $25,000, an unheard-of sum in those days. The Globetrotters had announced that they would pay him $50,000, but in fact their offer was about a third of that. Worse, Abe Saperstein, the famed owner of the Globetrotters, had enraged Russell by meeting with Russell and his college coach and negotiating with the coach as if Russell were not there. The racial overtones of the meeting were rich, the implicit sense that Russell was a boy, indeed a colored boy, who could not make a business decision himself; when the meeting was over there was no chance of Russell playing with the Globetrotters. It had been unlikely in the first place that someone with Russell's overwhelming pride would choose to play with a team of barnstorming black athletes who portrayed themselves as basketball buffoons, rather than to test himself against the best white professional talent in the country.

The next pick in the draft belonged to St. Louis. It was at this moment that Red Auerbach made his trade. He gave up a talented and popular player, center Ed Macauley—who averaged about twenty points a game but was spindly and was not exactly a power player and who wore down during the regular season—plus the draft rights to another potentially gifted player, Cliff Hagan, for the rights to Russell. Russell signed for $22,500. (Six thousand dollars was going to be held out because he joined the Celtics late, after leading the American team to an Olympic victory in Melbourne, but Walter Brown, the Celtic's owner, decided that was unfair and held out only three thousand, in effect splitting the difference with Russell.)

With that trade, Auerbach went from being very smart to being a genius. He told Russell to concentrate on rebounding and not to worry about scoring. "We'll count rebounds as baskets for you," he told him. In Russell's first year, the Celtics won the NBA championship, and Russell became not merely the best player in the league, but he began his tour as the most dominating team athlete of modern American sports. His first game came on December 22, in the Boston Garden against the St. Louis Hawks, on national television. Bob Cousy remembered it vividly: Even though Russell was new, there was an immediate sense on the part of his teammates that the future had arrived and that the game had changed because of him; he not only rebounded as Auerbach had promised, but he brought a different dimension to defense. There had never been anything like him before, Cousy thought at the time—the quickness, the superb timing, a big man playing with the agility and speed of a small man.

The Celtics were suddenly a brand-new team. (In his first game Russell had played only sixteen minutes but had gotten twenty-one rebounds.) A few days later, in a game in New York that was part of a doubleheader, he held Neil Johnston of the Warriors, then the game's third leading scorer, without a field goal for the first forty-two minutes. Russell also gathered in eighteen rebounds; the next night in another game against the Warriors, he took down *thirty-four* rebounds in twenty minutes of play, blocked a number of shots, and led the Celtic fast break. The new age had arrived. Even Auerbach, as shrewd as he was, Cousy thought, did not realize how much he was getting when he drafted Russell.

When Russell had been measured in college, the tape never indicated what a superlative athlete he was. He played a good deal taller than his height indicated. Even in college he had been surprised at the things he could do that other players could not. He had found that when he went up for a rebound, he was different from other players— not only did he seem to go higher (on one occasion in college he found he was looking down at the basket, which meant he was jumping at least forty-eight inches off the ground), but he seemed to hang in the air longer; the other players returned to the ground while he stayed in the air. In later years this would be known as hang time. Russell was both extremely agile and extremely powerful. Not only was he a superb jumper, he had exceptional timing; indeed, his hand-to-eye coordination and the timing of his jumps reflected a rare athletic skill. His intelligence matched his athletic ability; he seemed, he later noted, to be able to anticipate what the player he was guarding was going to do next. With him, playing defense in basketball became as much of an art as hitting was to a great baseball player like Ted Williams or Stan Musial. Among other things, Russell was left-handed, which meant that his more athletic hand was keyed to the shooting hand of most players he defended against. He was supremely

intelligent, a master not only at psyching teammates but intimidating his opponents, and he was
one of the proudest men ever to play any sport.

He played for the Celtics, but Boston was
never his home. He was acutely aware of the city's
prejudices, that the Celtics, though champions,
rarely sold out at home. He responded to the
schizophrenia of the white sports fan who covets
autographs but, at least in Russell's opinion, does
not covet black neighbors, by refusing to sign
autographs. He had once, as a collegian, been
invited to a conference at the White House, but
then had driven the segregated highway back to
his original home in Louisiana, where on stops
along the road he had been treated as "just another black boy, just so much dirt, with no rights,
with no element of human courtesy or decency
shown to me or mine." He had decided before he
even turned pro that he would always be polite
with fans, that he would speak only when spoken
to, but that he would not be a caricature of a
black—a dancing, joking buffoon.

His gifted teammate Bob Cousy, who was the
best passer of his era, was always intrigued by the
contradictions in Russell. Russell played the game
brilliantly, but he did not even particularly seem
to like the game. He was a notoriously poor practice player, perhaps the most indifferent one on
the team. But he played with a special fury in the
real games, as though this sport was the only out-
let, Cousy thought, for all the racial anger stored

up within him. *This,* the intensity of his play seemed to say, was his answer to prejudice and discrimination and to existing myths about things that blacks could not do but that whites could do. He was a great big-game player, although it was said that he was so tense before a game that he inevitably had to go to the locker room and throw up just before the tipoff. In those days the Celtics' archrivals were the St. Louis Hawks, and in St. Louis, then a Southern city, the crowd seemed to him to be the most racist in the league, the epithets the most vile; it was a place where even the coffee shops denied him service. He played particularly well in St. Louis.

In the past, the dominating big players had been white, usually strong but slow. When they blocked a shot, it was generally because the offensive player had taken a poor shot. Russell was something completely new, the forerunner of a different player in a different game, the big man who got down court faster than the other team's small men. He blocked shots that had never been blocked before. Players on other teams not only had to correct the arc of their shots but change the very nature of their offense when they played against him. When opponents brought the ball up the court, they always looked to see where Russell was. He averaged more than twenty rebounds a game, and his rebounding was so formidable that it unlocked the Boston offense, leading to the Celtics' fast break and what were often easy baskets. He changed, in the most elemental sense, the very tempo of the game. In the past a team had brought the ball up rather leisurely, passed it around, and a shot was taken. When that happened, the roles of the two teams changed, the offensive team going on defense, and vice versa, but they changed comparatively slowly—the offensive team had a few extra seconds to pull itself together, get back down court, and set up on defense, while the offensive team had somewhat leisurely taken a few seconds to rearrange itself and then take the ball up the court for offense. With Russell the tempo of the game seemed to have no break; now it was continuous, offense flowing into defense instantaneously. It was now a game for the swift and the agile. In Russell's first ten years in Boston, the Celtics won the championship nine times, including one stretch of eight championships in a row. In his thirteen seasons there, the Celtics won the title eleven times.

FORTY-FIVE

LATE IN HIS PRESIDENCY, Dwight Eisenhower came under increasing scrutiny personally. *Sputnik* was only the first of several psychological setbacks for America, the impact of which neither the President nor the men around him fully comprehended. Soon after, in November 1957, the Gaither report leaked out. It was prepared by the Security Resources Panel of the Science Advisory committee of the Office of Defense Mobilization and was officially titled "Deterrence and Survival in the Nuclear Age." It took its nickname from committee chairman Rowan Gaither and was a chilling piece of work. Based on information available to most laymen (and certainly with no knowledge of the Soviet weaknesses as sighted by the U-2), it implied that we were slipping in our nuclear capacity while the Soviets were becoming stronger all the time. The evidence, it reported, "clearly indicates an increasing threat which may become critical in 1959 or early 1960." The Russians seemed to be ahead of us in all aspects of defense and weapons technology, and even worse, their GNP was said to be growing at a faster rate than ours (a particularly preposterous idea, given the crude nature of Soviet industry). Clearly, the barbarians were not merely at the gate, they were able to fly over it with missiles and nuclear warheads. The Gaither committee recommended $25 billion for the building of bomb shelters all over the country and another $19 billion on increased budgeting for weaponry. William C. Foster, the head of Olin Mathieson Chemical Corporation, who was on the committee, said, "I felt as though I were spending ten hours a day staring straight into hell." Eisenhower was now in the embarrassing position of having appointed a blue-chip panel whose conclusions he would have to reject or at least ignore. This, after *Sputnik* and Little Rock, seemed to confirm the view of an administration of older men no longer in touch, unaware of how quickly the world was changing. Herblock, the talented and influential *Washington Post* cartoonist, was drawing Eisenhower as a slightly addled, goofy, ineffectual figure, confused by what he was doing and why he was doing it.

In a sense, the U-2 helped stabilize the relationship between the two superpowers. But because the information it provided could not be introduced into the democratic system, Eisenhower was oddly paralyzed. What he knew, ordinary citizens could not know. At one point, frustrated by all the pressure coming at him on the domestic front to intensify the arms race, Eisenhower said with some irritation, "I can't understand the United States being quite as panicky as they are."

Nevertheless, in the last three years of the Eisenhower administration, a debate began over an alleged missile gap, which did not, in fact, exist. In a way it was not without its own justice: The Republicans had won in the past in no small part because they had blamed the Democrats for losing countries to Communism; in the early part of the Cold War, the Republicans had exagerrated the natural anxieties of the Cold War. The result was that not only had the Democrats vowed never to be accused of being soft on Communism again, they were determined to find an issue that showed they were, if anything, even more vigilant and tougher. McCarthy's attacks guaranteed that the national debate would shift ever more to the right. With *Sputnik* and the so-called missile gap, the Democrats, though careful not to attack the President frontally, managed to make it seem as if his best days were behind him.

He had nothing to offer but himself and his word in defense of his policies. He had no proof. That lay locked in the CIA's vaults. But there was no guarantee, beloved and trusted as he was, that his word alone was good enough now. Part of this was the erosion caused by his health. His personal signature had always been his physical vigor, his ruddiness and vitality, but like Truman before him, he had found the brutal rigors of the American presidency in the postwar era to be a killing job. Truman, with his plowboy constitution and simple life-style, had withstood the physical erosion remarkably well, but Eisenhower was not as lucky. In September 1955, Eisenhower had suffered his first heart attack; less than a year later, he was struck with ileitis. He underwent a stomach operation, even though there was considerable nervousness among his doctors about subjecting a man who had so recently suffered a heart attack to so serious an operation. Then, in November 1957, he suffered a mild stroke. The exhausting quality of the job was taking its toll. The doctors told him to avoid "irritation, frustration, anxiety, fear, and above all anger." "Just what do you think the presidency *is*?" he asked.

In fact, he had never entirely wanted the job, nor for that matter did he like it very much after he got it. Cy Sulzberger, an old friend from Paris days, visiting him some twenty months into his administration, was surprised to find him "uneasy, irascible, crotchety, and not quite sure of himself. I felt sorry for him." He was surrounded by politicians, whom he tended to describe as sons of bitches, who came to see him when they needed help getting reelected but who in no way supported his program. The longer he stayed in office, the more disillusioned he became. After one meeting with congressional leaders late in his presidency, he turned to an aide and said, "I don't know why anyone should be a member of the Republican party." He would talk often of the time when his term was up and he would be a free man again. When Everett Dirksen and Charlie

Halleck spoke wistfully about the fact that it was a shame that he could not run again because of the Twenty-Second Amendment, he quickly disabused them of any desire he might have for a third term. Nor, he added, did he think anyone should be President after he was seventy. The job was taking its toll.

As the *Sputnik*-defense spending crisis deepened, his behavior seemed passive compared to the almost primal energy of Nikita Khrushchev. Khrushchev was something new for Americans to contemplate. Stalin had been a completely foreboding figure, the paranoiac as ultimate dictator, inflicting his dark vision on all those unlucky enough to fall under the rule of the Soviet empire. Khrushchev was quite different—ferocious, volatile, shrewd, vengeful, very much the angry peasant. If Stalin had represented the worst of Soviet Communism, then Khrushchev to many Americans was even more threatening, for he seemed to reflect the peasant vigor of this new state. Was America finally attaining a broad affluence only to find that the comforts of middle-class existence had weakened it? Crude, unpredictable, occasionally violent, Khrushchev seemed to be the embodiment of the sheer animal force of the Soviet Union, its raw power and, perhaps many Americans feared, its irresistible will.

There was something chilly about Khrushchev, pounding his shoe and threatening to bury capitalism, at the UN. Contrasting his own pov-

erty with the affluent backgrounds of those Western figures he dealt with, he seemed to imply their
good manners were a weakness. "You all went to
great schools, to famous universities—to Harvard, Oxford, the Sorbonne," he once boasted to
Western diplomats. "I never had any proper
schooling. I went about barefoot and in rags.
When you were in the nursery, I was herding cows
for two kopeks. . . . And yet here we are, and I can
run rings around you all. . . . Tell me, gentlemen,
why?"

Many Americans worried that the very material success of America in the postwar years—all
those cars, kitchen amenities, and other luxu-
ries—had made us soft and vulnerable to the Soviet Union, where people were tougher and more
willing to sacrifice for their nation. Was there
strength and truth in poverty? Styles Bridges, a
conservative Republican senator, seemed to talk
in this vein when he said that Americans had to be
less concerned with "the height of the tail fin in
the new car and be much more prepared to shed
blood, sweat and tears, if this country and the free
world are to survive."

Part of Eisenhower's problems, as he entered
the last phase of his presidency, was that he could
never bring himself to lobby the most important
members of the press on his own behalf, or even
on behalf of his policies. Because of network-tele-
vision news shows, the national press corps was
growing ever more influential as a force—if not in

policymaking, then certainly in the way policy was seen by the general public. Yet in his relations with the press, Eisenhower still saw himself as the general and the press as obedient privates and corporals who liked him personally, shared his vision of the war and, given the circumstances of the national effort, all but saluted him. Therefore he thought he had not needed to get into the pit and explain. All he had to do was give his version. A challenge to his policy from people who, in his opinion, did not have a tenth of his experience and training, who were outsiders and had never made a hard decision, would quickly ignite his anger. He had entered the presidency feeling that way and not having needed the press corps during his election run when their bosses, like Paley, Sarnoff, Whitney, and Sulzberger, had practically begged him to come in.

As President, he assumed the press would be properly respectful. A press corps that did otherwise was, to him, untrustworthy and quite possibly dishonest. It was not that he had not had opportunities to bring the press in. When he took office, various columnists volunteered to be insiders, to report what the administration was doing but could not say. The first and perhaps most brazen of these offers came from Joseph Alsop, who dropped by early in the administration to talk with Robert Cutler, Ike's national security secretary. Cutler was an old Boston friend, a fellow member of the Porcellian Club at Harvard.

Alsop pointed out the many Republican connections in his own family and suggested he could serve the administration with his column by publishing certain administration perceptions and thoughts without attribution. "Such a person, trusted by a President, could provide an anonymous channel to help shape public opinion," Alsop said. But Cutler told Alsop to get his information like any other reporter—by attending press conferences and talking with Jim Hagerty. The administration, Cutler said, was not interested in deals. Alsop was not pleased: This was clearly beneath him. Cutler clearly did not understand the new hierarchy of Washington journalism.

This was fairly typical. Ike barely knew the names of the men and women who covered the White House every day. He knew the names of only the most senior reporters who reported on him. He did not read the major papers, and when he did, it made him angry. To his mind, *The New York Times* was "the most untrustworthy paper in the world." He gave little access to its top people. Once the President asked Cy Sulzberger what Arthur Krock, the paper's conservative columnist, was doing lately. Writing his column three times a week, Sulzberger said. "Is that so?" said the President. Then Ike noted that he liked Krock, which came as a surprise to Sulzberger, who knew that Krock had been trying in vain to see the President for more than a year. The President continued: He also liked one other columnist, though he often had trouble with his name: "And you know who another good reporter is—that's that little fellow—what's his name?—that little fellow who works for—" Sulzberger asked if the President meant Roscoe Drummond. "Yes," said the President. "Roscoe, that's the fellow I meant."

Eisenhower disliked Walter Lippmann, the great sage of the era, and thought him usually wrong. He hated Ed Murrow: "I can't stand that gangster [Ed] Murrow. I can't stand looking at him. I have no use for him. He always looks like a gangster with a cigarette hanging out of his mouth." But it was Joe Alsop, who became, to his mind, the lowest of the low as the columnist began to establish himself as the foremost journalistic critic of Eisenhower's defense policies.

If there ever was a time and an issue when Eisenhower needed journalistic support, particularly from influential columnists, it was over his defense policies in the last three years of his administration. If ever there was an angry critic of them, it was Alsop. He was snobbish, vain, talented, hardworking, egocentric, and well connected to the powerful people in Washington, either through clubs, family connections, or the capacity to intimidate them by using his column as a lever. Close to hard-line Democrats like Acheson, Alsop soon became unusually influential in creating the impression that Eisenhower was somewhat confused, an ill-informed figure who was out of touch with reality and whose defense policies were putting American security in jeopardy. As he wrote his friend Isaiah Berlin in April 1958: "One prays—how odd it seems!—for the course of nature to transfer the burden to Nixon (who exactly resembles an heir to a very rich family . . . now utterly distraught because Papa has grown a little senile and spends his family fortune out the window—really he is like that). I lunched with him the other day and he all but asked me how it was possible to argue with a ramolli papa without getting disinherited yourself!"

. . .

Eisenhower's last three years as President saw him virtually alone on this issue, standing up to a powerful array of critics in insisting that America had more than enough defense, that there was no missile gap, and that the nation's security was not in jeopardy. Allied against him were such powerful and influential Democrats as Lyndon Johnson, Stuart Symington, and Jack Kennedy, who were busy positioning themselves for a shot at the presidency. With this issue they could show that not only were they *not* soft on Communism, but they actually wanted to strengthen America. They had their allies in the government, most notably in the Air Force, which always wanted more bombers and more missiles. The Democrats and the liberal-centrist columnists were in touch with influential military sources, who were not privy to the U-2 intelligence and who were absolutely sure that the Soviets were moving ahead of us. "At the Pentagon they shudder when they speak of the Gap, which means the years 1960, 1961, 1962 and 1963," the Alsops wrote typically in that period. "They shudder because in those years the American government will flaccidly permit the Kremlin to open an almost unchallenged superiority in the nuclear striking power that was once our superiority." At the moment, voices like those of the Alsops had a certain power; the tensions of the Cold War and the success of *Sputnik* had frightened many in the political center.

The truth was that as Eisenhower entered the final years of his presidency, his primary objective was to establish his legacy, which he saw as limiting the arms race. He knew from the U-2 photos that the Soviets were not a threat, so it seemed logical to get a test-ban treaty of some sort. In 1959 he said with some melancholy, "We haven't made a chip in the granite in seven years." His closest advisers urged him to let Symington and other Democratic critics see some of the photos taken by the U-2. That would end much of the criticism. But Eisenhower would not budge. He thought there was no way to keep the flights secret if the opposition leadership was let in. So the flights continued in secret. A spy satellite that would fly over the entire world would not be ready, it appeared, until some time in 1961.

His critics and his enemies became bolder. The Air Force generals were the worst, he believed. They seemed to be teaming up with the munitions people—he used the old-fashioned phrase from World War One to describe the booming new defense industry—to push for endless redundant military systems. "I'm getting awfully sick of the lobbies by munitions," he told the Republican leaders. Indeed, he sensed their primary motivation was greed: "You begin to see this thing isn't wholly the defense of this country, but only more money for some who are already fatcats."

When in the wake of *Sputnik* members of his own cabinet pushed for a dramatic increase in defense and space spending, he revealed his irritation. "Look," he had said. "I'd like to know what's on the other side of the moon, but I won't pay to find out this year." It was taking all his will to keep the military and the defense contractors from escalating the arms race. Even when he did increase defense spending substantially, he told his aide Andrew Goodpaster that two thirds of the increase was for public opinion. "God help the nation when it has a President who doesn't know as much about the military as I do," he would say.

It is our contradictions that make us interesting. Eisenhower, the famed general, wanted more to be a man of peace than a man of war. Jingoism in other men had always made him uneasy. When he heard the news of the success of the atomic bomb on Hiroshima, though it meant a quick end to the war in the Pacific, he was left with a feeling of severe depression, caused by the arrival of a new and terrifying chapter in man's capacity to destroy man. Mary Bancroft, Allen Dulles's acute lady friend, even thought that Ike's hatred of war was a weakness, not unlike, she said, a prostitute who values her chastity. He was a curious combination of qualities: part shrewd and conniving, and alternately innocent, naive, and trusting. He was the most political of generals, and yet he thought politicking on the part of others unseemly. He was a man who knew that his greatest asset, as a leader not just in the United States but throughout the world, was that the entire world seemed to trust him and believe in him, but he sharply increased the use of clandestine operations to overthrow governments that he disliked in underdeveloped countries. He had hoped, after the war, for a rapprochement with the Russians, but his anti-Communism seemed to harden during much of his administration. He could barely restrain his contempt toward Adlai Stevenson when he raised the issue of limiting nuclear testing in 1956, and yet in the final years of his administration he hungered, more than anything, for some form of accord with the Russians on limiting nuclear testing and perhaps even on limiting the production of nuclear weapons.

By 1958 he had begun to reduce the number of U-2 flights. He had always been uneasy with them. He knew they were provocative, and he himself would point out that nothing would move the United States more quickly to war than the knowledge that the Soviets were overflying us and taking pictures. In 1959 he became even more cautious. He was beginning to build new links to Khrushchev, and he did not want them jeopardized by the U-2 flights. There was a constant tug-of-war between him and Allen Dulles and Richard Bissell, who was in charge of the flights; the CIA always seemed to want one more flight, one more picture, or a new flight pattern just a little deeper into Soviet airspace. Soon there was a byplay, Bissell and Dulles asking for more flights, and Ike trying to hold the line and giving them fewer than they wanted and more than he wanted.

What the President did not know was that the U-2 pilots themselves were becoming more nervous. There was evidence by the fall of 1958 that the Soviets were not only tracking them with radar but firing SAMs (surface-to-air missiles) that were coming, as Powers put it, uncomfortably close. The U-2 pilots, Powers noted later, knew that the Soviets were having problems with their guidance systems, but by 1960 new SAM-2 missiles were being installed throughout the country. They had a far greater range than their predecessors, and the CIA estimated that they could hit a target seventy thousand feet high. At the same time the planes themselves were becoming heavier as more equipment was being added.

Powers was fast becoming the most senior pilot in the group: His personal life was something of a ruin; he and his wife spoke often of divorce. There was no brilliant Air Force career waiting; it was as if he had found his niche in this demanding but boring job, which above all else required endurance. He seemed so ordinary that it was hard to think of him as a spy. As James Donovan, one of the intelligence men who handled him later, said, he was just the kind of man the CIA would want. "Powers was a man, who, for adequate pay, would do it (fly a virtual glider over the Soviet Union) and as he passed over Minsk, would calmly reach for a salami sandwich." The world of the White House, of course, and the world of the U-2 pilots did not intersect. Dwight Eisenhower might have his doubts about the continued viability of the flights, and Francis Gary Powers, his doubts, but they did not share them. In 1959 a new engine arrived, stronger and able to fly at higher altitudes, but there was an increasing edginess among the pilots.

In 1959 Eisenhower invited Khrushchev to visit America, thinking that it would be for two or three days, but somehow in the confusion Khrushchev accepted for ten days. Someone asked the President what he wanted the Soviet leader to see, and the response was Eisenhower at his best: Levittown, he said. It was a town "universally and exclusively inhabited by workmen." (This was not an entirely accurate statement.) He wanted the premier to fly in a chopper with him and see the District. In addition, he wanted Khrushchev to go to Abilene, "the little town where I was born," and see for himself "the story of how hard I worked until I was twenty-one, when I went to West Point." The President noted that when Nixon had debated Khrushchev in Moscow, the Soviet leader had said that Americans knew nothing of hard work. Well, said the President, "*I* can show him the evidence that *I* did and I would like for him to see it." But most of all, he added, "I want him to see a happy people. I want him to see a free people, doing exactly as they choose, within the limits that they must not transgress the rights of others."

When Khrushchev finally came, it was a circus; every journalist in America turned out, for Americans had never seen a Soviet dictator in the flesh before, and this was no ordinary Soviet dictator—for Khrushchev always provided, if nothing else, good theater. Eisenhower and Khrushchev got on fairly well, although there was a sense that the boisterous Khrushchev was a bit much for the restrained Eisenhower. In private meetings, they minimized the differences between the countries. How was it, Khrushchev asked, that a general, a man whose entire mission in life had been waging war, was so committed to finding the peace? There might have been some moments of exhilaration during the last war, but "now war has become nothing more than a struggle for survival," the President answered. He was not afraid to say that he was afraid of nuclear war, and everyone else should be.

On the whole the trip went well. Khrushchev invited Eisenhower not just to come to Russia himself but to bring along his whole family. Ike, in one of his better moods, said, "I'll bring along the whole family. You'll have more Eisenhowers than you know what to do with." For Eisenhower, this was everything he had hoped for: He would visit Moscow and bring back a limited test ban treaty; personally, he would end the worst of the Cold War. This was why he had become President. In the summer of 1960 he would attend a summit meeting with the French, British, and Russians in Paris and from there fly on to Moscow. A process of peace might truly begin and this, surely, would be the triumph of his presidency.

· · ·

The less frequently the U-2 pilots flew, the more difficult each flight became. There were indications that the program was losing some of its secrecy. A model-airplane magazine published an article about the plane in March 1958, complete with drawings. It was also said that the official paper of the Soviet air force had reported on the flights and called the plane "the black lady of espionage." An American mole working in Soviet intelligence reported that the Soviets had a great deal of intelligence on the U-2, something that apparently surprised both Dulles and Bissell. In addition, in the summer of 1958 Hanson Baldwin, the military writer for *The New York Times,* spotted one of the U-2s on the tarmac while he was in West Germany and understood immediately what the plane's purpose was. He lunched with Robert Amory, one of Allen Dulles's top people, and said he was going to do a story—after all, he had seen it without violating security. *"Jesus, Hanson, no!"* Amory said. It would undermine America's most important intelligence program. They argued for a time and in the end Allen Dulles talked to Arthur Hayes Sulzberger, the *Times* publisher, who decided to hold the story. But, as Sulzberger told Dulles, the story had been set in type—in case someone like Drew Pearson got it, too. Gradually, the top people in Washington journalist circles, like Arthur Krock and Scotty Reston and Chal Roberts, of *The Washington Post,* found out about the U-2 but did not write it up. As Michael Beschloss noted, knowing about the U-2 became something of a status symbol on the Washington dinner-party circuit.

In Washington, in late April 1960, Eisenhower was preparing for the summit and wanted no more flights. "If one of these aircraft were lost when we were engaged in apparently sincere deliberations, it could be put on display in Moscow and ruin my effectiveness," he said to one aide. But Dulles and Bissell pleaded for one last flight, claiming it was unusually important: They wanted one more good look at the Soviet missile installation at Tyuratam. Again Eisenhower, accustomed over the years to listening to his subordinates, went against his better judgment and relented.

At the U-2 base in Turkey, Powers, by this time the only remaining member of the original group, was assigned the flight. For the first time, a U-2 would fly all the way across the Soviet Union. The flight would begin in Peshawar, Pakistan, and would end nine hours and 3,800 miles later in Bodo, Norway.

In the language of the pilots, the flights had been getting dicier and dicier all the time; this flight took these anxieties a step further. The pilots has always had unanswered questions about what to do in case they were shot down. Was there anyone they could contact? Powers had asked one of the briefing officers. No, he was told. How much should he tell? he asked. "You may as well tell them everything because they're going to get it out of you anyway," he was told.

The flight was delayed several times because of weather and was finally set for the last day of April. Powers slept poorly. He was not pleased with the plane he had been assigned; it was, he thought, a lemon—plagued by malfunctions. He carried his regular identification—a violation of the rules and a sign that the pilots were becoming complacent—and a new piece of equipment: a silver dollar with a pin. In case of capture by the Soviets, the pilots were to stick the pin in a groove, from which would seep out a sticky brown substance. Injecting yourself with the substance would make it appear that you had died from eating bad shrimp. The pilots had agreed among themselves they would not use the pin even if worst came to worst.

Fully dressed in his sealed flight suit, Powers climbed into the plane that morning at 5:20 A.M. and waited for the final clearance to come from the White House. It was clear to him by this point that Washington was approving each flight. As he sweated, a friend outside took off his shirt and held it over the cockpit in order to shield him from the sun. Finally, at 6:26 he was allowed to take off. He soon picked up the trail of a Russian jet. It was traveling at supersonic speed toward him. But he remained confident; Soviet planes still flew far below him. Unfortunately, he soon began to have problems with his own plane. When he put it on automatic pilot it began to malfunction, so he flew it manually. For a moment he considered aborting the mission, but then decided to go ahead. He was flying toward Sverdlovsk (formerly known as Ekaterinburg) for what would be the first U-2 trip over that city when he heard a dull thump. The aircraft pitched forward. A tremendous orange flash hit the cockpit and lit the sky around him. *My God,* he thought to himself. *I've had it now.* Later, Powers decided (and Kelly Johnson agreed) that what had happened to him was a near miss, which tore the fragile plane apart but spared his life.

He struggled with the plane, fearing the ejection seat. The plane was completely out of control, spinning wildly and hurtling toward the ground. He was sure that both wings had been severed. He finally managed to get out of the plane: For a time he fell rapidly through the air, an exhilarating feeling, even better, he thought, than floating in a swimming pool. Finally, he got his parachute open. When he landed, he was quickly picked up by a local farmer and turned over to the KGB.

In Washington on the afternoon of May 1, Dwight Eisenhower was notified by Andrew Goodpaster that a U-2 was missing and had apparently been shot down. They both lamented the death of the brave young pilot. The one thing Allen Dulles had promised Dwight Eisenhower was that if the Russians shot down a plane, the pilot would not live. It was a question Eisenhower had raised on several occasions. Dulles would always answer that it was unlikely the Soviets could shoot one down, and if they did, the pilots would blow up the planes before taking their own lives. That they would *never* capture a live pilot was the great given, thought John Eisenhower, the President's son, who was serving as his aide at the time and going over the U-2 requests. There was no reason to think that even though a U-2 was missing a major crisis was in the works. With the amount of fuel Powers had on board the plane, Andy Goodpaster, the President's closest aide, said, "there is not a chance of his being alive." In the White House, aides started working on a cover story.

At first Powers was sure the Soviets were going to execute him. But then he was moved from Sverdlovsk to Moscow, and he began to believe for the first time that he might be permitted to live and that the Soviets might use him in the propaganda war. Perhaps Khrushchev, he thought, might take him to the upcoming summit and present Powers to Eisenhower as something which belonged to him.

Years later Chip Bohlen, one of the top American Kremlinologists, said that Khrushchev took the U-2 as a personal insult; it was a personal embarrassment, because he had promised his colleagues in the Politburo that Eisenhower could be trusted. (Khrushchev himself later said that the U-2 affair was the beginning of the end for him in terms of his ability to hold power.) Khrushchev decided to bait a trap for the Americans. On May 5, he announced that the Russians had shot down a spy plane. He seemed, however, to be allowing some room to maneuver for the President, who could say that he had not known what the CIA was doing. Unfortunately, Eisenhower was already under severe criticism for not being the master of his own house. Khrushchev did not let on that the pilot was alive. In Washington the administration came up with a cover story about a weather plane that had flown off course, and thereby walked right into the baited trap. Eisenhower was confident that Khrushchev had no proof. At best there had been a quick flash on the radar, and perhaps some wreckage.

On May 7, six days after Powers had been shot down, Khrushchev announced to the Supreme Soviet that he had the wreckage of the plane and the live pilot and, of course, the film. "The whole world knows that Allen Dulles is no great weatherman," he said. He mentioned the gold rings and gold watches that Powers, like other U-2 pilots, carried with him in case he needed to barter with the local people. "Perhaps he was supposed to fly still higher, to Mars, and seduce the Martian ladies!" He showed some of the photos taken by the plane. "Here—*look at this*! Here are the airfields—*here*! Fighters in position on the ground. Two little white strips. *Here they are!* . . ."

For the next day American officials squirmed and pointed fingers at each other, trying to decide what the next cover story would be and who would take the fall. Some suggested the commander of the base in Turkey be relieved. Others thought that Allen Dulles should resign for the good of his country, thus protecting the President and perhaps saving the summit. Eisenhower, however, was not a man who liked scapegoats. (When his son, John, told him he should get rid of Allen Dulles because Dulles had misled him on the issue of whether a pilot could survive, the President was very angry. "I am *not* going to shift the blame to my underlings!" he had said.) Gradually, the truth began to seep out. The President was responsible for flights like this, came a statement.

But whatever victory Khrushchev had scored overseas, he was sure he was the loser at home, the man who had preached trust but who, on the eve of so important a meeting as the summit, had been betrayed by the Americans. He now felt isolated, vulnerable to the hard-liners, who hated his efforts to deal with the West.

The Americans took a terrible beating in the propaganda game; the only question now was whether the summit could be saved. Eisenhower told reporters he still intended to go to Paris but that he would not be able to go to Moscow. Allen Dulles was allowed to meet with a group of eighteen select congressional leaders, and he and an aide showed some of the U-2 photos as a means of justifying them. What pleasure there was in knowing that the Soviet threat was overrated vanished in shards of shattered diplomacy.

The Paris summit was a disaster. Khrushchev chose to thunder his way through it. He shouted so loudly that de Gaulle, the host, tried to quiet him by saying, "The acoustics in this room are excellent. We can all hear the chairman." Eisenhower, listening to himself and his country being berated by the angry First Secretary, wrote a note to Christian Herter, who had replaced the ailing Foster Dulles as secretary of state: "I'm going to take up smoking again," he observed mordantly. Khrushchev told de Gaulle that he could not understand why Eisenhower had admitted his involvement with the U-2. To him it was not a sign of American candor but of contempt for himself personally and for Russia as a nation.

For Eisenhower there would be no trip to Moscow, no sightseeing with the Khrushchevs, no warm toasts, and no test-ban treaty. That which he had wanted most desperately—a genuine beginning of peace—had been shot down along with Powers. His administration would end, he said somewhat bitterly, much as it had begun—without any real progress. "I had longed," he said just before he died, "to give the United States and the world a lasting peace. I was able only to contribute to a stalemate." Yet Eisenhower may have underestimated the most important achievement of of his Administration—the fact that the worst did not happen. In the years of his Presidency both superpowers developed the hydrogen bomb along with intercontinental delivery systems. Yet his own essential decency, and the respect his own nation held for him, allowed him to soften the most terrible furies of that time and permit a relatively safe passage through those years.

Some thought the failure was Powers's. What had happened to great patriots like Nathan Hale? wondered the liberal educator Robert Hutchins. Hanson Baldwin was shocked that Powers had not committed suicide. Was Powers yet another reflection of a too affluent America gone soft? William Faulkner thought the Russians might release him immediately as a reflection of their contempt for what America had become. The Russians at least were not about to execute him. They sentenced him to ten years.

FORTY-SIX

The AMERICAN clandestine campaign against Fidel Castro began so tentatively that the people who were its authors did not even realize they were taking a fateful step. By the late 1950s those who posed legal and moral questions about clandestine operations were considered naive. The success of the coup in Guatemala was a precedent for covert action elsewhere in the region, and American policy had apparently been established: essential indifference to the needs of the people living there in favor of the interests of the large American companies in the region, most notably United Fruit. Given the increased feelings of nationalism in much of the area because of advances in modern communications, it was not a happy situation.

The CIA agents who had engineered the Guatemalan coup were now considered to be experts, though in general their knowledge of the region was marginal, few spoke Spanish, and they tended to seek out only far right-wing military men as agents. In Cuba the government of Fulgencio Batista had to come apart in the latter part of the fifties. Few countries were headed by so greedy or cruel a dictator as Batista. His base of popular support was surprisingly small, and Cuba boasted, by Latin American standards, an increasingly sophisticated urban middle class. That power was slipping from Batista's hands and that his armed forces were corrupt and of dubious loyalty were not exactly secrets either in Havana or in Washington.

The Cuba of the fifties was an ugly and decadent place, a playland for rich Americans who wanted to escape the puritanical atmosphere of their home country, where they could gamble legally and buy whatever they wanted in terms of sexual gratification. It was a place of gambling, drinking, sex shows, prostitution. One mulatto star of the sex shows was known by the Americans as Superman, because of the heroic size of his penis, which was a tourist attraction of sorts, a must-see for many Americans on their Havana vacations. Superman would pretend to have sex with a number of women onstage every night. He did not particularly like his job, but he made $25 a night for it, which was for him a great deal more money than he could make working in the cane fields for United Fruit.

The gambling casinos were run by the American mob, and a healthy percentage of the profits went to Batista himself. Nothing worked without bribes and kickbacks. The key players in the regime—the secret police, the top military, and the bagmen who were responsible for the deliveries of money back and forth to the casinos—were handsomely rewarded with large cash bonuses, given out personally by the dictator each month in unmarked brown envelopes. This method implied that the dictator could, if he so chose, withhold the bribe the following month if things did not go to his liking. It was all surprisingly well organized. Batista's control of the Cuban political and military process, wrote John Dorschner and Roberto Fabricio, "resembled the organization of a large criminal mob more than it did a traditional government."

A regimental commander had to pay Batista $15,000 a month in kickback money from the gambling houses in his area. That alone gave Batista more than $1 million a year. But the main casinos in Havana were the heart of the action. They were controlled by the American mobster Meyer Lansky, and the dictator's take was a neat $1.28 million a month. It was always paid on Monday at noon. Someone from Lansky's operation would slip into the presidential palace with a briefcase full of money. From there a portion of the money would percolate down through the Batista system—to the secret police and the torturers, of course.

Batista had ruled Cuba, directly or indirectly, legally or illegally, for much of the preceding two decades. He had risen to power through the army, taking over in a coup while still a sergeant in 1940. Shrewd and tough, he skillfully exploited Cuba's potential for corruption. Taking a brief sabbatical after his first tour of office, he returned at the beginning of the fifties, shed his first wife, and married a young, ambitious woman who coveted social acceptance from Havana's snobbish aristocracy. Since Batista was the son of a cane cutter and a mulatto, that was not a realistic aspiration. He was blackballed at the elegant Havana Yacht Club—the vote against him was said to be one of the rare free elections in Cuba.

He proceeded to extract his revenge by accumulating fabulous wealth—including cattle ranches, sugar plantations, and his own airline. He and his wife were world-class shoppers and clotheshorses. He loved to eat and turned it into something of an art form; during endless meals, he would periodically go off to vomit so that he could eat more. He loved to play cards with his pals, and rich though he was, even here he cheated, using waiters to tip him off about his opponents' cards. He delighted in his control of the political apparatus, and he started each day by meeting with a trusted aide from the secret police, who brought him up to date on gossip gathered from wiretaps. "The novel," the briefing was called and it was the dictator's favorite moment of each day. A man like that has enemies and Batista went everywhere surrounded by teams of bodyguards, equipped with machine guns.

The key to his survival, of course, was the support of the United States, which in the past had committed itself to him unwaveringly: It was a policy set in part by hoods like Lansky, in conjunction with the more respectable businessmen from United Fruit, who were getting what they wanted out of Batista's Cuba. But by 1957 his power declined. There was a growing debate within the State Department about Batista's effectiveness as an agent of American policy. The top people in the Latin American division of the State Department thought that Batista's reign was already in its twilight, and that the United States should separate itself from supporting him so uncritically. The U.S., they thought, should work quickly to help create an alternative government, one far more liberal and democratic, which could keep up with the increasing demands for social change in the country. If we did not, the choice of Batista's successor might well be outside our control. Worse, there was the likelihood that this violent, oppressive regime on the right might well create its mirror image, a brutal regime of the left.

Yet Batista had one important American supporter: Earl E. T. Smith, a wealthy contributor to Eisenhower's campaign and the American ambassador to Cuba. Smith liked to say that he was the second most powerful man and occasionally the most powerful man in Cuba, and he managed to sabotage the attempts of moderates in Havana, including church leaders, to find some kind of moderate successor to Batista.

Smith's policy was perfect for Batista, because the two got on so well. Smith was very conservative. The only Cubans he talked to were wealthy, right-wing ones. Of the U.S. he would say, "I have lived in two eras, One when the country was run by the classes, and now when it is run by the masses. Something in between is probably best but I'll be honest. I enjoyed it more when it was run by the classes." Almost his entire embassy dissented from his view that Batista (or a Batista proxy) was a valid instrument of American policy, but Smith silenced them by refusing to sign off on their reporting. When it was clear that Batista was on his way out, Smith still continued to sabotage the attempts of moderate leaders in Cuba to bring some kind of moderate coalition government to power. Years later, Wayne Smith, a young political officer at the time, wrote of Earl Smith that he had come to see Batista as "a bulwark against Communism. In fact Batista was exactly the opposite; it was Batista who brought about the conditions that opened the door to radical solutions."

Yet time had already passed Batista by. He ruled by force, had no popularity among the peasants, and his army was commanded by men who held their ranks for political reasons. The brutality of his regime offended almost everyone. In an age of modern communications, his attempts at manipulation were pathetically transparent. Even as Batista's government was collapsing in 1958 and Fidel Castro was gathering his forces for the final military strike, Batista was sending out press releases on his forces' alleged victories to journalists whom he bought and sold—but Castro was using his own rebel radio to reach the Cuban masses. In Havana, given the nature of the regime, almost nothing the government said was believed, while almost everything that came from Castro's radio had credibility, born of the fact that he was challenging a tyrant.

William Wieland, the State Department's director for Caribbean and Mexican affairs, was the leader of those officials anxious to get rid of Batista and replace him with someone more centrist. Wieland wanted Batista out in no small part because he feared the coming of someone like Castro. In 1958 he had told colleagues at a State Department meeting that if "Batista was bad medicine for everyone, Castro would be worse."

Such fears were justified: If there was a growing disgust with Batista and his police brutality in Havana, then up in the hills of the interior, a guerrilla force was growing, pledged not only to bring Batista down but to install a revolutionary government in his place. Thirty years after he had come to power, Fidel Castro would appear to many in the West merely as an anachronism, a surviving Stalinist, a man who had sported his beard, fatigues, and Marxist rhetoric for too long. But when he first came to power, he possessed the mystique of the brave young rebel who risked his life to bring down a hated dictator and who seemed to promise a more enlightened, freer Cuba. He had gained immensely from the sheer cruelty of the Batista regime.

By the time he came down from the mountains, his myth was greater than his actual military power. Ironically, in contrast to Batista, Castro was the child of privilege, the son of a successful planter who leased large land holdings from United Fruit and sold his cane back to it. Fidel was sent to Jesuit schools and to the University of Havana law school, but from the start he had been a rebel. As a student he was part of a plot against Trujillo, the Dominican dictator, and after Batista retook power in Cuba in 1952 by means of a coup, it was the young Castro who led a group of rebels against a regimental garrison headquarters on July 26, 1953. Most of his men were captured then, and some sixty-nine were tortured and murdered either in prison or in hospitals. That brutality shocked many Cubans, and church leaders intervened with Batista, demanding that if any more rebels were caught, they be tried. That probably saved Castro, who was captured about a week after the attack.

Castro had a natural instinct for the dramatic, and he represented himself at his trial. Thus allowed to cross-examine state witnesses, he used the trial as a means of highlighting Batista's brutality and corruption. He read voraciously while in prison, and wrote a pamphlet, "History Will Absolve Me," which outlined the historical and legal case for overthrowing tyrants. After close to two years he was released in a general amnesty. By this time he had become a national figure and, as far as Batista was concerned, a marked man. In December 1956, he led a small band of followers to Oriente province, where he hoped to start a guerrilla movement. Instead he was ambushed by government forces. About sixty of his men were killed or taken prisoner, and only about twenty made it into the rugged mountains.

As Castro hid with two of his colleagues that first night after the ambush, he talked about the revolution he intended to lead and of how he would defeat Batista. Even though he was staring total annihilation right in the face that night, he was not given to doubting himself. Clearly, he saw himself as a man of destiny. He was a true believer in himself and his cause, and so in time were his men. As he and a handful of men moved into the rugged terrain of the interior on those first days, he asked a peasant. "Are we already in the Sierra Maestra?" The peasant said that they were. "Then the revolution has triumphed," Castro said. In Havana the Batista forces put out an announcement that Fidel Castro was dead. It was picked up and sent all over the world by the United Press, an act for which Castro never forgave the agency.

In the beginning his forces were tiny, but he received a major break when a *New York Times* journalist and editorial writer, Herbert Matthews, appeared at his camp only two months after Castro arrived. Matthews was something of a romantic, in the view of his *Times* colleague Tad Szulc. His liberal politics had been profoundly shaped during the time he covered the Spanish Civil War. He had hated the idea of Franco's victory. Matthews was instantly taken with Castro, whom he viewed as a brave, attractive young nationalist fighting against the dark forces of despotism. For Matthews Cuba was a replay of Spain, Szulc believed. He was fifty-seven when he met Castro, easily old enough to be Castro's father, and he seemed to feel almost paternal toward the younger Cuban rebel.

Castro did a masterful job of making his small unit seem much larger. He kept Matthews in camp and dispatched different men to what were supposed to be other camps; guerrillas, supposedly from different rebel headquarters, reported in to Castro in front of Matthews. It was, wrote Tad Szulc, quite literally guerrilla theater. Matthews stayed for a few days and then filed his reports to the *Times*. "Fidel Castro, the rebel leader of Cuba's youth, is alive and fighting hard and successfully in the rugged, almost impenetrable vastness of the Sierra Maestra," he began. He portrayed Batista's forces as frustrated by Castro's charismatic force. "The personality of the man is overpowering. It was easy to see that his men adored him and also to see why he has caught the imagination of the youth of Cuba all over the island. Here was an educated, dedicated fanatic, a man of ideals, of courage and of remarkable qualities of leadership." When Matthews' stories were printed they had immense impact, not least by proving that Castro was alive, not dead as Batista had claimed.

In the making of the legend of Fidel Castro, the Matthews stories played a crucial role. There was something exceptionally romantic about the young leader leaving his privileged life and going into the mountains with a few men and vowing never to return until he could walk into Havana with his revolution. It was a timeless myth, part Robin Hood, part Mao, and given the excesses of Batista, it found wide acceptance. Fidel Castro might have been hundreds of miles away in the distant mountains, but with those articles, in the minds of millions of Cubans, he *lived*.

From his mountain base, he waged a guerrilla campaign similar to the Chinese Communists' under Mao and the Vietminh's in Vietnam. They attacked only when their strength was superior, then slipped quickly back into the mountains. The purpose of every engagement was to capture more weapons, not to kill. They lived simply, largely off the soil. The officers ate after the men and they ate the same rations. They treated the peasants well and never stole from them. They treated captured soldiers generously as well, often converting them. The life was hard, which was fine with Castro—he wanted hard men of conviction and purpose, not summer soldiers.

Slowly, his band grew in size. In March 1958, after some sixteen months, he opened a second front in the northern section of Oriente. His forces, compared to those of Batista, were still small, but their deeds were greatly magnified by rumors. In the spring of 1958 Batista opened a major offensive against him. Some ten thousand men were used to drive Castro's men into a tiny defensive perimeter, but at that critical point the Batista troops pushed no further.

From then on there was a complicated dynamic at work: Castro was becoming stronger, and Batista was becoming weaker, and it was clear that American policymakers were becoming increasingly uneasy. The Americans no longer had confidence in Batista, but they had no one with whom to replace him. It was getting very late, and with the passage of time, not only was Castro's reputation growing more powerful, but his claim to succeed Batista was seen as more and more legitimate in the eyes of most Cubans. There was still considerable talk at the higher levels of the State Department's Latin American affairs section of a third force—nationalist, liberal, tainted neither by Batistaism nor Castroism. The problem with the third force, here as in other countries, most notably Vietnam, was that the Americans could not readily invent one at the last minute. The role of leader had to be *earned* and the only person earning the title, the respect, and the love of his fellow Cubans was Fidel Castro.

In November 1958, Castro began to take his men down from the hills. If he was not entirely ready for the final strike, he was nonetheless aware that Batista was near collapse and he was wary that the Americans might take his prize and give it to someone else. At the time he began his final assault on Havana, Castro probably had several thousand men, while Batista had 40,000 soldiers and an additional 30,000 police officers. But as Castro moved forward it became more and more of a rout. Real battles were relatively rare. Instead, there were more and more instances when the Batista forces simply surrendered en masse. The Batista regime at the end was like "a walking corpse," in the words of one observer. Castro's growing victory march, his ever easier road to Havana, came as much from the old order collapsing of its own weight as it did from his exceptional military leadership of the rebels. It was a government literally rotting away.

In Havana Earl Smith had wanted to continue to support Batista, but in December he was told to tell Batista to leave the country. In the final hours of the Batista regime, there was a desperate attempt to have Colonel Ramon Barquin take over the government as an anti-Castro leader. But if he had once been something of a hero, who had tried to lead a coup against Batista, he had been taken out of play by the failure of his movement and his years in Batista's prison. What might have worked twenty months earlier was now a useless footnote to the fast-moving stream of history. No one knew this better than Barquin. "What can I do?" he asked a friend in the CIA. "All they left me with is shit."

The Americans had ended up with no one whose deeds spoke for themselves and whose charisma might match that of Castro. The third-force policy had produced nothing of consequence. The Americans were, wrote Wayne Smith, "like a bridge player who had held his aces too long until they were trumped."

On January 8, 1959, Castro entered Havana as a victorious conqueror. Rarely had anyone present seen a celebration quite like it. Like Moses parting the Red Sea, one journalist said. Havana, as he entered, was still filled with armed Batista loyalists. Some of Castro's soldiers wanted to precede him as he walked through the streets, for the city was still dangerous, but Castro would have none of it. Like MacArthur landing in Tokyo in August 1945 and walking around unarmed, he understood the power of the symbolic gesture, as few around him did. The people, he had said, would protect the revolutionaries. He would walk ahead of this massive parade and he would do it unarmed. "I will prove that I know the people," he said. Of the joy that ran throughout the country there was no doubt, and of his immense broad-based popularity there was no doubt; and also of the dilemma for American policymakers there was also no doubt.

How far left was Castro? Was he a Communist? And what should American policy be now? These were the critical questions for the Eisenhower administration. There was little in the way of definitive proof that Castro was actually a Communist. In the beginning, at least, there was the strong possibility he was a nationalist with no larger allegiance to any doctrine. In fact, there was a Communist party in Cuba, which had joined with Castro only relatively late in his struggle. His success had been largely indigenous. The weapons he used were primarily captured from Batista's troops. Asked by Washington whether Castro was a Communist or not, the embassy put together a very careful report that said he had no links to the Communist party; nor, for that matter, did he have much sympathy for it. But there was much about him that gave cause for concern. Wayne Smith's analysis noted at the time, for ". . . he seemed to have gargantuan ambitions, authoritarian tendencies, and not much in the way of an ideology of his own. He was also fiercely nationalistic." Given the history of relations of the two countries, "he did not hold the U.S. in high regard. One could imagine him turning to the Communists. All depended on what he thought would best advance his interests—and Cuba's as he interpreted them." The CIA largely concurred with this analysis. As late as November 1959, the deputy director of the CIA told a Senate committee, "We believe that Castro is not a member of the Communist Party and does not consider himself to be a Communist."

On his first trip to the United States in April 1959, at the invitation of the American Society of Newspaper Editors, an invitation that greatly irritated Dwight Eisenhower, Castro was on his best behavior and generally said all the right things. He was against dictatorships. He was for a free press, which he said was the first enemy of a dictatorship. His nominally conservative hosts gave him a standing ovation. He laid a wreath at the Lincoln Memorial. He told the Senate Foreign Relations Committee he would not expropriate United States property. The one person he did not charm was Vice-President Nixon, who met with him for three and a half hours as Eisenhower's proxy. Shrewd and analytical, Nixon knew in this instance that his own career was very much at stake—he had attacked the Democrats for losing China, and after all, now here was Cuba only ninety miles away with an unknown radical as its leader.

In some ways Nixon was impressed with Castro. He found him intelligent and forceful. He could well understand his appeal in Cuba, but he was bothered by Castro's answers on why he did not hold elections (the Cuban people, Castro answered, did not want them) and why he was executing some of his opponents without fair trials (the Cuban people did not want them to be given trials). In a long memo to the President and Secretary of State Christian Herter, who had replaced Foster Dulles, Nixon wrote, "Castro is either incredibly naive about Communism or is under Communist discipline." He had reason to worry, for Castro was soon to be his responsibility.

Nixon himself was fast approaching a critical moment in his career: his run for the presidency in 1960. After serving as Vice-President for almost seven years, he was seething with frustration and resentments. The vice-presidency is a job largely without portfolio in the best of circumstances, and these were hardly the best of circumstances, for he raged at his treatment by Ike. By 1958 Nixon was caught in a political bind, one partly of his own making. He needed to upgrade his image to that of someone worthy of the presidency. He had to redo himself and make a move to the center, without changing so completely that the Republican right did not turn on him. Yet at the same time improvements in communications technology were making it more difficult to tailor speeches for specific audiences without there being a record. Some of his speeches in the Rocky Mountain states during the 1956 campaign had caused considerable controversy, but the local papers had not done a particularly serious job of covering them.

In 1958 *The New York Times* sent Russell

Baker, then a young reporter, to cover him with a tape recorder. At the first stop, when Baker had pushed the recorder up so that it could catch Nixon at a press conference, Nixon had seen the machine, had understood the game immediately, and had answered Baker's first question with a diatribe against his paper. It was clearly going to be harder than ever to be a hydra-headed candidate in American politics. Which Nixon would he choose to be as he entered his presidential run—the combative anti-Communist Nixon of the earlier, harsher campaigns, or the new Nixon, more centrist, less partisan, acceptable to the entire country? During the 1960 campaign Ken Galbraith asked Kennedy if he was tired from the brutal daily campaign routine. No, he was not tired, Kennedy answered, but he felt sure that Nixon was and he felt sorry for him. Why? Galbraith asked. "Because I know who I am and I don't have to worry about adapting and changing. All I have to do at each stop is be myself. But Nixon doesn't know who he is, and so each time he makes a speech he has to decide which Nixon he is, and that will be exhausting."

Escaping the past and moving from one constituency to another was not easy, even for someone as politically nimble as Richard Nixon. In an off-record interview with David Astor, the British publisher, Nixon addressed the ugliness of the 1950 campaign against Helen Gahagan Douglas: "I'm sorry about that episode. I was a very young man." When a version of the interview came out in *The New Republic,* Nixon angrily denied the statement and claimed that he had nothing to apologize for.

He was still wary of being accused of being soft on Communism. The one thing, he wrote in a memo to his speechwriters in July 1959, that they should never put in his speeches was an endorsement of the idea of peaceful coexistence. "This is the Acheson line in the State Department and I will not put it out!!!!!! Cushman [his Marine aide and NSC liaison, Major Bob Cushman], tell all of them—it is never to be used again . . . or whoever does it will be shipped [out] on the next plane."

In the summer of 1959, he had scored a coup in his so-called "kitchen debate" with Khrushchev. Nixon had gone to Moscow as the head of a large delegation to open a trade fair. Ambassador Llewellyn Thompson warned Nixon on arrival that the Russians were primed for a fight because of their anger over the Captive Day resolution, which Washington annually issued and to which no one, of course, paid virtually any attention except the Soviets. When Nixon went to the Kremlin for his first meeting with the Soviet leader, Khrushchev observed that Senator McCarthy might be dead but apparently his spirit lived on. Nixon tried to change the subject, but Khrushchev pushed on, earthy as ever: "People should not go to the toilet where they eat. This resolution stinks. It stinks like fresh horse shit, and nothing smells worse than that!" Nixon, remembering that the Russian leader had been a pig farmer, said there was one thing that smelled worse "and that is pig shit." With that Khrushchev smiled and agreed to change the subject.

But the tone had been set. From then on it seemed a mutual boasting competition. Whatever America did, the Russians did better. As the two men toured a model American house, which was a part of the exhibition, Nixon claimed that though the Soviet Union might be ahead in rocket power, America was ahead in middle-class housing. But the house was not good enough for the Soviet first secretary: The Russians would build better housing than the West, he boasted, housing that would last for several generations.

When Nixon tried to talk about the new consumer devices that made life easier in these houses, Khrushchev scorned them. Some of them, he said, were probably out of order. Others were worthless. "Don't you have a machine that puts food into the mouth and pushes it down?" he asked sardonically. "You do all the talking and you do not let anyone else talk," Nixon finally complained. "I want to make one point. We don't think this fair will astound the Russian people, but it will interest them. . . . To us, diversity, the right to choose, the fact that we have a thousand different builders, that's the spice of life. We don't want to have a decision made at the top by one government official saying that we will have one kind of house. That's the difference."

But Khrushchev was not Nixon's problem as 1959 became 1960 and the campaign for the presidency began. The problem was Castro. If Nixon and the Republican party were vulnerable on any one issue, it was Cuba. Vietnam had been a close call, but the President had shrewdly managed to put the blame on our allies. But Cuba was a wild card. Castro had come to power, our influence with him was minimal, and yet the President did not seem very interested in Cuba; his mind was elsewhere. He, unlike Richard Nixon, did not have to run for the presidency in 1960. Whatever else Dwight Eisenhower thought about Cuba, it had nothing to do with his political future.

A new ambassador, Phillip Bonsal, a highly professional career officer, had replaced Earl Smith, and Bonsal had made it clear that he wanted to create some kind of dialogue with Castro. But it was increasingly apparent by the fall of 1959 that Castro was on a course to the left: Both his words and actions were increasingly upsetting to American authorities. In October 1959 Huber Matos, one of the top men in the revolution, criticized the rising influence of the Communists in Castro's inner circle; Matos was immediately arrested and sentenced to twenty years in prison. By November 1959, almost all of Castro's moderate ministers were gone, replaced by men either from the Communist party or sympathetic to it. In November a Soviet trade delegation arrived and was given the red-carpet treatment, and in February 1960, Anastas Mikoyan visited Cuba, to an unusually warm welcome. More and more, Castro seemed to be on a deliberate collision course with Washington.

Castro continued his brutal executions of former Batista sympathizers, and his rhetoric was increasingly hostile to the United States. Perhaps both sides carried too much baggage from the past to be friends now. When a French ship that was unloading munitions exploded, Castro angrily blamed the United States, though there was no evidence of American involvement, nor did any show up later. Wayne Smith, a man not averse to criticizing American policy, felt that the explosion was probably caused by carelessness. But the incident seemed to mark the point of no return. Castro started buying petroleum products from the Soviet Union, and when Soviet tankers arrived, the three local refineries—two of them American, one British—refused to refine the crude. With that, Castro nationalized the refineries. By the end of the summer he had nationalized a large amount of American property. The Americans, in retaliation, ended the Castro sugar quota, refusing to buy the remaining 700,000 tons of it.

On his second visit to the United States, Castro was not so amiable a guest. He arrived for the United Nations General Assembly in September

1960 and stayed at the Hotel Theresa in Harlem—in itself a major political statement. He dined with Khrushchev at the Soviet mission in New York. With such moves Castro was thinking not of his place in Cuba but of his place in the world. Even the sympathetic Herbert Matthews, Wayne Smith noted, had written about Fidel's "Messiah complex." "Fidel," Matthews had written, "has all along felt himself to be a crusader if not a saviour." For a man like this, Cuba was too small a stage. He wanted to be a major figure on the international stage, and to do that he had to be free of the United States.

To Tad Szulc, the distinguished *New York Times* reporter who covered Castro for years and later wrote a major biography of him, that explanation made the most sense. Castro, Szulc believed, was a man of instinct and circumstances as much as he was of ideology. He was shrewd, emotional, extremely talented, and overwhelmingly ambitious. Given Castro's view of himself, given his desire to be a worldwide revolutionary figure, it was inevitable, Szulc thought, that he would go the way he did. It was not by chance that he kept the fatigues and the beard long after he had left the Sierra Maestra. His decision was, thought Szulc, not at all very ideological, but rather very pragmatic—indeed instinctive. Therefore the question for American policymakers was not whether or not the Eisenhower administration had played him incorrectly in those important early months, for there was simply no right way to play him. He was going in a very different direction because it was the way he wanted to go. He could not be a major revolutionary figure of world-wide status and yet be an ally of the leading capitalist power.

Nevertheless, America was largely without a policy toward Cuba. As the unthinkable happened—a radical, left-wing, quite possibly Marxist, government had taken power—the American response was almost automatic. On January 18, 1960, the CIA division responsible for the Western Hemisphere held its first meeting on Castro and Cuba. As the regulars assembled, everyone's spirits were high. Many of them were veterans of the successful coup against Arbenz six years earlier and looked forward to a repeat success. When Jake Engler (a professional pseudonym), one of the men in charge, called David Atlee Phillips, who had run the radio station during the Arbenz coup, he gave Phillips three guesses what they were going to deal with. The answer was easy: "Cuba. Cuba. And Cuba," Phillips said. When Phillips was reunited with Howard Hunt, who had been one of the high-level operatives in the Guatemalan coup, Hunt was excited. "Welcome aboard, Chico," he said. They were all so confident; it was, they thought, like a reunion; Guatemala had been a piece of cake, and Cuba now would be a bigger one. The operating group proceeded enthusiastically, ignoring all intelligence estimates from the embassy and from the CIA, which portrayed Castro as remarkably invulnerable to guerrilla insurrection. Rather, they showed a far more sophisticated and developed country than Guatemala, and also that Castro was a truly formidable figure, in no way a target comparable to Arbenz. If he was losing some popularity through his increasingly brutal tactics of suppressing all domestic political opposition, then he compensated by developing his own secret police.

Wayne Smith vacationed in Miami in the summer of 1960 and found the city rife with surprisingly detailed accounts of a new clandestine operation which was obviously intended to topple Castro. "We're going to take care of Castro just like we took care of Arbenz," one man, obviously a CIA agent, told Smith. "It was easy then and it'll be easy now." The smugness of the CIA men stunned Smith and others. There was one CIA agent who liked to move around the Miami exile community telling Cuban exiles that he carried the revolution with him in his checkbook.

The planning for the anti-Castro operation was all done in a rush. The driving force was Richard Bissell, who had been so successful in the development of the U-2. Though Bissell was inexperienced in running an operation like this, he was a fierce taskmaster and pushed things through ruthlessly. Time was of the essence. Cuban pilots were said to be learning to fly MiGs in the Soviet Union, and any operation needing air cover would lose its advantage when they returned. Pressure was also being applied by Richard Nixon, who much more so than Eisenhower supported the operation. Eisenhower remained ambivalent about Cuba. He did not like Castro and he was irritated by what Castro was doing, but his second tour was almost done. His warnings to the CIA people were not unlike those he had made in the past; if it was to be done, he wanted it to succeed. It was all or nothing for him. But he clearly had his doubts. At one meeting in March 1960, Eisenhower said Cuba might be "another black hole of Calcutta."

Nixon, though, did not want Castro's Cuba to be an issue in the 1960 campaign. "How are the boys doing at the Institute?" Nixon would ask his liaison with the NSC, Robert Cushman referring to the CIA's operation in Cuba. It was clear, Cushman thought, that Nixon wanted the operation to take place before the election. Predictably, things did not develop smoothly. The ablest top-level CIA officer, Dick Helms, who was involved in something of a power struggle with Bissell at the time, wanted no part of it. Throughout the Agency, the word was out that Helms was staying away from the Cuba thing—a signal to many other of the Agency's more senior people to stay away as well. Helms, as Peter Wyden noted in his book on the Bay of Pigs, was known to have "a nose for incipient failures."

There were four parts to the operation: the

creation of what was called a responsible government in exile, a powerful propaganda effort, a
covert intelligence operation inside Cuba, and,
most important, the training of a paramilitary
Cuban force in exile. On March 17, 1960, Eisenhower gave his official approval to go ahead on
the paramilitary unit. The plan called for training
twenty-five Cuban exiles, who would in turn train
other exiles to overthrow Castro. From then on,
what happened was a striking case of an ill-conceived, ill-advised policy being carried forward by
its own institutional momentum. Many people
thought the plan was foolish and ill-conceived,
but no one wanted to take responsibility for stopping it; finally, it became impossible to stop.

In mid-August, 1960, Ike approved a budget
of $13 million for the covert operation. But still
things lagged behind schedule. The presidential
election was heating up. Bissell was confident that
Nixon would approve the final plan. Of Kennedy
he was not so sure. Nixon, thought his aide Robert Cushman, was getting very restless. There was
constant pressure from him to find out how things
were going. The truth was, Cushman thought,
they were not going that well. Early operations in
which agents were dropped into Cuba backfired,
and the agents were easily picked up. It was decided that the operation needed to be bigger, with
a fifty-kilowatt radio station, a rebel air force
based in Nicaragua, and a full-scale landing in
Cuba of more than one thousand men. It was now

not so much a covert operation as an invasion. Eisenhower was still ambivalent. "Where's our government in exile?" he kept asking Allen Dulles. In the late fall, he showed his skepticism yet again at a meeting with Dulles and Bissell. "I'm going along with you boys, but I want to be sure the damned thing works."

Soon it became clear there would not be time to launch the operation while Eisenhower was still President. And with that perhaps the last chance to kill the operation had died. For it would have been easy for Eisenhower, an experienced military man with solid anti-Communist credentials, to call off his own program; it was not so easy for a young Democratic President, vulnerable to accusations of a lack of experience and being insufficiently anti-Communist to stop a program that was so far advanced.

So the plan moved forward and continued to grow. Soon it was six hundred men instead of four hundred; then it was seven hundred fifty, and then over one thousand. Then it became less a covert guerrilla force and more a full-scale landing from the sea, supported by a small hired air force. That was one of the most difficult maneuvers of all in military terms. The more men were needed, the less secrecy there would be and the more the operation would depend on increased airpower. In fact the operation had become something of an open secret by the fall of 1960. Castro had agents everywhere, and even if he had not, the size of the force, the swagger of its members as they boasted of what they would do, had guaranteed that Castro would know many of the details.

. . .

That meant that Richard Nixon's worst nightmare about the 1960 campaign had come true. The Cuban dilemma had not been settled, Castro was sticking his finger in America's eye from his safe haven ninety miles away, and the formation of an exile expeditionary force lagged well behind schedule. The Democrats, as he had suspected, were about to nominate John Kennedy, who would make a formidable opponent.

Kennedy was young, attractive, contemporary, skilled as few politicians of his generation were at using television. He also represented the resurgence of the Democrats as hard-liners. Accused of being soft on Communism in the past, they were now determined to show that if anything, they were tougher foes of Communism than the Republicans. They did this somewhat deftly: They did not actually accuse the Republicans of being soft on Communism; instead, they claimed that the country had lost its edge during the Eisenhower years. America had become self-satisfied and lazy, and the world was leaving America behind, particularly in the race for friends in the third world. They spoke of a missile gap (which did not exist) and again and again of Castro's Cuba.

John Kennedy was a cool and very controlled young man, privileged, well educated, but in some ways very much the son of his Irish-immigrant father. If the passions and rage of Joe Kennedy had been obvious, those of his son were not: He appeared not as an angry immigrant but, thanks to the tailoring of Harvard, as reserved and aristocratic—the first Irish Brahmin. Be more Irish than Harvard, the poet Robert Frost would ask of him at his inauguration a year later. The Kennedy signature was a kind of rugged masculinity, a physical and emotional toughness. Kennedy men did not cry, and they did not make themselves vulnerable on issues of anti-Communism. "Isn't he marvelous!" an excited Joe Alsop had said to a colleague after watching Kennedy's announcement for the presidency. "A Stevenson with balls."

Because he was as good at listening as speaking, he soon recognized that the country's anxieties over the Cold War now had more to do with Castro than with Khrushchev. All he had to do was mention, as he did frequently, that Cuba was only ninety miles away, eight minutes by jet, and the audience would explode in anger and frustration. Typically, in a speech on October 15, in Johnstown, Pennsylvania, he said: "Mr. Nixon hasn't mentioned Cuba very prominently in this campaign. He talks about standing firm in Berlin, standing firm in the Far East, standing up to Khrushchev, but he never mentions standing firm in Cuba—and if you can't stand up to Castro, how can you be expected to stand up to Khrushchev?" So ironically, Kennedy attacked Nixon for the administration's softness on Castro, but Nixon, privy to the CIA's preparation of the clandestine operation, could not respond.

If television played a role in previous presidential elections, this was the first in which it became the dominating force. In past elections, Kennedy might have been denied the nomination because the party bosses (most of them, ironically, Catholic) were against him, fearing an anti-Catholic backlash. But Kennedy used the primaries to prove he could win predominantly Protestant strongholds, and the key to that was his skillful use of television.

Kennedy had been a natural on television—from the start the camera had liked him. He was attractive, he did not posture, and he was cool by instinct: Television was a cool medium—the more overheated a candidate, the less well he did on it. Kennedy's gestures and his speaking voice seemed natural—perhaps it was a reaction to the old-fashioned blarney of his Irish-American grandfather, who had campaigned by singing Irish songs. John Kennedy did not like politicians who gave florid speeches; he greatly preferred understatement. His own speeches were full of humor, irony, and self-depreciation, and that helped him in what was to be the defining moment of the 1960 campaign—the first presidential debate.

By contrast, television was a problem for Nixon. Not only were his physical gestures awkward, but his speaking tone was selfconscious and artificial. What often came through was a sense of insincerity. To Eisenhower's secretary, Anne Whitman, "The Vice-President sometimes seems like a man who is acting like a nice man rather than being one." That was a critical distinction, particularly for a man entering the television age, because if there was one thing the piercing eye of the television camera was able to convey to people, it was what was authentic and what was artificial.

The first debate changed the nature of politics in America, and it also crowned the importance of television politically and culturally. From then on, American politics became a world of television and television advisers; the party machinery was soon to be in sharp decline as the big-city political bosses no longer had a monopoly on the ability to assemble large crowds—television offered much larger ones. Until that night in Chicago, Kennedy had been the upstart, a little-known junior senator who had hardly bothered to take the Senate seriously. Nixon, on the other hand, had been Vice-President for eight years; he was experienced, had visited endless foreign countries and met with all the leaders of the world. He also fancied himself a not inconsiderable debater, and he was confident he would do well against Kennedy.

Kennedy, who viewed Nixon with a cool snobbishness, arrived in Chicago early. He had spent much of the previous week in California, and he was tanned and glowing with good health. Knowing that this was the most important moment in the campaign, he had minimized his campaign schedule and spent much of his time in his hotel resting. He also practiced with his staff members, who posed likely questions and likely Nixon answers.

Nixon, by contrast, arrived in terrible shape. He had been ill earlier in the campaign with an infected knee, and he had never entirely recovered. Others on his staff tried to tell him to rest and prepare himself, but no one could tell him anything. Old and once trusted advisers had been cut off. Frustrated by Eisenhower's treatment of him for the last seven and a half years, Nixon had become megalomaniacal in 1960 as far as his veteran staff was concerned, determined to be his own campaign manager as well as candidate. Ted Rogers, his top television adviser, found that Nixon would not even talk with him about planning for the coming debates. Rogers kept calling the Nixon campaign plane to see how the candidate was doing and how he looked, and the answer always come back that he was doing well and looked fine.

At one point Rogers flew out to Kansas City to talk with Nixon about the debate but had not been able even to see him. Have you got him drinking milkshakes? Rogers asked the staff on the plane, and was assured that the candidate looked just fine. The first debate was set for Monday, September 26. Nixon, ill and exhausted, flew out late on Sunday night and went on a motorcade through Chicago, stopping for rallies in five wards and getting to bed very late. Then on Monday, even though he was clearly exhausted, he made another major campaign appearance in front of a labor union. His staff prepared possible questions and answers for him, but he was in no mood to look at their work. Late Monday afternoon, Rogers was permitted a brief meeting. He was stunned by how badly Nixon looked. His face was gray and ashen, and his aides had not even bothered to buy him new shirts—so his shirt hung loosely around his neck like that of a dying man. The only thing he wanted to know from Rogers was how long it would take to get from his hotel to the studio.

At the studio, both candidates turned down the makeup offered by the station. It was gamesmanship: Each man feared that if he used any makeup, then the next day there would be newspaper stories about it, or, even worse, a photo. But Kennedy had a good tan and his aide Bill Wilson did a slight touch-up with commercial makeup bought at a drugstore two blocks away. Because of his dark beard, Nixon used something called Shavestick. The CBS professionals were as shocked by Nixon's appearance as Ted Rogers had been. Don Hewitt, the producer (later to be the executive producer of *60 Minutes*), was sure that a disaster was in the making and that CBS would later be blamed for Nixon's cosmetic failures (which in fact happened).

Nixon was extremely sensitive to heat, and he sweated profusely when the television lights were on (years later, as President, he gave fireside chats from the White House with the air-conditioning turned up to the maximum so that he would not sweat). He had started out in the debates by looking ghastly, gray and exhausted. Then while some 80 million of his fellow Americans watched, it got worse. He began to sweat. Soon there were rivers of sweat on his gray face, and the Shavestick washed down his face. In the control room Rogers and Wilson were sitting with Hewitt, who, Rogers decided, was the most powerful man in the country at that moment because he controlled the camera. Earlier, during the negotiations, both sides had agreed on the number of reaction shots that could be used—that is, how many times the camera would focus on one candidate while the other candidate was speaking. At first Wilson had called for more reaction shots of his man, Kennedy, and Rogers had called for more reaction shots of his man. But soon they had switched sides: Watching Nixon in a kind of cosmetic meltdown, Wilson called for more shots of *Nixon* and Rogers called for more of *Kennedy*—anything to get that relentlessly cruel camera off Nixon's gray face as it dissolved into a river of sweat. "That night," Russell Baker wrote thirty years later, "image replaced the printed word as the natural language of politics."

Nixon had been warned by others that he must not attack too harshly, that otherwise he would seem like the Nixon of old; even Eisenhower had told him that he must not be too glib. That had stung, for it was nothing less than a rebuke, the President's way of saying that he thought Nixon was, in fact, too glib (what stung even more was learning that Ike did not even bother to watch the debate). When it was all over, Nixon thought he had won. Kennedy knew otherwise, particularly when the door to WBBM opened and there was Dick Daley, the boss of the Chicago Democratic machine, who had so far shunned Kennedy in Chicago. Now he was eager to congratulate him, eager to come aboard. The next day Kennedy drew huge crowds wherever he went, and the people seemed to feel a personal relationship with the candidate. For Nixon the news was a great deal worse. The parents of Rose Woods, his longtime secretary, called from Ohio to ask if there was anything wrong with him. Even Hannah Nixon called Rose to inquire about her son's health.

Later, Ted Rogers mused that eight years of Nixon's experience as Vice-President had been wiped out in one evening. Rogers wondered how Nixon could have been so careless about so vital a moment in the campaign, and later he decided that it was the sum of everything that had gone before: anger over his treatment by Eisenhower as Vice-President; his subsequent determination to make all the important decisions in this campaign himself and to listen to none of his old advisers; and finally, his belief that because of the Checkers speech, he was an expert on television. Unfortunately, anyone who understood television could have warned him that Kennedy was a formidable foe in front of a television camera.

. . .

The debate between these two young men, each born in this century, each young enough to be Dwight Eisenhower's son, seemed to underscore how quickly the society had changed in so short a time. It showed not only how powerful the electronic medium had become, but also how much it was already speeding the pace of life in America. Not everyone was pleased by the change wrought in American politics by television. Dean Acheson was not moved by either candidate as he watched the debate and it had made him feel older. To him both candidates appeared to be cold, mechanistic figures who had, with the aid of pollsters and advertising executives, figured out, down to the last decimal point, what stand to take on every issue. "Do you get a funny sort of sense that, so far at least, there are no human candidates in this campaign?" he wrote Harry Truman. "They seem improbable, skillful technicians. Both are surrounded by clever people who dash off smart memoranda, but it is not all pulled together on either side, by or into a man. The ideas are too contrived. . . . These two . . . bore the hell out of me."

Author Interviews *for* The Fifties

Ralph Abernathy, Tom Adams, Naohiro Amaya, Michael Arlen, Harry Ashmore, Russell Baker, James Bassett, Laura Pincus Bernard, Hans Bethe, Stanley Booth, Herbert Brownell, Will Campbell, M.C. Chang, John Chancellor, David Cole, Bob Cousy, Geoff Cowan, Keith Crain, Robert Cumberford, Mike Dann, David E. Davis, Anthony De Lorenzo, Sophie Pincus Dutton, Jock Elliot, Dan Enright, Jerry Evans, Jules Feiffer, Estelle Ferkauf, Eugene Ferkauf, David Fine, Karl Fleming, Al Freedman, Don Frey, Betty Friedan, Betty Furness, Frank Gibney, Paul Gillian, Herman Goldstine, Dick Goodman, Dick Goodwin, Katharine Graham, Harold Green, Wayne Greenhaw, Sidney Gruson, Oscar Hechter, Thomas Hine, Mahlon Hoagland, Sandra Holland, Townsend Hoopes, Robert Ingram, Evelyn Pincus Isaacson, Joe Isaacson, Ray Jenkins, W. Thomas Johnson, Kensinger Jones, Chuck Jordan, Ward Just, Stanley Katz, Alfred Kazin, Murray Kempton, Bunkie Knudsen, Florence Knudsen, Julian Krainan, A.J. Langguth, William Levitt, Ira Lipman, Susan McBride, David McCall, Frank McCullough, Dick McDonald, Jay Milner, Frederic Morrow, Stan Mott, Leona Nevler, Stan Parker, Knox Phillips, Sam Phillips, John Alexis Pincus, Michael Pincus, Earl Pollock, Johnny Popham, Bill Porter, G.E. Powell, Waddy Pratt, Joel Raphaelson, Richard Rhodes, David Riesman, Matthew Ridgway, Kermit Roosevelt, Sr., Al Rothenberg, Harrison Salisbury, Gerald Schnitzer, Don Schwarz, Sheldon Segal, Joel Selvin, Robert Serber, Don Silber, Claude Sitton, Reggie Smith, Dick Starmann, Herb Stempel, Tad Szulc, Henry Turley,

Fred Turner, Sander Vanocur, Bill Walton, Tom Watson, Jr., Thomas Weinberg, Victor Weisskopf, Wallace Westfeldt, Marina von Neumann Whitman, Jerome Wiesner, Kemmons Wilson, Sloan Wilson, Bill Winter, Andy Young

ADDITIONAL AUTHOR INTERVIEWS

Roger Ailes, Louis Cowan, Helen Gahagan Douglas, Albert Gore, Leonard Hall, Averell Harriman, Don Hewitt, Larry L. King, Murrey Marder, Earl Mazo, Mollie Parnis, Rosser Reeves, James Reston, Ted Rogers, Pierre Salinger, David Schoenbrun, Dan Schorr, C.L. Sulzberger, Bill Wilson

Bibliography

Abernathy, Ralph. *And the Walls Came Tumbling Down.* New York: Harper Perennial, 1989.

Acheson, Dean. *Present at the Creation: My Years in the State Department.* New York: Norton, 1969.

Adams, Sherman. *First-Hand Report.* New York: Harper and Row, 1961.

Alabama Oral History Project: Interview with Virginia Durr, *Memoir Vol. II,* November 24, 1976.

Allen, Fred. *Treadmill to Oblivion.* Boston: Little, Brown and Co., 1954.

Alsop, Joseph W. *I've Seen the Best of It: The Memoirs of Joseph W. Alsop.* New York: W.W. Norton & Co.

Alsop, Joseph and Stewart Alsop. *We Accuse!: The Story of the Miscarriage of American Justice in the Case of J. Robert Oppenheimer.* New York: Simon and Schuster, 1954.

Alvarez, Luis W. Alvarez: *Adventures of a Physicist.* New York: Basic Books, 1987.

Ambrose, Stephen. *Eisenhower, Vol. 2: The President.* New York: Simon & Schuster, 1984.

Ambrose, Stephen. *Nixon: The Education of a Politician, 1913–1962.* New York: Simon & Schuster, 1987.

Anderson, Kent. *The History and Implications of the Quiz Show Scandals.* Westport: Greenwood, 1978.

Andrews, Bart. *The I Love Lucy Book.* New York: Doubleday & Co., 1985.

Appelbaum, Irwyn. *The World According to Beaver.* New York: Bantam Books, Inc., 1984.

Appleman, Roy. *South to the Naktong, North to the Yalu.*

June–November, 1950. Washington D.C.,: Office of the Chief of Military History, Department of the Army, 1961.

Ashmore, Harry. *Hearts and Minds: The Anatomy of Racism from Roosevelt to Reagan.* New York: McGraw Hill, 1982.

Aspery, William. *John von Neumann and the Origins of Modern Computing.* Cambridge, Massachusetts: Massachusetts Institute of Technology Press, 1990.

"Attack on the Conscience," *Time.* Vol LXIX: February 18, 1957.

Barmash, Isadore. *More than They Bargained for: The Rise and Fall of Korvettes.* New York: Lebhar-Friedman Books, 1981.

Barnouw, Erik. *A History of Broadcasting, Vol II: The Golden Web.* New York: Oxford University Press, 1968.

Barnouw, Erik. *A History of Broadcasting, Vol. III: The Image Empire.* New York: Oxford University Press, 1970.

Bates, Daisy. *The Long Shadow of Little Rock.* Fayetteville: The University of Arkansas Press, 1962.

Bayley, Edwin. *Joe McCarthy and the Press.* Madison, Wisonsin: University of Wisconsin Press, 1981.

Bayley, Stephen. *Harley Earl and the Dream Machine.* New York: Knopf, 1983.

Berg, Stacey Michelle. Undergraduate thesis, Harvard University.

Berghaus, Erik. *Reaching for the Stars.* New York: Doubleday, 1960.

Bernays, Edward. *Biography of an Idea: Memoirs of Public Relations Council Edward L. Bernays.* New York: Simon & Schuster, 1965.

Bernstein, Jeremy. *Hans Berthe: Prophet of Energy.* New York: Basic Books, 1980.

Beschloss, Michael. *The Crisis Years: Kennedy and Khrushchev, 1960–1963.* New York: HarperCollins, 1991.

Beschloss, Michael. *Mayday: Eisenhower, Khrushchev, and the U-2 Affair.* New York: Harper and Row, 1986.

Blair, Clay. *Ridgway's Paratroopers.* New York: Doubleday & Co., 1985.

Blair, Clay. *The Forgotten War: America in Korea, 1950–1953.* New York: New York Times Books, 1987.

Blossom, Virgil. *It Happened Here.* New York: Harper and Row, 1959.

Blumberg, Stanley and Gwinn Owens. *Energy and Conflict: The Life of Edward Teller.* New York: Putnam, 1976.

Booth, Stanley. *Rythym Oil.* New York: Pantheon, 1992.

Bradley, Omar with Clay Blair. *A General's Life.* New York: Simon & Schuster, 1983.

Branch, Taylor. *Parting the Waters: America in the King Years, 1954–1963.* New York: Simon & Schuster, 1988.

Brochu, Jim. *Lucy in the Afternoon: An Intimate Biography of Lucille Ball.* New York: William Morrow & Co., 1990.

Bundy, McGeorge. *Danger and Survival: Choices About the Bomb in the First Fifty Years.* New York: Random House, 1988.

Cal Fullerton Archives: Interviews with Jane Milhous Beeson, Elizabeth Cloes, Guy Dixon, Douglas Ferguson, Saragrace Frampton, Olive Mashburn, Oscar Mashburn, Charles Milhous, Dorothy Milhous, Lucile Parson, Hubert Perry, Paul Ryan, Ralph Shook, Paul Smith, Madeline Thomas, Lura Walfrop, Samuel Warner, Merel West, Marcia Elliot Wray, and Merton Wray.

Carey, Gary. *Marlon Brando: The Only Contender.* New York: St. Martin's Press, 1985.

Cassady, Carolyn. *Off the Road: My Years with Cassady, Kerouac, and Ginsberg.* New York: Morrow, 1990.

Caute, David. *The Great Fear: The Anti-Communist*

Purge Under Truman and Eisenhower. New York: Simon & Schuster, 1978.

Chambers, Whittaker. *Witness.* New York: Random House, 1952.

Christenson, Cornelia V. *Kinsey: A Biography.* Bloomington: Indiana University Press, 1971.

City vs. Charlotte Colvin. Transcript from the circuit court of Juvenile Court and Court of Domestic Relations, Montgomery County, Alabama, March 18, 1955.

Clarke, Arthur, ed. *The Coming of the Space Age.* New York: Meredith Press, 1967.

Coffey, Thomas M. *Iron Eagle: The Turbulent Life of General Curtis LeMay.* New York: Crown Publishing Group, 1987.

Cohen, Marcia. *The Sisterhood: The True Story Behind the Women's Movement.* New York: Simon & Schuster, 1988.

Collins, Joseph Lawton. *War in Peacetime: The History and Lessons of Korea.* Boston: Houghton Mifflin, 1969.

Cooke, Alistair. *A Generation on Trial.* New York: Knopf, 1982.

Costello, William. *The Facts About Nixon.* New York: Viking Press, 1960.

Cotten, Lee. *The Elvis Catalog.* New York: Charlton Associates, 1987.

Coughlin, Robert. "Dr. Edward Teller's Magnificent Obsession." *Life,* No. 37, September 6, 1954.

Cray, Ed. *Chrome Colossus: General Motors and its Times.* New York: McGraw Hill, 1980.

Cray, Ed. *General of the Army: George C. Marshall.* New York: W.W. Norton, 1990.

Currie, Majorie Dent, ed. *Current Biography Yearbook.* New York: H.W. Wilson Co., 1949.

Currie, Majorie Dent, ed. *Current Biography: Who's*

News and Why-1953. New York: H. W. Wilson Co., 1954.

Currie, Majorie Dent, ed. *Current Biography Yearbook*. New York: H.W. Wilson Co., 1956.

Dalton, David. *James Dean: The Mutant King*. New York: St. Martin's Press, 1974.

Davidson, Sarah. "Dr. Rock's Magic Pill." *Esquire,* December, 1983.

Davis, K. Charles. *Two-Bit Culture: The Paperbacking of America*. Boston: Houghton Mifflin Co., 1984.

Davis, Nuell Pharr. *Lawrence and Oppenheimer; The Da Capo Series in Science*. New York: Da Capo Press, 1986.

Dean, William with William Worden. *General Dean's Story*. New York: Viking, 1954.

Diamond, Edwin and Stephan Bates. *The Spot: The Rise of Political Advertising on Television*. Cambridge: MIT Press, 1988.

Diggins, John Partrick. *The Proud Decades*. New York: Norton, 1988.

Donovan, Robert J. *Conflict and Crisis: The Presidency of Harry S. Truman, 1945–1948*. New York: Norton, 1972.

Donovan, Robert J. *Tumultuous Years: The Presidency of Harry S. Truman, 1949–1953*. New York: Norton, 1982.

Dornberger, Walter. *V-2*. New York: Viking, 1952.

Dorschner, John and Robert Fabricio. *The Winds of December*. New York: Coward, McCann and Geoghegan, 1980.

Dulles, Eleanor L. *Eleanor Lansing Dulles: Chances of a Lifetime: A Memoir*. New York: Prentice Hall, 1980.

Dundy, Elaine. *Elvis and Gladys*. New York: Macmillan, 1988.

Dunleavy, Steve. *Elvis: What Happened*. New York: Ballantine, 1982.

Edwards, Anne. *Vivien Leigh.* New York: Simon & Schuster, 1977.

Eisenhower, Dwight D. *Mandate for Change.* New York: Doubleday, 1963.

Escot, Colin and Martin Hawkins. *Sun Records: The Brief History of a Legendary Record Label.* New York: Quick Fox, 1975.

Fall, Bernard. *Hell in a Very Small Place: The Siege of Dien Bien Phu.* Philadelphia: J. B. Lippincott Co., 1967.

Farre, Robert, ed. *The Diaries of James C. Hagerty.* Bloomington, Indiana: Indiana University Press, 1983.

Faubus, Orval. *Down from the Hills,* Vol I. Little Rock: Pioneer Press, 1980.

FBI Documents on J. Robert Oppenheimer, May 27, 1952– Albuquerque Office.

Fehrenbach, T.R. *This Kind of War: A Study in Unpreparedness.* New York: Macmillan, 1954.

Fenton, John. *In Your Opinion.* Boston: Little, Brown, 1960.

Ferrell, Robert H., ed. *Dear Bess: The Letters from Harry to Bess Truman, 1910–1959.* New York: Norton, 1983.

Ferrell, Robert H., ed. *Off the Record: The Private Papers of Harry S. Truman.* New York: Harper & Row, 1980.

Fiore, Carlo. *Bud: The Brando I Knew.* New York: Delacorte Press, 1974.

Fox, Stephen. *The Mirror Makers.* New York: Morrow, 1984.

Friendly, Fred. *Due to Circumstances Beyond Our Control.* New York: Random House, 1967.

Gans, Herbert J. *The Levittowners: Ways of Life and Politics in a New Suburban Community.* New York: Pantheon, 1967.

Garrow, David. *Bearing the Cross.* New York: William Morrow & Co., 1986.

Geller, Larry and Joel Specter with Patricia Romanowski. *"If I Can Dream": Elvis's Own Story.* New York: Simon & Schuster, 1989.

Gifford, Barry and Lawrence Lee. *Jack's Book.* New York: St. Martin's Press, 1978.

Goldman, Albert. *Elvis.* New York: McGraw-Hill, 1981.

Goldman, Eric. *The Crucial Decade: America 1945–1955.* New York: Knopf, 1956.

Goodchild, Peter. *J. Robert Oppenheimer: Scatterer of Worlds.* Boston: Houghton Mifflin, 1981.

Goodwin, Richard N. *Remembering America: A Voice from the Sixties.* Boston: Little, Brown & Co., 1988.

Gorman, Joseph Bruce. *Kefauver.* New York: Oxford University Press, 1971.

Goulden, Joseph. *The Best Years: 1945–1950.* New York: Atheneum, 1976.

Goulden, Joseph C. *Korea: The Untold Story.* New York: Times Books, 1982.

Gray, Madeline. Margaret Sanger: *A Biography of the Champion of Birth Control.* New York: R. Malek, 1979.

Green, Harold P. "The Oppenheimer Case: A Study into the Abuse of Law." *The Bulletin of the Atomic Scientist,* September, 1977.

Greenshaw, Wayne. *Alabama on My Mind.* Boulder: Sycamore Press, 1987.

Grossman, James K. *Black Southerners and the Great Migration.* Chicago: University of Chicago Press, 1989.

Guiles, Fred L. *Legend: The Life and Death of Marilyn Monroe.* Toronto: Madison Press Books, 1985.

Guiles, Fred L. *Norma Jean: The Life of Marilyn Monroe.* New York: Paragon House, 1993.

Gunther, John. *Inside USA.* New York: Harper, 1947.

Guralnick, Peter. *Feel Like Going Home.* New York: Perennial Library, 1989.

Hagerty, James C. *The Diary of James C. Hagerty: Eisenhower in Mid Course.* Bloomington: Indiana University Press, 1983.

Haining, Peter, ed. *Elvis in Private.* New York: St. Martin's Press, 1987.

Halberstam, David. *The Reckoning.* New York: Morrow, 1986.

Halberstam, David. *The Powers that Be.* New York: Knopf, 1979.

Harris, Warren G. *Lucy & Desi.* New York: Doubleday & Co., 1990.

Hastings, Max. *The Korean War.* New York: Simon & Schuster, 1987.

Hearings of the Subcommittee of the Committee on Interstate and Foreign Commerce, Eighty-Sixth Congress, II, Vol. 51.

Hendrik, George. *The Selected Letters of Mark Van Doren.* Baton Rouge: LSU Press, 1987.

Hewlett, Richard and Francis Duncan. *Atomic Shield: A History of the U.S. Atomic Energy Commission.* University Park: Pennsylvania State University Press, 1969.

Higham, Charles. *Brando: The Unauthorized Biography.* New York: New American Library, 1987.

Hine, Thomas. *Populuxe.* New York: Knopf, 1986.

Hiss, Tony. *Laughing Last: Alger Hiss.* Boston: Houghton Mifflin Co., 1977.

Holmes, John Clellon. *Go.* New York: Thunder's Mouth Press, 1988.

Hopkins, Jerry. *Elvis: The Final Years.* New York: Berkley, 1983.

Hoopes, Townsend. *The Devil and John Foster Dulles.* Boston: Little, Brown and Co., 1973.

Hoover, J. Edgar. *Masters of Deceit: The Story of Communism in America and How to Fight It.* New York: Henry Holt, 1958.

Horowitz, Irving L. *C. Wright Mills: An American Utopian.* New York: The Free Press, 1983.

Huckaby, Elizabeth. *Crisis at Central High: Little Rock 1957–1958.* Baton Rouge: LSU Press, 1980.

Hughes, John Emmet. *The Ordeal of Power.* New York: Atheneum, 1963.

Huie Letters at Ohio State University.

Hunt, Howard. *Give Us This Day.* New Rochelle: Arlington House, 1971.

Immerman, Richard. *The CIA in Guatemala: The Foreign Policy of Intervention.* Austin: University of Texas Press.

Institutional VFM Interview

Jackson, Kenneth T. *Crabgrass Frontier: The Suburbanization of the United States.* New York: Oxford University Press, 1985.

James, Clayton D. *The Years of MacArthur: Triumph and Disaster, 1945–1964,* Vol. III. Boston: Houghton Mifflin, 1985.

Johnson, Haynes. *The Bay of Pigs.* New York: Norton, 1964.

Kazan, Elia. *A Life.* New York: Knopf, 1988.

Keats, John. *The Crack in the Picture Window.* Boston: Houghton Mifflin, 1957.

Kempton, Murray. *Part of Our Time.* New York: Delta Books, 1955.

Kennan, Erland A. and Edmund H. Harvey. *Mission to the Moon.* New York: Morrow, 1969.

Kennedy, David. *Birth Control in America.* New Haven: Yale University Press, 1970.

Kerouac, Jack. *On the Road.* New York: NAL/Dutton, 1958.

King, Martin Luther, Sr. and Clayton Riley. *Daddy King: The Autobiography of Martin Luther King, Sr.* New York: William Morrow & Co., 1980.

Kluger, Richard. *Simple Justice: The History of Brown vs. the Board of Education & Black America's Struggle for Equality.* New York: Alfred A. Knopf, 1975.

Knox, Donald with additional text by Alfred Coppel. *The Korean War: An Oral History-Pusan to Chosin.* San Diego, California: Harcourt Brace Jovanovich, 1985.

Kroc, Ray with Robert Anderson. *Grinding It Out: The Making of McDonald's.* Chicago: Contemporary Books, 1977.

Lamm, Michael. *Chevrolet 1955: Creating the Original.* Stockton, CA: Lamm-Morada Inc., 1991.

Lamont, Lansing. *Day of Trinity.* New York: Atheneum, 1965.

Lapp, Ralph. *The Voyage of the Lucky Dragon.* New York: Harper and Row, 1958.

Larrabee, Eric. "Six Thousand Houses That Levitt Built." *Harper's,* No. 1971: September, 1948.

Lewis, Richard. *Appointment on the Moon.* New York: Viking, 1968.

Lilienthal, David. *The Journals of David Lilienthal: The Atomic Energy Years, 1945–1950,* Vol. 2. New York: Harper and Row, 1964–1983.

Love, John. *McDonald's: Behind the Arches.* New York: Bantam, 1986.

Lurie, Leonard. *The Running of Richard Nixon.* New York: Coward, McCann, and Geoghegan, 1972.

Lyon, Peter. *Eisenhower: Portrait of a Hero.* New York: Little, Brown, 1974.

Maharidge, Dale and Michael Williamson. *And Their Children Came After Them.* New York: Pantheon, 1990.

Mailer, Norman. *Marilyn.* New York: Warner Books, 1975.

McCann, Graham. *Marilyn Monroe: The Body in the Library.* New Brunswick: Rutgers University Press, 1988.

McCullough, David. *Truman.* New York: Simon & Schuster, 1992.

The McDonald's Museum, Oak Park, CA; Tapes and letters.

McDougall, Walter A. *The Heavens and the Earth.* New York: Basic Books, 1985.

McKeever, Porter. *Adlai Stevenson: His Life and Legacy.* New York: William Morrow, 1989.

McLellan, David and Dean Acheson, eds. *Among Friends: The Personal Letters of Dean Acheson.* New York: Dodd Mead, 1980.

Manchester, William. *The Glory and the Dream: A Narrative History of America 1932–1972.* Boston: Little, Brown and Co., 1973.

Manchester, William Raymond. *American Caesar: Douglas MacArthur.* Boston: Little, Brown, 1978.

Marshall, S.L.A. *The River and the Gauntlet.* New York: William and Co., 1953.

Martin, John Bartlow. *Adlai Stevenson of Illinois: The Life of Adlai Stevenson.* New York: Doubleday, 1976.

Mathews, Herbert L. *A World in Revolution.* New York: Scribners, 1971.

Mayer, Martin. *Madison Avenue, USA.* New York: Harper and Bros., 1954.

Mazo, Earl. *Nixon: A Political and Personal Portrait.* New York: Harper and Bros., 1959.

Medaris, John B. *Countdown for Decision.* New York: G.P. Putnam's Sons, 1960.

Meehan, Diana. *Ladies of the Evening: Women Characters of Prime-Time Television.* Metchuen, NJ: Scarecrow Press, 1983.

"Meeting of Minds," *Time.* Vol LXXII: September 15, 1958.

Michelmore, Peter. *The Swift Years: The Robert Oppenheimer Story.* New York: Dodd, Mead, and Co., 1969.

Miles, Barry. *Ginsberg: A Biography.* New York: Simon & Schuster, 1989.

Miller, Arthur. *Timebends: A Life.* New York: Grove Press, 1987.

Miller, Merle. *Plain Speaking.* New York: G.P. Putnam's Sons, 1974.

"Mr. Little Ol' Rust," *Fortune.* Vol XLVI: December, 1952.

The Montgomery Advertiser, July 10, 1954.

Morella, Joe and Edward Z. Epstein. *Forever Lucy: The Life of Lucille Ball.* New York: Carol Publishing Group, 1986.

Morgan, Ted. *Literary Outlaw.* New York: Henry Holt, 1988.

Moritz, Michael. *Going for Broke: The Chrysler Story.* Garden City, New York: Doubleday, 1981.

Morris, Roger. *Richard Milhous Nixon.* New York: Henry Holt, 1989.

Morris, Roger. *Richard Nixon: The Rise of an American Politician.* New York: Henry Holt, 1990.

Mosley, Leonard. *Dulles: A Biography of Eleanor, Allen, and John Foster Dulles and their Family Network.* New York: Dial Press, 1978.

Moss, Norman. *Men Who Play God: The Story of the H-bomb and How the World Came to Live With It.* New York: Harper and Row, 1968.

"Most House for the Money," *Fortune.* Vol. XLVI: October, 1952.

Museum of Radio and Television Broadcasting; Tapes.

Nader, Ralph. *Unsafe at Any Speed.* New York: Grossman, 1965.

Nelson, N. Walter Henry. *Small Wonder: The Amazing Story of Volkswagen.* New York: Little, Brown & Co., 1967.

The New York Times, Vol. VIII: April 8, 1934, 6:4

Nicosia, Gerald. *Memory Babe: A Critical Biography of Jack Kerouac.* Fred Jordan, ed. New York: Grove Press, 1983.

Nixon, Julie. *Pat Nixon: The Untold Story.* New York: Simon & Schuster, 1986.

Norton-Taylor, Duncan. "The Controversial Mr. Strauss." *Fortune.* Vol. L: January, 1955.

Oates, Stephen B. *Let the Trumpet Sound: The Life of Martin Luther King, Jr.*, New York: Harper & Row, 1982.

O'Reilly, Kenneth. *Hoover and the Un-Americans: The FBI, HUAC, and the Red Menace.* Philadelphia: Temple University Press, 1983.

Oshinsky, David. *A Conspiracy So Immense.* New York: Free Press, 1983.

Ottley, Roi. *The Lonely Warrior: The Life and Times of Robert S. Abbot.* Chicago: Henry Regnery, 1955.

Packard, Vance Oakely. *The Hidden Persuaders.* New York: Pocket Books, 1981.

Parry, Albert. *Russia's Rockets and Missiles.* New York: Doubleday, 1960.

Patterson, James T. *Mr. Republican.* Boston: Houghton Mifflin, 1972.

Pauly, Phillip. *Controlling Life: Jacques Loeb and the Engineering Ideal in Biology.* New York: Oxford University Press, 1987.

Pepitone, Lena and William Stadiem. *Marilyn Monroe Confidential.* New York: Simon & Schuster, 1979.

Phillips, David Atlee. *The Night Watch.* New York: Atheneum, 1972.

Pomeroy, Wardell B. *Dr. Kinsey and the Institute for Sex Research.* New York: Harper and Row, 1972.

Potter, David. *People of Plenty.* Chicago: University of Chicago Press, 1954.

Powers, Francis Gary with Curt Gentry. *Operation Overflight.* New York: Holt Rinehart and Winston, 1970.

Powers, Richard. *G-Men: Hoover's FBI in American Popular Culture.* Carbondale: Southern Illinois University Press, 1983.

Powers, Richard. *Secrecy and Power: The Life of J. Edgar Hoover.* New York: Free Press, 1987.

Prados, John. *The Sky Would Fall.* New York: Dial Press, 1983.

Prados, John. *The Soviet Estimate.* New York: Dial Press, 1982.

Presley, Dee and Billy, Rich, and David Stanley with Martin Torgoff. *We Love You Tender.* New York: Delacorte Publishing, 1980.

Press, Howard. *C. Wright Mills.* Boston: Twayne Publishers, 1978.

Pringle, Peter and James Spigelman. *The Nuclear Barons.* New York: Holt, Rinehart, and Winston, 1981.

Quain, Kevin, ed. *The Elvis Reader.* New York: St. Martin's Press, 1992.

Raines, Howell. *My Soul is Rested: Movement Days in the Deep South Remembered.* New York: Putnam Publishing Group, 1977.

Ratcliff, J. D., "No Father to Guide Them," *Colliers.* March 20, 1937.

Reed, James. *From Private Vice to Public Virtue.* New York: Basic Books, 1978.

Rhodes, Richard. *The Making of the Atomic Bomb.* New York: Simon & Schuster, 1986.

Ridgway, Matthew. *The Korean War.* New York: Doubleday & Co., 1967.

Roosevelt, Kermit. *Countercoup: The Struggle for the Control of Iran.* New York: McGraw Hill, 1979.

Rosenbaum, Ron. "The House that Levitt Built." *Esquire,* No. 100, December, 1983.

Rothe, Anna and Evelyn Lohr, eds. *Current Biography: Who's News and Why, 1952.* New York: H. W. Wilson Co., 1953.

Rovere, Richard. "What Course for the Powerful Mr. Taft?" *The New York Times Magazine,* March 22, 1953.

Roy, Jules. *The Battle of Dien Bien Phu.* London: Faber, 1965.

Rubin, Barry. *Paved With Good Intention: The American Experience and Iran.* New York: Oxford University Press, 1980.

Russell, Bill. *Go Up for Glory.* New York: Berkley Publishing, 1980.

Ryan, Mary P. *Womanhood in America: From Colonial Times to the Present.* Danbury, CT: Franklin Watts, Inc., 1975.

Sakharov, Andrei, trans. Richard Lourie. *Memoirs.* New York: Knopf, 1990.

Salisbury, Harison. *Without Fear of Favor:* The New York Times *and Our Times.* New York: Times Books, 1980.

Schlesinger, Stephen and Stephen Kinzer. *Bitter Fruit: The Untold Story of the American Coup in Guatamala.* New York: Doubleday, 1982.

Schwartz, Bernard and Stephan Lesher. *Inside the Warren Court, 1953–1969.* New York: Doubleday & Co., 1983.

Schwartz, Bernard. *Super Chief: Earl Warren and His Supreme Court, A Judicial Biography.* New York: New York University Press, 1983.

Selvin, Joel. *Ricky Nelson: Idol for a Generation.* Chicago: Contemporary Books, 1990.

Selznick, Irene Mayer. *A Private View.* New York: Knopf, 1983.

Serrin, William. *The Company and the Union: The Civilized Relationship of the General Motors Corporations and the United Automobile Workers.* New York: Knopf, 1973.

Sheehan, Robert. "How Harland Curtice Earns his $750,000." *Fortune,* No. 53, February, 1956.

Shepley, James and Clay Blair. *Hydrogen Bomb: The Men, The Menace, The Mechanism.* Westport, CT: Greenwood Publishing Group, 1971.

Shickel, Richard. *Brando: A Life in Our Times.* New York: Atheneum, 1991.

Simon, James F. *The Antagonists: Hugo Black, Felix Frankfurter, and Civil Liberties in Modern America.* New York: Simon & Schuster, 1989.

Smith, Alice Kimball and Carles Weiner, eds. *J. Robert*

Oppenheimer: Letters and Recollections. Cambridge, Mass.: Harvard University Press, 1980.

Smith, Richard Norton. *Thomas Dewey and His Times.* New York: Simon & Schuster, 1982.

Smith, Wayne. *The Closest of Enemies.* New York: Norton, 1987.

Sochen, June. *Movers & Shakers: American Women Thinkers and Activists, 1900–1970.* New York: Times Books, 1974.

Stern, Philip M. *The Oppenheimer Case: Security on Trial.* with the collaboration of Harold P. Green, special commentary by Lloyd K. Garrison. New York: Harper & Row, 1969.

Stone, Joseph and Tim Yohn. Prime Time and Misdemeanors. New Brunswick: Rutgers University Press, 1992.

Strauss, Lewis. *Men and Decisions.* Garden City, N.Y.: Doubleday, 1962.

Street, James H. *The New Evolution in Cotton Economy.* Chapel Hill: University of North Carolina Press, 1957.

Sullivan, William C. *The Bureau: My Thirty Years in Hoover's FBI.* New York: Norton, 1979.

Sulzberger, C.L. *The Last of the Giants.* Boston: Macmillan, 1970.

Sulzberger, C.L. *A Long Row of Candles: Memoirs and Diaries 1934–1954.* New York: Macmillan, 1969.

Summers, Anthony. *Goddess: The Secret Lives of Marilyn Monroe.* New York: NAL/Dutton, 1986.

Szasz, Verenc Morton. *The Day the Sun Rose Twice: The Story of the Trinity Site Nuclear Explosion, July 16, 1945.* Albequerque: University of New Mexico Press, 1984.

Szulc, Tad. *Fidel: A Critical Portrait.* New York: Morrow, 1986.

Talese, Gay. *Thy Neighbor's Wife.* New York: Doubleday & Co., 1980.

Taylor, Robert. *Fred Allen: His Life and Wit.* Boston: Little, Brown and Co., 1989.

Theoharis, Athan G. and John Stuart Cox. *The Boss: J. Edgar Hoover and the Great American Inquisition.* Philadelphia: Temple University Press, 1988.

Theoharis, Athan G. *The Yalta Myths: An Issue in U.S. Politics, 1945–1955.* Columbia, Mo.: University of Missouri Press, 1970.

Thomas, Evan and Walter Issacson. *The Wise Men: Six Friends and the World they Made.* New York: Simon & Schuster, 1988.

Tilman, Rick. *C. Wright Mills: A Native Radical and His American Intellectual Roots.* University Park: Penn State University Press, 1984.

Truman, Margaret. *Harry S. Truman.* New York: William Morrow and Co., 1973.

Ulam, S.M. *Adventures of a Mathematician.* New York: Scribner's, 1976.

Van Doren, Mark. *The Autobiography of Mark Van Doren.* New York: Harcourt, Brace, Jovanovich, 1958.

Vaughan, Paul. *The Pill on Trial.* New York: Coward-McCann Inc., 1970.

Vineberg, Steven. *Method Actors.* New York: Schirmer Books, 1991.

Wakefield, Dan. *New York in the Fifties.* New York: Houghton Mifflin, 1992.

Ward, Ed and Geoffrey Stokes and Ken Tucker. *Rock of Ages:* The Rolling Stone *History of Rock & Roll.* New York: Simon & Schuster, 1986.

Warren, Earl. *The Memoirs of Earl Warren.* New York: Doubleday & Co., 1977.

Watson, Thomas H. and Peter Petre. *Father, Son and Co.* New York: Bantam, 1990.

Weaver, John D. *Earl Warren: The Man, The Court, The Law.* Boston: Little, Brown, Inc., 1967.

Weinstein, Allen. *Perjury: The Hiss-Chambers Case.* New York: Knopf, 1978.

Wertheim, Arthur. *The Rise and Fall of Milton Berle in American History, American Television.* New York: Times Books, 1978.

Weyr, Thomas. *Reaching for Paradise: The Playboy Vision of America.* New York: Times Books, 1978.

White, G. Edward. *Earl Warren: A Public Life.* New York: Oxford University Press, 1987.

Whitfield, Stephen. *A Death in the Delta.* New York: Free Press, 1988.

"Who's a Liar," *Life.* Vol. 30, No. 14: April 2, 1951.

Wickware, Francis Still. "Report on Kinsey." *Life,* August 2, 1948.

Wilford, John Noble. "Wernher von Braun, Rocket Pioneer Dies," *The New York Times.* Vol. CXXVI: June 18, 1977.

Williams, Edwina Dakin as told to Lucy Freedman. *Remember me to Tom.* New York: G. P. Putnam's Sons, 1963.

Williams, Robert Chadwell. *Klaus Fuchs, Atom Spy.* Cambridge, Massachusetts: Harvard University Press, 1987.

Williams, Tennessee. *Memoirs.* Garden City, New York: Doubleday and Co., 1975.

Wilson, Sloan. *The Man in the Gray Flannel Suit.* New York: Simon & Schuster, 1955.

Windham, Donald. *Lost Friendships.* New York: William Morrow and Co., 1983.

Wise, David and Tom Ross. *The Invisible Government.* New York: Bantam, 1964.

Wise, David and Tomas B. *The U-2 Affair.* New York: Random House, 1962.

Wyden, Peter. *Bay of Pigs.* New York: Simon & Schuster, 1979.

Ydigoras, Miguel Fuentes. *My War with Communism.* Englewood Cliffs, NJ: Prentice Hall, 1963.

Yeakey, Lamont. *The Montgomery Bus Boycott, 1955–1956.* Unpublished Phd. thesis, Columbia University.

Yergin, Daniel. *Shattered Peace.* New York: Penguin, 1990.

Yergin, Daniel. *The Prize: The Epic Quest for Oil, Money and Power.* New York: Simon & Schuster, 1991.

York, Herbert F. *The Advisors: Oppenheimer, Teller and the Superbomb.* Stanford, Ca.: Stanford University Press, 1989.

Notes

CHAPTER ONE

p. 2 ALL MIDDLE CLASS CITIZENS OF: Smith, *Thomas Dewey and His Times,* p. 554.

5 TOM DEWEY HAS NO REAL: Patterson, *Mr. Republican,* p. 269.

5 THE BAREFOOT BOY FROM WALL: Smith, p. 306.

6 THE CHOCOLATE SOLDIER: Smith, p. 487.

6 IF YOU READ THE *CHICAGO*: Smith, p. 35.

6 COLD—COLD AS A FEBRUARY: Smith, p. 299.

7 HE STRUTS SITTING DOWN: Patterson, p. 547.

7 THOSE CONGRESSIONAL BUMS: Smith, p. 513.

7 CAMPAIGNING FOR THE PRESIDENTIAL NOMINATION: Smith, p. 529.

7 SMILE, GOVERNOR: Smith, p. 26.

8 HE HAD FORBIDDEN ONE OF: Smith, p. 471.

8 YOU CAN'T SHOOT AN IDEA: Smith, p. 487.

9 GOING AROUND LOOKING UNDER BEDS: Smith, p. 507.

9 HIS FACE WAS SO SMALL: Interview with Herbert Brownell.

9 HIS PLATFORM, SAID SAMUEL ROSENMAN: Smith, p. 504.

10 TO THESE HISTORIC FOUR SENTENCES: Patterson, p. 425.

11 INTO THE WRONG WAR: Caute, *The Great Fear: The Anti-Communist Purge Under Truman and Eisenhower,* p.41.

13 COMMUNISM AND REPUBLICANISM: Caute, p. 26.

13 PARTY LABELS DON'T MEAN ANYTHING: Morris, *Richard Nixon: The Rise of an American Politician,* p. 745.

13 WHEN I TOOK UP MY: Chambers, *Witness,* p. 741.

14 WHO GOES OUT EVERY MORNING: Patterson, p. 477.

14 I WATCH HIS SMART-ALECK: Thomas and Isaacson, *The Wise Men: Six Friends and the World They Made,* p. 547.

15 SHAVE IT OFF: Caute, pp. 42–43.

15 MY MOTHER'S ENTHUSIASM FOR THE: McLellan and Acheson, *Among Friends: The Personal Letters of Dean Acheson,* p. 2.

15 WAS NOT A MODERN, CENTRALIZED: McLellan, p. 189.

18 IF YOU AND ALGER ARE: Weinstein, *Perjury: The Hiss Chambers Case,* p. 10.

18 DON'T WORRY LITTLE ONE: Weinstein, p. 8.

18 AN AMERICAN GENTLEMAN, ONE OF: Cooke, *A Generation on Trial,* pp. 107–8.

19 LET'S WASH OUR HANDS OF: Cooke, p. 15.

19 NIXON HAD HIS HAT SET: Cooke, pp. 16–17.

20 I AM AN OUTCAST: Chambers, pp. 148–49.

20 THERE WAS NO ONE WHO: Interview with Murray Kempton.

22 AS 1949 WENT ON: Goldman, *The Crucial Decade,* p. 104.

23 THERE WAS A STRONG DESIRE: Cooke, p. 9.

24 EACH GOT THE OTHER WRONG: Interview with Murray Kempton.

24 THAT, ACCORDING TO ONE OF: Hiss, *Laughing Last,* p. 132.

25 HE RECKLESSLY LUMPS SOCIALISTS, PROGRESSIVES: Weinstein, p. 519.

26 WE KNEW THAT AT YALTA: Theoharis, *The Yalta Myths,* p. 93.

27 IT SEEMS THAT THE ONLY: Theoharis, pp. 78–79.

27 I DO NOT INTEND TO: Goldman, p. 134.

28 CHRIST'S WORDS SETTING FORTH COMPASSION: Goldman, p. 134.

28 HAD HE, MUSED SCOTTY RESTON: McLellan, p. 221.

28 A TREMENDOUS AND UNNECESSARY GIFT: Goldman, pp. 134–35.

28 ONE MUST BE TRUE TO: McLellan, p. 227.

29 WE HAVE GOT TO UNDERSTAND: Goldman, p. 125.

30 WE ARE FACED WITH EXACTLY: Yergin, p. 350.

CHAPTER TWO

32 THE GREAT WHITE JAIL: Truman, *Harry S Truman,* p. 260.

32 TWO-DOLLAR WORDS: Truman, p. 26.

33 HAD BREAKFAST IN THE COFFEE SHOP: Ferrell, *Dear Bess: The Letters from Harry to Bess Truman, 1910– 1959,* p. 468.

33 HIS UNUSUALLY BAD EYESIGHT: McCullough, *Truman,* p. 41.

34 THANKS TO THE RIGHT LIFE: Ferrell, p. 478.

34 THREE THINGS RUIN A MAN: McCullough, p. 181.

35 BRIGHT GRAYNESS: McCullough, p. 333.

36 A MAN OF IMMENSE DETERMINATION: Truman, p. 268.

36 STRAIGHTFORWARD, DECISIVE, SIMPLE, ENTIRELY HONEST: McCullough, p. 351.

37 HE MUSED ABOUT HOW MANY: Donovan, *Tumultuous Years,* p. 155.

38 SHORTLY AFTER TRUMAN'S INAUGURATION AS: Truman, p. 415.

38 IF IT EXPLODES—AS I: Blumberg and Owens, *Energy and Conflict: The Life of Edward Teller,* p. 149.

39 NOW I KNOW WHAT HAPPENED: Moss, *Men Who Play God: The Story of the H-Bomb and How the World Came to Live with It,* p. 34.

39 THE ARMY THOUGHT THE SOVIETS: Blair and Shepley, *The Hydrogen Bomb: The Men, the Menace, the Mechanism,* p. 13.

39 THAT THE RUSSIANS COULD NOT: Rhodes, *The Making of the Atomic Bomb,* p. 760.

40 WHEN HE FIRST MET THE HEAD: Davis, *Lawrence and Oppenheimer,* p. 260.

41 ARE YOU SURE?: Moss, p. 24.

41 HE THEN SPECULATED THAT CAPTURED: Lilienthal, *The Journals of David Lilienthal,* p. 571.

41 I'M NOT CONVINCED THAT RUSSIA: Moss, p. 25.

42 WHAT WE'D FEARED EVER SINCE: Lilienthal, p. 570.

42 THIS IS NOW A DIFFERENT: Donovan, p. 99.

42 RUSSIA HAS SHOWN HER TEETH: Donovan, p. 103.

42 STAY STRONG AND HOLD ON: Davis, p. 294.

42 THE ERA WHEN WE MIGHT: Pringle and Spigelman, *The Nuclear Barons*, p. 88.

43 INDEED AMERICA'S DEMOBILIZATION: Donovan, *Conflict and Crisis: The Presidency of Harry S Truman, 1945–1948*, p. 127.

44 AROUND A TABLE WAS A: Collins, *War in Peacetime: The History and Lessons of Korea*, p. 39.

45 UNKNOWN TO TRUMAN AT THE: Lamont, *Day of Trinity*, p. 261.

46 A SCIENTIST CANNOT HOLD BACK: Lamont, p. 261.

46 IN THE LAST MILLISECOND: Szasz, *The Day the Sun Rose Twice: The Story of the Trinity Nuclear Explosion, July 16, 1945*, p. 89.

47 NOW WE'RE ALL SONS: Lamont, p. 242; Szasz, p. 90.

47 OPPENHEIMER HIMSELF WENT BACK: Oppenheimer, *Letters and Recollections*, p. 297.

47 WHEN JAMES CONANT RETURNED: Szasz, p. 203.

47 YOU WILL BELIEVE THAT THIS: Oppenheimer, p. 297.

48 GIVEN THE FACT THAT IN: Rhodes, p. 563.

48 THE MORE WE WORKED: Rhodes, pp. 416–17.

49 BETTER BE A SLAVE UNDER: Blumberg and Owens, p. 121.

49 AN IMMENSE GULF BETWEEN THE: Bundy, *Danger and Survival: Choices About the Bomb in the First Fifty Years*, p. 198.

50 THE BOMB, WHOSE GLARE ILLUMINATED: Alsop, Joseph and Stewart, *We Accuse*, p. 6.

51 I. I. RABI, THE NOBEL LAUREATE: Davis, p. 185.

51 THERE, JOHNNY VON NEUMANN: Alvarez, *Alvarez: Adventures of a Physicist*, p. 130.

52 A SPIRIT OF ATHENS: Davis, p. 186.

52 WHEN ANYONE MENTIONS LABORATORY DIRECTORS: Davis, p. 182.

52 HE WAS SO MUCH SMARTER: Interview with Victor Weisskopf.

52 YOU DON'T UNDERSTAND ENOUGH ABOUT: Interview with Victor Weisskopf.

53 ASK ME A QUESTION IN LATIN: Blumberg and Owens, p. 76.

53 I WAS AN UNCTUOUS, REPULSIVELY: Pringle and Spigelman, p. 114.

53 YEARS LATER, DESPITE HIS IMMENSE: Oppenheimer, pp. 61 and 300.

54 THERE WAS A TERRIBLE SADNESS: Interview with Victor Weisskopf.

54 TROUBLE IS THAT OPPIE IS: Michelmore, *The Swift Years: The Robert Oppenheimer Story,* p. 20.

54 I GOT OUT OF THERE: Blair and Shepley, pp. 32–33; and Michelmore, p. 23.

54 THERE'S A HUGE DIFFERENCE BETWEEN: Davis, p. 51.

56 WHY I CHOSE THAT NAME: Oppenheimer, p. 290.

56 IF THE RADIANCE OF A: Lamont, p. 297.

56 THE DAY AFTER THE NAGASAKI: Davis, p. 251.

57 IF YOU ASK: Rhodes, p. 758.

57 LET THE SECOND TEAM TAKE: Davis, p. 251.

57 HE REALLY IS A TRAGIC: Lilienthal, p. 69.

58 MOST IMPORTANT MILITARY RESOURCE: Rhodes, p. 751.

58 ON WHICH HE DREW LITTLE: Acheson, *Present at the Creation: My Years in the State Department,* p. 153.

59 MISTER PRESIDENT, I HAVE BLOOD: Donovan, p. 155.

60 THE GREATEST EVENT IN THE: Pringle and Spigelman, p. 93.

60 TOTAL POWER IN THE HANDS: Pringle and Spigelman, p. 93.

61 WOULD PUSH THE ADMINISTRATION: Donovan, vol. 2, p. 152.

61 WHAT SHALL WE DO: Rhodes, p. 767.

61 I'M NOT WORRYING ABOUT THE: Rhodes, p. 768.

62 FAILING TO GET OPPENHEIMER: Bernstein, *Hans Bethe: Prophet of Energy,* p. 94.

63 EDWARD, I'VE BEEN THINKING IT: Moss, p. 53.

63 I HAVE EXPLAINED THIS TO: Bernstein, p. 94.

64 SO MUCH SO THAT LESLIE: Goodchild, *J. Robert Oppenheimer: Shatterer of Worlds,* p. 93.

64 TRUMAN TOLD LILIENTHAL THAT STRAUSS: Lilienthal, p. 89.

64 BUT IN 1917, WHEN HE: Strauss, *Men and Decisions,* p. 6.

65 WHEN DO YOU WANT TO: Strauss, p. 8.

65 HE HAS MORE ELBOWS THAN: Norton-Taylor, "The Controversial Mr. Strauss," *Fortune,* January 1955.

65 ALL PLIABILITY: Alsop and Alsop, p. 19.

66 VERY SMART AND VERY VAIN: Donovan, p. 150.

66 FAR LESS IMPORTANT THAN ELECTRONIC: Stern, *The Oppenheimer Case: Security on Trial,* p. 130; and Davis, pp. 289–90.

67 IT SEEMS TO ME THAT: Blumberg and Owens, p. 202.

68 ON THE OTHER HAND: Donovan, p. 152.

70 ELFRIEDE SEGRE WOULD WATCH HIM: Lamont, p. 78.

70 STANISLAW ULAM, THE BRILLIANT MATHEMATICIAN: Williams, *Klaus Fuchs: Atom Spy,* pp. 40 and 76.

72 WHAT CONCERNS ME IS REALLY NOT: Oppenheimer, pp. 89–90.

73 OVER MY DEAD BODY: Stern, p. 138.

73 THERE ARE GRADES OF MORALITY: Lilienthal, p. 581.

73 MAKES ME FEEL I WAS: Lilienthal, p. 581.

74 ONLY PSYCHOLOGICAL: Davis, p. 312.

74 AS LONG AS YOU PEOPLE: York, *The Advisors: Oppenheimer, Teller, and the Superbomb,* p. 65.

75 ENOUGH EVIL HAD BEEN BROUGHT: Bundy, p. 216.

76 I DON'T BLITZ EASILY: Lilienthal, p. 594.

76 WE KEEP SAYING: Lilienthal, p. 577.

77 I DON'T THINK SO: Williams, p. 2.

77 ON JANUARY 27, 1950, AN: Williams, p. 116.

78 HE DID NOT, THE PRESIDENT: Williams, p. 116.

79 CAN THE RUSSIANS DO IT: Lilienthal, Vol. 2, pp. 632–33.

79 THE ROOF FELL IN TODAY: Lilienthal, p. 634.

79 SENATOR BRIEN MCMAHON, LEWIS STRAUSS: Blumberg and Owens, p. 213.

80 IT WAS ALWAYS MY INTENTION: Williams, p. 134.

81 YES SIR, I'LL TELL THEM: Sakharov, *Memoirs,* p. 160.

81 THE SOVIET GOVERNMENT: Sakharov, p. 99.

CHAPTER THREE

83 IN THE MIDDLE OF A SPEECH: Bayley, *Joe McCarthy and the Press,* pp. 17–18.

85 "HOWARD SHIPLEY," MCCARTHY WROTE: Bayley, p. 29; author interview with Frank McCullough.

90 WHEN SOME CRITICISM OF MCCARTHY'S ATTACKS: Bayley, p. 14.

91 IN ONE OF HIS FIRST SPEECHES: Patterson, *Mr. Republican,* p. 444.

92 HE WAS, SAID HIS OLD FRIEND: Oshinsky, *A Conspiracy So Immense,* p. 503.

92 THEN HE ROARED WITH LAUGHTER: Bayley, p. 73.

92 "HE WAS," SAID SENATOR PAUL DOUGLAS: Oshinsky, p. 15.

93 HE GOES FORTH TO BATTLE: Oshinsky, p. 397.

93 "I WASN'T OFF PAGE ONE: Oshinsky, p. 118.

94 SO THE REPORTERS SAT THERE: Bayley, p. 130.

94 "JOE COULDN'T FIND A COMMUNIST: Bayley, p. 68.

95 HE NEVER HAS ANY PLANS.": Bayley, p. 151.

95 TYDINGS, USING A SUBCOMMITTEE: Caute, *The Great Fear,* p. 36.

97 "HOW STUPID CAN YOU GET?": Beschloss, *Mayday,* p. 83.

97 "IF THE NEW DEAL IS STILL IN CONTROL: Oshinsky, p. 50.

97 WHERRY OF NEBRASKA, FAMOUS FOR: Oshinsky, p. 36.

97 AND WHELKER OF IDAHO, WHO FANCIED: Oshinsky, p. 133.

98 HE REFERRED TO PEOPLE IN THE STATE DEPARTMENT: Patterson, p. 443.

99 IT PORTRAYED TAFT AS THE SPOILED CHILD: Patterson, pp. 458–59.

100 HE SHOULD "KEEP TALKING AND IF ONE CASE: Patterson, p. 455.

101 BUT, AS ROVERE LATER WROTE: Rovere, "What Course for the Powerful Mr. Taft?," p. 9.

101 WHEN SPILLANE'S FIRST BOOK, *I, THE JURY: Life,* June 23, 1952.

102 HE WAS THE AVENGER: Kenneth Davis, *Two Bit Culture,* p. 181.

103 TERRY SOUTHERN NOTED: *Esquire,* July 1963.

104 VICTOR WEYBRIGHT, THE CHIEF EDITOR: *Fortune,* September 1963.

104 THE EVIL OF THE COMMUNISTS: Davis, p. 182.

105 JAMES SANDOE OF THE *HERALD TRIBUNE: Life,* June 23, 1952.

105 "NO, ANYBODY CAN BE A WINNER: *Esquire,* July 1963.

CHAPTER FOUR

106 "IF THE BEST MINDS HAD SET OUT: Goulden, *Korea: The Untold Story of the War,* p. 3.

106 "A SOUR LITTLE WAR,": Thomas and Isaacson, *The Wise Men,* p. 507.

108 THEY WERE, HE SAID, "THE SAME BREED: Blair, *The Forgotten War: America in Korea, 1950–1953,* p. 38.

108 "I AM NOT SUFFICIENTLY FAMILIAR: Blair, p. 39.

109 "REGARDING AMERICAN POLICY," HE ADDED: Hastings, *The Korean War,* p. 39.

109 "ITS POLITICAL LIFE IN THE COMING PERIOD": Blair, p. 41.

111 DEIGNING TO COME TO SEOUL: Blair, p. 44.

113 "DEAN REALLY BLEW IT: Author interview with Averell Harriman.

114 "[THE CHINESE PEOPLE] HAD NOT OVERTHROWN: Acheson, *Present at the Creation,* pp. 355–56.

114 TO OMAR BRADLEY, IT COULD: Bradley, *A General's Life,* p. 474.

114 THE TRUMAN DEFENSE BUDGET, CABELL PHILLIPS: Manchester, *American Caesar,* p. 550.

114 AS ACHESON ONCE NOTED, THE FOREIGN POLICY: Thomas and Isaacson, p. 338.

116 AS CHIANG COLLAPSED OF HIS OWN WEIGHT: Hastings, p. 43.

118 TRUMAN, REFLECTING THE FEARS OF MANY: Thomas and Isaacson, p. 544.

118 WHEN LT. GEN. MATTHEW RIDGWAY SAW THE FIRST: Ridgway, *The Korean War,* p. 192.

118 "WE ARE GOING TO FIGHT,": Blair, p. 67.

118 "BY GOD I AM NOT GOING TO: Blair, p. 67.

119 WE HAD TO DRAW THE LINE SOMEWHERE: Bradley, p. 535.

120 EVENTS WERE TAKING OVER: Bradley, p. 539.

121 ACCORDING TO GENERAL WILLIAM DEAN: Dean, *General Dean's Story,* p. 29.

121 "THEY HAD ENLISTED,": Fehrenbach, *This Kind of War,* p. 148.

121 ONLY AS THEY BOARDED THE PLANES: Knox, *The Korean War,* p. 33.

121 WHEN WORD OF THE NORTH KOREAN: Knox, p. 6.

121 MOST OF ITS TRAINING HAD: Knox, p. 10.

123 ONE OF ITS OFFICERS WROTE LATER: Blair, p. 93.

123 ONE COLONEL IN THE 34TH INFANTRY: Fehrenbach, p. 109.

124 THE KOREANS CHEERED THEM AS THEY: Knox, p. 17.

125 NO THOUGHT OF RETREAT OR DISASTER: Blair, p. 98.

125 "THOSE ARE T-34 TANKS, SIR: Knox, p. 19.

127 INSTEAD OF A MOTLEY HORDE: Blair, p. 102.

129 BY JULY 10, JUST SIX DAYS: Blair, p. 101.

130 ONE DAY AFTER ARRIVAL IN-COUNTRY: Appleman, *South to Naktong,* p. 214–15.

131 WHEN ONE BATTALION COMMANDER, MORGAN: Blair, p. 214.

131 "WE ARE FIGHTING A BATTLE: Appleman, pp. 207–8.

134 MACARTHUR WAS SUPREMELY CONFIDENT: Blair, p. 188.

CHAPTER FIVE

136 FROM THEIR YEARS TOGETHER IN THE PHILIPPINES: Blair, *The Forgotten War: America in Korea, 1950–1953,* pp. 78–79.

136 EISENHOWER THOUGHT A YOUNGER COMMANDER: Blair, pp. 78–79.

137 "ARTHUR MACARTHUR," ONE OF HIS AIDES: Manchester, *American Caesar,* p. 30.

137 ON THE DAY OF HIS FINAL EXAM: Manchester, p. 47.

138 "YOU MUST GROW UP TO BE: Manchester, p. 41.

138 "I AM DEEPLY ANXIOUS: Manchester, p. 93.

138 "CONSIDERING THE FINE WORK: Manchester, p. 93.

138 SHE WROTE PERSHING: Manchester, p. 134.

139 WHEN HER SON BECAME CHIEF: Manchester, p. 144.

140 A DISTINGUISHED PORTRAIT PAINTER: Manchester, p. 111.

140 "NOT ONLY HAVE I MET HIM: Manchester, p. 166.

140 IN THEM THE CODE WORD: Manchester, p. 184.

142 ONLY MEDIOCRE COMMANDERS TRIED: Manchester, p. 369.

144 ROOSEVELT, WHO HAD ALWAYS RECOGNIZED: Manchester, pp. 357–58.

144 IT WILL BE LIKE AN ELECTRIC FAN: Hastings, *The Korean War,* p. 100.

145 "MAKE UP A LIST OF AMPHIBIOUS: Manchester, p. 574.

145 "I CAN ALMOST HEAR THE TICKING: Blair, p. 232.

145 REAR ADMIRAL JAMES DOYLE, WHOSE JOB: Manchester, p. 576.

145 THE NEXT DAY SHERMAN WAS AS NERVOUS: Blair, pp. 232–33.

146 "THE SORCERER OF INCHON: Thomas and Isaacson, *The Wise Men,* p. 537.

147 FROM THEN ON, MATT RIDGWAY: Ridgway, *The Korean War,* p. 44.

148 "PSYCHOLOGICALLY, IT WAS ALMOST: Blair, p. 237.

149 "AND WHAT TO DO WITH MR. PRIMA DONNA: Margaret Truman, *Harry S Truman,* p. 260.

149 "IF HE'D BEEN A LIEUTENANT: Miller, *Plain Speaking,* p. 294.

149 YEARS LATER, JOE COLLINS: J. Lawton Collins, *War in Peacetime,* p. 215.

CHAPTER SIX

150 "PLEASE DON'T TALK TO ME: Blumberg and Owens, *Energy and Conflict,* p. 21.

150 "WHEN HE WAS SIX: Blumberg and Owens, p. 3.

151 ANOTHER TEACHER ADDRESSED HIS: Blumberg and Owens, p. 23.

153 WE, MEN LIKE WEISSKOPF AND I: author interview with Hans Bethe.

154 STAN ULAM LATER WOULD REMEMBER: Ulam, *Adventures of a Mathematician,* p. 164.

154 "THAT I WAS NAMED TO HEAD: Bernstein, *Hans Bethe,* p. 81.

155 "ONE MIGHT SAY," BETHE COOLY NOTED: Bernstein, p. 81.

155 AS TELLER'S POSITION ON THE H-BOMB: interviews with Bethe and Weisskopf.

156 "HE WAS," SAID ENRICO FERMI: Blumberg and Owens, p. 185.

157 A FEW MONTHS LATER, A LIBRARIAN: interview with Serber.

157 INCREASINGLY HE BECAME FRIENDLY: interviews with Bethe and Weisskopf.

158 AND YET NONE KNEW BETTER: Stern, *The Oppenheimer Case,* p. 160.

159 SOMEWHAT TO HIS SURPRISE, SAKHAROV: interview with Jerome Weisner.

160 BECAUSE AN ELECTRON WEIGHED: Watson, *Father, Son, and Co.,* p. 189.

161 "BECAUSE WE ARE SHARING: Watson, p. 135.

162 BECAUSE OF THIS OBSESSION: Aspery, *John von Neumann and the Origins of Modern Computing,* p. iv.

163 "IT ALL CAME SO EASILY FOR HIM: interview with Herman Goldstine.

164 WEYL INDEED SOLVED IT: interview with Herman Goldstine.

164 VON NEUMANN TURNED TO HERMAN: interview with Herman Goldstine.

165 IT WAS, ULAM THOUGHT: Ulam, p. 207.

166 EGALITARIAN SOCIETIES LIKE AMERICA: interview with Goldstine.

167 IT WAS IN DANGER: Watson, pp. 189–90.

168 OPPENHEIMER JOINED THEM: Ulam, p. 217.

168 THAT HELPED CONVINCE ULAM: Ulam, pp. 223–24.

169 ALL TELLER COULD SAY: interview with Bethe.

169 YET TO HIS SCIENTIFIC PEERS: interview with Bethe.

170 EARLIER GAC SKEPTICISM ABOUT: Rhodes, p. 772.

170 HIS EGOCENTRISM BECAME SOMETHING: Ulam, p. 212.

171 IT WEIGHED SOME SIXTY-FIVE TONS: Farre, ed., *The Diaries of James C. Hagerty,* p. 6.

171 AT THE TIME HE USED TO JOKE: Blumberg and Owens, p.290.

171 AS THE NEEDLE ON THE SEISMOGRAPH: Rhodes, p. 777.

172 TELLER SAID THAT HE: Rhodes, p. 296.

CHAPTER SEVEN

176 BUT THEIR WEAKNESSES WERE NOTED: Fehrenbach, *This Kind of War,* p. 300.

177 LATER HE CAME TO REFER TO THEM: Hastings, *The Korean War,* pp. 142–43.

179 "AFTER ALL," HE SAID: Hastings, p. 130.

180 "BY THAT TIME I COULD FEEL THE HAIR: Blair, *The Forgotten War: America in Korea, 1950–1953,* p. 371.

181 ONE NCO THOUGHT THE SITE: Knox, *The Korean War,* pp. 434–38.

181 SOME 600 MEN IN THE REGIMENT: Ridgway, *The Korean War,* p. 58.

181 DURING WORLD WAR TWO MACARTHUR: Acheson, *Present at the Creation,* p. 424.

181 JACK CHILES, ALMOND'S G-3: Blair, p. 377.

183 THEY HAD STRUCK WITH GREAT SUCCESS, Acheson, p. 466.

184 BUT, HE NOTED, "WE SAT AROUND: Thomas and Isaacson, *The Wise Men,* p. 537.

185 "IF SUCCESSFUL, THIS SHOULD FOR ALL: Blair, pp. 534–35.

185 AS CLAY BLAIR NOTED, IT TIPPED: Blair, pp. 534–35.

185 INSTEAD HE PLUNGED NORTHWARD: Ridgway, p. 86.

186 MACARTHUR, JOE COLLINS WROTE: Collins, *War in Peacetime,* p. 142.

187 "WE'RE STILL ATTACKING AND WE'RE: Blair, p. 462.

187 THE MOMENT ALMOND FLEW AWAY: Blair, p. 463.

188 "MY FRIEND, I'M SORRY: Marshall, *The River and the Gauntlet,* pp. 318–20.

190 VANDENBERG GAVE HIM A LONG LOOK: Ridgway, p. 62.

190 "THIS WAS," ACHESON LATER NOTED: Acheson, p. 475.

191 THEN MACARTHUR TOLD HIM: Ridgway, p. 83.

192 "HE WAS," NOTED A WEST POINT: Blair, *Ridgway's Paratroopers,* p. 6.

192 I'D SAY, "MATT, GET THE HELL: Blair, *Ridgway's Paratroopers,* p. 111.

193 THE MEN SEEMED TO GO ABOUT: Ridgway, p. 86.

193 "WE COULD GET OFF INTO: Ridgway, p. 89.

193 WHAT HE WANTED TO CREATE: Ridgway, p. 90.

194 "THE STRENGTH AND MEANS WE HAVE: Blair, *The Forgotten War: America in Korea, 1950–1953,* p. 159.

195 "MICHAELIS," HE ASKED, "WHAT: Blair, *The Forgotten War: America in Korea, 1950–1953,* p. 605.

195 ANOTHER HIGH OFFICER SAID: Blair, *The Forgotten War: America in Korea, 1950–1953,* p. 634.

196 "RIDGWAY ALONE," SAID COLLINS: Collins, p. 255.

196 AS OMAR BRADLEY, NOT A MAN: Bradley, *A General's Life,* p. 608.

196 YEARS LATER NOTING THAT AMERICA: Hastings, p. 188.

196 IN 1954 MACARTHUR TOLD JIM LUCAS: Ridgway, p. 159.

197 BY THIS TIME THE TOP BRITISH: Hastings, p. 200.

197 IN ORDER TO DO THIS HE WAS: Bradley, p. 616.

198 "I'VE COME TO THE CONCLUSION: Truman, *Off the Record,* pp 210–11.

199 HE KNEW THIS, HE SAID: Blair, *The Forgotten War: America in Korea, 1950–1953,* p. 801.

202 TRUMAN, TYPICALLY WAS BLUNTER: James, *The Years of MacArthur, Triumph and Disaster,* p. 616.

CHAPTER EIGHT

203 SHE SITS BESTRIDE THE WORLD: Goulden, *The Best Years: 1945–1950,* p. 426.

204 HE OWNED A CAR AND A HOUSE: Yergin, *The Prize: The Epic Quest for Oil, Money, and Power,* p. 541.

204 HAD MARX WITNESSED THE INDUSTRIAL EXPLOSION: Author interview with Naohiro Amaya.

206 IN 1949, COAL ACCOUNTED FOR TWO THIRDS: Yergin, p. 546.

206 LIKE MANY RETURNING VETERANS: Author interview with William Levitt.

207 WE AT GENERAL MOTORS: Cray, *Chrome Colossus: General Motors and Its Times,* p. 7.

208 THE TREATY OF DETROIT: Serrin, *The Company and the Union: The Civilized Relationship of the General Motors Corporation and the United Automobile Workers,* p. 170.

210 PEOPLE DON'T WANT THE KIND OF CAR: Cray, p. 348.

211 TYPICALLY, WHEN TWO BROTHERS: Author interview with Dick McDonald.

211 IMPRACTICAL TOYS: Serrin, p. 94.

213 I BELIEVE IT IS REASONABLE: Serrin, p. 91.

213 THE GROWTH OF CORPORATE ENTERPRISE: Cray, p. 278.

214 A BUYER COULD CHOOSE A CAR: Halberstam, *The Reckoning,* p. 96.

214 WE HAD NO STAKE: Bayley, *Harley Earl and the Dream Machine,* p. 29.

214 AFTER WORLD WAR TWO: Moritz, *Going for Broke: The Chrysler Story,* p. 52.

215 WERE BROUGHT ABOUT BY A DELIBERATE: Bayley, pp. 16–17.

216 THE TROUBLE WITH SMALL MODELS: Bayley, p. 38.

216 I'M HERE WITH HARLOW: Author's group interview with GM designers: Chuck Jordan, Bill Porter, Stan Parker, Paul Cillian, and Don Schwarz.

217 MY SENSE OF PROPORTION TELLS ME: Hine, *Populuxe,* p. 95.

217 AT THE LOWER HEIGHT: Author's group interview.

218 THE WORLD STANDS ASIDE: Author's goup interview.

218 THE COST TO THE COMPANY: Author interview with Robert Cumberford.

218 NO SON OF MINE: Author interview with Robert Cumberford.

219 EVEN HIS SHOES LOOKED: Author's group interview.

220 WELL THE NEXT TIME: Author's group interview.

220 IF IT HAD NOT, HE: Author's group interview.

221 HOW CAN YOU COMPLAIN: Author's group interview.

221 AT FORD HE WAS KNOWN: Author interview with Don Frey.

221 IS IT RESPONSIBLE TO CAMOUFLAGE: Hine, p. 93.

222 THE 1957 FORD WAS GREAT: Hine, p. 99.

223 GENERAL MOTORS IS IN BUSINESS: Author interview with Robert Cumberford.

224 LISTEN, I'D PUT SMOKE STACKS: Author interview with Stan Mott.

224 IT GAVE THEM [THE CUSTOMERS]: Hine, p. 83.

224 DYNAMIC OBSOLESCENCE: Hine, p. 85.

224 I AM A WRENCH AND PLIERS MAN: Halberstam, p. 322.

225 WHEN MOTHER NATURE FORMED PETROLEUM: Halberstam, p. 323.

226 FOUNDED BY WOODBRIDGE FERRIS: Author interview with Anthony De Lorenzo.

226 HE COULD SEE BEYOND THE FIGURES: Author interview with Anthony De Lorenzo.

226 HARLEY, WHAT DO YOU DRIVE: Author interview with Anthony De Lorenzo.

227 YOU NEVER STAND STILL: Cray, p. 354.

227 THE LAST PERSON TO REALLY RUN: Cray, p. 380.

228 YOU KNOW WHAT THE BOSS: Sheehan, "How Harland Curtice Earns His $750,000," *Fortune,* February 1956, p. 135.

228 FIFTY PERCENT, HELL: Author interview with Bunkie Knudson.

CHAPTER NINE

229 $5,000, WHICH WAS THEN: Fenton, *In Your Opinion,* p. 25.

229 RIGHT AFTER THE WAR: Goulden, *The Best Years: 1945–1950,* p. 426.

230 GRADUATE CARPENTERS: Author interview with William Levitt.

230 LEVITTOWN HOUSES WERE SOCIAL CREATIONS: Jackson, *Crabgrass Frontier: The Suburbanization of the United States,* p. 236.

230 NO MAN WHO OWNS HIS: Larrabee, "Six Thousand Houses That Levitt Built," *Harpers,* September 1948, p. 84.

232 THE NAVY PROVIDED HIM: Author interview with William Levitt.

232 JUST BEG, BORROW, OR STEAL: Author interview with William Levitt.

234 THE REAL ESTATE BOYS: Jackson, p. 233.

234 IN 1944 THERE HAD BEEN ONLY: Jackson, p. 233.

234 WE BELIEVE THAT THE MARKET: Larrabee, p. 87.

235 THE ORIGINAL NAME WAS SOMETHING: Author interview with William Levitt.

238 THE SAME MAN DOES THE SAME THING: "The Most

House for the Money," *Fortune,* October 1952, p. 152.

239 EIGHTEEN HOUSES COMPLETED: Author interview with William Levitt.

241 A RETIRED MARX BROTHER: Larrabee, p. 79.

241 MY FATHER ALWAYS TAUGHT ME: Larrabee, p. 83.

242 THE JOB OF THE UNION: Author interview with William Levitt.

242 IF ONLY IN THREE-CENT STAMPS: Larrabee, p. 83.

243 FOR LITERALLY NOTHING DOWN: Keats, *The Crack in the Picture Window,* p. 7.

244 A MULTITUDE OF UNIFORM, UNIDENTIFIABLE: Jackson, p. 244.

245 ABOUT THE HORROR OF BEING: Rosenbaum, "The House that Levitt Built," *Esquire,* December 1983, p. 380.

246 NOW LEWIS MUMFORD CAN'T CRITICIZE: Gans, *The Levittowners: Ways of Life and Politics in a New Suburban Community,* p. 9.

246 I THINK BY NOW WE'VE SHOWN: Rosenbaum, p. 386.

247 THE NEGROES IN AMERICA: Currie, *Current Biography Yearbook* (1956), p. 375.

248 IN THE THIRD LEVITTOWN: Gans, p. 9.

249 BY 1955 LEVITT-TYPE SUBDIVISIONS: Jackson, p. 233.

CHAPTER TEN

Major sources: author interviews with Eugene and Isabelle Ferkauf and *More Than They Bargained For: The Rise and Fall of E.J. Korvetts* by Isadore Barmash.

CHAPTER ELEVEN

270 WE WERE BOTH PUSHING LIGHTS: Author interview with Dick McDonald.

271 PAT, I THINK YOU'VE OUTLIVED: Author interview with Dick McDonald.

271 WE WEREN'T GOING TO SELL: Author interview with Dick McDonald.

272 I CAN'T GIVE YOU THE FULL: Author interview with Dick McDonald.

272 MY GOD, THE CARHOPS WERE SLOW: Love, *McDonald's: Behind the Arches,* p. 14.

273 THE MORE WE HAMMERED AWAY: Love, p. 14.

274 POSING AS A FREE-LANCE WRITER: Author interview with Dick McDonald.

275 OUR WHOLE CONCEPT WAS BASED: Love, p. 14.

276 IN THIS, THEY WERE GREATLY: Love, p. 17.

277 IN 1952 THEY WERE ON: Love, p. 20.

277 I HAVE NEVER SEEN ANYTHING: Love, p. 25.

278 WHAT THE HELL FOR: Love, p. 22.

278 WE ARE GOING TO BE: Love, p. 23.

280 ON THE DAY OF THE SENIOR: Kroc with Anderson, *Grinding It Out: The Making of McDonalds,* p. 39.

281 YOU COULD MIX CONCRETE: Kroc, p. 6.

281 IN 1939 HE STARTED HIS OWN: Love, p. 34.

282 HE IMMEDIATELY LIKED WHAT HE: Kroc, p. 6.

283 MR. MULTIMIXER: Kroc, p. 8.

283 SOMETIME LATE IN THE NIGHT: Author interview with Fred Turner.

283 HAVE YOU FOUND A FRANCHISING: Love, p. 40.

284 IT WAS PRACTICALLY LIFE OR DEATH: Love, p. 47.

285 THESE WERE THE FORERUNNER: Author interview with Fred Turner.

286 THE PEOPLE WHO WOULD EAT: Author interview with Waddy Pratt.

286 I'VE MADE UP MY MIND THAT: Author interview with Waddy Pratt.

287 THAT DEMANDED A CONDIMENT STATION: Love, p. 142.

288 WE HAVE FOUND OUT, AS YOU HAVE: Love, p. 31.

289 EVERY NIGHT YOU'D SEE HIM: Love, p. 71.

289 HE GAVE HIS TOP PEOPLE: Author interview with Fred Turner and Dick Starmann.

290 THAT SOB BETTER BE GOOD: Love, p. 91.

290 MY NAME'S RAY KROC, AND I'M: Author interview with Waddy Pratt.

291 I GUESS YOU WISH YOU: Author interview with Dick Starmann.

291 FROM THE START HIS RESTAURANT: Love, p. 73.

291 NOTHING IN THE WORLD CAN: From tapes at the McDonald's Museum in Oak Park.

292 TO THE DAY HE DIED: Author interview with Turner and Starmann.

292 KROC WENT BALLISTIC AND DEMANDED: Author interview with Dick Starmann.

293 RAY, WHAT IN GOD'S NAME: Author interview with Waddy Pratt.

293 WHEN BEEF, STEAKS, AND CHOPS: Letter written December 17, 1969; in the McDonald's Museum.

294 RAY, YOU'VE GOT TO BE CRAZY: Love, p. 73.

296 HE TREATED HIS SUPPLIERS WELL: Love, pp. 129–30.

297 I PUT THE HAMBURGER ON: Love, p. 211.

297 RIDICULOUS TO CALL THIS: Institutional VFM interview.

298 IF THEY WERE DROWNING: The McDonald's Museum.

298 CONSIDER, FOR EXAMPLE, THE HAMBURGER BUN: Kroc, p. 92.

298 TOWARD THE END OF HIS LIFE: Author interview with Dick Starmann.

300 ART, I'M NOT NORMALLY A VINDICTIVE MAN: Love, p. 201.

CHAPTER TWELVE

Major sources: "Kemmons Wilson," *Time* magazine, June 12, 1972; "Kemmons Wilson and Holiday Inn," by Ed Weathers, *Memphis* magazine, September 1985. Author interviews with friends and family.

CHAPTER THIRTEEN

312 A DEVICE THAT PERMITS PEOPLE: Taylor, *Fred Allen: His Life and Wit,* p. 284.

312 TELEVISION WAS ALREADY CONDUCTING ITSELF: Allen, *Treadmill to Oblivion,* p. 238.

313 SOUNDED LIKE A MAN WITH FALSE TEETH: Taylor, p. 3.

313 WHY DON'T YOU LOOK UP: Taylor, p. 284.

314 HE'S AFRAID GOD MIGHT RECOGNIZE HIM: Taylor, p. 250.

315 SITUATED ON THE SHORES: Allen, p. 80.

315 YOU WOULDN'T DARE TALK TO ME: Taylor, p. 239.

316 EVEN WITHOUT THE COMING OF TELEVISION: Allen, p. 238.

316 A MEDIUM THAT DEMANDS ENTERTAINMENT: Allen, p. 239.

317 REDUCED TO ESSENTIALS A QUIZ SHOW: Allen, p. 106.

318 FOR ME MORE INTERESTING THAN LINDBERGH'S: Taylor, p. 289.

318 WHEN TELEVISION BELATEDLY FOUND ITS WAY: Allen, p. 239.

319 IT IS THE STORY OF A RADIO SHOW: Taylor, p. 353.

319 IN 1950 THERE WERE 108 DIFFERENT SERIES: Barnouw, *A History of Broadcasting: The Golden Web,* Vol. 2, p. 285.

320 IN NEW YORK CITY, FIFTY-FIVE THEATERS CLOSED: Barnouw, p. 286.

322 YOU TAKE A KID AT THE AGE OF FIVE: Berle, *Milton Berle: Current Biography* (1949), p. 69.

323 ACCORDING TO VARIETY, OF THE: Wertheim, *The Rise and Fall of Milton Berle in American History, American Television,* p. 72.

324 PEOPLE WHO CALLED HIM AT HOME: Wertheim, p. 74.

CHAPTER FOURTEEN

326 PART OF HIS SUCCESS WITH ORDINARY PEOPLE: Author interview with Albert Gore.

326 I'VE MET MILLIONS OF SELF-MADE: Halberstam, *The Powers that Be,* p. 226.

327 WELL, ESTES, YOU'RE A CONGRESSMAN: Gorman, *Kefauver,* p. 6.

327 SHAME ON YOU, ESTES KEFAUVER: Gorman, p. 7.

328 WE ARE ANXIOUS TO GET EVERYTHING: Gorman, p. 46.

328 PET COON FOR THE SOVIETS: Gorman, pp. 48–49.

329 DON'T YOU WANT TO BE VICE-PRESIDENT: Author interview with Katharine Graham.

331 BY SOME ESTIMATES ONLY 1.5 PERCENT: Gorman, p. 91.

333 SOME 70 PERCENT OF NEW YORK: Manchester, *The Glory and the Dream: A Narrative History of America, 1932–1972,* p. 600.

333 THE WEEK OF MARCH 12, 1951: "Who's a Liar," *Life,* April 2, 1951, pp. 19–25.

336 HE COULD NOT ATTEND THE AWARDS: Gorman, p. 102.

CHAPTER FIFTEEN

Major sources: Andrews, *The I Love Lucy Book;* Brochu, *Lucy in the Afternoon;* Diggins, *The Proud Decades;* Fox, *The Mirror Makers;* Harris, *Lucy & Desi;* Morella and Epstein, *Forever Lucy.*

CHAPTER SIXTEEN

350 "IF THEY DO NOT," HE SAID: James, *The Years of MacArthur,* p. 610.

350 THE SENATE HEARINGS THAT FOLLOWED: Collins, *War in Peacetime,* p. 290.

352 AS WILLIAM MANCHESTER WROTE, MACARTHUR'S: Manchester, *American Caesar,* p. 628.

352 MACARTHUR STILL, ON OCCASION: Manchester, p. 182.

353 BUT ON THE PRO SIDE, HE WROTE: Patterson, *Mr. Republican,* p. 505.

353 IT WAS A CARTOON OF A DINOSAUR: Patterson, p. 561.

354 BUT EVEN AS A PARTISAN FIGURE: Patterson, p. 440.

354 ROOTED AS IT WAS IN THE MIDWEST: Patterson, p. 519.

354 HE FINISHED FIRST IN HIS CLASS: Patterson, p. 30.

355 HAVE I MENTIONED ANYTHING: Patterson, p. 43.

356 "MODERN WAR," HE SAID, OPPOSING: Patterson, p. 243.

358 IN 1946–47 *FORTUNE*: Smith, *Thomas Dewey and His Times,* p. 442.

358 ON ANOTHER OCCASION HE WAS: Patterson, p. 215.

358 WHY ARE ALL THESE PEOPLE COMPLAINING: Patterson, p. 214.

360 WHEN HE WAS FINISHED, MACARTHUR PATTED: Alsop, *I've Seen the Best of It,* p. 338.

360 IN 1948, IMMEDIATELY FOLLOWING HIS DEFEAT: Smith, p. 554.

361 HE TOLD HIS FRIEND BILL ROBINSON: Beschloss, *Mayday,* p. 293.

361 " . . . NOW AS ALWAYS AN OPPORTUNIST: Sulzberger, *A Long Row of Candles,* Vol. 1, p. 685.

361 "A VERY STUPID MAN: Sulzberger, p. 702.

361 IN MAY 1951 EISENHOWER WROTE: Lyon, *Eisenhower,* pp. 428–29.

361 AS HE WAS BEING PULLED INTO: Sulzberger, p. 752.

362 A REPRESENTATIVE FROM *MCCALL'S:* Lyon, p. 430.

362 AS THE POLITICAL PRESSURE GREW: Sulzberger, p. 754.

363 "DON'T CALL ME," EISENHOWER SAID: Sulzberger, p. 715.

364 IN FACT HE RESEMBLED NO ONE: interview with Jock Elliot.

365 AT ONE POINT, JOHN WAYNE: Smith, p. 591.

366 "I LIKE IKE," SAID EISENHOWER'S: Patterson, p. 519.

367 TAFT WAS AMUSED AND REPLIED: Patterson, p. 571.

367 BACK CAME THE MESSAGE: Patterson, p. 558.

367 AFTERWARD HE SHOOK NIXON'S: Smith, p. 394.

368 FROM THEN ON NIXON BECAME: Morris, *Richard Milhous Nixon,* p. 684.

368 HE WAS, IN THE WORDS OF DEWEY'S: Smith, p. 591.

368 "I THOUGHT THE CONVENTION HAD TO: Smith, p. 596.

368 "WHAT ABOUT NIXON: Smith, p. 596.

368 HENRY CABOT LODGE, IKE'S OFFICIAL: Morris, p. 733.

379 "WHY DON'T YOU GRAB THIS FELLOW: Martin, *Adlai Stevenson of Illinois,* p. 269.

379 "AM FORTY-SEVEN TODAY—STILL: McKeever, *Adlai Stevenson,* p. 104.

379 "NEVER WENT TO OXFORD: Martin, p. 278.

380 WHEN ARVEY CAME BY, STEVENSON: Martin, p. 279.

380 FOR A TIME STEVENSON HEDGED: McKeever, p. 113.

380 WHEN ARVEY READ STEVENSON'S: McKeever, p. 114.

381 DURING ONE FIGHT LEWIS HAD: McKeever, p. 26.

382 GEORGE BALL, ONE OF THE BRIGHT: Martin, p. 380.

382 FOR MUCH OF HIS ADULT CAREER: McKeever, p. 70–71.

383 WHEN DREW PEARSON WROTE THAT: McKeever, p. 166.

385 "HE COULDN'T UNDERSTAND IT: McKeever, p. 179.

385 "WHAT ARE YOU TRYING TO TELL: McKeever, p. 180.

386 "I THINK WE HAVE TO LEAVE: McKeever, p. 185.

386 HE NEVER HAD TO DO IT: McKeever, p. 37.

CHAPTER SEVENTEEN

388 DUFFY DECIDED THAT THEY HAD TO RECAST IKE: Author interview with Jock Elliot.

390 MY SECRET SELF: Fox, *The Mirror Makers,* pp. 189, 191.

391 WELL, FIRST I'VE GOT TO GET: Mayer, *Madison Avenue, USA,* pp. 35–36.

391 WERE THE MOST HATED COMMERCIALS: Fox, p. 188.

391 NOT BAD FOR SOMETHING WRITTEN: Diamond and Bates, *The Spot,* p. 40.

392 IF WE EVER GET OUT OF PACKAGED: Mayer, p. 55.

392 WHEN HIS FRIENDS COMPLAINED: Author interview with David McCall.

392 WITHOUT SUBTLETY, AND WITHOUT CONCERN: Fox, p. 193.

392 THE MOST UNCONFUSED MIND: Mayer, p. 49.

393 THIS NEW MEDIUM OF TELEVISION WAS: Author interview with Rosser Reeves.

393 THE PRINCE OF HARD SELL: Fox, p. 192.

393 ON OCCASION IT WOULD BE KNOWN: Fox, p. 189.

394 THE UNCHECKABLE CLAIM: Mayer, p. 50.

394 I HAD SOME OIL INTERESTS: Diamond and Bates, p. 53.

394 THE QUICKEST, MOST EFFECTIVE AND CHEAPEST: Diamond and Bates, p. 54.

396 YOU LOSE PENETRATION: Mayer, p. 296.

397 EISENHOWER, MAN OF PEACE: Author interview with Rosser Reeves.

397 YOU GET THE AUDIENCE BUILT UP: Diamond and Bates, p. 54.

398 YOU TEND TO LOWER YOUR HEAD: Author interview with David Schoenbrun.

399 HE'S NOT GOING TO SAY IT: Author interview with Rosser Reeves.

399 TO THINK THAT AN OLD SOLDIER: Author interview with Rosser Reeves; and Mayer, p. 297.

399 REAL PEOPLE IN THEIR OWN CLOTHES: Diamond and Bates, p. 57.

400 NO, NOT IF WE HAVE A SOUND: Diamond and Bates, pp. 599–600.

400 ROSSER, I HOPE FOR YOUR SAKE: Author interview with David Ogilvy.

400 IT WAS PIONEER WORK: Author interview with Rosser Reeves.

400 FACED WITH THIS DILEMMA: Fox, p. 310.

401 EISENHOWER HITS THE SPOT: Halberstam, *The Powers That Be,* p. 236.

402 REEVES REMEMBERED CLEVELAND: Author interview with Rosser Reeves.

402 AN UNINFORMED ELECTORATE CAN LEAD: Mayer, p. 303.

402 THIS IS THE WORST THING: Author interview with Louis Cowan.

403 TO BOTH REPUBLICANS AND DEMOCRATS: Halberstam, p. 229.

403 LOU, OLD BOY, WE: Author interview with Louis Cowan.

405 TONIGHT I WANT TO TALK: Museum of Radio and Television Broadcasting.

406 THE NEW G.I. BILL INTELLECTUALS: Author interview with Michael Arlen.

407 HE'S TOO ACCOMPLISHED AN ORATOR: Barnouw, *The Golden Web,* p. 298.

407 IN HIS ALMOST PAINFUL HONESTY: McKeever, *Adlai Stevenson: His Life and Legacy,* p. 249.

408 SURE, ALL THE EGGHEADS: Goldman, *The Crucial Decade: America 1945–1955,* p. 222.

409 I FIND MYSELF CONSTANTLY BLACKMAILED: McKeever, p. 252.

409 BUT, I DON'T HAVE TO WIN: McKeever, p. 213.

410 WHEN AN AMERICAN SAYS: Goldman, p. 221.

410 THE MEN WHO HUNT COMMUNISTS: Martin, *Adlai Stevenson of Illinois: The Life of Adlai Stevenson,* p. 658.

411 THEY ARE SO POOR THEY: Morris, *Richard Milhous Nixon: The Rise of an American Politician,* p. 757.

412 OUR THINKING WAS THAT: Morris, p. 760.

412 TELL THEM ABOUT THE $16,000: Morris, p. 772.

413 OF WHAT AVAIL IS IT: Lyon, *Eisenhower, Portrait of a Hero,* p. 456.

414 THE LITTLE BOY CAUGHT WITH JAM: Morris, p. 791.

415 GENERAL, I NEVER THOUGHT SOMEONE: Author interview with Ted Rogers.

416 SHERM, IF YOU WANT TO KNOW: Mazo, *Nixon: A Political and Personal Portrait,* p. 125.

418 YOU'LL KNOW. YOU'LL JUST KNOW: Author interview with Ted Rogers.

418 WHY DO WE HAVE TO TELL PEOPLE: Morris, p. 831.

418 WALKING OFF THE SET INTO: Author interview with Ted Rogers.

418 WELL, ARTHUR, YOU SURELY GOT: Mazo, p. 132.

418 BEN, TONIGHT WILL MAKE HISTORY: Lyon, p. 461.

420 HE MAY ASPIRE TO THE GRACE: Morris, p. 856.

420 A DISTURBING EXPERIENCE: Morris, p. 854.

421 THERE WAS JUST ONE THING: Morris, p. 854.

421 FUCK 'EM; WE DON'T NEED: Author interview with Ted Rogers.

CHAPTER EIGHTEEN

423 STEADY MONTY, YOU CAN'T SPEAK: Bradley and Blair, *A General's Life,* p. 330.

434 NO, MARDER SPECULATED, HIS BEAT: Author interview with Murrey Marder.

435 JOE, YOU'RE A REAL SOB: Oshinsky, *A Conspiracy So Immense,* p. 132.

435 A PIMPLE ON THE PATH OF PROGRESS: Hagerty, *The Diary of James C. Hagerty: Eisenhower in Mid-Course,* p. 27.

436 I KNOW THAT CHARGES OF DISLOYALTY: Oshinsky, p. 236.

436 NOT JUST HIS DEMOCRATIC OPPONENTS: Cray, *General of the Army: George C. Marshall,* p. 369.

436 IT TURNED MY STOMACH: Bradley and Blair, p. 656.

436 HYPOCRITICALLY CALLING INTO QUESTION: Bradley and Blair, p. 655.

437 HE TOLD HIS GODDAUGHTER: Cray, p. 728.

437 BUT EISENHOWER'S HATRED OF MCCARTHY: Adams, *First Hand Report,* p. 148.

437 HE DON'T TAKE SHOVIN'!: Adams, p. 15.

437 I KNOW ONE FELLOW I'D: Oshinsky, p. 359.

437 I WILL NOT GET IN THE GUTTER: Adams, p. 135.

438 COULDN'T YOU TELL THEM: Oshinsky, p. 287.

439 ON THE MORNING OF THEIR APPEARANCE: Oshinsky, p. 287.

438 SO FAR AS I'M CONCERNED: Oshinsky, p. 290.

439 KISS MY ASS, VAN: Oshinsky, p. 504.

CHAPTER NINETEEN

442 HER LADYSHIP IS FUCKING BORED: Edwards, *Vivien Leigh,* p. 178.

446 THIS CHARACTER HAS NEVER HAD: Williams, T., *Memoirs,* p. 136.

448 HOW DID YOU LIKE YOU'SELF: Williams, E., *Remember Me to Tom,* p. 148.

449 SOMEWHERE DEEP IN MY NERVES: Williams, T., p. 17.

449 I WAS NOT A YOUNG MAN: Williams, T., p. 52.

450 AUNT ELLA AND AUNT BELLE: Williams, T., p. 117.

451 HE DID IT EVERY MORNING: Kazan, *A Life,* p. 261.

453 HE PUT WRITING BEFORE KNOWING: Windham, *Lost Friendships,* p. 113.

454 WHY ME? WHY ME?: Selznick, *A Private View,* p. 295.

455 I AM SURE YOU MUST HAVE: Kazan, p. 329.

456 I COME FROM A FAMILY: Kazan, pp. 190–191.

457 IT'S FINE, LEAVE IT: Kazan, p. 19.

458 WHY YOU NOT LEARNING SOMETHING: Kazan, p. 40.

459 HEY, GEORGE, YOU GOT A DEAD ONE: Kazan, p. 70.

459 HOW CONFIDENT THEY WERE: Kazan, p. 40.

460 FOUR YEARS OVER IN MASSACHUSETTS: Kazan, p. 49.

461 VERY HIGH CLASS: Kazan, p. 91.

461 TELL US WHAT YOU WANT: Kazan, p. 57.

462 ALL THEY WANT IS A STAGEHAND: Kazan, p. 100.

464 WELL, WHAT IS IT: Higham, *Brando: The Unauthorized Biography,* p. 76.

465 HE WAS ABOUT THE BEST-LOOKING: Williams, p. 131.

466 I HATE ULTIMATUMS: Fiore, *The Brando I Knew,* p. 60.

468 THIS PUPPY THING WILL BE: Carey, *Marlon Brando: The Only Contender,* p. 13.

470 I TAUGHT HIM NOTHING: Higham, p. 38; and Carey, p. 15.

CHAPTER TWENTY

472 "GOD," HE NOTED, "WHAT A: Christenson, *Kinsey,* pp. 117–18.

472 "AS YOU MAY KNOW WE ARE: Pomeroy, *Dr. Kinsey and the Institute for Sex Research,* p. 191.

474 "YEARS AGO MY BANKER: Pomeroy, p. 50.

475 HE ONCE TOLD A COLLEAGUE, WARDELL: Pomeroy, p. 8.

475 AFTER HIS DEATH WARDELL POMEROY: Pomeroy, p. 472.

476 "NOW, BRUCE," KINSEY SAID: Pomeroy, p. 29.

476 TO ONE YOUNG MAN WHO APPLIED: Pomeroy, p. 71.

476 AS A BOY HE COLLECTED STAMPS: Pomeroy, p. 16.

477 HE WROTE HIS FIRST BOOK: Christenson, p. 29.

477 EARLE MARCH, A SAN FRANCISCO: Pomeroy, p. 166.

478 CLARA KINSEY WAS KNOWN ON: Wickware, "Report on Kinsey," p. 98.

479 WHEN HE BEGAN HIS STUDIES: Pomeroy, pp. 72–73.

479 BY 1939 HE WROTE TO A: Christenson, p. 107.

480 THOSE WHO THOUGHT HE WOULD DO: Christenson, p. 113.

481 THE WAR MADE THINGS HARDER: Christenson, p. 114.

484 HIS CRITICS WERE, HE NOTED: Pomeroy, p. 284.

485 "AND THEN THERE ARE SOME: Pomeroy, p. 147.

487 KINSEY TURNED HIM DOWN: Pomeroy, p. 346.

487 THEN THE FIRESTORM BEGAN: Pomeroy, p. 364.

487 THE WORST THING ABOUT THE REPORT: Christenson, p. 162.

487 AGAIN KINSEY WAS DISHEARTENED: Pomeroy, p. 160.

488 LATER IN ANOTHER LETTER TO RUSK: Christenson, p. 190.

488 "DAMN THAT RUSK: Pomeroy, p. 16.

489 ANDERSON PLEADED WITH HIM: Christenson, p. 193.

489 "IT IS A SHAME," HE NOTED: Christenson, p. 199.

CHAPTER TWENTY-ONE

492 IT WAS SHE WHO INTRODUCED US: Gray, *Margaret Sanger: A Biography of the Champion of Birth Control,* pp. 58–59.

493 I AM ANARCHIST, TRUE, BUT: Gray, p. 74.

493 OH, JULIET, THERE NEVER WAS: Gray, p. 159.

494 LOOK THE WHOLE WORLD IN THE FACE: Kennedy, *Birth Control in America,* p. 1.

497 IT WAS NO LONGER MY LONE FIGHT: Reed, *From Private Vice to Public Virtue,* p. 112.

497 IF YOU LIKE MY RELIGION: Gray, p. 158.

497 IT IRKS MY VERY SOUL: Reed, p. 112.

499 RICH AS CROESUS: Vaughan, *The Pill on Trial,* p. 25.

500 HE WAS RATHER SHOCKED: Gray, p. 438.

500 YOU HAVE THE POWER TO CHANGE: Author interview with Oscar Hechter.

501 BUT THIS IS JUST A CRUISING: Author interviews with Laura Pincus Bernard, John Alexis Pincus, and Oscar Hechter.

501 A CONTENTED JEWISH PEASANTRY: Pauly, *Controlling Life: Jacques Loeb and the Engineering Ideal in Biology,* p. 185.

502 SCARED PEOPLE, CREATING VISIONS: Reed, p. 321.

502 RABBITS BORN IN GLASS: *The New York Times* (April 8, 1934), VIII 6:4.

502 PICTURED PINCUS AS A SINISTER: Reed, p. 321.

503 MAN'S VALUE WOULD SHRINK: Ratcliff, *Colliers,* March 20, 1937, p. 73.

508 PINCUS WAS VERY GENTLE: Author interview with John Pincus.

508 LIZUSKA, EVERYTHING IS POSSIBLE: Vaughn, p. 6.

509 GOODY, HOW DID YOU GET: Author interview with Oscar Hechter.

CHAPTER TWENTY-TWO

512 IF THERE WAS ONE FIGURE WHO: Nicosia, *Memory Babe,* p. 475.

513 "WELL, WELL!" CARR SAID: Miles, *Ginsberg,* p. 36.

514 HE HAD TO BE A GENIUS: Morgan, *Literary Outlaw,* p. 102–3.

514 GINSBERG WROTE IN HIS JOURNAL: Morgan, p. 89.

515 DETERMINED TO BE A WRITER: Gifford and Lee, *Jack's Book,* p. 34.

515 KEROUAC'S FIRST IMPRESSION: Miles, p. 44.

515 GINSBERG WROTE HIS OLDER: Miles, p. 39.

516 BURROUGHS, GINSBERG AND KEROUAC: Gifford and Lee, p. 38.

517 THE DEAN LOOKED AT HIM: Miles, p. 60.

518 THESE YOUNG REBELS DID NOT: Morgan, p. 96.

518 THEY ASPIRED TO BECOME: Gifford and Lee, p. 39.

518 "THESE JERKS," BURROUGHS ONCE: Morgan, pp. 139–40.

518 "WHERE IS YOUR FORMER, FINE: Miles, p. 59.

521 SHARING THE SUBWAY CAR WITH: Holmes, *GO,* pp. 140–41.

521 IN *GO* HOLMES DESCRIBED: Holmes, p. 36.

522 THE FIRST WORDS THAT NEAL CASSADY: Cassady, *Off the Road,* p. 2.

523 MARIJUANA, THEN KNOWN AS TEA: Holmes, p. 141.

523 AS BARRY GIFFORD AND LAWRENCE: Gifford and Lee, p. 170.

523 LATER, THE DEFINITION WAS REINVENTED: Morgan, p. 154.

523 MALCOLM COWLEY, THE DISTINGUISHED: Gifford and Lee, p. 187.

525 THAT, GREGORY CORSO LIKED TO: Gifford and Lee, pp. 180–81.

525 HOLMES NOTED THAT DOWN DEEP: Gifford and Lee, p. 129.

525 KEROUAC DESCRIBED HIM IN: Kerouac, *On the Road,* p. 5.

526 WHAT HE EXEMPLIFIED, TED MORGAN: Morgan, p. 159.

527 "WHEN NEAL CAME TO TOWN: Gifford and Lee, p. 127.

527 KEROUAC SEEMED A MAN: Gifford and Lee, p. 129.

528 ON THIS POINT HOLMES HELD: Holmes, pp. xx–xxi.

529 HE WROTE IT, HIS FRIEND JOHN: Gifford and Lee, p. 156.

529 IT WAS, IN HOLMES'S WORDS: Gifford and Lee, p. 157.

529 THE PROBLEM, HE ADDED: Cassady, p. 187.

530 GIL MILSTEIN, A TALENTED: Gifford and Lee, p. 170.

531 IT WAS TIME, HE DECIDED: Miles, p. 135.

531 HE WROTE KEROUAC, "I AM: Miles, p. 185.

531 THE RESULT WAS POETRY AS IF: Miles, p. 188.

532 FERLINGHETTI AGREED TO PUBLISH: Miles, p. 193.

532 "IT HAD," TED MORGAN LATER: Morgan, p. 256.

532 "THIS POEM WILL MAKE YOU FAMOUS: Miles, p. 196.

533 FERLINGHETTI SENT GINSBERG A CABLE: Morgan, p. 257.

533 *ON THE ROAD* OFFERED A NEW VISION: Kerouac, p. 3.

533 WHAT KEROUAC DID, TED MORGAN: Morgan, p. 288.

534 QUITE THE CONTRARY: "THE FIRST: Miles, p. 232.

CHAPTER TWENTY-THREE

535 ALL THEY TALKED ABOUT WAS: Adams, *First Hand Report,* p. 20.

538 I HAVE TO NOMINATE THAT DIRTY: Morris, *Richard Milhous Nixon: The Rise of an American Politician,* p. 734.

539 A LITTLE MAN IN A BIG HURRY: Morris, p. 739.

539 PLAYS BOTH SIDES AGAINST THE MIDDLE: Morris, p. 447.

540 THE COMMIES DON'T LIKE IT: Morris, p. 564.

542 HIS TELEVISION ADVISER IN HIS SUCCESSFUL: Personal interview with Roger Ailes.

542 THOUGH THE FAMILY LIVED ON A FARM: Ambrose, *Nixon,* p. 20.

543 AS NIXON'S COUSIN JESSAMYN WEST: Morris, p. 25.

543 HE WAS NOT A QUAKER: Interviews with Paul Smith, Guy Dixon, Douglas Ferguson, Hubert Perry, Merton Wray, Paul Ryan, Merel West, Olive and Oscar Mashburn, Dorothy Milhous, Charles Milhous, Jane Milhous Beeson, Ralph Shook, Lucile Parson, Samuel Warner, Madeline Thomas, Elizabeth Cloes, Marcia Elliot Wray, Saragrace Frampton, and Laura Walfrop from the archives of the Cal Fullerton Library.

543 THE HARDEST PIECE OF SOIL: Cal Fullerton Library.

544 HE NEVER MADE A PENNY: Cal Fullerton Library.

545 I AM NOT GOING TO WEAR: Cal Fullerton Library.

545 WHEN THE OIL BOOM STRUCK: Lurie, *The Running of Richard Nixon,* p. 22.

546 HE ALWAYS CARRIED SUCH A WEIGHT: Morris, p. 61.

546 THERE WERE, SHE THOUGHT, TOO: Lurie, p. 22.

547 ONE WHO HAS KNOWN RICHARD: Morris, p. 848.

548 NOR FOR THAT MATTER WAS BEWLEY: Cal Fullerton Library.

548 SHE DID HER PART NICELY: Ambrose, p. 99.

549 WHEN SHE PRETENDED NOT TO BE: Nixon, *Pat Nixon: The Untold Story,* p. 58.

549 YES—I KNOW I'M CRAZY: Nixon, p. 58.

550 IT IS OUR JOB TO GO FORTH: Nixon, p. 68.

550 THEIR WEDDING RING COST $324.75: Nixon, p. 68.

551 TOO MANY RESTRICTIONS ETC.: Nixon, p. 82.

551 WHETHER IT'S THE LOBBY: Nixon, p. 83.

552 I AM WRITING YOU THIS SHORT: Morris, p. 271.

554 NIXON LIFE STORY LIKE FILM: Morris, p. 606.

555 I THINK: WILL IT PACK: Nixon, p. 187.

556 YOU CANNOT BE TIRED, YOU: Ambrose, p. 96.

557 I DETEST TEMPER; I DETEST SCENES: Nixon, p. 21.

561 THE MANAGER OF OUR DEPARTMENT: Nixon, pp. 47–48.

562 NIXON HAD THE MOST HATEFUL FACE: Author interview with Larry King.

562 IT WAS, ROGERS LATER DECIDED: Author interview with Ted Rogers.

563 HE WAS MOST COMFORTABLE: Author interview with Helen Gahagan Douglas.

563 I GUESS I CAN MAKE IT: Nixon, p. 115.

563 I DON'T THINK I CAN: Nixon, p. 122.

564 IN PUBLIC, HE WOULD ALWAYS PRAISE: Author interview with James Bassett.

564 OUR HEARTS WERE BREAKING: Nixon, p. 424.

564 JIM BASSETT, WHO WORKED WITH NIXON: Author interview with James Bassett.

566 HE'S NEVER LIKED ME: Author interview with Len Hall.

567 NO, NO, DEAR DON'T DO THAT: Author interview with Mollie Parnis.

567 HOW COULD THAT BE: Ambrose, p. 801.

CHAPTER TWENTY-FOUR

568 INDEED OPPENHEIMER LATER JOKED: Stern, *The Oppenheimer Case,* p. 206.

569 HE EVEN APOLOGIZED LIGHTLY: Stern, p. 111.

570 THEY SHOULD LEAVE THIS TO OPPIE: interview with Victor Weisskopf.

570 "HE WAS," WEISSKOPF SAID DRILY: interview with Weisskopf.

571 "THE DIFFERENCE WITH ME: interview with Hans Bethe.

571 "SOME PEOPLE PROFESS GUILT: Ulam, *Adventures of a Mathematician,* p. 224.

572 "OUR PLANE SEEMED TO STAND: Blair and Shepley, *The Hydrogen Bomb,* p. 63.

573 AT THE TIME, HERBERT MARKS: Stern, *The Oppenheimer Case,* p. 206.

574 "HARRY," GREEN SAID: interview with Harold Green.

575 STRAUSS BROOKED NO DISSENT: Joseph and Stewart Alsop, *We Accuse,* p. 19.

577 YET WHAT WAS TAKING PLACE: interview with Green.

578 OPPENHEIMER, IN THE WORDS OF THE AEC: Green, "The Oppenheimer Case."

580 HIS JOB WAS SOON DISSOLVED: Sullivan, *The Bureau,* p. 108.

580 HIS LUNCH RARELY VARIED: Powers, *Secrecy and Power,* p. 314.

580 IN TRUTH, HE OFTEN BET: Sullivan, p. 87.

581 HOOVER WOULD STAY IN: Powers, p. 314.

581 HE ENSHRINED THE AMERICAN: Hoover, *Masters of Deceit,* p. 16.

583 AS TWENTIETH-CENTURY STANDARDS: Powers, pp. 3–4.

584 THEREAFTER THE ANTEROOM: Powers, *G-Men,* p. 114.

584 BUT HOOVER FOUGHT OFF: Powers, *G-Men,* p. 115.

585 "NO ORGANIZATION THAT I KNOW: Theoharis and Cox, *The Boss,* pp. 160–61.

585 WHEN WILLIAM SULLIVAN JOINED: Sullivan, p. 33.

586 WHEN HOOVER WAS ASKED IN LATER: Sullivan, p. 37.

586 "ANYTIME I NEED: Sullivan, p. 38.

586 FROM THAT MOMENT ON, WROTE: Sullivan, p. 38.

587 "WE GAVE MCCARTHY EVERYTHING: O'Reilly, *Hoover and the Un-Americans,* p. 337.

587 WHEN A REPORTER FROM THE: Powers, *Secrecy and Power,* p. 321.

588 THE HOUSE SUBCOMMITTEE ON THE: O'Reilly, p. 325

590 IN THE FALL OF 1952: Stern, p. 195.

592 IN THE COPY TO HOOVER: Blumberg and Owens, *Energy and Conflict,* p. 304.

593 EISENHOWER ORDERED THAT A "BLANK: Stern, p. 221.

593 "JACK, I'M SORRY": Michelmore, p. 206.

594 HE SAT THAT FIRST DAY: Stern, p. 232.

595 "WHAT YOU SHOULD SAY: interview with Weisskopf.

595 HE DID NOT, HE WROTE: Stern, p. 233.

597 "THE SUN'S RISING IN: Moss, *Men Who Play God,* p. 8.

598 "SOME KIND OF WHITE SAND: Lapp, *The Voyage of the Lucky Dragon,* p. 34.

598 "THE INDIVIDUALS WERE UNEXPECTEDLY: Lapp, p. 53.

600 "YOU LOOK LIKE A NEGRO: Lapp, p. 56.

600 "FROM THIS DAY ON, UNHAPPINESS: Lapp, p. 87.

600 ONE OF THE SEAMEN TOLD: Moss, p. 90.

601 AT ONE POINT HE CRIED: Lapp, p. 169.

601 "IF I WERE THE REDS: Hagerty, *The Diary of James C. Hagerty,* p. 42.

601 ON APRIL 2, 1954: Hagerty, p. 40.

603 LUIS ALVAREZ, ANOTHER OPPENHEIMER: Alvarez, *Alvarez,* p. 180.

603 "SOMEHOW," WEISSKOPF WROTE: Stern, p. 255.

604 ASKED WHY HE HAD TOLD: Stern, p. 280.

604 "THERE HADN'T BEEN A PROCEEDING: Stern, p. 305.

605 HE WAS SORRY TO HEAR ABOUT: Stern, p. 335.

605 AFTER BEING RECRUITED BY STRAUSS: FBI documents on J. Robert Oppenheimer, May 27, 1952, Albuquerque office to director.

606 WHEN ROBB ASKED TELLER: Blumberg and Owens, p. 361.

606 THIS WAS THE CRITICAL: Blumberg and Owens, pp. 362–63.

607 FINALLY CAME THE DENOUEMENT: Coughlin, "Dr. Teller's Magnificent Obsession," p. 74.

607 OPPENHEIMER, IN A POLITE VOICE: Coughlin, p. 74.

607 WHEN OPPENHEIMER HAD BEEN ASKED: Stern, p. 380.

608 *YOU DOUBLE-DEALING, LYING:* interview with Green.

608 HE DID IT, GREEN NOTED: interview with Green.

609 EISENHOWER BECAME NERVOUS: Hagerty, p. 43.

609 LATER, AFTER THE REVIEW BOARD: Hagerty, p. 61.

610 OPPENHEIMER SMILED AND ANSWERED: Stern, p. 451.

610 "THE LOS ALAMOS LABORATORY: Davis, *Lawrence and Oppenheimer,* p. 316.

611 WHILE A ROOM FULL OF PROMINENT: Stern, p. 447.

611 FRIENDS HEARD THEIR YOUNG DAUGHTER: Stern, p. 378.

616 IT WAS ONE OF THE MOST COMPLETE: Coffey, *Iron Eagle,* p. 165.

616 NOT EVERYONE IN THE AIR FORCE: Coffey, p. 246.

617 LEMAY ANSWERED, "IT DOESN'T: Coffey, p. 272.

617 HE BELIEVED, RIGHT UP UNTIL: Coffey, p. 331.

617 "SOME OF US," HE WOULD ADD: Coffey, pp. 331–32.

618 HE THOUGHT ARMY BASE SECURITY: Coffey, p. 311.

618 "THIS AFTERNOON," HE TOLD THEM: Shepley and Blair, *The Hydrogen Bomb,* p. 192.

CHAPTER TWENTY-FIVE

622 A WORD FROM ONE [BROTHER]: Schlesinger and Kinzer, *Bitter Fruit: The Untold Story of the American Coup in Guatemala,* p. 108.

623 THE GENERAL MANAGER OF THE WAR: Candee, *Current Biography: Who's News and Why—1953,* p. 580.

623 GODDAMNIT, LET'S HAVE IT OUT: Lyon, *Eisenhower: Portrait of the Hero,* p. 328.

623 I LOVE THAT MAN: Lyon, p. 367.

623 COLD FISHY EYE: Mosley, *Dulles: A Biography of Eleanor, Allen, and John Foster Dulles and Their Family Network,* p. 283.

624 HE WAS A SMALL MAN: Roosevelt, *Countercoup: The Struggle for Control of Iran,* p. 4.

624 ROOSEVELT, IF YOU CAN'T KEEP: Roosevelt, p. 4.

624 SO THIS IS HOW WE GET: Roosevelt, p. 8.

625 AS I LISTENED TO HIM: Rubin: *Paved with Good Intentions: The American Experience and Iran,* p. 74.

625 INARTICULATE AS USUAL BUT ENTHUSIASTIC: Roosevelt, p. 18.

625 WE SHOULD PROCEED: Roosevelt, p. 17.

626 THAT'S THAT THEN: Roosevelt, p. 18.

626 THE LAST PERSON YOU'D EXPECT: Mosley, p. 326.

627 ONE PERCENT OF THE POPULATION: Rubin, p. 22.

627 BY CONTRAST, THE AMERICAN EMBASSY: Rubin, p. 54.

627 IN 1950, THE BRITISH GOVERNMENT: Lyon, p. 488.

627 YOU DO NOT KNOW HOW CRAFTY: Rubin, p. 66.

628 DON'T YOU REALIZE THAT RETURNING: Rubin, p. 68.

630 TO EMBODY IRAN PERSONALLY, ITS: Rubin, p. 59.

630 BUT BEING CALLED ON SO OBVIOUS A PLOY: Acheson, *Present at the Creation: My Years at the State Department,* p. 504.

630 ESSENTIALLY A RICH REACTIONARY: Acheson, p. 504.

631 PULL UP YOUR SOCKS: Roosevelt, p. 115.

633 IT WAS A GREAT ADVENTURE: Roosevelt, p. 138.

633 HE WAS BARELY LITERATE: Roosevelt, pp. 138–40.

634 THE OLD BUGGER: Roosevelt, p. 163.

634 ROOSEVELT ALSO BROUGHT WITH HIM: Rubin, p. 82.

635 I WISH YOUR IMPERIAL MAJESTY: Roosevelt, p. 168.

636 HAPPY TO REPORT: Roosevelt, pp. 190–91.

636 AS A SOUVENIR OF OUR RECENT ADVENTURE: Roosevelt, p. 201.

636 THE SHAH IS A NEW MAN: Lyon, p. 552.

637 WELL I CAN SAY THAT THE STATEMENT: Wise and Ross, *The Invisible Government,* p. 113.

637 YOUNG MAN, IF I HAD BEEN: Roosevelt, p. 207.

637 OUR AGENT THERE, A MEMBER: Lyon, p. 552.

CHAPTER TWENTY-SIX

639 HIS EYES . . . GLEAMING: Roosevelt, *Countercoup: The Struggle for the Control of Iran,* p. 4.

639 BUT ROOSEVELT FIGURED THAT: Author interview with Kermit Roosevelt.

643 IF THAT COLONEL OF YOURS: Beschloss, *Mayday: Eisenhower, Khruschev, and the U-2 Affair,* p. 126.

643 YOU DON'T KNOW WHAT YOU'RE: Schlesinger and Kinzer, *Bitter Fruit: The Untold Story of the American Coup in Guatemala,* p. 146.

644 I'LL TELL THE TRUTH TO DICK RUSSELL: Beschloss, p. 129.

644 FOR UNFRIENDLY COUNTRIES: Beschloss, p. 126.

644 ALLEN, CAN'T I EVER MENTION A NAME: Beschloss, p. 128.

645 ALAS, NO, BUT I WISH: Mosley, *Dulles: A Biography of Eleanor, Allen, and John Foster Dulles and Their Family Network,* p. 125.

645 HE REFUELED HIMSELF ON PARTIES: Mosley, p. 282.

645 HIS AFFAIRS WERE SO NOTORIOUS: Mosley, p. 125.

646 DELICIOUS SENSE OF SIN: Dulles, *John Foster Dulles,* p. 2.

646 I CAN MAKE AN EDUCATED GUESS: Mosley, p. 282.

647 SMITH APPARENTLY THOUGHT DULLES TOO: Mosley, p. 294.

650 AS IN THE PAST, HE RESERVED: Schlesinger and Kinzer, p. 108.

650 THAT GOOD INDIAN LOOK ABOUT HIM: Hunt, *Give Us This Day,* p. 117.

650 I WANT YOU ALL TO BE DAMN: Lyon, *Eisenhower: Portrait of the Hero,* p. 611.

651 IT ALSO CONTROLLED EITHER DIRECTLY: Schlesinger and Kinzer, p. 12.

651 BY 1950, THE COMPANY REPORTED: Immerman, *The CIA in Guatemala: The Foreign Policy of Intervention,* p. 73.

652 WILD AND DANGEROUS BEAST: Immerman, p. 32.

652 SO! YOU TOO ARE A COMMUNIST: Ydigoras, *My War with Communism,* p. 26.

652 THEN IT'S TRUE: Ydigoras, p. 36.

653 POLITICAL REVOLUTION WAS NO PROBLEM: Bernays, *Biography of an Idea: Memoirs of a Public Relations Council,* pp. 757–58.

653 HIS IDEALISM COINCIDED WITH THE: Immerman, p. 46.

654 THE BANANA MAGNATES, CO-NATIONALS: Schlesinger and Kinzer, p. 47.

655 JUST GIVE ME THE ARMS: Mathews, *A World in Revolution,* 262.

657 A STAR-SPANGLED-BANNER GUY: Schlesinger and Kinzer, p. 55.

658 THE GOVERNMENT WILL FALL IN: Sulzberger, *The Last of the Giants,* p. 826.

658 SEEMED MUCH MORE CIA THAN STATE: Sulzberger, p. 826.

658 AGRARIAN REFORM HAD BEEN INSTITUTED: Immerman, p. 138.

658 WE ARE MAKING OUR FOURTH OF JULY: Immerman, p. 141.

659 IF ARBENZ IS NOT A COMMUNIST: Schlesinger and Kinzer, p. 139.

659 ALLEN DULLES HAD ANOTHER AGENT: Immerman, p. 155.

660 WELL BOYS, TOMORROW AT THIS: Schlesinger and Kinzer, p. 13.

660 IN FACT, THE NEWS WAS SO PUBLIC: Immerman, p. 3.

661 MEXICO CITY WAS NOT AN ONEROUS: Author interview with Sidney Gruson.

662 YOU'RE CRAZY, YOU KNOW YOU: Author interview with Sidney Gruson.

662 TURNER, WE CAN DO THIS: Author interview with Sidney Gruson.

663 SYDNEY, WE WANT YOU TO STAY: Author interview with Sidney Gruson.

664 A MAJOR GENERAL, A NO-NONSENSE: Salisbury, *Without Fear or Favor: The New York Times and Its Times,* p. 477.

665 HE BEGAN TO PRESS THE HEAD: Salisbury, pp. 479–82.

667 MR. PRESIDENT, WHEN I SAW HENRY: Eisenhower, *Mandate for Change,* pp. 424–26.

667 THINKING OF THE TERRIBLE LOSSES: Phillips, *The Night Watch,* p. 50.

668 PEOPLE WERE COMPLAINING THAT: Immerman, p. 141.

668 AND THAT IF HE HAD BROUGHT: Schlesinger and Kinzer, p. 195.

669 COLONEL, YOU'RE JUST NOT CONVENIENT: Schlesinger and Kinzer, pp. 206–7.

669 IT WOULD BE BETTER IN: Schlesinger and Kinzer, pp. 207–8.

670 HE WOULD, HE SAID, MAKE EVERYTHING: Immerman, p. 181.

670 THERE WAS NOTHING CONCLUSIVE: Immerman, p. 186.

670 BECAUSE OF MY RESPECT FOR: Salisbury, p. 481.

671 A MAN HAVING HIS [GRUSON'S]: Salisbury, p. 482.

671 MY JUDGMENT, FORMED ON THE BASIS: Salisbury, p. 482.

671 CYRUS SULZBERGER, WHO BELIEVED GRUSON: Author interview with Cyrus Sulzberger.

CHAPTER TWENTY-SEVEN

672 AS REINHOLD NEIBHUR: Hoopes, *The Devil and John Foster Dulles,* p. 37.

673 YES, SAID DULLES, AND HE: Hoopes, p. 74.

673 THERE WERE REPORTS THAT AT THE LAST: Hoopes, p. 137–38.

674 HE COMPLAINED TO CLOSE AIDES: Hoopes, p. 129.

674 STILL HE HONORED EISENHOWER: Adams, *First-Hand Report,* p. 89.

675 EISENHOWER, ON THE OTHER HAND: Hoopes, pp. 200–201.

675 "MR. DULLES MAKES A SPEECH: Hoopes, p. 149.

676 THE WRITER CAME AWAY: Hughes, *The Ordeal of Power,* p. 70.

677 AT THAT POINT CRONKITE NOTED: Hoopes, p. 132.

677 ALEXANDER CADOGEN, AN ASSISTANT: Dulles, *John Foster Dulles,* pp. 119–20.

677 IKE LATER SAID HE ANSWERED: Prados, *The Sky Would Fall,* p. 26.

678 THE ITALIANS OF COURSE WERE: Mosley, *Dulles,* p. 329.

679 WHEN JOHN FOSTER WAS FIVE, HIS MOTHER: Hoopes, p. 11.

680 SEEING HIS YOUNGER SISTER CRYING: Mosley, p. 19.

681 YEARS LATER, WHEN SHE WAS ASKED: Mosley, p. 30.

681 "IT MADE THEM BOSSY: Dulles, p. 81.

681 "HE KNEW," HIS SISTER LATER: Dulles, p. 80.

682 HE REMAINED "A MAN OF WATERTOWN: Dulles, p. 91.

685 HUMPHREY SEEMED TO SPEAK: Hoopes, p. 196.

686 SOON THERE WERE A VARIETY: Hoopes, p. 200.

689 USING THE KIND OF WORDS: Fall, *Hell in a Very Small Place,* p. 28.

690 IN 1946 GENERAL JACQUES PHILIPPE LECLERC: Halberstam, *Ho,* p. 84.

691 NAVARRE WAS NOT ENTHUSIASTIC: Roy, *The Battle of Dien Bien Phu,* p. 7.

691 EVEN MORE OMINOUS WAS A WARNING: Roy, pp. 8–9.

691 "IN THAT CASE THEY ARE DONE: Roy, pp. 8–9.

691 THE WARNING FROM SALAN: Roy, p. 68.

692 "NOT ONE SOU: Prados, p. 96.

692 GEORGE HUMPHREY, THE SECRETARY: Prados, pp. 27–28.

694 THEY HAD THE MOST PRIMITIVE: Roy, pp. 72–73.

694 WHEN GIAP'S NAME WAS: Roy, p. xix.

694 SPEAKING OF THE FRENCH ARROGANCE: Roy, p. xix.

695 THE NAME DIEN BIEN PHU: Prados, p. 3.

695 IN NOVEMBER 1953, RESPONDING: Fall, pp. 35–36.

696 AS BERNARD FALL, THE HISTORIAN: Fall, p. 49.

696 YEARS LATER, MAJOR MARCEL: Fall, p. 5.

697 WHEN NAVARRE HIMSELF VISITED: Fall, p. 103.

697 ONCE AGAIN THEY HAD MADE: Roy, p. 52.

697 THEY COULD CARRY UP TO: Roy, p. 105.

698 IT WAS NOTHING OF THE SORT: Roy, p. 131.

698 HE SHRUGGED HIS SHOULDERS: Roy, p. 174.

698 "I AM COMPLETELY DISHONORED: Fall, p. 156.

699 "LET'S HAVE NO ILLUSIONS: Roy, p. 179.

700 "FIRST WE SEND THEM PLANES: Prados, p. 49.

701 "YOU COULD TAKE ALL DAY TO DROP: Prados, p. 92.

701 "THE DAMN REPUBLICANS: Halberstam, *The Best and the Brightest,* p. 139.

703 BUT THE FRENCH DEMURRED: Fall, p. 307.

703 "I HAVE SPENT MORE TIME: Prados, p. 96.

703 AT ONE POINT IN EARLY APRIL: Prados, p. 105.

703 A FEW DAYS LATER, AT A PRESS: Prados, p. 115.

704 RIDGWAY SAW AIRPOWER: interview with Ridgway.

705 WHEN HE BRIEFED EISENHOWER: interview with Ridgway.

707 AS THE IDEA OF INTERVENTION: Fall, p. 309.

707 THAT NIGHT ALL FRENCH: Fall, pp. 415–16.

708 IN APRIL THAT YEAR THE *TIMES:* Prados, p. 89.

708 "WE HAVE A CLEAN BASE: Hughes, p. 208.

710 IT WAS, HE NOTED, "A MODERN: Hoopes, p. 310.

710 "YOU HAVE TO TAKE CHANCES: Hoopes, p. 310.

710 HEARING LATER OF DULLES'S BOASTS: Fall, p. 459.

CHAPTER TWENTY-EIGHT

713 FRANKFURTER REFERRED TO BLACK: Schwartz, *Super Chief,* p. 81.

713 HIS CLOSE FRIEND, JUDGE LEARNED HAND: Schwartz and Lesher, *Inside the Warren Court,* p. 130.

713 HE SAID OF BLACK: Schwartz and Lesher, p. 52.

713 OF A BLACK OPINION: Schwartz and Lesher, p. 52.

713 BLACK, WHO WAS AWARE: Schwartz and Lesher, p. 53.

713 IN A LETTER TO HAND: Schwartz and Lesher, p. 53.

713 DOUGLAS RETURNED THE SENTIMENTS: Schwartz and Lesher, p. 53.

713 ONCE AFTER HEARING AN UNUSUALLY LONG: Schwartz and Lesher, p. 24.

715 "THIS MAN," PHILIP ELMAN: Schwartz, p. 73.

715 THEY WERE, HE THOUGHT: Simon, *The Antagonists,* p. 200.

717 THE DISPARITY WAS EVEN: Kluger, *Simple Justice,* p. 257.

717 IF THE PACE WITH WHICH: Kluger, p. 217.

718 SO, HE NOTED, HE HAD "WRAPPED: Kluger, p. 224.

718 "THE FOURTEENTH AMENDMENT: Kluger, p. 222.

719 "JUSTICE BROWN, IN SHORT: Kluger, p. 80.

720 IN A PASSIONATE DISSENT: Kluger, p. 82.

720 HE ADDED: "THE WHITE: Kluger, p. 82.

720 WHEN THE COURT MET: Schwartz and Lesher, p. 23.

721 "WE CAN'T CLOSE OUR EYES: Schwartz and Lesher, p. 23.

721 "THIS IS THE FIRST INDICATION: Kluger, p. 656.

721 SPECULATION BEGAN TO CENTER: Schwartz, p. 17.

722 THE POVERTY OF HIS FATHER'S LIFE: Warren, *The Memoirs of Earl Warren,* p. 16.

723 THAT THEY HAD NOT YET RISEN UP: Weaver, *Warren,* p. 105.

723 IN JUNE 1943, WARREN: Kluger, p. 662.

724 LATER HE EXPRESSED CONSIDERABLE: White, *Earl Warren,* p. 77.

724 THAT A RECORD OTHERWISE: interview with A.J. Langguth.

724 HIS CRITICS THOUGHT HIM: White, p. 180.

724 FROM THEN ON, HE INCLUDED: Warren, p. 161.

725 WHEN HIS LAW CLERKS TWITTED: Schwartz and Lesher, p. 143.

725 "WARREN'S GREAT STRENGTH: Schwartz and Lesher, p. 33.

725 EDGAR PATTERSON, HIS DRIVER: Schwartz, p. 97.

725 JOHN GUNTHER, ONE OF THE VERY BEST: Gunther, *Inside U.S.A.,* p. 18.

727 HIS LAW CLERK, EARL POLLOCK: Kluger, p. 695.

727 WARREN, HUGO BLACK WROTE: Simon, p. 222.

727 "EARL WARREN," ANTHONY LEWIS: Kluger, p. 667.

728 PREVIOUS CASES, HE LATER TOLD: Kluger, p. 678.

728 THE LAW, HE SAID: Kluger, p. 679.

729 WARREN WANTED A MINIMUM: Kluger, p. 679.

729 JUSTICE TOM CLARK HAD: Kluger, p. 706.

730 "THESE ARE NOT BAD PEOPLE: Schwartz and Lesher, p. 87.

730 WHEN FRANKFURTER CIRCULATED: Kluger, p. 37.

731 THE MIXING OF THE RACES: Kluger, p. 60.

733 FINALLY THE CHIEF JUSTICE MADE: Kluger, p. 698.

733 "THERE ARE MANY CONSIDERATIONS: Schwartz and Lesher, p. 87.

734 JACKSON'S CLERK, BARRETT: Kluger, p. 697.

The major source for the remainder of this chapter is an author interview with Frederic Morrow.

CHAPTER TWENTY-NINE

748 HIS MOTHER, MAMIE BRADLEY, WORKED: Whitfield, *A Death in the Delta,* p. 15.

749 THE AVERAGE WHITE ADULT HAD: Whitfield, pp. 23–24.

751 A CROSSROADS MARILYN MONROE: Whitfield, p. 110.

754 WE'VE GOT TO HAVE OUR MILAMS: From the Huie letters at Ohio State.

754 THE WHITES OWN ALL THE PROPERTY: Huie letters.

755 I AM CAPABLE OF DRINKING: Huie letters.

756 WHAT ELSE COULD WE DO: Huie letters.

757 HAVE YOU EVER SENT A LOVED SON: Whitfield, p. 23.

761 I'VE GOT ALL THESE REPORTERS: Whitfield, p. 23.

762 A DELTA SHERIFF COULD OFFICIALLY: Whitfield, p. 27.

763 MORNIN' NIGGERS: Author interview with Jay Milner and Murray Kempton.

764 CLARENCE, AS FORMER GOVERNOR BILL: Author interview with Bill Winter.

764 HE HAD THREE PLANES FOR CROP: Whitfield, pp. 29–30.

765 THIS NIGGER SAID THERE'S: Whitfield, p. 37.

765 WASN'T IT JUST LIKE THAT: Whitfield, pp. 31–32.

766 WHEN A CLARKSDALE RADIO STATION: Whitfield, p. 37.

766 THE MOST HE NEEDED WAS: Whitfield, p. 37.

766 YOUR ANCESTORS WILL TURN OVER: Whitfield, p. 34.

766 WELL, I HOPE THE CHICAGO NIGGERS: Whitfield, p. 34.

767 IT WOULD HAVE BEEN A QUICKER DECISION: Whitfield, p. 34.

CHAPTER THIRTY

769 JOURNALISTS, AS THE NOTED: Author conversation with James B. Reston.

771 IN THE LATE 19TH: Grossman, *Black Southerners and the Great Migration,* p. 13.

772 THEY COULD GET THE WRINKLE: Ottley, *The Lonely Warrior: The Life and Times of Robert S. Abbot,* p. 159.

772 WHY THE MINIMUM WAGE IN THE PACKING: Grossman, p. 15.

772 INSTEAD, IN HIS PAGES, A BLACK: Ottley, p. 110.

773 A COLORED MAN CAUGHT WITH: Ottley, p. 110.

773 IT WAS ESTIMATED THAT TWO THIRDS: Grossman, p. 75.

773 A RELIGIOUS PILGRIMAGE: Ottley, p. 163.

774 COME NORTH WHERE THERE IS MORE: Ottley, p. 161.

774 WITH TREMBLING AND FEAR: Grossman, p. 110.

777 IT WAS, HE CONFIDED TO HIS BROTHER: Maharidge and Williamson, *And Their Children Came After Them,* p. 40.

777 AT AN EARLY AGE HE: "Mr. Little Ol' Rust," *Fortune,* December 1952.

778 I KNEW I HAD HOLD OF SOMETHING: "Mr. Little Ol' Rust," *Fortune.*

778 GOOD HEAVENS, RUST, YOU CAN'T: Rust, "The Origin and Development of the Cotton Picker," Monograph.

779 WHEN THE RUST MACHINE FIRST: "Mr. Little Ol' Rust," *Fortune.*

780 THE MISSING LINK IN THE MECHANICAL: "Mr. Little Ol' Rust," *Fortune.*

780 I SINCERELY HOPE THAT YOU: Maharidge and Williamson, pp. 42–43.

780 E. H. CRUMP, THE POLITICAL BOSS: Street, *The New Evolution in Cotton Economy,* p. 125.

780 IF IT DOES MY WORK: Maharidge and Williamson, p. 42.

781 THERE WAS A LONG TIME: Author interview with G. E. Powell.

781 WHEN IN 1949, IT FINALLY: Maharidge and Williamson, p. 105.

782 A GOOD PICKER CAN AVERAGE: Goulden, *The Best Years,* p. 128.

784 EVERYONE WAS ENTHUSIASTIC: Author interview with Powell.

790 SOME ESTIMATED THAT BY 1955: Street, p. 170.

791 IN 1952 THE NATIONAL COTTON COUNCIL: "Mr. Little Ol' Rust," *Fortune.*

792 SO ESPY'S TELEVISION PEOPLE SHOT: Author interview with Bill Winter.

CHAPTER THIRTY-ONE

The section on Elvis Presley is based on a number of books, including biographies by Albert Goldman; Elaine Dundy; Steve Dunleavy; Dee Presley, Rich Stanley, and David Stanley; Stanley Booth; Kevin Quain; Larry Geller and Joel Spector; Peter Haining; Jerry Hopkins; Lee Cotten; Peter Guralnick; Colin Escot and Martin Hawkins; and Geoffrey Stokes, Ed Ward, and Ken Tucker, as well as interviews with Sam Phillips of Sun Records and a number of other Elvisologists. In addition I spent four years as a reporter on the *Nashville Tennessean* covering, among other things, the music beat. That allowed me, through the courtesy of my friend, Chet Atkins, who ran the RCA studio, to watch sessions of Elvis recording during those early days in Nashville. I also knew Colonel Tom Parker quite well in those days, and much to my surprise he kept his promise to let me be the one reporter allowed on Elvis's train when the singer returned from the Army.

Section on James Dean:

837 IN A BOOK THAT WAS IN NO SMALL PART: Schickel, *Brando,* p. 1.

837 DEAN "WAS SO ADORING: Kazan, *A Life,* p. 538.

838 ON OCCASION DEAN SIGNED: Dalton, *James Dean: The Mutant King,* p. 159.

838 DEAN WAS, WROTE STEVEN VINEBERG: Vineberg, p. 187.

839 DICK SCHICKEL NOTED THE ADVANTAGES: Schickel, p. 11.

839 DEAN ANSWERED THAT IT CAME: Dalton, p. 248.

840 HIS TALENT, ESPECIALLY HIS ABILITY: Dalton, p. 92.

842 "THEY'RE LIKE FIGHTERS: Dalton, p. 153.

843 "HE WAS SHOWING OFF: Kazan, p. 534.

843 "THERE WAS NO POINT IN TRYING: Dalton, p. 162.

843 THEN, PLAYING ALONG WITH: Dalton, p. 154.

843 THE TECHNICIANS WORKING ON THE SET: Kazan, p. 535.

844 THAT DELIGHTED KAZAN: Kazan, p. 535.

844 "MUST I ALWAYS BE MISERABLE: Dalton, p. 159.

845 THAT PLEASED KAZAN: Kazan, p. 537.

845 "HE'D SHOW ME THE GODDAMN: Dalton, p. 194.

845 ON THE SET OF *GIANT:* Dalton, p. 238.

846 DEAN IS, ONCE AGAIN: Dalton, p. 238.

847 IN TRUTH HE WAS NOT FOND: Kazan, pp. 538–39.

848 SUDDENLY *ALIENATION* WAS A WORD: Schickel, p. 6.

CHAPTER THIRTY-TWO

849 BY ROUGH ESTIMATES, 49.3 MILLION: Cray, *Chrome Colossus* p. 362.

851 ZORA ARKUS-DUNTOV, A TOP GM DESIGNER: interview with David. E. Davis.

853 INSTEAD HE TURNED TO HIS AIDE: interview with Al Rothenberg.

854 AS THEY WERE HEADING BACK: interview with Tony de Lorenzo.

855 HEADING THE CORPORATION AFTER HEADING: interview with Tom Adams.

856 IN ADDITION THE STYLING OF THE CAR: Cray, p. 363.

861 COLE'S MOTTO, A FRIEND NOTED: Lamm, *Chevrolet 1955,* p. 6.

861 HE SCOURED THE COMPANY: Lamm, p. 10.

862 ALMOST EVERYTHING ABOUT THE 1955: Lamm, p. 6.

862 IT WAS, CLARE MACKICHAN: Lamm, p. 30.

862 "HELL, I WOULDN'T WANT TO MAKE: Lamm, p. 29.

863 "IT SURE AS HELL IS: interview with David Cole.

863 "HE WANTED THE AVERAGE GUY: Lamm, p. 39.

863 OR AS HARLEY EARL SAID TO HARLOW: Lamm, p. 29.

864 THAT WAS WHAT THE PUBLIC WANTED: interview with Al Rothenberg.

CHAPTER THIRTY-THREE

865 IN THE HOME IT WAS TO BE: Hine, *Populux,* p. 15.

865 POPPY CANNON, A FOOD WRITER: Hine, p. 24. The material on Betty Furness comes from an author interview with her.

873 [WE] DISCOVERED, SAID ROSSER: Diamond and Bates, *The Spot,* p. 40.

873 THE SPEED WITH WHICH TELEVISION'S: Fox, *The Mirror Makers,* p. 210.

873 "SHOW THE PRODUCT," SAID BEN: Fox, p. 211.

874 MANY ADVERTISERS DID THAT: Fox, p. 211.

874 IT WAS, ROSSER REEVES SAID: Diamond and Bates, p. 40.

874 THE ADVERTISING FIRMS THAT ADAPTED: Fox, pp. 175, 210.

875 "WHY DON'T YOU BE ONE OF THOSE: Fox, p. 208.

875 "ADVERTISING," HE WROTE, "NOW COMPARES: Potter, *People of Plenty,* p. 167.

875 STUDIES COMPARING THE HEALTH: Fox, p. 209.

876 "I SOLD MY INTEREST: Mayer, *Madison Avenue, USA,* p. 11.

877 BUT IN THE NEW AGE OF TELEVISION: interview with David McCall.

878 A KIND OF MISGUIDED ETHIC: interviews with Don Frey, Tom Adams, and Campbell Ewald.

879 "OUR SOD-BUSTING DELIVERY: Fox, pp. 222–23, 225.

880 HIS CHILDREN BARELY SAW: Fox, p. 224.

881 OF THE ORIGINAL ADS: interview with David McCall.

881 THE ADS BEGAN TO TALK ABOUT: Packard, *The Hidden Persuaders,* p. 21.

882 THERE WAS A NEW WESTERN SONG: Packard, p. 21.

882 "CAPITALISM IS DEAD: Packard, p. 21.

883 WINTHROP ALDRICH, THEN THE HEAD: interview with David McCall.

884 ERNEST DICHTER, ONE OF THE FIRST: Packard, p. 57.

884 THIS WAS, HE BELIEVED: Packard, p. 58.

CHAPTER THIRTY-FOUR

The main sources for this chapter are author interviews with friends of Ricky Nelson, Joel Selvin's *Ricky Nelson: Idol for a Generation, The World According to Beaver* by Irving Applebaum, and *Ladies of the Evening: Woman Characters in Prime Time* by Diana Meehan.

CHAPTER THIRTY-FIVE

911 "WITHOUT TALKING ABOUT IT MUCH: Wilson, *The Man in the Gray Flannel Suit,* p. 3.

912 "FEW PEOPLE CONSIDERED GREENTREE: Wilson, p. 109.

912 WHEN THE NEIGHBORS GATHERED: Wilson, p. 109.

913 TRY FOR $15,000, ONE OF HIS: Wilson, p. 4.

913 THEN SHE SIGHS: Wilson, p. 6.

914 "WHEN YOU COME RIGHT DOWN: Wilson, p. 7.

914 HE COULD ALSO HAVE WRITTEN: Wilson, p. 8. The biographical material on Sloan Wilson is based on material from an interview with Wilson by the author.

921 "I HAVE NEVER KNOWN," HE: Press, *C. Wright Mills,* p. 13.

921 MILLS'S WORK WAS IMPORTANT: interview with Stanley Katz.

922 WHEN IT WAS HIS TURN TO RESPOND: Tilman, *C. Wright Mills,* p. 8.

924 ALIENATION CAME NATURALLY TO HIM: Press, p. 13.

924 HIS PARENTS FORCED HIM TO SING: Horowitz, *C. Wright Mills,* p. 6.

925 HE ONCE WROTE KURT WOLFF: Horowitz, p. 84.

925 AFTER AN UNHAPPY START: Wakefield, *New York in the Fifties,* p. 256.

926 CLARENCE AYRES, A PROFESSOR: Tilman, p. 6.

926 IN THIS LETTER WRITTEN: Tilman, p. 7.

927 IN MADISON, HE SEEMED TO MAKE: Horowitz, p. 47.

927 MILLS, HE SAID, WAS "AN EXCELLENT: Horowitz, p. 72.

928 IN MADISON HE MARRIED: Horowitz, p. 6.

928 HE TOLD MILLS TO "STICK: Horowitz, p. 58.

928 HE WAS TAKING POLITICS: Horowitz, p. 62.

928 HIS ATTITUDE AS IRVING: Horowitz, p. 66.

929 "ORGANIZE THE WORKERS: Press, p. 50.

930 THE LIBERALISM OF THE SOCIETY: Horowitz, p. 70.

930 "I WROTE MY WAY OUT OF THERE: Wakefield, p. 35.

931 "MILLS," WROTE HOROWITZ, "WAS CAUGHT: Horowitz, p. 83.

931 HE WOULD LATER SAY OF *WHITE COLLAR:* Wakefield, p. 35.

931 "WE WERE BOTH CONGENITAL: Horowitz, p. 77.

931 THEY BOTH HAD, HE NOTED: Horowitz, p. 77.

931 HE WAS, THOUGHT WAKEFIELD: Wakefield, p. 33.

933 AS HOROWITZ NOTED, IT HIT ON: Horowitz, p. 244.

933 RIESEMAN THOUGHT THERE WAS: interview with Rieseman.

934 THERE MIGHT BE, HOFSTADER: Horowitz, p. 251.

935 BELL'S CRITICISM STUNG: Tilman, p. 203.

937 AMERICA, HE THOUGHT, WAS: Tilman, p. 12.

937 HE CONTINUED TO SMOKE AND DRINK: Horowitz, p. 6.

938 "MILLS," AS IRVING HOROWITZ: Horowitz, p. 283.

CHAPTER THIRTY-SIX

941 SHE TOLD HIM TO GO RIGHT: Garrow, *Bearing the Cross,* p. 12.

942 BUT IF SHE HAD NOT PLANNED: Garrow, p. 12.

944 ONCE VIRGINIA DURR HAD TURNED: Yeakey, *The Montgomery Bus Boycott, 1955–1956,* p. 275.

944 AS THE BUS DRIVER CONTINUED TO SHOUT: Oates: *Let the Trumpet Sound: The Life of Martin Luther King, Jr.,* p. 8.

945 DID THEY BEAT YOU: Yeakey, p. 255.

946 OH, THE WHITE FOLKS WILL KILL YOU: Durr, *Memoir, Vol. II,* (Nov. 24, 1976); and Yeakey, p. 275.

946 IF YOU THINK WE CAN GET: Yeakey, p. 275.

947 WELL, I'LL TELL YOU ONE: Raines, *My Soul is Rested,* p. 44.

948 EVEN GOD CAN'T FREE PEOPLE WHO: Abernathy, *And the Walls Came Tumbling Down,* p. 17.

949 ATTEMPTS ON THE PART OF BLACK: Yeakey, p. 97.

949 THERE IS GOING TO BE A SECOND DAY: *The Montgomery Advertiser,* July 10, 1954, pp. 1A–5A; and Yeakey, p. 90.

951 SHE INSISTED SHE WAS COLORED: from transcript of *City vs. Claudette Colvin* in the circuit court of Juvenile Court and Court of Domestic Relations, Montgomery County, Alabama (March 18, 1955); and Yeakey, p. 235.

955 NOW, LET US SAY THAT WE: King, "Speech at Holt Church"; cited in Yeakey, p. 668.

956 FIVE YEARS BEFORE THE BUS BOYCOTT: Yeakey, p. 17.

958 I'LL KILL YOU, KILL YOU: King, Sr., *Daddy King,* p. 47.

958 A MAN'S ANGER GETS THE BEST OF HIM: King, Sr., p. 47.

959 NOW, KING, YOU KNOW GOD DOESN'T LOVE: King, Sr., p. 14.

960 WHY, REVEREND KING, YOU MUST BE FIXIN': King, Sr., p. 22.

960 YOU'RE JUST NOT COLLEGE MATERIAL: King, Sr., p. 75.

960 APPARENTLY, YOU CAN START CLASSES: King, Sr., p. 77.

962 HE WAS THE MOST PECULIAR CHILD: Oates, p. 8.

963 THE SHACKLES OF FUNDAMENTALISM WERE: Oates, p. 19.

966 YOU WILL NOT BE MARRYING ANY ORDINARY: Oates, p. 45.

967 AT FIRST BAPTIST, THEY DON'T MIND THE PREACHER TALKING: Abernathy, pp. 118–119.

967 KEEP MARTIN LUTHER KING IN THE BACKGROUND: Oates, p. 48.

968 JOHNSON WAS AMUSED WHEN, IN THE MIDDLE: Author interview with W. Thomas Johnson.

968 I DON'T WANT TO LOOK LIKE AN UNDERTAKER: "Attack on the Conscience," *Time,* February 18, 1957, p. 19.

968 THEY PREACHED THE GOSPEL: Abernathy, p. 114.

968 COMES THE FIRST RAINY DAY: Oates, p. 75.

970 THE NEGROES ARE LAUGHING: Yeakey, p. 487.

971 SHOOTIN' MARBLES, FOR EXAMPLE: Yeakey, p. 397.

973 AN ALMOST PERFECT CROSS BETWEEN: Author interview with Karl Fleming.

973 WE LOVE OUR CITY HERE: Greenhaw, *Alabama on My Mind,* p. 60.

974 HE SPOKE MORE AND MORE SCATHINGLY: Author interviews with Robert Ingram, Ray Jenkins, Wallace Westfeldt, Karl Fleming, Wayne Greenhaw, Claude Sitton, Tom Johnson, and Harry Ashmore.

974 THE KINDEST THING THAT COULD BE SAID: Author interviews.

977 AND YOU NEVER KNOW WHAT COLOR: Author interview with Wallace Westfeldt.

979 I WOULDN'T TRADE MY SOUTHERN BIRTHRIGHT: *Time,* February 18, 1957, p. 19.

979 I HAVE THE FEELING: Oates, p. 95.

980 MARTIN LUTHER, STAND UP FOR: Oates, pp. 88–89.

980 VISION IN THE KITCHEN: Branch, *Parting the Waters,* p. 202.

981 THEY GON' TO KILL MY BOY: Oates, p. 93.

981 I HAVE BEGUN THE STRUGGLE: Oates, p. 93.

983 GET ME MY CHICKEN GUN: Author interviews with Wayne Greenhaw and Ray Jenkins.

CHAPTER THIRTY-SEVEN

Major sources for the section on Marilyn Monroe are *Timebends* by Arthur Miller; *Marilyn: A Biography* by Norman Mailer; *Marilyn Monroe: The Body in the Library* by Graham McCann; *Norma Jean: The Life of*

Marilyn Monroe and *Legend: The Life and Death of Marilyn Monroe* by Fred Lawrence Guiles; *Goddess: The Secret Lives of Marilyn Monroe* by Anthony Summers; and *Marilyn Monroe Confidential* by Lena Pepitone with William Stadiem. The major sources for the section on Hugh Hefner and *Playboy* are *Thy Neighbor's Wife* by Gay Talese and Thomas Weyr's *Reaching for Paradise: The Playboy Vision of America.*

CHAPTER THIRTY-EIGHT

1008 "BECAUSE YOU WOULDN'T HAVE LET: Davis, *Two-Bit Culture,* p. 257.

1008 "BUT IF YOU GO BENEATH: Toth, *Inside Peyton Place,* p. 1.

1012 KENNETH DAVIS NOTED IN HIS BOOK: Davis, p. 259.

1012 "FOR PERHAPS THE FIRST TIME IN POPULAR: Davis, p. 255.

1015 "HOW COULD YOU BE SO STUPID: Toth, p. 49.

1016 "I AM TRAPPED: Toth p. 60.

1019 "I KNOW THIS IS A BIG BOOK: Toth, p. 94

1019 BY CONTRAST MESSNER LOOKED: Toth, p. 94.

1019 LATER SHE DECIDED THAT WHAT: interview with Leona Nevler.

1021 INTERESTINGLY ENOUGH, A CRITIC: Toth, p. 145.

1021 THE PEOPLE IN NEW YORK: interview with Nevler.

1021 "THIS BOOK BUSINESS: Toth, p. 151.

1022 YEARS LATER GEORGE METALIOUS: Toth, p. 178.

1022 ALMOST AS SOON AS THE INTERVIEW: Toth, p. 163.

1023 "OUR MOTHER HAD TO BE TOLD: Toth, p. 225.

CHAPTER THIRTY-NINE

1026 A POLL OF BOTH MEN AND WOMEN: Ryan, *Womanhood in America,* p. 188.

1026 AT THE BEGINNING OF THE NEW DEAL: Sochen, *Movers and Shakers,* p. 162.

1027 THE *LADIES HOME JOURNAL* EVEN PUT: Ryan, p. 188.

1027 IN JUST TWO YEARS SOME TWO MILLION: Ryan, p. 190.

1033 "WHEN JIM COMES HOME," SAID: Hine, *Populux,* p. 55.

1033 "THE TWO BIG STEPS: Hine, p. 31.

The material on Betty Friedan comes from an interview with the author, *It Changed My Life* and *The Feminine Mystique,* both by Ms. Friedan, and *The Sisterhood* by Marcia Cohen.

CHAPTER FORTY

1050 HE BEGAN TO FIT SOME OF HIS: Davidson, "Dr. Rock's Magic Pill," p. 100.

1051 "DEAR MADAM," HE WROTE BACK: unpublished manuscript by Mahlon Hoagland.

1053 "HE [PINCUS] WAS A LITTLE SCARY: Vaughan, *The Pill on Trial,* p. 32.

1053 "THEY DID IT," THE YOUNG HOAGLAND: interview with Mahlon Hoagland.

1054 "AFTER ALL, IF YOU COULD PATENT: Vaughan, p. 21.

1056 "THE R.C. CHURCH," SHE WROTE: Gray, *Margaret Sanger,* p. 435.

1056 BY DOING SO HE WAS ABLE TO "LIBERATE: Pauly, *Controlling Life,* p. 194.

1057 HE WOULD TELL HIS AUDIENCES: Pauly, p. 194.

1057 "TO MARGARET SANGER," HE WROTE: Kennedy, *Birth Control in America,* p. vii.

1057 OF IT CLARE BOOTH LUCE: Davidson, p. 108.

1058 WHEN THE STORY WAS RELAYED TO CHANG: interview with M. C. Chang and Mahlon Hoagland.

CHAPTER FORTY-ONE

1061 WE DESPISE THE FRENCH: McDougall, *The Heavens and the Earth,* p. 44.

1062 THESE MEN, HUZEL BELIEVES, TEND: Lewis, *Appointment on the Moon,* p. 24.

1062 MY NAME IS MAGNUS VON BRAUN: McDougall, p. 44.

1062 TOO YOUNG, TOO FAT, TOO JOVIAL: Rothe and Lohr, *Current Biography: Who's News and Why—1952,* p. 608.

1062 THIS WILL MAKE BUCK ROGERS: McDougall, p. 44.

1063 WE WERE IMPRESSED WITH THEIR: McDougall, p. 70.

1063 THIS IS ABSOLUTELY INTOLERABLE: McDougall, p. 44.

1064 FOR MY CONFIRMATION: Noble, "Wernher von Braun, Rocket Pioneer Dies," *The New York Times,* June 18, 1977, p. 24.

1064 I WAS ECSTATIC: Berghaus, *Reaching for the Stars,* p. 40.

1066 DO YOU REALIZE WHAT WE: Clarke, *The Coming of Space,* p. 49.

1066 OUR MAIN OBJECTIVE FOR A LONG TIME: Medaris, *Countdown for Decision,* p. 38.

1067 WITH SUCH WEAPONS, HUMANITY: Medaris, p. 38.

1067 WHAT I WANT IS ANNIHILATION: Dornberger, *V-2,* p. 103.

1068 VON BRAUN CHECKED IT OUT: Berghaus, p. 78.

1071 SHADOWS AND IMAGES IN THE STRANGE: Berghaus, p. 29.

1072 FORMER GERMAN SCIENTISTS WHO: Medaris, p. 117.

1072 BUT IT WAS NO SMALL IRONY, AS: McDougall, p. 99.

1073 THEY QUICKLY PICKED UP THE SECOND TIER: Parry, *Russia's Rockets and Missiles,* p. 115.

1073 THE POINT IS THAT THE V-2: McDougall, p. 53.

1075 I DON'T WANT TO EXAGGERATE: McDougall, p. 59.

1076 HE HELD THE JOB FOR ELEVEN MONTHS: McDougall, p. 105.

1077 THIS COUNTRY, HE ONCE NOTED: McDougall, p. 126.

1078 BY THE SUMMER OF 1955, THE AIR FORCE: Wise and Ross, *The U-2 Affair,* p. 46.

1081 A JET WITH THE BODY: Powers and Gentry, *Operation Overflight,* p. 22.

1082 YOU'LL NEVER CONVINCE ME: Wise and Ross, p. 43.

1084 I'VE FIGURED OUT WHAT YOU'RE DOING: Powers and Gentry, p. 39.

1084 ONCE ON, IT FELT LIKE: Powers and Gentry, p. 22.

1085 SITTING ON A LOADED SHOTGUN: Powers and Gentry, p. 62.

1088 IT IS ONLY LOGICAL TO ASSUME: McDougall, p. 119.

1089 I WOULDN'T CARE IF THEY DID: Manchester, *The Glory and the Dream,* p. 787.

1092 A USELESS HUNK OF IRON: Kennan and Harvey, *Mission to the Moon,* p. 62.

1092 A SILLY BAUBLE IN THE SKY: Parry, p. 190.

1093 AS FAR AS THE SATELLITE IS CONCERNED: Ambrose, *Eisenhower the President,* pp. 429–30.

1093 YES, DEAR, AND IN SIX MONTHS: Lewis, p. 55.

1094 A BOOK CALLED: Manchester, p. 793.

1095 ONE CRITIC NOTED THAT AS: Parry, p. 190.

1095 YOU AMERICANS HAVE A BETTER: Manchester, p. 793.

1095 CELESTIAL BROTHERS: McDougall, p. 286.

1096 THEY'LL CALL ME SOON: Berghaus, p. 327.

1097 IT SEEMED AS IF THE GATES OF HELL: Clarke, p. 19.

1097 PHUT GOES U.S. SATELLITE: Lewis, p. 58.

1097 THAT WAS SPUTNIK: Parry, p. 191.

1099 THEY HEAR HER, WERNHER, THEY: Berghaus, p. 321.

1099 SHE IS EIGHT MINUTES LATE: Lewis, p. 67.

1099 LET'S NOT MAKE TOO GREAT: McDougall, p. 168.

CHAPTER FORTY-TWO

The material for the section on advertising and General Motors is based on interviews with Kennsinger Jones, Gerald Schnitzer, Al Rothenberg, and Barney Knudsen. Sources used for the section on the Volkswagen and the Corvair are *Small Wonder: The Amazing*

Story of Volkswagen by Walter Henry Nelson, *Unsafe at Any Speed* by Ralph Nader, and author interviews with David E. Davis, Don Frey, and several General Motors executives.

CHAPTER FORTY-THREE

1125 BUT $64,000 GETS INTO THE REALM: Anderson, *Television Fraud: The History and the Implications of the Quiz Show Scandals,* p. 6.

1126 SHE DID NOT HESITATE TO MAKE: Author interview with Geoff Cowan.

1127 IT PROVED EVERY AMERICAN HAD: Author interview with Geoff Cowan.

1127 NOBODY LEAVES THIS ROOM: Barnouw, *The History of Broadcasting: The Image Empire,* p. 56.

1127 WE'RE ALL PRETTY MUCH ALIKE: Anderson, p. 39.

1128 ANY BETS ON HOW LONG: Friendly, *Due to Circumstances Beyond Our Control,* p. 77.

1129 A NEW TELEVISION PROGRAM SPONSORED: Barnouw, p. 58.

1130 THE CONSERVATISM OF A FATHER: Anderson, p. 9.

1130 LET YOUR MODERATION BE KNOWN: Anderson, p. 9.

1131 IF YOU'RE SYMBOLIC OF THE MARINE CORPS: Anderson, p. 20.

1132 IT HELPED. IT HELPED: *Hearings of the Subcommittee of the Committee on Interstate and Foreign Commerce, Eighty-sixth Congress, II,* Vol. 51, p. 811.

1133 WE WROTE THE QUESTIONS INTO: Author interview with Russell Baker.

1133 LATER HE TOLD JOE STONE: Stone and Yohn, *Prime Time and Misdemeanors,* pp. 206–7.

1135 DO WHATEVER YOU HAVE TO DO: Author interview with Dan Enright.

1135 YOU CANNOT ASK RANDOM QUESTIONS: Stone and Yohn, p. 119.

1136 THUS HE WAS ABLE TO RATIONALIZE: Author interview with Enright.

1137 THE WALKING ENCYCLOPEDIA: Author interview with Herb Stempel.

1138 IF YOU SAW HIM: Author interview with Enright.

1138 ENRIGHT MADE STEMPEL GET: Author interview with Enright.

1139 STEMPEL WAS EVEN TOLD TO WEAR: *Hearings,* p. 26.

1139 YOU'RE NOT PAYING ATTENTION: *Hearings,* p. 29.

1139 IT WAS A CRUEL THING TO DO: Author interview with Enright.

1140 I THINK I'VE GOT THE RIGHT: Author interview with Enright.

1142 YOU CAN BE ERUDITE AND LEARNED: Author interview with Al Freedman.

1143 IT TOOK HIS BREATH AWAY: Author interview with Dick Goodman.

1144 CHARLIE, DID YOU KNOW THAT: Author interview with Al Freedman.

1145 NOT MUCH OF A BUSINESSMAN: Van Doren, *The Autobiography of Mark Van Doren,* p. 16.

1146 THE DIFFICULT ATTAINABLE THROUGH: Van Doren, p. 275.

1146 THE SUN WOULD GO DOWN JUST AS: Author interview with Alfred Kazin.

1146 VALUES YOUR LETTERS IF ONLY: Hendrick, *The Selected Letters of Mark Van Doren,* p. 136.

1147 REALLY, CHA, I'M NOT: Hendrick, p. 136.

1149 I FELT HERE WAS A GUY: "Meeting of Minds," *Time,* September 15, 1958.

1152 I FELT LIKE A BULLFIGHTER: Author interview with Dick Goodwin.

1153 'CAUSE WHEN I GO ON: "Meeting of Minds," *Time.*

1154 HE WAS NOT NEARLY AS BOTHERED: Author interview with Enright.

1155 DAN, I HOPE THIS TEACHES YOU: Author interview with Enright.

1156 DAN, HAVE I EVER ASKED YOU: Author interview with Enright.

1159 DICK, SOME DAY I HOPE: Author interview with Goodwin.

1161 A QUIZ SHOW INVESTIGATION WITHOUT: Author interview with Goodwin.

1164 THE DINNER WAS SUPERB: Goodwin, *Remembering America,* pp. 57–58.

1165 IF I WANTED TO DESTROY: Stone and Yohn, p. 251.

1168 OF THE IMPORTANT PLAYERS STILL: Author interview with Julian Krainan.

CHAPTER FORTY-FOUR

1171 NATURAL-BORN ROTARIAN: Author interview with Harry Ashmore.

1172 AT THE HEART OF THEIR: Author interview with Ashmore.

1173 TO FIND OUT WHY: Author interview with Ashmore.

1173 IN FACT, JUST ABOUT: Huckaby, *Crisis at Central High: Little Rock 1957–1958,* p. ix.

1174 NOBODY URGED ME TO GO: Blossom, *It Happened Here,* p. 82.

1175 YOU MAY DESERVE ORVAL FAUBUS: Ashmore, *Hearts and Minds: The Anatomy of Racism from Roosevelt to Reagan,* p. 253.

1175 GOVERNOR, JUST WHAT *ARE* YOU GOING: Blossom, p. 53.

1176 IF THE SOUTHERN STATES ARE PICKED: Blossom, p. 30.

1177 WHY DON'T YOU TELEPHONE HIM: Blossom, p. 54.

1178 HIS FATHER, SAM FAUBUS, SAID: Ashmore, p. 261.

1178 HE WAS, ASHMORE LIKED TO SAY: Author interview with Ashmore.

1178 LATER AFTER LITTLE ROCK HAD: Ashmore, p. 253.

1179 FAUBUS NEVER EVEN SAW A BLACK: Ashmore, p. 260.

1179 IT WAS HARD TO FIND WHITE: Blossom, pp. 50–51.

1180 I BROUGHT ORVAL DOWN FROM: Ashmore, p. 255.

1180 IN 1954 FAUBUS RAN FOR GOVERNOR: Faubus, *Down from the Hills,* p. 16.

1181 I'M SORRY, BUT I'M ALREADY: Ashmore, p. 259.

1182 KEEP THE NIGGERS OUT: Blossom, p. 84.

1185 HE WAS TERRIBLY FRIGHTENED FOR HER: Author interview with John Chancellor.

1188 YOU CAN DO WHAT YOU WANT: Author interview with Chancellor.

1189 A LOVELY MOZARTIAN UNITY: Author interview with Chancellor.

1190 A NATIONAL EVENING SEANCE: Author interview with Daniel Schorr.

1190 WITH TELEVISION EVERY BIT OF ACTION: Author interview with Chancellor.

1191 CAN YOU BELIEVE THIS: Author interview with Chancellor.

1194 LIPMAN ALWAYS HAD TO WHISPER: Author interview with Chancellor.

1194 WESTFELDT COULD SEE THEM CURSING: Author interview with Wallace Westfeldt.

1195 AT FIRST HE WOULD PANIC: Author interview with Chancellor.

1196 SHERIFF, THERE'S SOME SON: Author interview with Chancellor.

1197 A BAPTIST PREACHER BUT NEVER: Author interview with Will Campbell.

1199 THIS IS A SIN: Author interview with Campbell.

1200 I'M AN OLD MAN: Ashmore, p. 258.

1200 I'LL GIVE IT TO YOU IN ONE: Bates, *Long Shadow of Little Rock,* p. 93.

1201 BUT REMEMBER ORVAL: Author interview with Ashmore.

1202 IN FACT, THE STATE ATTORNEY GENERAL: Author interview with Herbert Brownell.

1203 THE MAN TO WHOM EISENHOWER: Sulzberger, *A Long Row of Candles: Memoirs and Diaries,* p. 649.

1204 THE ATTORNEY GENERAL WARNED THE PRESIDENT: Author interview with Brownell.

1204 HERB, CAN'T YOU GO DOWN THERE: Faubus, p. 257.

1205 I GOT THE IMPRESSION THAT: Faubus, p. 255.

1205 JUST BECAUSE I SAID IT: Ashmore, p. 269.

1205 WELL, YOU WERE RIGHT, HERB: Author interview with Brownell.

1206 A WEAK PRESIDENT WHO FIDDLED: McLellan and Acheson, *Among Friends: The Personal Letters of Dean Acheson,* p. 132.

1207 FOR THE FIRST TIME IN MY LIFE: Bates, p. 104.

1208 ALL SHE HAD DONE: Huckaby, p. 77.

1216 NL, THE TRADITIONAL NEWSPAPER ABBREVIATION: Author interview with Reggie Smith.

1218 THIS IS AN INDOOR SPORT AND TABOOS: Gunther, *Inside America,* p. 285.

1218 OF COURSE I'M GOING TO WORK: Russell, *Go Up for Glory,* p. 17.

1220 AT THE END OF THE '55: Author interview with Bob Cousy and Bill Walton.

1221 $6000 WAS GOING TO BE HELD OUT: Stout, "Scientist in Sneakers," *Boston* magazine, February 1989.

1221 WE'LL COUNT REBOUNDS AS BASKETS: Russell, p. 123.

1222 THERE HAD NEVER BEEN ANYTHING: Author interview with Cousy.

1224 JUST ANOTHER BLACK BOY: Russell, p. 37.

1225 *THIS,* THE INTENSITY OF HIS PLAY: Author interview with Cousy.

CHAPTER FORTY-FIVE

1228 I FELT AS THOUGH I WERE: Lyon, *Eisenhower: Portrait of a Hero,* pp. 756–57.

1228 I CAN'T UNDERSTAND THE UNITED: Ambrose, *Nixon,* p. 434.

1230 JUST WHAT DO YOU THINK: Beschloss, *Mayday,* p. 113.

1230 UNEASY, IRASCIBLE, CROTCHETY: Sulzberger, *The Last of the Giants,* p. 103.

1230 HE WAS SURROUNDED BY POLITICIANS: Sulzberger, *Giants,* p. 102.

1230 I DON'T KNOW WHY ANYONE: Ambrose, p. 596.

1232 YOU ALL WENT TO GREAT SCHOOLS: Beschloss, *The Crisis Years: Kennedy and Khruschev, 1960–1963,* p. 34.

1232 THE HEIGHT OF THE TAIL FIN: Beschloss, *Crisis,* p. 149.

1234 SUCH A PERSON, TRUSTED BY: Beschloss, *Mayday,* p. 94.

1234 TO HIS MIND, *THE NEW YORK TIMES*: Beschloss, *Mayday,* p. 2.

1235 ROSCOE, THAT'S THE FELLOW: Sulzberger, *A Long Row of Candles: Memoirs and Diaries,* p. 922.

1235 I CAN'T STAND THAT GANGSTER: Sulzberger, *Giants,* p. 579.

1236 ONE PRAYS—HOW ODD IT: Beschloss, *Mayday,* p. 153.

1237 WE HAVEN'T MADE A CHIP: Beschloss, *Mayday,* p. 7.

1238 YOU BEGIN TO SEE THIS THING: Ambrose, p. 516.

1238 LOOK, I'D LIKE TO KNOW WHAT'S: Ambrose, p. 433.

1238 EVEN WHEN HE DID INCREASE: Ambrose, p. 433.

1238 GOD HELP THE NATION WHEN: Beschloss, *Mayday,* p. 209.

1239 WHEN HE HEARD THE NEWS: Beschloss, *Mayday,* p. 7.

1241 POWERS WAS A MAN, WHO: Beschloss, *Mayday,* p. 350.

1242 I CAN SHOW HIM THE EVIDENCE: Ambrose, p. 536.

1243 HE WAS NOT AFRAID TO SAY: Beschloss, *Mayday,* p. 209.

1243 I'LL BRING ALONG THE WHOLE: Beschloss, *Mayday,* p. 213.

1243 THE BLACK LADY OF ESPIONAGE: Powers, *Operation Overflight,* p. 67.

1244 AS MICHAEL BESCHLOSS NOTED, KNOWING: Beschloss, *Mayday,* p. 234.

1244 IF ONE OF THESE AIRCRAFT: Beschloss, *Mayday,* p. 233.

1245 YOU MAY AS WELL TELL THEM: Powers, p. 71.

1246 INJECTING YOURSELF WITH THE SUBSTANCE: Powers, p. 69.

1247 THAT THEY WOULD *NEVER* CAPTURE: Beschloss, *Mayday,* p. 8.

1248 THERE IS NOT A CHANCE OF HIS: Beschloss, *Mayday,* p. 37.

1248 PERHAPS KHRUSHCHEV, HE THOUGHT, MIGHT: Powers, p. x.

1248 YEARS LATER, CHIP BOHLEN, ONE: Beschloss, *Mayday,* p. 239.

1248 THE WHOLE WORLD KNOWS THAT ALLEN: Beschloss, *Mayday,* pp. 59–60.

1250 I AM NOT GOING TO SHIFT: Beschloss, *Mayday,* p. 271.

1251 I'M GOING TO TAKE UP SMOKING: Beschloss, *Mayday,* p. 284.

1251 I HAD LONGED TO GIVE THE UNITED STATES: Beschloss, *Mayday,* p. 388.

CHAPTER FORTY-SIX

1254 SUPERMAN WOULD PRETEND TO HAVE SEX: Dorschner and Fabricio, *The Winds of December,* p. 21.

1255 RESEMBLED THE ORGANIZATION OF A LARGE: Dorschner and Fabricio, p. 65.

1256 SINCE BATISTA WAS THE SON OF A CANE: Dorschner and Fabricio, p. 63.

1256 HE LOVED TO EAT: Dorschner and Fabricio, p. 65.

1256 A MAN LIKE THAT HAS ENEMIES: Dorschner and Fabricio, p. 67.

1257 SMITH LIKED TO SAY THAT HE: Dorschner and Fabricio, pp. 48–49.

1258 I HAVE LIVED TWO ERAS: Dorschner and Fabricio, pp. 48–49.

1259 BATISTA WAS BAD MEDICINE: Smith, *The Closest of Enemies,* p. 36.

1260 IRONICALLY, IN CONTRAST TO BATISTA: Szulc, *Fidel: A Critical Portrait,* p. 105.

1260 HISTORY WILL ABSOLVE ME: Szulc, p. 297.

1261 ARE WE ALREADY IN THE SIERRA: Dorschner and Fabricio, p. 34.

1262 THE PERSONALITY OF THE MAN: Szulc, p. 413.

1265 THE BATISTA REGIME AT THE END: Smith, p. 38.

1266 WHAT CAN I DO: Dorschner and Fabricio, p. 461.

1266 THE AMERICANS WERE, WROTE WAYNE SMITH: Smith, p. 36.

1266 LIKE MOSES PARTING THE RED SEA: Dorschner and Fabricio, p. 492.

1267 FOR HE SEEMED TO HAVE: Smith, pp. 15–16.

1268 WE BELIEVE THAT CASTRO: Johnson, *The Bay of Pigs*, p. 25.

1269 CASTRO IS EITHER INCREDIBLY NAIVE: Wyden, *Bay of Pigs*, pp. 28–29.

1270 AT THE FIRST STOP WHEN BAKER: Author interview with Russell Baker.

1270 BECAUSE I KNOW WHO I AM: Halberstam, *The Best and the Brightest*, p. 98.

1270 I'M SORRY ABOUT THAT EPISODE: Ambrose, *Nixon: The Education of a Politician 1913–1962*, p. 220.

1271 THIS IS THE ACHESON LINE: Ambrose, p. 520.

1272 IT STINKS LIKE FRESH HORSE: Ambrose, pp. 522–23.

1272 YOU DO ALL THE TALKING: Ambrose, p. 524.

1274 WAYNE SMITH, A MAN NOT: Smith, p. 49.

1275 FIDEL HAS ALL ALONG FELT HIMSELF TO BE: Smith, p. 49.

1276 HE COULD NOT BE A MAJOR: Author interview with Earl Mazo.

1276 CUBA. CUBA. AND CUBA: Wyden, pp. 21–22.

1276 WELCOME ABOARD CHICO: Wyden, pp. 21–22.

1277 THERE WAS ONE CIA AGENT: Wyden, p. 31.

1278 IT WAS CLEAR, CUSHMAN THOUGHT: Wyden, p. 29.

1278 HELMS, AS PETER WYDEN NOTED IN: Wyden, p. 48.

1279 THE PLAN CALLED FOR TRAINING: Wyden, p. 25.

1280 I'M GOING ALONG WITH YOU: Wyden, p. 68.

1282 ISN'T HE MARVELOUS: Author interview with Mazo.

1282 MR. NIXON HASN'T MENTIONED CUBA: Kennedy, *Speeches of John F. Kennedy: Presidential Campaign of 1960,* p. 607.

1284 THE VICE-PRESIDENT SOMETIMES SEEMS: Ambrose, p. 601.

1288 EVEN HANNAH NIXON CALLED ROSE: Ambrose, p. 575.

1289 UNFORTUNATELY, ANYONE WHO UNDERSTOOD: Author interviews with James Bassett, Ted Rogers, Bill Wilson, Pierre Salinger, Don Hewitt, and Leonard Hall.

1289 DO YOU GET A FUNNY SORT OF SENSE: McLellan and Acheson, *Among Friends: The Personal Letters of Dean Acheson,* p. 193.

Index

Aaron, Henry, 1216
Abbott, Robert S.,
    771–75
ABC, 316, 1103
Abernathy, Ralph, 948,
    967, 968–69, 979
Ace, Goodman, 324
Acheson, Dean, 672, 676,
    684, 688, 1235–36,
    1271
  on anti-Communists,
    96, 100–101
  background of, 14–16
  Guatemalan policy and,
    656, 657
  Hiss affair and, 16–17,
    22, 27–29
  Korean War and, 106,
    113, 120, 183–84
  on Little Rock
    desegregation
    efforts, 1206
  on loss of China,
    113–14
  MacArthur and, 146,
    190, 199–200
  McCarthy and, 91, 92
  Mossadegh's meeting
    with, 630–31
  on Nixon-Kennedy
    debate, 1289–90
  nuclear weapons policy
    and, 61, 75–76,
    78–79
  Oppenheimer's briefing
    of, 58–59
  Truman's relationship
    with, 32–33, 36,
    37–38
Adams, Sherman, 362, 416,
    535, 565, 1092,
    1211–12
Adams, Tom, 855, 858
Adler, Julius Ochs, 664–65
Adler, Mortimer, 1166
Adler, Stella, 468, 470
Adventures of Ozzie and
    Harriet, The, 890–94
advertising, 344, 388–94,
    867–83, 1129–32
  by Chevrolet, 1102–10
  consumerism and,
    882–86
  political, 388–89, 390
  television spot, 390,
    392–93
  tobacco industry and,
    878–82
Advertising Age, 1100, 1102
Agate, Betty, 295–96
Agate, Sandy, 295–96
Agee, James, 932

Agriculture Department, U.S., 296
Ailes, Roger, 542
Air Force, U.S., 39, 63, 123, 124, 569, 590, 1078–79, 1236, 1238
Alabama Journal, 972
Aldrich, Winthrop, 883
Alfhem, 659, 663
alienation, 848, 923–24, 927
Allen, Fred, 312–23, 347
Allen, George, 406–7
Allen, Lee, 327
Allen, Steve, 834–35
All My Sons (Miller), 455
Almond, Ned, 180, 181–82, 186–87
Alsop, John, 408
Alsop, Joseph, 50, 65, 409, 575, 626, 1233–34, 1235, 1237, 1282
Alsop, Stewart, 50, 65, 408, 575
Alvarez, Luis, 603
Amaya, Naohiro, 204
Ambrose, Stephen, 433, 542–43
American Century, 204, 357
American Civil Liberties Union, 574, 973
American Dilemma, An (Myrdal), 716
American Heritage Foundation, 812
American Mercury, 136
American Restaurant, 277
Anderson, Edgar, 479, 488–89

Anderson, Kent, 1130
Angeli, Pier, 844–45
Annie Get Your Gun, 812
anti-Semitism, 151, 163, 380, 503, 517, 683
Appleton (Wis.) *Post Crescent,* 90–91
Appointment on the Moon (Lewis), 1061–62
Arabs, Oil, and History (Roosevelt), 626
Arbenz Guzmán, Jacobo, 640, 641, 648, 649, 654–59, 661, 662, 663, 666–69, 670, 1276
Ardrey, Robert, 462
Arevalo Bermejo, Juan Jose, 653
"Arguing the Case for Being Panicky," 1094
Arkansas Democrat, 1171, 1200
Arkansas Gazette, 1171, 1179, 1193, 1200, 1211
Arkus-Duntov, Zora, 851
Arlen, Michael, 406
Armstrong, Park, 670
Army, U.S., 39, 1089
Army-McCarthy hearings, 93, 437–39, 568
Arnaz, Desi, 338–47
Arnaz, Desi, Jr., 346, 347, 888
Arneson, R. Gordon, 37, 75
Arno, Peter, 482–83

Arnold, Henry, 72, 77
Arthur Godfrey Show, The,
    337–38
Arvey, Jake, 378, 380,
    382–84, 385
Ascoli, Max, 327
Ashmore, Harry, 1171,
    1178, 1180, 1191,
    1199–1200, 1201,
    1211
Asphalt Jungle, The, 990
Associated Press, 84, 94,
    365, 376, 439, 976,
    1008, 1187
Atkins, Chet, 807
Atlantic, 407
Atlee, Clement, 373
atomic bomb, 49, 58, 107,
    570, 571, 1239
    Korean War and, 189,
        196
    Soviet Union and,
        38–45
    Trinity and, 46–47, 56
    U.S. monopoly of,
        38–41, 42–43, 44
Atomic Energy
    Commission (AEC),
        41, 60, 64, 66, 67,
        73, 76, 78, 79, 170,
        573
    Oppenheimer's ouster
        and, 577–78,
        592–94, 599, 603–4
Atwood, Bill, 380
Atwood, Wallace, 504–5
Aubrey, Jim, 345
Auerbach, Arnold "Red,"
    1218, 1220, 1221–23

Avedon, Richard, 877, 984
Ayers, Clarence, 926
Aykroyd, Dan, 897–98
Ayres, Harold, 123
Ayres, W. E., 780
Azbell, Joe, 975

Bagley, S. P., 271–72
Bainbridge, Kenneth,
    46–47
Baird, Gil, 872
Baker, Bob, 1195
Baker, Carlos, 1020–21
Baker, Newton, 138
Baker, Russell, 1269–70,
    1288
Baldwin, Hanson, 1244,
    1252
Baldwin, James, 961–62
Ball, George, 382, 400
Ball, Lucille, 338–47, 888
Bancroft, Mary, 1239
Bankhead, Tallulah, 463
Banks, Ernie, 1216
Barkley, Alben, 386
Barnard, Allan, 1007–8
Barnouw, Erik, 319, 320
Barquin, Ramon, 1265–66
Barry, Jack, 1139, 1147,
    1150, 1156
Barton, Bruce, 419
Baruch, Bernard, 679, 682
Barzun, Jacques, 1146
Bassett, Jim, 563, 565–66
Bates, Charley, 575–76
Bates, Daisy, 1175, 1182,
    1207, 1209, 1211
Bates, Ted, 392, 395–96,
    876

Batista, Fulgencio, 652, 1253–65
Battle of Angels (Williams), 452
Bayley, Stephen, 215
Bay of Pigs operation, 641, 645, 1278–81
Beat Generation, 512–34
Beat the Jackpot, 1132
Beilenson, Murray, 263, 264
Bell, Daniel, 935
Benny, Jack, 315, 348–49
Benton, Barbie, 1004
Benton, William, 876
Beria, Lavrenti Pavlovich, 81, 82
Berkner, Lloyd, 1091–92
Berle, Milton, 320–25, 339, 348, 416, 833
Berlin, Isaiah, 409, 1236
Bernays, Edward, 660–61
Bernstein, Leonard, 793–94
Berry, Chuck, 822, 824, 1215
Berryman, John, 1146
Beschloss, Michael, 1077, 1244
Bethe, Hans, 62, 79, 153–55, 156, 158, 169, 170
Better Homes and Gardens, 1033
Bidault, Georges, 710
Bigart, Homer, 1195
Big Board, The, 1132
Bigeard, Marcel, 696
Big Kill, The (Spillane), 103
Big Moment, The, 1132
Binford, Lloyd, 801, 812
Bird, Robert S., 1195

birth control movement:
  Comstock laws and, 498
  McCormick and, 498–500
  Pill and, 1046, 1051, 1053–55
  Planned Parenthood and, 497, 508, 1047, 1052, 1057, 1059
  see also Pincus, Gregory Goodwin "Goody"; Sanger, Margaret
Bissell, Richard, 1079, 1240, 1244, 1245, 1277, 1278, 1280
Bitter Fruit (Schlesinger and Kinzer), 651
Black, Bill, 797
Black, Hugo, 712, 713, 714, 715, 727
blacks:
  Levittown discrimination against, 247
  migration of, 769–75
  music and, 807–11, 1215
  see also civil rights movement
Blake, J. F., 940–41, 945
Block, Felix, 159
Blossom, Virgil, 1170–72, 1173, 1175–76, 1177–78, 1179, 1180, 1181
"Blue Moon of Kentucky," 798

Bohlen, Charles E. "Chip,"
   26, 146, 438, 1248
Bohr, Niels, 152
Bonanza, 1103
Bonesteel, Charles, 107
Bonsal, Phillip, 1273
Booth, Stanley, 800, 813
Borden, William, 572, 591,
   592
Bowes, Major Edward,
   314
Bowles, Jerry, 831
Boyle, Hal, 1008, 1020
Bradbury, Norris, 169
Bradley, Mame, 748–49,
   757–58, 766
Bradley, Omar, 74, 76, 78,
   114, 115, 119, 120,
   139, 148, 197, 436,
   686–87
   on MacArthur, 350
   on Ridgway, 196
Brando, Marlon, 443, 445,
   463–71, 794, 806,
   836, 838, 840, 842,
   845, 847, 848, 1148
   background of, 465–69
   career of, 441–42,
   468–70
   Dean's admiration of,
   837–38
   style of, 469–70
Breech, Ernie, 1115
Breen, Joseph, 443
Bricker, John, 97, 435
Bridges, Styles, 8, 9, 116,
   1232
Brinkley, David, 1191–92
brinksmanship, 710

Brockway, George, 1039,
   1043
Brothers, Joyce, 1134
Brown, Edmund G. "Pat,"
   723
Brown, Henry Billings, 719
Brown, Jim, 1217–18
Brown, John Mason, 610
Brown, Minniejean, 1207,
   1209
Brown, Oliver, 716
Brown, Walter, 1221
Brownell, Herbert, 9, 368,
   1202, 1204–5
Brown v. *Board of
   Education,* 716, 725,
   734–35, 743, 745–49,
   758–59, 793, 947,
   949, 1169, 1174,
   1176, 1202
Brown v. *Board of
   Education II,* 734,
   1170
Bruce, David, 656
Brundage, Percival, 1093
Bryant, Carolyn, 750, 751
Bryant, Roy, 750–58, 763,
   765, 766, 767
Buckley, Oliver, 73
Bunche, Ralph, 717, 1203
Burnett, Leo, 879–81, 1101
Burroughs, William,
   515–16, 518–19
Burton, Harold, 713–14,
   733
Butler, Hugh, 15, 97
Buttenweiser, Helen, 25
Byrnes, James F., 379, 733
Bystrom, Art, 94

Cadaret, Bob, 863
Cadogan, Alexander, 677
Caldwell, Erskine, 1012
Calhern, Louis, 990
Call, The, 493
Campbell, Will, 1196–99
Cannon, Poppy, 865
Capote, Truman, 469, 519
Car and Driver, 1123–24
Carnation company, 278
Carnegie, Mrs. Dale, 1033
Carr, Lucien, 513–15, 516,
    519
Carter, John Franklin, 353
Cartier-Bresson, Henri, 984
Cash, Johnny, 820
Cassady, Neal, 522, 523,
    525–28
Castillo Armas, Carlos
    Enrique, 650, 666,
    668
Castro, Fidel, 922, 936,
    1253, 1258–81
    Bay of Pigs and,
        1280–81
    guerrilla campaign of,
        1263–64
    myth of, 1259–60
    New York Times and,
        1261–63
    U.S. visits of, 1268,
        1274–75
Catholic Church, 490–91,
    497–98, 1049–50,
    1056
Catledge, Turner, 357, 662,
    760
Caute, David, 11–12

CBS, 339–40, 342–43, 344,
    345–46, 364, 407,
    415, 637, 673, 736,
    738, 826–27, 829,
    830, 888, 1103,
    1127, 1131, 1210,
    1286–87
Central Intelligence Agency
    (CIA), 669, 1267–68
    anti-Castro operation
        and, 1276–77
    Guatemala coup and,
        640–67, 1253
    Iran coup and, 621,
        623–38
    U-2 and, 1078–82,
        1085, 1240–49
Chamberlain, Wilt, 1219
Chambers, Whittaker,
    13–25
Chambrun, Jacques,
    1018–19
Champion, Albert, 853–54
Chancellor, John, 1185–99,
    1206, 1210
Chandler, Harry, 726
Chang, M. C., 504, 506,
    509, 510–11, 1046,
    1052, 1053, 1058
Chase, Hal, 518, 526
Chatham, Gerald, 766
Checkers speech, 416, 547,
    563, 1289
Cheever, John, 1007
Chiang Kai-shek, 14, 96,
    98, 112, 114,
    115–16, 120, 147,
    149, 175, 198, 201

Chicago Daily News, 377, 385, 773

Chicago Defender, 771–74

Chicago Tribune, 4, 6, 11, 83, 90, 93, 370–72, 373, 540

Chiles, Jack, 181–82

Chiles, Morris, III, 586

China, Nationalist, 14, 15, 90, 98, 100, 114
   see also Chiang Kai-shek

China, People's Republic of, 44, 113, 146, 175–86, 197, 537, 689, 691, 709, 711

China Lobby, 116

Chotiner, Murray, 416

Christy, Robert, 611

Chrome Colossus (Cray), 849

Churchill, Winston, 36, 39, 49, 402, 634, 637, 675, 703, 706, 1063

City Lights Bookstore, 530, 532–33

civil rights movement, 36, 100, 327, 715, 730–32, 941, 974, 982
   black migration and, 769–75
   mechanical cotton picker and, 776–81
   national media and, 748, 758–62, 767, 972, 1188–96
   Till case and, 748–68, 769, 788, 979, 1187
   white resistance to, 745–49, 949–50, 969–70
   see also Brown v. *Board of Education*; Little Rock integration crisis; Montgomery bus boycott; *specific leaders*

Clark, Jim, 1214

Clark, Tom, 714, 721, 729–30

Clement, Frank, 422

Clements, Earle, 703

Cleveland, Harlan, 401–2

Cleveland Press, 853

Clift, Montgomery, 463, 842, 846

Cline, Ray, 1086

Clurman, Richard M., 793

Coca, Imogene, 834

Cockcroft, John, 77

Coffey, Thomas, 616

Cogny, René, 695–96

Cold War, 46, 165, 536, 623–24, 638, 660, 676, 711, 922–23, 936, 1237, 1243
   computer technology and, 167
   covert operations and, 642
   Hiss affair and, 23
   Korean War and, 147
   see also Soviet Union

Cole, David, 859, 862
Cole, Dolly, 861
Cole, Ed, 857–64, 1103,
    1110, 1119–23
Cole, Nat King, 819
Colliers, 503, 829
Collins, James, 277
Collins, J. Lawton, 44,
    119–20, 145, 186,
    195
"Coming Ice Age, The"
    (Friedan), 1039
Commerce Department,
    U.S., 740
"Committee of One
    Hundred," 495
Communism, see
    McCarthyism,
    McCarthy era;
    specific countries and
    conflicts
Communist party, U.S., 8,
    16, 55, 68, 83, 86,
    462
Compton, Arthur, 48–49
computers, 160, 776
    H-bomb and, 160
    von Neumann and,
        160–68
Comstock, Anthony, 494,
    495
Conant, James, 47, 59, 62,
    67–68, 73–74, 169,
    570, 590, 604
Condon, Edward, 54
Cone, Fairfax, 392
Congress, U.S., 7, 10, 12,
    15, 37, 38, 75, 90,
    327, 541, 579, 659,
    714, 720–21
    Comstock law and, 494,
        498
    covert operations and,
        642
    MacArthur's address
        to, 200–201
    Oppenheimer's
        testimony to, 42
    Rhee and, 110
    UMT and, 45
    Van Doren and, 1163
Connally, Tom, 27, 42
Conner, Fox, 432
Connor, Eugene "Bull,"
    1214
consumerism, 882
Cooke, Alistair, 11, 18,
    22–23
Cooke, Sam, 1215
Corcoran, Thomas G., 648
Corso, Gregory, 525
Costello, Frank, 332–33
cotton picker, mechanical,
    776–81
Courts, Gus, 746–47
Cousy, Bob, 1220,
    1222–23, 1224–25
Cowan, Lou, 402–3,
    1125–28, 1131
Cowley, Malcolm, 105,
    523–24, 529–30, 533
Crabgrass Frontier
    (Jackson), 235
Craft of Intelligence, The
    (Dulles), 645
Crawford, James, 579

Cray, Edward, 849
Crime in America
(Kefauver and
Shalett), 334
Cronkite, Walter, 676,
869
Crosby, John, 403, 829
Crucial Decade, The
(Goldman), 22
Crudup, Arthur, 797–98
Crump, Ed, 327–28, 780,
801
Cuba, 922, 936, 937,
1253–81, 1282–83
Cumberford, Robert,
220–21, 222–23
Curtice, Harlow, 216, 218,
225–28, 852–53, 855,
863, 1111, 1120,
1121
Cushman, Robert, 1271,
1279
Cutler, Robert, 1233–34

Daily Express (London),
1097
Daily Herald (London),
1097
Daily Mail (London),
1097
Daley, Richard J., 1288
Damone, Vic, 845
Dann, Mike, 342
Davis, Bob, 428
Davis, John W., 387, 679,
730
Davis, Kenneth, 102, 104,
1012

Davis, Miles, 522
"Day Camp in the
Driveways"
(Friedan), 1038
Dean, James, 469, 794,
806, 837–48
Dean, William, 121, 122,
124–25
deCastries, Christian Marie
Ferdinand de la
Croix, 698
de Chevigne, Pierre, 698
Defense Department, U.S.,
110, 178, 190, 625,
1077, 1083, 1098,
1237
de Gaulle, Charles, 691,
1250–51
DeLorean, John, 227
De Lorenzo, Tony, 226
DeMille, Cecil B., 217
Democratic party, U.S., 7,
89, 98, 386, 387,
562, 676, 701, 923,
1229
Kefauver hearings and,
330, 335
1952 election and, 378,
620
Southern wing of, 720
World War II and, 1–3,
11–12
Denver Post, 84
Depression, Great, 1, 2, 3,
55, 206, 210, 233,
271, 922, 1026
Derounian, Steve, 1162
Desmond, Frank, 84

Dewey, Thomas E., 2, 5–11, 353, 358–59, 360, 362, 363, 365, 366, 367, 375, 377, 394, 415, 536, 552, 673
Diaz, Carlos Enrique, 668
Dichter, Ernest, 884
Diddley, Bo, 798, 830–31
Diem, Ngo Dinh, 708, 711
Dien Bien Phu, battle of, 688, 693–701, 704, 707, 708–9
Dietch, Bob, 1111
Dietrich, Marlene, 828
Diggs, Charles, 764–65
Dillinger, John, 579, 584
DiMaggio, Joe, 992–94
Dirksen, Everett, 96, 366, 377, 1230–31
discount stores, 251–52, 255, 265
    see also E. J. Korvettes
Dodds, Harold, 484
Dodge, Mabel, 492
Dogan, Harry, 767, 788
Doherty, John, 669
Domino, Fats, 905, 1215
domino theory, 704
Donner, Frederic, 1111–13
Donovan, James, 1241
Donovan, William J., 626
"Don't Be Cruel," 833
Dornberger, Walter, 1066, 1067, 1069
Dorschner, John, 1255
Doud, John, 430
Douglas, Helen Gahagan, 96, 367, 540, 554, 562, 1270–71

Douglas, Paul, 92, 335, 379–80, 383
Douglas, William O., 712, 713, 714, 727
Doyle, James, 145
DuBridge, Lee, 73, 74, 590
Duffy, Ben, 388, 419, 873–74
Dulles, Allen, 621, 622, 625–26, 634, 637, 642, 643–50, 659, 664, 665, 667, 670, 671, 680, 683, 1082–83, 1085, 1086, 1239, 1240, 1244, 1245, 1247, 1249, 1250, 1280
Dulles, Eleanor, 645, 680, 681
Dulles, John Foster, 17, 22, 96, 366, 438, 621, 622, 624, 625, 631, 639, 640, 642, 644–46, 648, 650, 665, 669–70, 674, 721, 1085–86, 1094, 1251
    background and personality of, 678–82
    brinksmanship and, 710
    Eisenhower contrasted with, 674–76
    Indochina conflict and, 700–711
    massive retaliation and, 685–86
    1952 election and, 676–77

Republicans and,
672–73
Durant, William C., 212
Durr, Clifford, 943, 946
Durr, Virginia, 943–44
Dykstra, Lillian, 7

Earl, Harley, 215–24,
226–27, 862, 863
Eastland, James, 1176
East of Eden (film), 838,
844, 845, 847
East of Eden (Steinbeck),
842
Eberhart, Richard, 534
Eckert, Pres, 161, 162, 166
Eckford, Elizabeth,
1182–85, 1196
Eckstine, Billy, 819
Eden, Anthony, 630, 677,
706
*Edible Wild Plants of North
America* (Kinsey),
478
EDVAC (Electronic
Discrete Variable
Arithmetic
Calculator), 162
Edwards, Willard, 83, 93
Eggs of Mammals, The
(Pincus), 504
Einstein, Albert, 82, 152
Eisenhower, David,
426–27, 428, 934
Eisenhower, Dwight D., 2,
44–45, 56, 65, 114,
115, 136, 148, 159,
207, 227, 319–20,
346, 394, 410, 513,
535, 538, 542, 569,
588, 601, 617, 639,
641–42, 684, 685,
687, 688, 709, 721,
728, 739, 1059,
1061, 1089, 1092–93,
1099, 1257, 1267,
1268, 1273, 1278,
1284, 1288
background of, 422–34
Bay of Pigs and,
1278–80
career of, 430–34
civil rights and, 730,
736–38, 741–42
domino theory of,
703–4
Dulles contrasted with,
674–76
farewell address of,
1076
Guatemala coup and,
647–50, 659, 667,
669
health of, 1229–30
Indochina conflict and,
700, 701, 704
Iran coup and, 621,
622, 634, 636, 638
Khrushchev's visit and,
1241–43
Little Rock integration
crisis and, 1201–5
MacArthur and, 139,
140, 351–52, 359
McCarthy and, 434–38
media and, 1232–36
missile gap debate and,
1227–30

Eisenhower (*continued*)
  1952 election and,
    359–67, 377–78, 384,
    385
  Nixon disdained by,
    566–67
  Oppenheimer case and,
    592–93, 609
  secret fund affair and,
    413–20, 547
  Stevenson contrasted
    with, 406–8
  television image of,
    388–89, 397–400
  U-2 affair and, 1237,
    1244–51
  U-2 development and,
    1078–79, 1085–87
Eisenhower, Ida Stover,
    426, 427–28
Eisenhower, John,
    1247–48, 1250
Eisenhower, Mamie Doud,
    389, 400, 430–31,
    432–33, 567
Eisenhower, Milton,
    360–61, 398–99, 425,
    429, 433, 649
E. J. Korvettes, 255
  name of, 258
  public offering of, 268
  success of, 265–67
  see also Ferkauf,
    Eugene
election of 1952, 2–3,
    388–420, 436–37,
    538, 563, 721, 869
  Checkers speech and,
    416–21

  Democrats and, 378,
    620
  Dulles and, 676–77
  Eisenhower and,
    359–67, 377–78, 384,
    385
  isolationists and, 351,
    353, 360
  McArthur and, 351–52
  Nixon and, 365–69,
    411–21
  Republicans and,
    351–53, 365–67, 395,
    408–9, 620
  secret fund affair and,
    411–17
  Stevenson and, 378–87,
    402–21
  Taft and, 351–53,
    358–59, 361, 365–67,
    377–78, 384
  television and, 388–403
  Truman and, 362, 378,
    383–85, 386
elections, U.S.:
  of 1932, 3, 362
  of 1936, 362
  of 1939, 327
  of 1940, 5, 362, 717
  of 1944, 34, 362, 552
  of 1946, 26–27, 37–38,
    95, 97, 367, 537, 552
  of 1948, 6–11, 95,
    327–28, 358–59, 360,
    379–81, 382–83, 394,
    673
  of 1950, 95, 540, 554,
    562, 1270–71
  of 1951, 335

of 1954, 565–66,
  1180–81
of 1955, 747
of 1956, 422, 566, 708,
  869, 1170, 1269
of 1958, 1211
of 1960, 538–39, 1056,
  1269, 1273, 1278,
  1281–88
of 1968, 542, 557
Ellis, Havelock, 495
Elman, Philip, 715
Enforcer, The, 334
ENIAC (Electronic
  Numerical
  Integrator and
  Computer), 160,
  161, 162
Enright, Dan, 1134–43,
  1149–55, 1156, 1167
Ertegun, Ahmet, 823
Espy, Mike, 792
Esquire, 246, 992
Evans, Ward, 607
Evers, Medgar, 765–66

Fabricio, Roberto, 1255
Faith, Don Carlos, 187
Fall, Bernard, 696, 698
Farnham, Marynia, 1030
Fassett, John, 732
fast food:
  mechanization of,
    273–75
  quality control and, 296
  standardization of, 286,
    287
  see also McDonald's
Father Knows Best, 894, 898

Faubus, Orval, 1169–82,
  1201–5, 1207,
  1210–11, 1213
Faulkner, William, 452,
  1252
Federal Bureau of
  Investigation (FBI),
  16, 91, 156, 548,
  583, 585–86
  AEC and, 575–78
  Dillinger case and, 584
  Fuchs case and, 72
  Hiss affair and, 16–17
  Oppenheimer case and,
    589–90, 593, 595,
    604, 608, 610
Federal Trade
  Commission, 879
Fehrenbach, T. R., 121
Feminine Mystique, The
  (Friedan), 1040–41,
  1045
Ferguson Innes, J. E., 109
Ferkauf, Eugene, 251–69
  Fortune article on, 268
  success of, 264
Ferlinghetti, Lawrence,
  530, 532, 533
Fermi, Enrico, 48, 52, 73,
  74, 154, 156, 158,
  168, 604, 610
Ferris, Woodbridge, 226
Fine, Benjamin, 1173,
  1184–85, 1196
Flanders, Ralph, 93
Fleeson, Doris, 99–100
Fleming, Bob, 94
Fleming, Karl, 973, 1195
Floyd, Pretty Boy, 584

Food and Drug
    Administration,
    U.S., 1057
Ford, Henry, 203, 213–15,
    229, 230, 237, 276,
    776, 1115
Ford, Henry, II, 206–7,
    1115, 1117
Ford Motor Company,
    206, 208–9, 213,
    317, 864
Forgotten War, The (Blair),
    127
Forrestal, James, 65
Fortune, 208, 228, 242, 268,
    358, 590, 776, 865,
    866, 935, 1025
Foster, William C., 1228
Fox, Neil, 278
Fox, Stephen, 874
France, 30, 376, 620, 678,
    688, 692, 701, 710,
    770
Franchi, Sergio, 828
franchising:
    Holiday Inn and,
        308–9, 311
    McDonald's and,
        278–79, 283–84,
        287–88, 294–97
Franck, James, 54
Frank, Reuven, 1187, 1189,
    1192
Frankfurter, Felix, 16, 22,
    712, 713, 714, 715,
    721, 727, 729,
    730–31, 734, 1158,
    1161

Fred Allen Show, The,
    312–18
Freed, Alan, 809–10
Freedman, Al, 1140–44,
    1148, 1153–55, 1156,
    1159, 1167
Freedman, Emmanuel,
    663–64
Frey, Don, 219, 1122–23
Friedan, Betty, 1035–45
Friendly, Fred, 1128
Frisch, Otto, 152
Frost, Robert, 1282
Fuchs, Klaus, 68–72,
    76–80, 573, 578
Furness, Betty, 867–72

Gable, Clark, 875, 988
Gaither, Rowan, 1227,
    1228
Galbraith, John Kenneth,
    1270
Gallup, George, 10, 350,
    397
Gans, Herbert, 245, 248–49
Garfield, John, 463
Garrett, Paul, 853
Garrison, Lloyd, 605
Gavin, James, 192–93
Gayle, W. A., 969, 979
General Motors, 206–28,
    849–56, 1100, 1113,
    1119
    annual model change
        and, 222
    Chevrolet division of,
        854–57, 862–64,
        1102–10

Corvair designed by,
1119–24
Curtice and, 216,
225–28
Earl and, 215–24
innovations of, 224–25
labor and, 207
market exploited by,
210–13
Sloan and, 211–16
Gentlemen Prefer Blondes,
994–95
Gerber, Will, 328
Germany, Nazi, 38, 46, 62,
360, 364, 608, 615,
642, 678, 682–83,
928, 1061–69, 1077
Gerth, Hans, 927
Giant, 845
Giap, Vo Nguyen, 690,
694, 697, 710
Gibney, Frank, 1002–3
Gifford, Barry, 523
Ginsberg, Allen, 513–19,
527, 529, 530–34,
1146
Glass Menagerie, The
(Williams), 445, 446,
448, 453
Glazer, Nathan, 932
Gleason, Jackie, 832
Godfrey, Arthur, 338
Go (Holmes), 518, 521,
523, 528
Gold, Don, 1002
Gold, Harry, 70–71
Goldberger, Paul, 230
Goldman, Eric, 22, 28, 611

Goldstine, Herman, 162,
163–64, 166
Goldwater, Barry, 538–39
Goodkind, Howard, 1020
Goodpaster, Andrew, 1238,
1247, 1248
Goodwin, Richard N.,
1149, 1152, 1158–62,
1164
Gore, Albert, 326
Graham, Billy, 487
Graham, Phil, 329, 434
Great Britain, 4, 30, 43–44,
59, 66, 116, 147,
197, 357, 373, 376,
677, 770
Fuchs and, 68, 69–70,
79, 80
Indochina conflict and,
701, 705–8
Iran coup and, 627–31,
632, 637
Great Fear, The (Caute),
11–12
*Great Treasury of Western
Thought, The* (Van
Doren), 1167
Green, Ernest, 1193,
1209–10
Green, Harold, 573–78,
593–94, 608
Greenberg, Carl, 554
Greene, Graham, 626–27
Gregg, Alan, 485–86
Griffin, Marvin, 1177,
1180–81
Griffith, Andy, 834
Groves, Leslie, 56, 57, 64

Gruenther, Alfred M., 363, 623
Gruson, Sydney, 661–66, 670, 671
Guatemala, 640–70
    CIA coup in, 640–70, 1253, 1276–77
Guillain, Robert, 698
Gunther, John, 35, 370–72, 373, 725–26, 1218
Guttmacher, Alan, 1046

Hackett, Alice Payne, 103–4
Hagerty, James, 413, 601–2, 1096, 1099, 1234
Haislip, Ham, 191, 194
Haley, Bill, 801, 822, 824
Hall, Grover Cleveland, Jr., 972–75
Hall, Leonard W., 566
Halleck, Charles A., 1230–31
Halley, Rudolph, 332, 335
Hammerstein, Oscar, 340, 827
Hand, Augustus, 498
Hand, Learned, 713, 724
Hanrahan, William, 533
Harlan, John Marshall, 720
Harper's, 242, 407, 1039
Harriman, Averell, 15, 106, 113, 133–34, 147, 384, 628–29, 676, 677, 684
Harris, Julie, 847, 1038
Harris, Richard, 971

Harris, Roy, 1177, 1180–81
Harrison, George, 47
"Harry S Truman, A Study in Failure" (Cooke), 11
Hart, Ed, 92
"Harvest Moon Ball," 826
Hastings, Max, 189, 196
"Have We Gone Soft?" (Steinbeck), 1165
Hawkins, David, 547
Haywood, William D. "Big Bill," 492
"Heartbreak Hotel," 833
Heasley, Morgan, 131
Hebert, F. Edward, 19
Hechter, Oscar, 500, 506, 509, 1048–49, 1056
Hefner, Hugh, 995–1006
Hefner, Millie Williams, 999–1000
Heiskill, J. N., 1199–1200
Helms, Richard M., 1278
Henderson, Dion, 439
Henderson, Loy, 625, 627
Hepburn, Katharine, 338
Herblock, 353, 1228
Herter, Christian, 1251, 1269
Hewitt, Don, 1287
Hicks, Jim, 764–65
Hidden Persuaders, The (Packard), 1043
"Hidden Struggle for the H-Bomb: The Story of Dr. Oppenheimer's Persistent Campaign to Reverse U.S.

Military Strategy,
The" (Murphy),
590–91
Hiss, Alger, 13–26, 91, 97,
330, 367, 537, 539,
540, 565
"History Will Absolve
Me" (Castro),
1260–61
Hitler, Adolf, 69–70, 152,
375, 682, 1066,
1067–68, 1077, 1115
Hoaglund, Hudson, 504–6,
1049, 1053, 1058
Hobbing, Enno, 669
Ho Chi Minh, 690, 708,
710
Hodge, John, 108–9, 111
Hoffman, Abbie, 929
Hofstader, Richard, 930,
934
Holiday Inn, 301–11, 823
competitors and,
310–11
concept of, 301–3
franchising and, 308–9,
311
naming of, 304
success of, 307–11
Holland, Henry, 666–67
Holmes, John Clellon,
518–19, 521, 524,
527, 528
Holmes, Oliver Wendell,
16–17, 540–41
Hook, Sidney, 25
Hoopes, Townsend, 674–75
Hoover, Herbert, 2, 3, 4,
64–65, 202, 374

Hoover, J. Edgar, 16, 539,
592, 923
assessment of, 578–89
McCarthy and, 91, 439,
587–88
Oppenheimer as seen
by, 576, 577–78
secret files of, 578–79,
588–89
Truman and, 586–87
Hopper, Dennis, 839, 845
Hopper, Hedda, 442
Horn, W. J. Clayton, 534
Horowitz, Irving, 924–25,
928, 931, 938
"Hound Dog," 833
House Judiciary
Committee, 329
House of Representatives,
U.S., 327, 678, 1132
House Subcommittee on
the Judiciary, 588
House Un-American
Activities
Committee
(HUAC), 17–19, 44,
330, 537, 571, 587
housing:
mass production and,
230–32, 236–40
racism and, 247
World War II and,
233–34
see also Levittown
"How Dulles Averted
War" (Shepley), 709
"Howl" (Ginsberg),
532–34
Howling Wolf, 817

Huckaby, Elizabeth,
1208–9
Hucksters, The
(Wakeman), 875
Hudson, Richard, 975
Hughes, Emmet John,
675–77, 708
Huie, William Bradford,
753–54, 755, 757,
767
Hulton, Graham, 369
Humphrey, George, 684,
685, 692–93
Huncke, Herbert, 523
Hunt, E. Howard, 622,
645, 650, 1276
Huntley, Chet, 1191
Huzel, Dieter, 1061–62
hydrogen bomb, 45–82,
150, 569, 572,
590–91, 594, 1251
Air Force and, 63
computer technology
and, 160
debate over, 45–49
development of, 72–82
Lucky Dragon incident
and, 595–602
Oppenheimer and,
48–68, 72–74
politics and, 61, 65–68
Soviet Union and,
80–82, 172–74
Teller and, 57–63,
74–75, 79, 156–58
tests of, 169–72
Truman's decision on,
61, 72, 76, 78–79

I Aim at the Stars, 1072
I Love Lucy, 416, 878
I, the Jury (Spillane),
101–3
"I'm All Right, Mama,"
797
Immerman, Richard, 653
"I'm Walkin'," 905
Indochina War, 620,
688–92, 699–711
Inside Peyton Place (Toth),
1013
Institute for Sex Research
of Indiana
University, 482
*Invasion of the Body
Snatchers, The,* 245
Iran, 621
CIA coup in, 623–38,
640
Irvin, Monte, 1216
Irwin, James, 1054–55
"I Say He's a Wonderful
Guy" (Pat Nixon),
555
Isbell, Marion, 311
isolationism, isolationists,
6, 11–12, 96, 115,
535, 641, 642
McCormick and,
369–78
1952 election and, 351,
353, 360
Taft and, 357–58

Jackman, Richard, 1136
Jack's Book (Gifford and
Lee), 523

Jackson, Kenneth, 235, 250
Jackson, Robert, 712, 713,
    714, 727, 729,
    731–32, 734
Jackson (Miss.) *Daily
    News,* 780
Japan, 26, 44, 46, 106, 108,
    109, 142, 599,
    600–601, 615–16,
    642
Jenner, William, 26, 92, 97,
    435, 437, 590
Jewish Farmer, 501
JOHNNIAC, 167
Johns, Vernon, 948, 967
Johnson, Kelly, 1078,
    1079–80, 1082, 1247
Johnson, Louis, 78–79
Johnson, Lyndon B., 90,
    702, 705, 1094, 1236
Johnson, Tom, 968
Johnson, Wallace, 307
Johnston, Neil, 1222
Joint Chiefs of Staff, 26,
    76, 114, 119–20,
    145, 178, 182, 183,
    190, 684, 686, 687,
    688, 692, 1077
Joint Committee on Atomic
    Energy, 60, 572, 592
Jones, Curtis, 749, 750,
    751, 757
Jones, Kensinger,
    1100–1110
Jones, Margo, 465
Jordan, Will, 828
Joy of Reading, The (Van
    Doren), 1167

Jurist, Edward, 1135
Justice Department, U.S.,
    207, 227, 582, 949

Kael, Pauline, 845
Kammerer, Dave, 516
Kazan, Elia, 442–45, 451,
    452, 455–65, 471,
    837, 838, 842–47
Kazan, Molly Day
    Thacher, 452, 461,
    462
Kazin, Alfred, 1146
Keats, John, 234, 243
Keck, John, 1062
Kefauver, Estes, 326–36,
    384, 386
Keiser, Laurence "Dutch,"
    188
Keller, K. T., 1076
Kelley, Tom, 989, 995, 996
Kempton, Murray, 20, 23,
    24, 762
Kennan, George, 23, 29,
    109–10, 146, 570,
    604
Kennedy, John F., 159,
    542, 1056, 1059,
    1166, 1214, 1236,
    1270, 1279, 1281,
    1282–88
Kern, Nathan, 789
Kerouac, Jack, 513,
    514–15, 517–30, 531,
    532, 534
Kerr, Deborah, 875
Kerr, Robert S., 350
Kessel, Barney, 908

Kessie, Jack, 1002
Kettering, Charles, 209,
    224–25, 1117–18
Keyes, Evelyn, 985
Keynes, John Maynard,
    682
Khrushchev, Nikita, 113,
    1073, 1075, 1091,
    1095, 1231–32, 1240,
    1275, 1282–83
  "kitchen debate" and,
    1271–73
  U-2 affair and, 1248–51
  U.S. visit of, 1241–43
Killian, James, 1079
Kim Il Sung, 110–13
King, B. B., 817, 818
King, Coretta Scott,
    964–65, 966, 968
King, Martin Luther, Jr.,
    948, 1217
  background of, 956–69
  boycott and, 953–56,
    971, 972, 974,
    979–82
  media and, 1212–15
  as speaker, 954–55
King, Martin Luther, Sr.,
    957, 960, 962, 963,
    965, 966
King's Row (Winsor),
    1017–18
Kinsey, Alfred, 473–89,
    1000
Kinzer, Stephen, 651
Kiss Me Deadly (Spillane),
    103
Kistiakowsky, George, 46,
    52

"kitchen debate," 1271–73
Kitts, Clara, 782–83
Kluger, Richard, 717, 720,
    728
Knight, Shirley, 1108
Knowland, Joe, 726
Knowland, William F.,
    96–97, 366, 415, 538
Knudsen, Semon
    "Bunkie," 228,
    1111–13
Knudsen, William S. "Big
    Bill," 855, 856
Koplin, Mert, 1133
Korean War, 106–34,
    143–49, 158, 172,
    175–202, 258, 365,
    562–63, 620–21, 684,
    685, 691, 701, 705,
    935
  Acheson's speech and,
    113
  atomic bomb
    considered in, 189,
    196
  casualties of, 133
  Chinese intervention in,
    149, 175–86
  Gauntlet in, 188–89
  Inchon landings and,
    144–45
  MacArthur and, *see*
    MacArthur,
    Douglas
  media and, 126–27
  onset of, 116–24
  prelude to, 106–34
  Pusan perimeter and,
    132

Ridgway and, 118, 127,
129, 133–34, 146,
185, 190–99
Soviet Union and,
111–12, 117, 144
Task Force Smith and,
125–26
Korolev, Sergei, 1073–75
Krainan, Julian, 1167–68
Kramer, Stanley, 441
Kreisker, Marion, 796, 820
Kreitzer, Catherine, 1130
Kretchmer, Arthur, 1005–6
Kroc, Ray, 279–300
background of, 279–81
franchising and, 294–97
McDonald brothers
bought out by,
297–300
philosophy of, 288
quality control and, 296
thriftiness of, 293–94
Krock, Arthur, 1234, 1244
Krutch, Joseph Wood, 1146
Kuboyama, Aikichi,
598–600
Kun, Béla, 151

labor, 3, 4, 99, 205, 207,
782–84
Ladies' Home Journal,
1027, 1030–31, 1042
Lahey, Ed, 385
Land, Edwin H., 1079,
1082
Landon, Alfred M., 2
Langguth, A. J., 724
Laniel, Joseph, 692, 707
Lansdale, Jack, 593

Lansky, Meyer, 1255, 1257
Lark, The, 1038
Larrabee, Eric, 241
Larsen, Arthur, 437
Larsen, Roy, 915–18
Laughton, Charles, 835
Lawrence, Bob, 1104
Lawrence, Ernest, 55,
56–57, 68, 590
Leave It To Beaver, 893–94
"Leaves of Grass"
(Whitman), 533
Leclerc, Jacques Philippe,
690–91
Leddy, Mark, 828
Lee, George, 746–47, 748
Lee, Lawrence, 523
Leffingwell, Russell, 213
Legion of Decency, 443–44
Lehman, Herbert, 96
Leigh, Vivien, 442–43
Lemann, Nicholas, 788
LeMay, Curtis, 42, 612–19
LeMay, Helen, 619
Lennon, John, 794
Levin, Michael, 395
Levitt, Alfred, 231–33, 238,
241
Levitt, William J., 206,
230–49, 251, 276,
892
first Levittown of,
234–36
innovations of, 230–32,
236–38
Mumford's criticism of,
244–46
segregation and, 247
success of, 237–43

Levittown, 234–40, 243–49, 254
Lewis, Anthony, 727–28
Lewis, Flora, 662
Lewis, Fulton, Jr., 604
Lewis, Jerry, 827
Lewis, Jerry Lee, 820–21
Lewis, John L., 204
Lewis, Richard, 1061–62
Libby, Leona Marshall, 171
Liberal party, U.S., 410
Life, 333, 675, 677, 709, 865, 869, 877, 1094, 1195, 1211
Lights Out, 342
Lilienthal, David, 41, 42, 47, 57, 60, 64, 76, 78–79, 591, 603, 604
Linares, Gonzales de, 691
Lindsay, Howard, 1145
Lipman, Ira, 1192–94
Lippmann, Walter, 420, 1235
Listen, Yankee! (Mills), 937
Little Richard, 822, 824, 1215
Little Rock integration crisis, 1169–1212
  Eckford episode and, 1182–85
  federal troops and, 1206–7
  media and, 1188–96
Lodge, Henry Cabot, 363, 368–69, 375, 1093
Loeb, Jacques, 502
Loeb, William, 8

Loewy, Raymond, 221
London Spectator, 557
Lonely Crowd, The (Glazer and Reisman), 848, 932
Long Time Till Dawn, A, 840
Long Wait, The (Spillane), 103
Longworth, Alice Roosevelt, 5, 6
Look, 753, 1046
Lopez-Herrarte, Marian, 657
Los Angeles Examiner, 554
Los Angeles Times, 563, 902
Loth, David, 1050
Louis, Joe, 315
Louisville Courier Journal, 10
Love, John, 276
Love Happy, 990
Lovett, Robert, 590, 684
Lowell, A. Lawrence, 53
Lubell, Samuel, 395
Lucas, Jim, 196
Lucas, Scott, 96
Luce, Clare Boothe, 1057–58
Luce, Henry, 204, 357, 683, 935–36
Luciano, Lucky, 332
Lucky Dragon, The, 597–601
Luman, Bob, 831–32
Lundberg, Ferdinand, 1030
Lyons, Alfred, 345

M*A*S*H, 127
MacArthur, Douglas, 32,
    191, 351–52, 361,
    363, 396, 664, 687
  background of, 135–39
  Bradley on, 350
  Chinese threat
    misjudged by, 175–86
  Congress addressed by,
    200–201
  Eisenhower and, 139,
    140, 351–52, 359
  failure of, 184–90, 196
  Inchon landings and,
    144–45
  Joint Chiefs and, 145,
    178, 182, 183, 190
  1952 election and,
    351–52
  onset of Korean War
    and, 118–20, 129,
    133–34, 147, 195
  personality of, 139–43
  political ambition of,
    135–36, 350–52
  political decline of,
    350–52
  prelude to Korean War
    and, 108, 111
  sycophants of, 181
  Truman's firing of, 97,
    198–99, 202, 352
  Truman's meeting with,
    148–49, 182
Macauley, Ed, 1221
McCall, David, 877
McCall's, 362, 1032, 1040,
    1041

McCardle, Carl, 669–70
McCarran, Patrick A., 590
McCarten, John, 136
McCarthy, Joseph, 26,
    83–101, 365, 368,
    404, 406, 409–10,
    564, 565, 587–88,
    609, 618, 1229, 1271
  alcoholism of, 91–92
  Army hearings and, 93,
    437–39, 568
  Eisenhower and, 434–38
  Hoover and, 91, 439,
    587–88
  Oppenheimer case and,
    590, 591–92
  political decline of,
    434–40
  Wheeling speech of,
    83–84, 100
McCarthyism, McCarthy
    era, 83–101, 408,
    409, 568–69
  effect of, 89
  media and, 93–95
  popular literature and,
    101–5
  Republicans and,
    96–100
  Stevenson on, 404–6
  Taft and, 95, 97–101,
    437–38
McCloy, John J., 58, 107,
    604, 673–74
McCormick, Katharine
    Dexter, 490,
    498–500, 508, 511,
    1048, 1052, 1055

McCormick, Robert R., 4, 6, 90, 369–78, 382
McCulloch, Frank, 84, 85–86
McCutcheon, Richard, 1130–31, 1133
McDonald, Dick, 211, 270–79, 282–88, 297, 299–300
Macdonald, Dwight, 931
McDonald, Maurice "Mac," 211, 270–79, 282–88, 297, 299–300
McDonald's, 272–300, 885
  Coke and, 290–91
  first store of, 272
  franchising and, 278–79, 283–84, 287–88, 294–97
  mechanization and, 273–77
  quality control and, 296
  standardization and, 286, 287
  success of, 277
  see also Kroc, Ray
McDougall, Walter, 1072, 1076, 1089–90
McElroy, Neil, 1095–96
McGee, Frank, 976–78, 1193
McIntyre, O. O., 313
McKellar, Kenneth, 328
MacKichan, Clare, 862
McMahon, Brien, 60, 79, 572
McMath, Sid, 1180

McMillin, Miles, 94
Mademoiselle, 1031
Major Bowes' Original Amateur Hour, The, 314–15
Make Room for Daddy, 898
Malenkov, Georgi, 1073
Malone, George "Molly," 84
Manchester, William, 352
Manchester Guardian, 11
Manhattan Project, 46, 53, 57, 71, 607
Man in the Gray Flannel Suit, The (Wilson), 848, 911–15, 919
Mannes, Marya, 400–401
Mansfield, Jayne, 986
Mao Tse-tung, 113, 117, 123, 147, 149, 1263
Marbury, William, 17–18
Marcantonio, Vito, 328
March, Earle, 477
March, Fredric, 463
March, Hal, 1131
Marder, Murrey, 95, 434
Markel, Hazel, 1093
Marker, Russell, 510
Marks, Herbert, 573, 593
Marlboro cigarettes, 881
Mars, Florence, 788–89
Marshall, George C., 183
  Dewey and, 8
  Eisenhower and, 411, 434, 435–36
  MacArthur and, 135, 141, 178, 181
  Ridgway and, 192

right-wing attacks on,
97, 98, 408–9,
435–36
Stevenson and, 379,
408–9, 411
UMT supported by, 45
Marshall, S. L. A., 188
Marshall, Thurgood,
717–18
Mars Project (von Braun),
1060
Martin, Dean, 827
Martin, Joseph W., Jr., 198
Martineau, Pierre, 881
Marty, 1151
Marx, Groucho, 990
Marx, Karl, 204, 581–82
Masaryck, Jan, 23
Massey, Raymond, 842,
844
"massive retaliation"
doctrine, 685–86
Masters of Deceit
(Hoover), 581–82
Matos, Huber, 1273
Matthews, Herbert,
1261–63, 1275
Mauchly, John, 161, 162,
166
"Maybellene," 822
Mayer, Louis B., 454
Mays, Willie, 1216
Medaris, John, 1072, 1088
Meet the Press, 385–86
*Memphis
Commercial-Appeal,*
780
Memphis Press Scimitar,
782

Men, The, 441
Merton, Thomas, 1144,
1146
Messner, Julian, 1007, 1018
Messner, Kitty, 1018–19,
1024
Mesta, Perle, 1094
Metalious, George, 1015,
1017, 1020, 1023
Metalious, Grace, 1007–24
Metalious, Marsha, 1015,
1023
Michaelis, John "Mike,"
127, 195
Middleton, Troy, 434
Mikoyan, Anastas, 1274
Milam, J. W., 750–58, 763,
765, 766, 767
Miller, Arthur, 455, 984,
985, 993–94
Miller, Edward, 655–56
Miller, Merle, 32
Miller, Mitch, 823
Miller, Warren, 1022–23
Millikan, Robert, 53
"Millionaire's Wife"
(Friedan), 1038
Mills, C. Wright, 920–38
alienation and, 923–24,
927
New Left and, 922, 924,
929, 930
Millstein, Gilbert, 530
Milwaukee Journal, 94,
439–40
Minton, Sherman, 714, 733
Mirror Makers, The (Fox),
874
missile gap debate, 1227–30

Mitchum, Robert, 469
*Modern Woman: The Lost
Sex* (Lundberg and
Farnham), 1030
Mohammed Reza Shah
Pahlavi, 624, 628,
630, 632–38, 639
Monde, Le (Paris), 698
Monitor, 1187
Monnet, Jean, 682
Monroe, Bill, 798
Monroe, Marilyn, 984–96
Montgomery Advertiser,
968, 970, 972,
974–76, 978, 982
Montgomery bus boycott,
946–56, 969–83
idea for, 946–47
King and, 953–56, 971,
972, 974, 979–82
precipitating incident
of, 939–42
Montgomery Improvement
Association (MIA),
953, 971
Moondog Show, The, 810
Moore, Scotty, 797–98
Morgan, Ted, 526, 533
Morrison, Philip, 571
Morrow, Frederic, 735–44,
1211–12
Mossadegh, Mohammed,
621, 624, 628–38,
639
motels, *see* Holiday Inn
Mott, Stan, 223
"Move On Up a Little
Higher," 808
Mumford, Lewis, 244–46

Mundt, Karl, 18, 21–22,
97, 404, 591
Murchison, Clint, 581
Murphy, Charles J. V., 590
Murphy, Gardner, 337–38
Murphy, George, 13
Murphy, Robert, 78
Murrow, Edward R., 487,
1128, 1210, 1235
Musial, Stan, 1223
music, 794
black culture and,
807–11, 1215
new generation and,
824
Sam Phillips and,
812–23
technology and, 821
My Favorite Husband,
338–39
My Gun Is Quick
(Spillane), 103
"My Happiness," 796
Myrdal, Gunnar, 716
My Three Sons, 1103

Nader, Ralph, 1124
Nashville Tennessean, 1194
Nation, 1145
National Association for
the Advancement of
Colored People
(NAACP), 717, 731,
735, 746, 764, 765,
766–67, 942, 943,
946, 954, 957,
1174–75, 1182
National Coalition
Council, 791

National Security Council (NSC), 685, 692
Navarre, Henri, 689, 691–95, 697, 699
Navasky, Victor, 589
Navy, U.S., 39, 144, 145, 1089–90, 1096
NBC, 319, 321, 323, 324, 342, 415, 978, 1093, 1103, 1151, 1152, 1156, 1157, 1160–61, 1185–86, 1187, 1189, 1192, 1193, 1210
NBC Nightly News, 1192, 1194
Nearing, Vivienne, 1153
Nedelin, Mistofan, 173
Nelson, David, 896, 902, 904
Nelson, Harriet, 887, 894–96, 904
Nelson, Ozzie, 887, 890, 893–908
Nelson, Ricky, 896–909
Nevler, Leona, 1018, 1019
Newborn, Phineas, 817
New Deal, 2, 3–5, 10, 13, 22, 26, 36, 99, 135–36, 372, 376, 378, 412, 540, 553, 654, 722, 733, 805, 1026–27
New Left, 922, 924, 929, 930
"New Look," 684, 686, 700, 704
Newman, Paul, 843
New Republic, 105, 358, 930, 1165, 1271

Newsweek, 321, 973, 1195
New World Writing, 530
New York Daily News, 407, 826, 830
New Yorker, 351–52, 392, 407, 482–83, 917
New York Herald Tribune, 27, 105, 237
New York Post, 24, 412–13, 762, 1156
New York Times, 11, 28, 115, 230, 236, 334, 341–42, 357, 385, 444, 483, 497, 502–3, 534, 661, 664–65, 671, 719, 760, 845, 928, 974, 1091, 1092, 1173, 1184, 1195, 1196, 1234, 1244, 1261–63, 1269–70, 1275
New York Times Book Review, 530
New York Times Magazine, 530
New York World-Telegram, 1021, 1155–56
Ngo Dinh Diem, 708, 711
Nichols, Kenneth, 61, 575, 593
Niebuhr, Reinhold, 483, 672, 965
Night Beat, 1022
Nitze, Paul, 23
Nixon, E. D., 943–47, 952–54, 975
Nixon, Frank, 543–46
Nixon, Hannah Milhous, 543, 545–49

Nixon, Pat Ryan, 417–18, 548–67
Nixon, Richard M., 17, 571, 592, 741, 1093, 1202, 1236, 1268, 1270, 1273
  background of, 542–50
  Checkers speech of, 416–21, 547, 563, 1289
  early career of, 536–42
  Eisenhower's disdain for, 566–67
  Hiss affair and, 17, 19, 21, 22, 28
  Kennedy's debate with, 1283–88
  "kitchen debate" and, 1271–73
  1952 campaign and, 365–69, 411–21
  1960 campaign and, 1270, 1273, 1278, 1281
  political career of, 550–67
  secret fund affair and, 411–17
Nixon, Tricia, 553, 555
No Adam in Eden (Metalious), 1024
"No Father to Guide Them" (Ratcliff), 503
Nordhoff, Heinz, 1115–16
Norris, George, 585
North, Sterling, 1021
North Atlantic Treaty Organization (NATO), 98, 361

"Now They're Proud of Peoria" (Friedan), 1038
nuclear weapons, 38–45, 700–701, 703, 1239
  massive retaliation and, 685–86
  see also atomic bomb; hydrogen bomb

O'Connell, William, 1050
Odets, Clifford, 461, 470–71
O'Dwyer, William, 334
Office of Strategic Services (OSS), 626, 634, 646
Ogilvy, David, 391–92, 400
O'Hanlon, Redmond, 1129–30
O'Hara, John, 1007
oil, 204–6, 626–29
Olivier, Laurence, 442–43, 985
Olsen, Edward, 85, 87, 88
One Lonely Night (Spillane), 103
On the Road (Kerouac), 524, 529, 530, 533
On the Waterfront, 836, 1148
Oppenheimer, J. Robert, 40, 42, 46–47, 81, 150, 156–58, 168, 169, 170, 171
  background and personality of, 53–55
  Congressional testimony of, 42

government's security
campaign against,
568–73, 576, 589–95,
603–10
Hoover's view of, 576,
577–78
hydrogen bomb and,
48–68, 72–74
Teller's relationship
with, 61–62, 63, 66,
153, 154, 172
Teller's testimony
against, 603–12
Trinity and, 56
Truman's meeting with,
59
von Neumann and,
165–66
Orbison, Roy, 820
Organization Man, The
(Whyte), 848
Ottley, Roi, 773
Our Town (Wilder), 319

Paar, Jack, 829
Packard, Vance, 1043
Paek Sun Yup, 179
Paley, William S., 339, 340,
1233
Paris Review, 530
Parker, Charlie, 522
Parker, Tom, 822, 834,
835
Parks, Bert, 317
Parks, Rosa, 939–47, 951,
979
Parnis, Mollie, 567
Parsons, Louella, 442
Patterson, Edgar, 725

Patton, George, Jr., 32,
139, 423, 432, 612
Payne, Robert, 203
PBS, 1167–68
Pearson, Billy, 784–88, 791
Pearson, Drew, 383, 396,
1244
Peck, Gregory, 919, 1142
Peierls, Rudolph, 80
Pendergast, Tom, 10, 34,
38
People of Plenty (Potter),
875
Pepper, Beverly, 1039
Pepper, Claude, 96, 376
Perkins, Carl, 820
Perry, Herman, 552
Pershing, John J., 138–39,
148
Persons, Jerry, 437
Person to Person, 487
Peurifoy, Jack, 657,
658–60, 663, 664,
665, 668–69
Peyton Place (Metalious),
1007–13, 1018–22,
1023
Philby, Kim, 623, 626, 646
Philip Morris company,
341–45, 878, 880
Phillips, Cabell, 114–15
Phillips, David Atlee,
667–68, 1276
Phillips, Dewey, 799–803,
808, 834
Phillips, Sam, 795–99,
812–23
Physics Today, 50
Pickering, William, 1098

Pincus, Gregory Goodwin
"Goody":
background of, 500–505
contraception research
of, 504–11, 1046–58
media's depiction of,
502–3
Sanger and, 511
Pincus, John, 501, 508
Piroth, Charles, 696–99
Placzek, George, 55, 153,
158–59
Planned Parenthood, 497,
508, 1047, 1052,
1057, 1059
Playboy, 997–1006
Plessy, Homer Adolph, 719
Plessy v. *Ferguson,* 718–21,
728
Pleven, René, 698
Pollock, Earl, 727
Pomeroy, Wardell, 475,
476
Pon, Ben, 1116
"Poor Little Fool," 907
Popham, John, 760–63,
767–68, 1195, 1196
Popular Mechanics, 1118
Porsche, Ferdinand, 116,
203, 1114–15, 1116
Porter, Arabelle, 530
Potsdam conference,
38–39, 100, 106
Potter, David, 875
Powell, G. E., 781
Power Elite, The (Mills),
932–35
Powers, Francis Gary,
1081, 1083–85,

1240–41, 1245–49,
1251
Powers, Richard Gid, 583,
1081
Prato, Gino, 1130, 1133
Pratt, Waddy, 290–91
Presley, Elvis, 469,
793–807, 822–25,
831–35, 847–48, 904,
906, 1215
background of, 803–7
Bernstein on, 793–94
first recording of,
795–98
Sullivan and, 830–31,
905
Presley, Gladys, 802–3,
804, 805, 832–33
Presley, Priscilla, 906
Prettyman, Barrett, 734
Prince, Earl, 280–81
*Prince and the Showgirl,
The,* 985
Providence Journal, 915
Purvis, Melvin, 584
Pusey, Nathan, 1094

Rabb, Max, 742–43
Rabi, I. I., 51, 73, 74, 172,
571, 604, 611
race, racism, 327, 731–32
housing and, 247
see also civil rights
movement
Radford, Arthur, 684, 685,
686, 687–88, 703,
706–7
radio, 1, 35, 126, 343, 372,
808, 876, 1125

television's overtaking
of, 312–25
Railton, Arthur, 1118
Rankin, John, 18, 327
Ratcliff, J. D., 503
Rauschenbusch, Walter,
965
Ray, Nicholas, 794, 846,
847
Rayburn, Sam, 562, 576
Raymond, Albert, 507
Reader's Digest, 396–97,
490, 555, 879
Rebel Without a Cause,
794, 846, 847
"Red, Hot and Blue," 799,
800
Redbook, 1031, 1042
Reece, B. Carroll, 13,
486
Reed, James, 502
Reed, John, 495
Reed, Stanley, 22, 730,
732–33
Reeder, Russell, 192
Reedy, George, 87, 94
Reeves, Rosser, 389–403,
873, 874, 878
Reno Gazette, 84
Reporter, 327, 401
Republican party, U. S.,
16, 31, 38, 98, 360,
367, 676, 701, 923,
1229
China Lobby and,
115–16
conservative wing of,
44, 375
Dulles and, 672–73

internationalism and,
535–36
McCarthyism and,
96–100
1948 campaign and,
6–11
1952 election and,
351–53, 365–67, 395,
408–9, 620
World War II effect on,
1–5
Yalta agreement
denounced by,
26–27
Reston, James "Scotty,"
28, 385, 769, 1244
Return to Peyton Place
(Metalious),
1022–23
Reuther, Walter, 207, 208
Revlon company, 1127,
1129, 1131–32, 1133,
1151
Revson, Charles, 1133
Revson, Martin, 1132,
1133–34
Rexroth, Kenneth, 531,
532
Rhee, Syngman, 110–11
Rhodes, Richard, 49
Rice, Thurman, 480
Richmond News-Leader,
982–83
Rickover, Hyman, 1094
Ridgway, Matthew, 685–86
Bradley on, 196
Indochina intervention
opposed by, 702,
704–5

Ridgway (*continued*)
  Korean War and, 118,
    127, 129, 133–34,
    146, 185, 190–99
  in World War II,
    192–93
Riedl, John, 90–91
Riesman, David, 932–34
River and the Gauntlet, The
    (Marshall), 188
Robb, Chuck, 792
Robb, Roger, 604, 605,
    606–7
"Robert Alphonso Taft
    Story, The," 99
Roberts, Chal, 1244
Robinson, Bill, 361
Robinson, Jackie, 1216
Robinson, Jo Ann, 950, 951
Rock, John, 499, 1047–53,
    1057
"Rock Around the Clock,"
    801
Rockefeller, Nelson, 539,
    624, 1093
Rockefeller, Winthrop,
    1181
Rockefeller Foundation,
    452, 481, 483,
    485–86, 488
Rodgers, Richard, 827
Rogers, Ted, 417–18, 419,
    421, 562, 1286–88
Rogers, Will, 437
Rogers, William P., 565,
    1202
Roosevelt, Eleanor, 586
Roosevelt, Franklin D.,
    1–2, 3, 6, 11–12, 26,
    31, 35, 106, 141,
    142–43, 205, 292,
    362, 372, 374–75,
    401–2, 417, 540–41,
    586, 626, 627, 654,
    683, 712, 733, 736,
    775
Roosevelt, Franklin D., Jr.,
    701
Roosevelt, Kermit, 621–22,
    624–26, 631–37, 639,
    641
Roosevelt, Teddy, 626, 633
Rosenbaum, Ron, 245, 246
Rosenhouse, Marty, 1135
Rosenman, Samuel, 9–10
Route 66, 1103
Rovere, Richard, 101, 116,
    420
Roy, Jules, 694
Rubin, Barry, 627, 630
Rusk, Dean, 107, 486, 488
Russell, Bill, 1218–26
Russell, Ray, 1001
Russell, Richard, 384, 644
Rust, John Daniel, 776–81,
    784, 786, 791
Rust, Mack, 777, 779, 781
Rust, Thelma, 791
Rustin, Bayard, 979
Ryan, Kate Halberstadt
    Bender, 559–60
Ryan, Will, 559–61

Sahl, Mort, 555, 1072
Saint, Eva Marie, 1148
Sakharov, Andrei, 80–81,
    159, 172–74
Salan, Raoul, 691, 694

Salisbury, Harrison, 664,
   671
Sandburg, Carl, 773
San Diego Evening Tribune,
   587–88
Sandoe, James, 105
Sanger, Bill, 491, 492–93,
   495
Sanger, Margaret, 490–500,
   508, 511, 1052, 1059
   background of, 491–94
   Catholic Church and,
      490–91, 497–98
   McCormick and, 490,
      498–500, 511, 1052
   Pincus and, 511, 1057
   Planned Parenthood
      and, 497, 508, 1047
Saperstein, Abe, 1220
Saturday Evening Post,
   305, 334, 407, 812
Saturday Night Live,
   897–98
Schickel, Richard, 837,
   839, 848
Schlesinger, Arthur, Jr.,
   116, 387
Schlesinger, Arthur, Sr., 496
Schlesinger, Stephen, 651
Schnitzer, Gerry, 1104–7
Schoenbrun, David, 398,
   673
Scholastic, 825
Schorr, Daniel, 1190
Scott, Hugh, 8
Searle Pharmaceutical
   Company, 506–7,
   1046, 1048, 1054,
   1058

Seay, Solomon, 949–50,
   975
Sedov, Leonid, 1095
Segre, Elfriede, 70
Sellers, Clyde, 979
Selvin, Joel, 901, 906
Selznick, David, 454
Selznick, Irene, 454–55,
   465
Senate, U. S., 34, 91, 96,
   350, 358, 379, 554,
   1124, 1268
   McCarthy censured by,
      439
Senate Armed Services
   Committee, 330,
   644, 700
Senate Committee on
   Government
   Operations, 438
Senate Finance Committee,
   213
Senate Foreign Relations
   Committee, 95, 1268
"Sepia Swing Club," 818
Serling, Rod, 840–41, 897
Sevareid, Eric, 407
Seven-Year Itch, The, 991,
   993
*Sexual Behavior in the
   Human Female*
   (Kinsey), 486–87
*Sexual Behavior in the
   Human Male*
   (Kinsey), 474, 480
Shah of Iran (Mohammed
   Reza Pahlavi), 624,
   628, 630, 632–38,
   639

"Shake Rattle and Roll,"
822
Shalett, Sidney, 334
Shapley, Harlow, 85–86
Sheehan, Robert, 228
Shelton, Ike, 747–48
Shepley, James, 709–10
Sher, Jack, 343
Sher, Marilyn, 343
Sherman, Forest, 145
Short, Dewey, 201–2
Silber, Don, 853
sitcoms, 343, 887–99
Sitton, Claude, 1195
$64,000 Challenge, The,
1132, 1133
$64,000 Question, The,
1125–34
60 Minutes, 1287
Sixty Years of Best Sellers
(Hackett), 103–4
Skardon, William, 72,
76–78, 80
Skin of Our Teeth, The
(Wilder), 463
Sloan, Alfred P., 207, 210,
211–16, 222, 227,
228, 853, 1110
Smathers, George, 96
Smith, Charles B. "Brad,"
122, 124, 125–26,
127
Smith, Dana, 411
Smith, Earl T., 1257, 1265,
1273
Smith, Herbert, 47, 53
Smith, Herman "Dutch,"
380
Smith, Lamar, 748

Smith, Loren, 125
Smith, Merriman, 1092
Smith, Paul, 546, 548
Smith, Walter Bedell
"Beetle," 622–24,
631, 636, 642,
643–44, 646, 648,
649, 655
Smith, Wayne, 1258, 1266,
1267, 1274, 1277
Snow, C. P., 58
Snow, Hank, 822
"Some Enchanted
Evening," 831
Somoza, Anastasio, 652,
655
Southern, Terry, 103–4,
105
Soviet Union, 12, 23, 29,
55, 58, 60, 63, 66,
70, 71, 74, 76, 77,
89, 97, 98, 146, 197,
371, 373, 537, 628,
633, 640, 642, 707,
708, 922–23, 929,
1063, 1076–77, 1085,
1089, 1231, 1237,
1241, 1249, 1250
atomic bomb and,
38–45
Cuba and, 1274
H-bomb and, 80–82,
172–74
Korean War and,
111–12, 113, 144
missile gap and,
1227–28
missile program of,
1072–76

postwar era and, 42–43, 44

Sputnik launched by, 1091–97

U-2 incident and, 1237–51

Yalta conference and, 26

Spillane, Mickey, 101–5, 1012

sports, 1215–26

Sputnik, 612, 1091–97, 1191, 1227, 1229, 1237, 1238

Sputnik II, 1096

Stage Show, 832

Stalin, Joseph, 26, 38, 41, 55, 96, 106–7, 112, 113, 118, 353, 371, 375, 569, 922, 929, 1063, 1073, 1074, 1231

Stassen, Harold, 8, 359, 365

State Department, U. S., 14, 23, 33, 83–84, 98, 100, 110, 622, 643, 648, 656, 657, 666–67, 672, 1085, 1257, 1259, 1271

State of the Union, 1145

Stehling, Kurt, 1096–97

Stein, Bob, 1042

Steinbeck, John, 842, 1165

Steinem, Gloria, 557–58

Stempel, Herb, 1136–41, 1148–58, 1159–60, 1162–63

Stennis, John, 700

Stephens, Tom, 420–21

Stevenson, Adlai E., 22, 389, 400, 410–11, 565, 617, 1165, 1239
background and career of, 378–87
Eisenhower contrasted with, 406–8
on McCarthyism, 404–6
1952 election and, 378–87, 402–21
television disliked by, 402–4

Stevenson, John, 341

Stewart, Homer, 1090

Stewart, Potter, 725

Stilwell, Joseph, 143

Stimson, Harry, 39, 45

Stone, Abraham, 1046

Stone, Harlan Fiske, 712

Stone, Joe, 1133, 1163

Stop the Music!, 316–17

Stout, Rex, 1146

Strasberg, Lee, 461

Strategic Air Command (SAC), 612–13, 617–19, 1076, 1078

Stratemeyer, George, 182

Strauss, Lewis, 64–67, 79, 157, 573–75, 590–95, 601–6, 608, 609, 612

Streetcar Named Desire, A (Williams), 441–46, 454, 456, 463, 471, 480, 836

Strider, Clarence, 761, 762, 763–65, 766–67, 788, 789, 791–92

Strider, Jesse, 792

Stripling, Robert, 19

Strong, Philip, 1078
Studio One, 867–68
Sullivan, Ed, 319, 826–31,
833–35, 905
Sullivan, Walter, 1091–92
Sullivan, William C., 585,
586–87
Sulzberger, Arthur Hays,
664–66, 670–71,
1244
Sulzberger, Cyrus, 361,
671, 1203–4, 1230,
1233, 1234–35
Summerfield, Arthur, 415,
419, 851–52
Summer Sentinel, 788
Supreme Court, U. S., 22,
574, 712–35, 741,
947, 981, 1171–74,
1190, 1217
Plessy decision of,
718–21, 728
Truman's appointments
to, 713–15
Warren's appointment
to, 727–28
see also Brown v. *Board
of Education*
Swados, Harvey, 925
Swango, Curtis, 761, 763
Swayze, John Cameron,
1186, 1187, 1191
Swillenberg, Joe, 258, 261
Symington, Stuart, 1236,
1237
Szulc, Tad, 1262, 1275–76

Taft, Alphonso, 354
Taft, Horace, 354, 356, 358

Taft, Martha Bowers, 7,
11, 355
Taft, Robert A., 4, 5, 11,
14, 539, 541–42,
672, 684, 687, 721
background and
personality of,
354–56
Fortune's description of,
358
isolationism and,
357–58
McCarthyism and, 95,
97–101, 437–38
1952 election and,
351–53, 358–59, 361,
365–67, 377–78, 384
politics of, 356–58
Truman on, 354
Taft, William Howard, 679
Take It Or Leave It, 1125
Talese, Gay, 992
Task Force Smith, 125–26
Taylor, Laurette, 448, 453
technology, 865–67
computers and, 160–68,
776
mechanical cotton
picker and, 776–81
music industry and, 821
teenagers and, 825–26
Ted Bates Agency, 389,
390, 392, 395–96,
876
teenagers, 825–26
television, 365, 372, 1100,
1101
advertising and, *see*
advertising

Benny's analysis of, 348–49
Berle and, 320–25
Checkers speech and, 416–21
Eisenhower's image and, 388–89, 397–400
family sitcoms on, 343, 887–99
I Love Lucy and, 339–47
journalism and, 348
Kefauver hearings and, 326–36
King and, 1212–15
Little Rock integration crisis and, 1188–96
movies and, 320
1952 election and, 388–403
Nixon-Kennedy debates and, 1283–90
political advertising on, 388–403
politics and, 337, 346
quiz shows on, 1125–40, 1165
radio overtaken by, 312–25
sports and, 1215
Sullivan and, 826–31
tobacco industry and, 878–82
Television Fraud (Anderson), 1130
Teller, Edward, 48, 68, 81, 163, 165, 594, 1094

background personality of, 150–54
egocentrism of, 168–70
H-bomb and, 57–63, 74–75, 79, 156–58
Oppenheimer's relationship with, 61–62, 63, 66, 153, 154, 172
Oppenheimer testimony of, 603–12
Teller, Mici, 153, 612
Texaco Star Theatre, 321
"That's When Your Heartaches Begin," 796
Theory of Games (von Neumann), 51
There Will Be No Time: The Revolution in Strategy (Borden), 572
Thomas, J. Parnell, 22, 44–45
Thomas, Rufus, 799
Thompson, Howard, 845
Thompson, Llewellyn, 1271
Thorndyke, Sybil, 985
Throckmorton, John, 179
Thurber, James, 317–18, 1146
Tic Tac Dough, 1132
Tight White Collar, The (Metalious), 1023
Till, Betty, 788–89
Till, Emmett, 748–66, 769, 788, 979, 1187
Time, 20, 31, 50, 85, 321, 331, 336, 569–70,

Time (continued)
689–90, 793, 1002,
1149
Times (London), 708
Today, 1152, 1210
Tolson, Clyde, 539,
578–81
Toman, Ed, 276, 283
Toriello (Guatemalan
foreign minister),
658, 668
Toth, Emily, 1013
Town and the City, The
(Kerouac), 528
Toys "R" Us, 268
Trainer, Harry, 574
Treadmill to Oblivion
(Allen), 319
Trilling, Lionel, 518, 1146
Trujillo, Rafael Leonidas,
652, 1260
Truman, Bess, 34
Truman, Harry S, 2, 6,
9–10, 13, 14, 15,
28–30, 68, 90, 96,
113, 114–15, 116–19,
135, 146–47, 175,
176, 182, 183, 189,
196, 205, 330, 334,
352, 540, 630, 631,
641–42, 676, 688,
721, 736, 1059,
1206, 1229–30, 1289
Acheson on, 36
assessment of, 31–38
background of, 33–35
demobilization and, 45
Guatemala coup and,
655, 656
H-bomb decision of,
61, 72, 76, 78–79
J. Edgar Hoover and,
586–87
MacArthur fired by, 97,
198–99, 202, 352
MacArthur's meeting
with, 148–49, 182
national emergency
declared by, 191
1952 election and, 362,
378, 383–85, 386
Oppenheimer's meeting
with, 59
Soviet A-bomb and,
40–42, 43
Supreme Court
appointees of,
713–15
on Taft, 354
Truman, Margaret, 30,
118
Truman Doctrine, 37
Tuck, James, 52
Tukhachevsky, Mikhail,
1074
Turner, Fred, 285, 289
Turner, Ike, 819, 1215
"Tutti Frutti," 822
Twenty-One, 1134–40,
1147, 1151, 1153,
1166
Twining, Nathan, 700–701
"Two Are an Island"
(Friedan), 1038
Two-Bit Culture (Davis),
102, 1012
Tydings, Millard, 95–96
Tyler, William, 880

U-2 aircraft, 1078–87, 1228
    Soviet downing of,
    1237–51
Ubico Castaneda, Jorge,
    647, 652
Ulam, Stanislaw, 70, 154,
    159, 165, 168,
    169–70, 571
unions, 205, 241–42
United Auto Workers
    (UAW), 207
United Fruit Company,
    647–48, 651–55, 656,
    660–61, 1253, 1254,
    1257, 1260
United Mine Workers,
    205
United Motors
    Corporation, 212–13
United Nations, 195, 379,
    382, 1231–32,
    1274–75
United Press, 87, 94, 1261
UNIVAC (Universal
    Automatic
    Computer), 166
Universal Military
    Training (UMT),
    45, 330
Urey, Harold, 590

Van Cleve, Edith, 468
Vandenberg, Arthur, 42
Vandenberg, Hoyt, 190,
    195
Van Doren, Charles,
    1140–68
Van Doren, Geraldine,
    1166

Van Doren, Mamie, 860,
    985
Van Doren, Mark, 1141,
    1144, 1145, 1146–47,
    1161, 1163
Van Dusen, Henry Pitney,
    483, 485, 487
Van Fleet, Jo, 842
Vannikov, Boris, 81
Van Susteren, Urban, 439
Variety, 323
Veblen, Oswald, 162
Venet, Nik, 887
Vengeance Is Mine
    (Spillane), 103
Vietminh, 688, 690–99,
    708, 710, 1263
Vietnam, 90, 126, 127,
    1263, 1273
    partition of, 708
Vineberg, Steven, 838
Vinson, Fred, 384, 714–15,
    720
Vivas, Eliseo, 928
Volkswagen Beetle,
    1113–19, 1123
Volpe, Joseph, 67, 593
Voluntary Parenthood
    (Loth), 1050
von Braun, Magnus, 1062
von Braun, Wernher, 608,
    1060–73, 1087,
    1097–98
Vo Nguyen Giap, 690, 694,
    697, 710
von Neumann, John, 51,
    160–68, 169, 170,
    571, 604
    background of, 163–66

von Neumann (*continued*)
    computer designed by,
        166–67
    personality of, 164–65
    politics of, 165–66
Voorhis, Jerry, 367, 537,
        551–52, 562

Wakefield, Dan, 930,
        931–32
Wakeman, Frederic, 875
Wald, Jerry, 1022
Walker, George, 222
Walker, Walton, 130–31,
        133, 179, 191
Wallace, George, 983, 1211
Wallace, Henry, 43, 96
Wallace, Mike, 1022, 1056
Wallis, Hal, 833
Wall Street Journal, 590
Walters, Vernon, 629
Ward, T. J., 951
Warner, Jack, 444
Warren, Earl, 200, 359,
        365, 368, 538,
        721–34
    background of, 722–24
    Brown decision and,
        734
    political career of,
        722–26
    on segregation, 730
Washington Post, 95, 329,
        353, 434, 1195,
        1228, 1244
Watergate scandal, 548,
        622, 645, 1155
Watson, Tom, Jr., 160–61,
        166–67

Watson, Tom, Sr., 166–67
Wayne, John, 365
Weismuller, Tony,
        294–95
Weisner, Jerome, 159
Weisskopf, Victor, 52, 54,
        55, 62, 153, 155,
        156, 570–71, 595,
        603
Welker, Herman R., 97
Wells, Herman, 480–82
Werblin, Sonny, 1156
West, Jessamyn, 543, 556
West, Rebecca, 645
Westfeldt, Wallace,
        1194–95
Westinghouse, 867–72
Weybright, Victor, 104,
        105
Weyl, Hermann, 163–64
"What I Found in the
        Underworld"
        (Kefauver), 334
"What Every Girl Should
        Know" (Sanger),
        493
What's My Line?, 334
Wheeler, John, 591
Wheeling Intelligencer, 84
Wherry, Kenneth S., 97
White, Bill, 11
White, William Allen, 7
White Citizens Council,
        746, 955, 969, 979,
        1177
White Collar (Mills), 848,
        931–34
Whitman, Ann, 567, 1284
Whitten, John, 754, 766

Why Johnny Can't Read—and What You Can Do About It (Flesch), 1094
Wieland, William, 1259
Wilder, Billy, 984, 986, 991
Wilder, Thornton, 319, 446, 463
Wild One, The, 467
Williams, Cornelius Coffin, 446–47
Williams, Edwina Dakin, 446–51
Williams, Hank, 975
Williams, Robert Chadwell, 69, 79
Williams, Rose, 447, 449–50
Williams, Ted, 1223
Williams, Tennessee, 441–56, 465, 471–73
Williams, William Carlos, 534
Willkie, Wendell, 2, 5, 359, 375, 1145
Willoughby, Charles, 181, 183
Wilson, Bill, 1286, 1287
Wilson, Charles E. "Engine," 207–8, 209, 225, 227, 625, 650, 684, 855, 1082, 1087–88, 1089, 1092, 1095
Wilson, Doll, 304–5
Wilson, Dorothy, 302–3, 307
Wilson, Kemmons, 301–11, 823

Wilson, Sloan, 911–19, 924
Windham, Donald, 453
Winstead, Charlie, 585
Winter, Bill, 764
Witness (Chambers), 13, 19–20, 25
Wolff, Kurt, 925
Woman Rebel, The, 494
women's movement:
employment and, 1025–30
Friedan and, 1035–45
magazines and, 1030–38, 1042–43
Metalious and, 1011–14
suburbs and, 250, 1031–34
see also Sanger, Margaret
Women's Political Council, 951
Wood, Audrey, 452, 453
Wood, Natalie, 985
Worchester Foundation for Experimental Biology, 505–8, 1049, 1053, 1058
World War I, 34, 64, 141–42, 771
World War II, 43, 44, 48, 114, 127, 141–43, 203, 206, 359, 372, 434, 626, 634, 646, 660, 759, 928, 929, 1027, 1210
black migration and, 771–75
colonialism and, 620

World War II (*continued*)
    Democrats affected by,
      1–3, 11–12
    housing and, 233–34
    LeMay and, 614–15
    Republicans affected
      by, 1–5
    Ridgway in, 192–93
    V-2 rocket and,
      1061–69
Wouk, Herman, 314, 319
Wright, Moses, 749, 750,
    755, 757, 765–66,
    769

Wyden, Peter, 1278
Wyrick, William, 124

Yalta conference, 26–27,
    100, 106
Yazoo City (Miss.) *Herald,*
    746
Ydigoras Fuentes, Miguel,
    652
Yergin, Daniel, 204
Yewl, Ken, 853
Yost, Norman, 84

Zemurray, Sam, 653

Author's Note

I am a child of the fifties. I graduated from high school in 1951, from college in 1955, and my values were shaped in that era. I wanted to write a book which would not only explore what happened in the fifties, a more interesting and complicated decade than most people imagine, but in addition, to show why the sixties took place—because so many of the forces which exploded in the sixties had begun to come together in the fifties, as the pace of life in America quickened. In large part this book reflects my desire as a grown man to go back and look at things that happened when I was much younger. I was a reporter in the South in the early days of the civil rights struggle; I went to Mississippi in 1955 immediately after graduation specifically because the Supreme Court had ruled on the Brown case the year before, and I thought therefore the Deep South was the best place to apprentice as a journalist. I was a reporter in West Point, Mississippi, when the Emmett Till trial took place in Sumner that summer. As I became aware of the vast press corps which was arriving in Tallahatchie County to cover the case, I knew instinctively that something important was taking place. I got an assignment from the old *Reporter* magazine to do a piece on the trial, and I faithfully read the various papers of the different reporters covering it. On my days off, I went over to watch them at work there. (I also managed to stay as far from Clarence Strider as I could—I still remember his threatening figure.) But when I sat down to write at the time, I was not able to pull off the piece I wanted, and it fizzled. Some thirty-eight years later I have taken what I sensed but could not articulate then, and tried to make it a part of this book. That is true of other experiences from those days as well. I have a clear memory, from countless visits to the bus stations in Nashville, Memphis, and Jackson, Mississippi, of large families of blacks headed North with all of their belongings. Clearly a great migration was then taking place, and I saw it, yet did not see it. This event of great historic importance went right by me until I finally understood its meaning some twelve years later when Andy Young talked to me about it one day while I was reporting on Martin King. Later, when I was a reporter in Nashville, I was assigned to cover the country music beat. That led to a friendship with Chet Atkins, the distinguished guitarist, who was also in charge of RCA's studios, and who would, on occasion, discreetly let me sit in when the young Elvis was recording there. Yet only later would I become fully aware of the importance of the new music as a sign of the political, economic, and social empowerment of the younger generation.

A book as long and demanding as this requires the help of many colleagues, and I would like to thank among others my editor Douglas Stumpf, and his assistants Leslie Chang, Erik Palma, and Jared Stamm. I am also grateful to Carsten Fries, Veronica Windholz, and Patty O'-Connell at Random House, Fernando Villagra, Amanda Earle, Danny Franklin, Martin Garbus, Bob Solomon, Gary Schwartz, Ken Starr, and Philip Roome, the staff of the New York Society Library where I spent long and happy hours, Pat Martin at the Worcester Foundation, Geoffrey Smith at the archives at Ohio State, who helped me look at Bill Huie's papers, Vicky Lem McDonald at the Museum of Broadcasting, and Keith Roachford in Senator Bill Bradley's office for helping me with the transcript of the Quiz Show hearings.

About the Author

DAVID HALBERSTAM *is the author of eleven previous books, including his highly praised trilogy on power in America,* The Best and the Brightest, The Powers That Be, *and* The Reckoning. *His recent book,* Summer of '49, *was a number one* New York Times *hardcover bestseller. He has won every major journalistic award, including the Pulitzer Prize. He lives in New York City.*